The Economy in Jewish History

THE ECONOMY IN JEWISH HISTORY

*New Perspectives on the Interrelationship
between Ethnicity and Economic Life*

Edited by
Gideon Reuveni and Sarah Wobick-Segev

Berghahn Books
NEW YORK • OXFORD

First published in 2011 by

Berghahn Books

www.berghahnbooks.com

©2011 Gideon Reuveni and Sarah Wobick-Segev

Library of Congress Cataloging-in-Publication Data

The economy in Jewish history : new perspectives on the interrelationship
between ethnicity and economic life / edited by Gideon Reuveni and Sarah
Wobick-Segev.
    p. cm.
  Includes bibliographical references and index.
  ISBN 978-1-84545-774-7
  1. Jews—Economic conditions. 2. Jewish businesspeople—History.
3. Economics—Sociological aspects—History. 4. Consumption
(Economics)—Social aspect—History. 5. Entrepreneurship—History.
I. Reuveni, Gideon. II. Wobick-Segev, Sarah.
  DS140.5.E36 2010
  330.089'924—dc22

2010025633

British Library Cataloguing in Publication Data

A catalogue record for this book is available from the British Library

Printed in the United States on acid-free paper.

ISBN: 978-1-84545-774-7 Hardback

CONTENTS

FOREWORD

Throughout the modern Western world, Jewish economic activity has been an object of awe and wonder. The Jews' economic influence has been often exaggerated, not only by anti-Semites searching for a culprit for overwhelming social ills, but also by philo-Semites identifying material manifestations of Jewish chosenness. From the mid-nineteenth century until the Second World War, Jewish writers directly engaged this language of Jewish economic exceptionalism with attitudes ranging from testy defensiveness to confident triumphalism to harsh self-criticism; meanwhile, Jewish economic difference remained prominent in Jewish self-consciousness. Then, in the wake of the Holocaust, talk about Jewish economic distinctiveness lost its respectability as even its benign forms were associated with Nazi anti-Semitism. Jewish scholars, in turn, ignored the subject, returning to it only in the past twenty years.

As the essays in this volume demonstrate, Jewish economic history is once again a lively subdiscipline, one that is characterized by an intriguing methodological tension. On the one hand, there is a push towards contextualization, that is, nuancing Jewish economic difference through comparison between Jews and mercantile minorities, niche and network theory, and models of sub- and supra-ethnic trading networks. The results are a minimizing of Jewish economic exceptionalism and a depiction of Jews as trading people that stops short of presenting *the* Jews as *a* trading people. The "cultural turn," which has encouraged study of consumption within the framework of bourgeois sensibility, further strengthens contextualist, as opposed to essentialist, presentations of Jewish economic behavior.

On the other hand, signs of Jewish economic uniqueness remain and demand explanation. Jews are unusual in having comprised a middleman minority lacking roots within an autochtonous national community. The Jews' historic status as a diaspora without a center (or, more accurately, with an ancient center that had long ceased to be a source of emigration) affected their economic lives in myriad ways, many of which have survived even in the state of Israel, in which Jews have belatedly become a sovereign middleman majority.

The essays in this volume deal with Jewish economic difference on four levels: significance within select fields, occupational structure, perception by others, and self-perception. The first originates with the traders and money-lenders of medieval Ashkenaz and early modern Poland's Jewish leaseholders, who were the life's blood of the manorial economy. In the ensuing centuries Jews were highly overrepresented, and even dominant, in a wide variety of economic fields: in Western and Central Europe, private banking in the eighteenth and early nineteenth centuries, then the stock market, then professions such as law and medicine; in Eastern Europe, agricultural industry and the financing of railroads; and in the fin de siècle Middle East, trade in colonial products such as ostrich feathers. On a lower economic register, Jewish peddlers were major suppliers of consumer goods to simple folk throughout Eastern Europe, North America, and South Africa. In the American West, social contact between natives and Europeans often took the form of an economic exchange with a Jewish peddler. Few mercantile communities have displayed such levels of involvement in all aspects of commerce.

Mercantile minorities are often feared and despised, though there are unusual features of perceptions of Jews as economic agents. (Chinese merchants have been called "the Jews of the Orient," but no one calls Jews the "Chinese of the West.") The reasons go far beyond economics and rest in the foundations of the Christian and Muslim faiths. The medieval Jewish moneylender, in reality and in fantasy, was a product of a theological anti-Judaism. When Christendom began its long, painful road toward toleration and, eventually, secularization, Jews and Judaism stood out as Europe's Other, on political and economic as well as religious planes. Throughout the West, the nineteenth-century critique of capitalism was shot through with anti-Semitism. Toward the end of the nineteenth century, the notion of awesome Jewish economic power was disseminated throughout the Arab Middle East in both the Christian and Muslim press. Here, Jewish economic influence was seen as both exemplary and baleful, being on the one hand a model of Semitic economic success that the Jews' Arab cousins should emulate, and on the other a disturbing explanation for the Zionist project's success.[1]

Just as the Jews produced a range of commercial agents from peddlers to high financiers, so has anti-Semitism targeted the starveling Jewish peddler as well as the wealthy banker. Jews have been attacked regardless of whether they were successful or failed, rich or poor. In contrast, Western criticism of colonized peoples focused on their alleged indolence (e.g., the British colonial construction of "Indian Economic Man" as yearning "only for Nirvana"[2]), and in postcolonial states the animosity toward mercantile minorities (e.g., ethnic Chinese in Indonesia) takes umbrage at their prosperity.

Jewish self-perception and self-definition, in turn, have depended more heavily on economic activity than has been case for other mercantile communities. Throughout the modern world, the Jews' status depended on how society judged Jews as economic agents. As a result, from the late eighteenth century onward Jews developed an elaborate matrix of economic self-evaluation, a matrix whose elements ranged from impassioned self-criticism (accepting the Gentile critique of Jewish economic behavior and calling upon Jews to move en masse from commerce to crafts and agriculture) to unapologetic triumphalism (proudly presenting Jews as the lifeblood of capitalism—indeed, as captalism's progenitors). In between these two extremes lay frank presentations of the Jews as a mercantile people, a *Handelsvolk,* whose collective existence was forged and maintained by commerce.

In Europe and North America, the subject-position of Jews as an ethno-religious minority seeking emancipation was different from that of indigenous merchant castes (as in India), mercantile minorities (ethnic Chinese in Southeast Asia), or, for that matter, Jews in the Ottoman Empire and Maghreb, who did not generate the apologetic economic rhetoric and complex, economically inflected identities that were so common in Europe. Until the late nineteenth century, Jews were unique among mercantile communities in their self-critique, particularly their call for radical occupational restructuring.

The state of Israel reflects its descent from a diasporic merchant people. Unlike other postcolonial states, whose newborn national economies depended upon the creation of an indigenous middle and managerial class, Israel was required to forge a farming and laboring class, that is to say, to create the preconditions for its very existence. Today, the country's leading high-technology sector displays traditional Ashkenazic proclivities for informality, improvization, fluidity, initiative, resourcefulness, tenacity, and resistance to hierarchy. In other words, in a state where a middleman minority has become the majority, its economic behavior remains that of the diasporic minority even though it now exercises sovereignty and domination over a national minority.

These aspects of Israel's history, like the relationship in general between economics and the Jews, were neglected for most of the second half of the twentieth century. Jewish historians hypostatized religion, then society, and most recently culture into independent variables. Now a new generation of scholars is adopting comparative and contextual approaches to the study of Jewish economic life while acknowledging the persistence of Jewish economic difference. This volume will enhance the recent trend toward integrating economics into Jewish civilization. It helps us better understand both the commonality of Jews and others as economic agents, and the singularities, whether real or perceived, of *Homo economicus judaicus*.

Derek Penslar
Samuel Zacks Professor of Jewish History, University of Toronto

Notes

1. On this point see Jonathan Gribetz, "Defining Neighbors: Religion, Race, and the Early 'Zionist-Arab' Encounter," PhD dissertation, Columbia University, 2010, chap. 3.
2. Ritu Birla, *Stages of Capital: Law, Culture, and Market Governance in Late Colonial India* (Durham, NC: Duke University Press, 2009), 2.

ACKNOWLEDGMENTS

This book is based on an interdisciplinary workshop, "Jewish History Encounters the Economy," held at the University of Wisconsin–Madison. During a stimulating two-day conference, Israeli, European, and North American scholars discussed the significance of the economy for our understanding of Jewish culture and history. The gathering marked a renewal of scholarly interest in a topic that until very recently had remained on the margins of Jewish studies. This collection of essays seeks to introduce to a wider audience the newest insights on the significance of the economy to Jewish history, and to lay a foundation for future studies on the topic.

The workshop was possible thanks to the generous support of the George L. Mosse Foundation. We would especially like to thank John Tortorice for his efforts in organizing the workshop, as well as David Sorkin for his encouragement and helpful advice. Additionally, many thanks go to Sonja Mekel for her assistance in organizing the Madison gathering.

In the time following the conference, other individuals contributed greatly to the completion of this volume. Helen Davies and Samuel Peter Koehne gave valuable comments on the first draft of the manuscript. Our two anonymous readers at Berghahn Books provided invigorating critique and support that substantially improved both individual contributions and the presentation of the volume as a whole. We would also like to thank our publisher for believing in this project despite the many difficulties and setbacks in its emergence. Those participants of the workshop who are not represented in this volume are also due thanks; their contributions helped us to think about the broader themes of this collection and improve our analysis. We would also like again to thank the George L. Mosse Foundation for providing us with funds for the completion of the book index. Finally, we would like to express our deep gratitude to the contributors to this book for their cooperation and endurance during the lengthy process of bringing this volume to fruition.

PROLEGOMENA

to an "Economic Turn" in Jewish History

Gideon Reuveni

A few years ago, when colleagues and friends heard I was preparing a collection of essays on the topic of Jewish sports, a common reaction was: "Oh, this
will no doubt be a short read."[1] A similar response to the study of the economic
aspects of Jewish life is almost inconceivable—indeed, the general image of the
Jews is overloaded with tropes and motifs taken from the sphere of economics.
Yet despite the centrality of economics to Jewish life and to the image of Jews
and Judaism in modern times, Jewish historiography has generally tended to
highlight religious, cultural, and political aspects of the Jewish past more intensively than its economic features. Moreover, if one looks to those occasional
studies of Jewish economic life over the past two centuries, one is struck by the
recurrent calls made by these scholars—suddenly and yet repeatedly aware of
the general neglect of the economy in Jewish studies—to intensify the study of
Jewish economics.[2]

With this volume, we seem to have arrived yet again at this stage. Its aim
is to suggest how scholarship would benefit by putting the "economy" back
on the agenda of Jewish studies. This endeavor is based on the notion that by
placing economics at the center of Jewish experience, we will not only open
still unexplored realms for historical research, but also evoke new readings of
Jewish history. For this purpose, the volume suggests that the term "economy"
should not refer only to the involvement and/or activities of Jews in the production, distribution, and consumption of goods and services. Instead, we call
for a much broader and culturally oriented approach to economic activities,
which, as the anthropologist Maurice Godelier suggested, "is organically linked

with other activities—political, religious, cultural, family—that along with it make up the content of life of [a] society."[3] This approach supposes that the very coherence of the economy and its ability to function depends very much on people's aptitude to interact with each other and to allocate values and norms, and on their willingness to share representations.[4] The eleven essays collected in this volume corroborate this approach. They explore the manifold aspects of the relationship between Jews, culture, and the economy, revealing the potential of a so-called economic turn in the context of Jewish history.

In his programmatic essay *Etwas über die rabbinissche Literatur* (On Rabbinic Literature) of 1818, Leopold Zunz (1794–1886), one of the most prominent German-Jewish intellectuals of the nineteenth century, demanded the inclusion of economic themes in the newly established discipline of *Wissenschaft des Judentums* (science of Judaism) and even pointed to the rich body of sources that could provide for this research.[5] Zunz's ambitious design for an all-encompassing science of Judaism had no followers. The newly founded *Wissenschaft des Judentums* shied away from economic themes and was, as later critics claimed, nothing more than a branch of philology that dealt primarily with philosophical texts.[6]

Not surprisingly, this critique originated from the circles of the Jewish nationalist movements that evolved in the late nineteenth century. As opposed to the *Wissenschaft des Judentums,* which understood Judaism predominantly as a religion, Jewish nationalists regarded Jews as a distinct national or ethnic group. This change of focus from the history of Jews as a religious community to the history of Jews as a people not only had serious political and ideological implications but also signified a methodological reorientation in the writing of Jewish history. An excellent example of this transition is found in the works of the historian Simon Dubnow (1860–1941), one of the leading personalities of the so-dubbed Diaspora-nationalism.[7] In his monumental ten-volume work *World History of the Jewish People,* Dubnow replaced the theological or intellectual view of history popularized by the *Wissenschaft des Judentums* with what he described as a "sociological perspective" of Jewish history, the foundation of which was the premise that Judaism created itself in the image of the social conditions of its national survival, not the other way around.[8] Thus, according to Dubnow, the challenge that faces Jewish historical writing is to record how, notwithstanding Jews' dispersing, a Jewish "social unity" was achieved out of the diversity of the Jewish experience(s). Dubnow hoped to create a valuable niche within this framework for the socioeconomic factors so neglected by the old school of Jewish historians.

While the interest of Jewish scholars such as Zunz and Dubnow in economic activities was informed by the attempt to understand Jewish history in its totality,[9] a further impetus for the growing interest in Jewish economic life came from non-Jewish scholars and the question of the role of Jews within the economy.

Perhaps the most prominent scholar writing on economic aspects of Jewish life in the nineteenth century was Wilhelm Georg Friedrich Roscher, founder of the German school of historical economy.[10] Indeed, Roscher's study of 1875 on "the position of Jews in the Middle Ages from the viewpoint of the general politics of commerce" is considered the cornerstone of modern research on the Jews and the economy.[11] The underlining question posed by Roscher was why one encountered a greater tolerance of the Jews in certain epochs than in others. Roscher recognized the reason for this in a general shift in attitudes toward Jews through social and economic developments. He saw the Jews as the "economic schoolmasters" of Europe—the only group in the early Middle Ages in a position to satisfy the demands of a burgeoning economic trading system.

According to Roscher, the modernizing role of the Jews explains the change in attitudes within the social majority: from tolerance and acceptance to exclusion and persecution. In other words, once, in the eyes of the majority, the role of the Jews becomes superfluous, resentments toward the Jews become more prevalent. This cycle in relations toward Jews, Roscher observed, was not specific to the relationship between Jews and non-Jews but was rather a general development among many peoples who allow their economies to be administered by a foreign and more highly cultivated people, but later, upon having reached the necessary level of development themselves, often after intense struggles, try to emancipate themselves from this tutelage. According to Roscher, "one may defiantly speak in this connection of a historical law here."[12]

A further impetus to the growing interest in Jewish economic life at the beginning of the last century was the so-called capitalism debate.[13] Here the issue was, above all, the problem of the cultural meaning of capitalism and the closely associated question of its historical origins, which ignited extensive controversy in the academic world of the time, a world deeply mired in historicism.[14] This was the case in Max Weber's famous study *The Protestant Ethic and the Spirit of Capitalism*, which was first published in 1904/5.[15] In this study, Weber established a link between the spirit of capitalism and Protestantism, and more specifically English Puritanism. Although Weber's thesis met with contradictory reactions, his basic approach to the search for the origins of capitalism in religion initiated a range of parallel efforts. The most well known example of this is to be found in Werner Sombart's 1911 book *Die Juden und das Wirtschaftsleben*, translated as *The Jews and Modern Capitalism*.[16] Sombart essentially accepted Weber's approach to the religious sources of modern capitalism and even offered his book as a direct development of Weber's study of Protestantism. However, he claimed that everything Weber had ascribed to Puritanism was actually rooted and more intensively practiced by the Jews. Finally, Sombart identified the Jews themselves, as opposed to Jewish culture or religion, as the originators and powerhouse of modern capitalism because of their alleged anthropological (racial) and physiological tendencies. Certainly,

Sombart's more than 450-page book was more of a reiteration of the age-old claim that Jews had a special affinity to money than an innovative explanation for the origin of modern capitalism. Even so, the book, which the liberal political economist Lujo Brentano characterized as "one of the most dreadful phenomena in the area of German social science," initiated vehement discussion.[17] The reason for this was not only Sombart's position as one of the most respected German sociologists of the early twentieth century, a position that gave academic credence to such notions, but also the debate on capitalism itself, which at the turn of the twentieth century reflected the consciousness of a deep-seated schism in the social development of the epoch. As a result, academic interest in the topic of Jews and the economy rose sharply. Jewish scholars in particular felt more duty-bound than most to analyze Jewish history from the perspective of economic primacy. In the center of this new interest stood the economic life of the Jews in the Middle Ages.

"How can it be explained," asked the Polish-born historian Yitzhak (Ignaz) Schipper in his dissertation on *The Beginnings of Capitalism in the early Middle-Ages,* published in 1906, "that the occidental Jews of the first half of the Middle Ages achieved such a strong position in business and differentiated themselves so sharply as an economic group from the rest of their social environment?" In contrast to the attempts to explain the special "Jewish business spirit" as an upshot of alleged race-based predispositions of the Jews, he emphasized the influence of social conditions on Jewish economic differentiation.[18] As an isolated and persecuted people, Schipper maintains, Jews were forced early on to acknowledge the magical power of money. Money, he contends, "afforded [the Jewish people] respect and prestige; money was their only defense amidst economically predatory peoples. It was a salvation and a balm; only money could make the oppressor mild."[19] Notwithstanding the importance Schipper ascribed to the influence of persecution and oppression in the course of Jewish history, he did not represent the Jews as a passive object of history, specializing in business only out of external pressure or innate disposition. For him, the Jewish business of money was the embodiment of Jewish interest and self-assertion. In this respect, Schipper, an active member of the left-wing Zionist movement (Poalei Zion left), is also an excellent representative of the Jewish nationalist interpretation of history, which sought to establish Jewish agency in the form of an autonomous Jewish national will that, as Simon Dubnow proclaimed, was "everywhere and at all times the subject and creative force of its own history, not only in the area of intellectual life but in social life as a whole."[20]

Yet the most notable expression of the new interest in Jewish economic history can be found in the work of the German-Jewish historian George Caro. In his comprehensive but never completed two-volume work *The Social and Economic History of the Jews in the Middle Ages and Modern Times,* Caro refuted all one-sided generalizations on the economic prominence of the Jews.[21] In the introduction to his first volume, published in 1908, he observed that the peculiarities of Jewish economic history preclude the possibility of a generally unified presentation. Jews, he claimed, did not always and everywhere special-ize in trade and finance. Referring to the situation of the Jews in the Middle Ages, Caro pointed out that in all countries where economic conditions had not developed far beyond those of Roman times, for example in the Orient or in the Mediterranean world, separation between the Jews and the rest of society focused primarily on religious distinctions and not on occupational or economic activities. The exclusive association of Jews with money and trade resulted, in his opinion, from times when Jews established themselves in eco-nomically underdeveloped countries. It was in those areas where Jews settled as a small minority among other religious groups that they began to fill in gaps in economic organizations and to secure their existence exclusively through hereditary activity in business.

Unlike Jewish scholars of national-Jewish orientation, such as Simon Dub-now or Yitzhak (Ignaz) Schipper, Caro stressed the significance of religion in Jewish history rather than the nation or social conditions. The history of the Jews, he wrote, is divided into internal (religious) and external (socioeconomic) realms. Whereas the religious sphere forms "the actual content of Jewish his-tory," he placed the possibility of fulfilling religious duties in the latter, external socioeconomic realm. According to Caro, "Wherever [the Jews] were able to establish themselves under tolerable circumstances, their intellectual life blos-somed."[22] Although Caro was speaking more about the economic activities of the Jews than about Jewish economics, he did not underestimate the role of the economy in the development and maintenance of an exclusive Jewish identity. The religious differences between Jews and their neighbors, he observed, even-tually contributed to the fact that the Jews formed a distinct class in almost all countries and lived in isolation from the rest of society.

Following the 1911 publication of Sombart's *Judenbuch*, this line of research, which challenged basic notions of Jewish historical writing such as the relation-ships between internal and external as well as intellectual and material factors in Jewish history, became controversial. Sombart's theses initiated impassioned apologetics among the majority of Jews, who for the most part reacted defen-sively to the one-sided treatment of the subject. It was felt that this representa-tion was an oversimplification of the Jew as *Homo economicus*, who, by dint of a special economic disposition, was unable to integrate into the social environ-ment. Yet by no means did Jewish reactions to Sombart form a united front. While liberal Jews strongly criticized Sombart as an antisemite, others, par-ticularly in the Zionist camp, praised him as a nonpartisan researcher and held up his theses as evidence of Jewish perseverance and acknowledgement of the Jews' special contribution. Sombart's controversial book was even translated into Hebrew in 1912 by a group of young Zionists in Kiev. In the introduction to this volume, they suggested that Sombart's work be considered part of the new Hebrew literary canon, illustrative not only of the phenomenal achievements of the Jewish people, but also demonstrating that the long period of suffering in exile had not been in vain.[23]

Jewish economic discourse thus became highly politicized and could hardly free itself from the long shadow of Sombart's book. The so-called renaissance of Jewish culture in the period between the wars contributed much to this tendency through, among other things, research institutes such as the Akademie für die Wissenschaft des Judentums (Academy for the Scientific Study of the Jewish People, founded in 1919), Die Gesellschaft für die Wissenschaft der Juden (The Society for the Social Science of the Jews, 1924), and YIVO (Yidisher Visnshaftlekher Institut, or the Jewish Scientific Institute, 1925), all of which strongly supported the systematic investigation of the social and economic position of the Jews.[24] Economic research was mobilized as a foundational aspect of Jewish nationalistic efforts. Modern social scientific methodology was applied to refuting the view of the Jews as simply a religious community and to driving the political and practical goals of the Jewish people forward.[25] Works that accentuated Jewish exceptionalism and resilience, like those of Wilhelm Roscher and Werner Sombart, formed the basis for this new direction in research.

It should be noted, however, that in the prewar period, investigation of Jewish economic life was not solely concerned with emphasizing Jewish distinctiveness or the existential vitality of the Jews. The Zionist economic discourse in particular had moments of intense cultural criticism and reformist zeal. Unlike liberal Jews, who recognized a positive relationship between material prosperity and Jewish identity, Zionist historians and social scientists maintained that the improved economic position in the Diaspora led to the decadence and decline of the Jews. Like other cultural critics of the day, Zionist social scientists such as Hayyim D. Horowitz, Arthur Ruppin, Jacob Lestschinsky, and Felix Teilhaber, among others, spoke of the decline of the (Jewish) *Volksgemeinschaft* as a result of modern capitalism and represented the Jews as victims of modernity.[26] This form of cultural pessimism was not limited to the small circle of European Zionists.

A similar argument about the risks that capitalism posed to Jewish endurance was put forth by the renowned historian Salo Wittmayer Baron. Although, in his 1937 three-volume work *A Social and Religious History of the Jews*, Baron still spoke of a kind of *metaphysical sympathy* between Jews and capitalism, he modified his position a few years later, stressing the dangers of modern capitalism to Jewish existence.[27] Modern capitalism, he wrote in his well-known essay on "Capitalism and the Fate of the Jews" of 1942, might offer many advantages to the Jews as individuals, but for Jewish religion and community, the individualism, materialism, rationalism, and secularism that are carried in capitalism represent a decisive threat.[28]

Notwithstanding these debates as well as the growing literature on different aspects of Jewish economic life during the interwar period, historian Bernard D. Weinryb, in an article from 1938, asserted that research on what he called "Jewish economy" was still on the margins of Jewish studies.[29] Almost twenty years later, in a programmatic essay published in the first volume of the newly founded *Leo Baeck Institute Yearbook* in 1956, he took upon himself the challenging task of reevaluating the place of the economy within Jewish history.[30] In this article, Weinryb critically reviewed the narrow approach of non-Jewish scholars that set out solely to examine the Jews' place and role in the economy. At the same time he reproached Jewish scholars, claiming that their interest in this topic was predominantly driven by apologetics designated to highlight the "contribution" of the Jews in order to refute antisemitic attacks, or as means to promote a certain political agenda. A similar view was voiced by the renowned English Jewish historian Cecil Roth, who a few years later bluntly stated that the "study of economic history of the Jews was in the past largely a matter of hit-and-miss."[31]

For Weinryb, the general tendency of Jewish economic historiography to overstress Jewish-Gentile relations and the contribution of the Jews to their surrounding society had, with the Second World War, come to a close. "Today," he wrote, "the return to internal Jewish history and thus 'to clear figures' and 'non-illusionistic' pictures seems to be a logical result of the new situation."[32] Based on this observation, Weinryb suggested that Jewish economic history should deal with the economic life of the Jews within the confines of their own "space" or "social field."[33] Moreover, as opposed to the so-called *Kleinarbeit* (micro-history) approach to Jewish history of the period between the world wars, Weinryb now suggested that placing Jewish economic history within "a large-scale synthetic narrative of Jewish history" would underpin general trends and parallels in the history of the Jews in different countries.[34] Like Leopold Zunz's ambitious design for an all-encompassing science of Judaism at the beginning of the nineteenth century, or Dubnow's sociological approach to Jewish history from the beginning of the twentieth century, Weinryb's scheme for a grand narrative of Jewish economic history still waits to be written.

Now, at the beginning of the twenty-first century, neither the question of the place of the Jews in the economy nor other economic aspects of Jewish life seem to arrest the same amount of attention as they did at the beginning of the last century. In fact, it appears that the "economy" has been pushed to the margins of the Jewish discourse in the decades since the end of the Second World War. Even the expanding discipline of Jewish studies appears to forgo economic topics. Consider the example of *The Oxford Handbook of Jewish Studies*, first published in 2002, which aims to cover all main areas currently taught and researched as part of Jewish studies in universities throughout the world.[35] The span of the volume chronologically and geographically is thus enormous.

It contains articles on a range of topics from biblical studies and Hebrew literature through Jewish philosophy and languages to Jewish women's studies, theater, and Israeli film, to mention but a few of the topics covered in this volume.
In this framework, however, economy is a non-topic. According to the detailed
subject index of the handbook, the term economy or economics occurs only
once in this volume of over a thousand pages. Other related terms like money
or even commerce do not appear at all. In this respect as well, the handbook
seems indeed to provide a precise snapshot of the current state of research in
Jewish studies, which focuses on the history, literature, religion, and culture of
the Jews more intensively than on economic features.

What is the meaning of this silence? Why are scholars of Jewish history
today inclined to shun economic topics? I would like to suggest three possible
answers to this question. As we saw above, especially after the publication of
Sombart's work, the economy and the way it was studied became an integral
part of the politics of being Jewish. Thus the politicization of this area of research might explain some scholars' reluctance to deal with economic issues
in Jewish life. Another factor that could explain the marginalization of the
economy from Jewish history is the general historiographical shift away from
political and social history toward cultural history. The "cultural turn" seems to
find harmony with the emerging field of Jewish studies, thus providing scholars
with a new framework to represent Jewish culture and history beyond the nation-state. Questions regarding Jewish experience and especially Jewish identity have become the focus of this new line of research, which still dominates
Jewish studies today.

And finally the third and probably most contentious reason for the tendency
to avoid economic issues in Jewish history is related in my view to the special
relationship between Jews and power. Money, as we all know, is power, and the
association of the two with Jews played an incisive role in Western culture.
Throughout history the affiliation of Jews to money fed anti-Jewish sentiments
and still to a large extent determines how we imagine Jews today. Indeed, the
figure of the mighty, greedy Jew still haunts us, although since the Shoah relat-
ing to Jews in terms of power has become a highly sensitive matter, one result of
which is the inclination to avoid representations of Jewish power altogether.

This volume cannot claim to fill this gap or for that matter even provide a
comprehensive overview of the vast sphere of the relations between Jews and
the economy. Its aim is to suggest how scholarship would benefit by putting the
"economy" back on the agenda of Jewish studies. A case in point is Jonathan
Karp's contribution to this volume, in which he explores how economic history
can date the inception of a Jewish modern period. At the core of Karp's reflections is the tension between two opposing perceptions of the relation between
Jews and modernity as they pertain to the question of the place of the Jews in
the economy. On the one hand, he refers to the close association between Jews

and modern capitalism. The stereotypical profile of the Jews as quintessential middlemen, traders, and moneylenders makes them modern even before modernity.[36] Yet at the same time, Karp points out that many of the central movements of modern Jewish history depicted Jews as a backward and unproductive group immersed in their traditions, thus setting as their aim the modernization of Jewish life. According to Karp, this paradoxical conception of the Jews as simultaneously avant-garde and retrograde is an upshot of changing economic doctrines in the period of the Enlightenment, which clearly reflects a change in the attitudes toward Jewish economic life. The irony of this new "modern" consciousness is that it is based upon a recognition of Jewish backwardness as opposed to earlier perceptions of the Jewish economic role that tended to regard the Jews as modernizers. By establishing the link between these new attitudes toward the Jews and the economic doctrines and ideologies of the Enlightenment, Karp demonstrates how economic history can help us date the onset of Jewish modernity.

There is much more to be said about the potential of this proposed "economic turn" in Jewish studies. Let us take as an example the issue of trust, no doubt one of the basic forms of social life and indeed a vital presupposition for the success of activities in the economic realm.[37] Was it simply utilitarian economic parameters, or were confessional and particular ethnic affiliations definitive for the trusting interactions between businesspeople of the same or different confessions and backgrounds? This question is to a large degree still unaddressed by historians of Jewish history. Within this context, the problem of access to credit is a source of exciting questions. Thus, for example, the availability of credit in the towns of the early modern period was tied to membership in particular corporations. Central to the honor of the merchants in the estate society stood the concept of the "merchant's credit," not just in the modern sense of creditworthiness, but also representing an estate-based reputation. A person's creditworthiness was closely identified with his trustworthiness. It is well known that Jews could not be members of guilds. To what extent and in which forms they were participants in this network of trust and confidence remains to be researched in more detail. Based on our knowledge today, it appears that since the Jews were bound into the estate system as a quasi-independent corporation, their creditworthiness as well as their economic transactions in general were identified with their Jewishness.

These observations corroborate with Susanne Bennewitz's work on Jewish middlemen activities in the Swiss city of Basel at the beginning of the nineteenth century. In her chapter in this volume, Bennewitz looks at a specific subtype of middlemen activities—informal brokerage, or schmoozing. Not the classical middleman, the schmoozer was not a trader or a third party amid producers and consumers, but a go-between, an intermediary and informal broker. He was an agent who was not involved legally in the business transaction itself.

What was typical about his services was his independence. The schmoozer not only mediated between two or more parties, he actually brought them together on a concrete deal. His work consisted in walking and talking, that is, in collecting information and networking. While schmoozers were predominantly Jewish, they interacted and had relationships with Jews and non-Jews alike, performing actions together, to use the language of present-day network analysts, that cause self-change and change in the system they formed.[38] Bennewitz observes that the schmoozer appears to blur distinctions between business relations and informal social interaction. Thus, what is particular about the schmoozer is that he transformed information and informal social relations into economic capital. Is the schmoozer then a forerunner of what contemporary observers refer to as "information economy" or "network society"? This is an interesting question that not only suggests how scholarship of Jewish economy could benefit from some of the recent developments in social sciences.[39] It also calls into question straightforward temporal disjunctures, according to which we now live in a time characterized by a radically different relationship between economy and culture than past eras, thus locating the question of Jewish modernity within wider debates regarding the nature of modernity.[40]

While Bennewitz explores the activities of small informal brokers in the pre-emancipation period, Helen Davies examines in her chapter the interplay between cultural heritage, political conviction, and economic activities of large-scale bankers and financiers in the second half of nineteenth century France. She provides a meticulous depiction of the brothers Emil and Isaac Pereire as children of the Sephardic community in Bordeaux, early socialists, innovative entrepreneurs, and adversaries of the Rothschild family. Moving to Paris at the beginning of the 1820s, the Pereires founded the *Crédit Mobilier* in 1852. As an investment bank, the *Crédit Mobilier* was influenced by Saint-Simonian ideas of a central banking system that would provide new sources of capital to contribute to the development of public and industrial credit based on principles of mutuality and the dissemination of interest-bearing banknotes. In a way, the business ideas of the Pereires call to mind more recent theories of social capitalism that contend, for example, that a strong social support network for the poor enhances capital output.[41] Yet, according to Davies, the social capitalism of the Pereires was not solely informed by Saint-Simonianism, but also drew upon elements that were derived from their Sephardic heritage. Thus, for example, she alludes to the significance of the Sephardic oligarchy of businessmen in the Pereires' conception of good governance. Another example is the Saint-Simonian doctrine to ensure the improvement of society's deprived classes, which, as Davies notes, was immediately comprehensible to men like the Pereires, for whom charity was a central constituent of their Judaism. Her observations suggest that closely associated with the complex of issues surrounding economic activities is the question of group identity.

Based on Marx's remark that "Judaism continues to exist not in spite of history, but owing to history," it was initially Marxist scholars who stressed the key role of the economy in the preservation of Jewish identity throughout history.[42] In the Middle Ages, for instance, the Marxist theoretician Karl Kautsky noted, in an essay published in 1890, that "to be a Jew meant not only to be a member of a particular nation, but also of a particular profession."[43] This notion of a "people-class" was enhanced and further developed by Abram Leon in his famous study on the Jewish Question, written in 1940. According to Leon, the concepts of class and people do not necessarily contradict each other. "It is because the Jews have preserved themselves as a social class," he maintains, "they have retained … certain of their religious, ethnic, and linguistic traits."[44] The significance of this theory does not merely lie in the association between Jews and certain professions, but in the finding that Jewish identity and survival is embedded in the economic and social system. Leon presents Judaism as an indispensable factor of precapitalist society. "It is no accident," he writes, "that a foreign element played the role of 'capital' in feudal society."[45] According to this view, "from the moment that capitalism begins to emerge from the womb of [the feudal] social system and takes the place of the borrowed organ, the Jew is eliminated and feudal society ceases to be feudal."[46] Thus, the "Jewish problem" is the dissolution of Jewish identity as a result of the evolution of modern capitalism.

Leon's approach did not find many followers in the postwar period. Echoing Georg Caro's perspective on the positive connection between economic prosperity and Jewish identity, historian Ellis Rivkin, for example, argued that "wherever anticapitalism or precapitalism has prevailed the status of the Jews and Judaism has either undergone deterioration or is highly precarious."[47] Writing in the heyday of the Cold War, Rivkin drew a direct connection between the degree to which capitalism is developed and the extent of freedom to perform and practice Jewishness. Based on this approach he even claimed that Jews enjoyed more freedom in the United States—the most advanced capitalist country—than in the developing Jewish state.

Yet a more prevailing approach today allocates the multifaceted interaction between economy and Jewish identity to the minority status of the Jews. "If the economic structure of an entire people is considered to be 'normal,' then the economic structure of a small and permanent minority must, by definition, be abnormal. If not, a minority would soon lose its identity as a specific group."[48] This is how the prominent economist Simon Kuznets identified the problem in his influential study "Economic Structure and Life of the Jews." Kuznets's groundbreaking work put the question of the "normalization" of Jewish economic life, which had played a central role in the history of European Jewry since the eighteenth century, in a new light and emphasized the importance of economics as fundamental to the development of group identity.[49] In recent years, this assessment has found broad support through the influence of concepts such as multiculturalism, postcolonialism, and the global Diaspora. An outstanding example for this is presented in Derek Penslar's groundbreaking book *Shylock's Children*.[50] For Penslar, the connection between group identity and economics is beyond question. This relationship applies to all minorities but especially to the Jews, whose concentration in particular economic sectors in the face of rampant modernization and secularization since the eighteenth century provided a structural firewall against the loss of collective identity. Given this analysis, Penslar considers the blurring of contemporary North American Jewry's economic distinctiveness as one of the major challenges facing modern Jewish identity.[51] These concerns call to mind similar apprehensions regarding the fate of German Jews in the Weimar years. Notwithstanding the rise of National Socialism, by the late 1920s some prominent Jewish social scientists were already expressing serious doubts as to whether German Jewry could retain its sense of communal identity after inflation and depression practically destroyed its distinctive social and economic fabric.[52]

If indeed the economy plays such a defining role in upholding a sense of Jewish distinctiveness, how, if at all, can "Jewish economy" illuminate economic life in general? But before we can even start thinking about this question it seems we have to come to terms with another, no less challenging matter—what is Jewish economy? According to Jacob Neusner, the notion that Jews have an economic history apparently "takes for granted that there is a single economically cogent group, the Jews, which has had a single ('an') economic history, and which, therefore, forms a distinctive unit of economic action and thought."[53] This reproach suggests that we should turn away from the notion that the Jews formed a single, linear, unitary group in all places and throughout history, and instead assume a more miscellaneous and fluid conceptualization of Jewishness that does not assume "master" narratives or "unchanging monolithic categories like 'nation' and 'religion.'"[54]

The eleven chapters collected in this volume confirm this approach to Jewish history. They do not amass a master narrative of a Jewish economy, but instead offer a range of perspectives on what we may refer to as Jewish economies. Most illustrative of this shift toward a multiplicity of historical perspectives is the section of the book that deals with Jewish economic activities in national and transnational settings. Here Michael Miller portrays the pivotal position of Moritz Jellinek in the economic modernization of Hungary. Unlike his more renowned two brothers Herman and Adolf, who left their hometown in Moravia to pursue careers in the world of letters in Germany and Austria, Moritz turned to the world of business and decided to pursue his fortune in Hungary. Miller suggests that Jellinek's pivotal position in the economic modernization of Hungary can be used as an indicator of the role Jews played as modernizers of Hungary at that time. Yet in the second half of the nineteenth century, the project of modernity was not restricted to the economic realm alone but was strongly bound to the creation of the nation-state. Indeed, as Miller shows, Jellinek was well aware of this connection, and although he had come to Hungary from abroad he developed strong nationalist sentiments, viewing himself as Hungarian and his financial and business activities as an integral part of the Hungarian nation-state building project.

While Miller shows how Jewish business activities were immersed in a national setting, Sarah Abrevaya Stein highlights the transnational aspects of Jewish commerce. Dealing with the ostrich feather trade at the turn of the last century, she is compelled to recognize the overwhelming presence of Jews in the commerce of this luxury good. Thus, instead of trying to underplay this particularity, she calls for situating this global commodity chain within a larger framework of colonialism and the emergence of modern consumer culture. According to Stein, only by placing the Jewish feather trade within this wider context can we start appreciating the multifaceted interplay between commerce and ethnicity, and illuminate the involvement of Jews in the modern flow of capital. Moreover, while Stein considers ethnicity an important force shaping the ostrich feather trade network, she contests notions that view Jews as a sealed, unified ethnos. By introducing the notion of sub-ethnicity, she reveals schisms and manifold distinctions between distinct groups of Jewish merchants, illuminating the different ways in which they were involved and practiced business. Thus, for example, Stein shows that while the Ashkenazi ostrich industry of South Africa profited considerably from colonial politics, the Sephardic ostrich feather trade of North Africa was adversely affected by European colonialism.

While Stein examines a global commodity chain that goes from the colonies to Europe, Adam Mendelsohn's chapter explores the opposite trajectory, from Europe to the colonies. He offers a fascinating case study of the involvement of Jews in a most unlikely commodity trade—Christian missionary Bibles. By exploring the trade in Bibles, Mendelsohn demonstrates how the focus on traditional colonial goods confines our understanding of the nature and scope of cultural exchange taking place across global trading routes to those products that make their way to major urban centers in Europe. One of the outcomes of this approach is a careful reassessment of the impact of Christian missionaries in the nineteenth century. According to Mendelsohn, the mass production of bootleg Bibles facilitated new markets for reading material, making book reading an agent of cultural change and modernization in different places outside of Europe. Jews were involved in this development in two main ways: as middlemen and traders, but also as consumers of these cheap, bootleg Bibles.

David De Vries explores another key commodity in the global network of luxury products—the diamond. Unlike Stein and Mendelsohn, who write the commodity chain network into the transnational histories of colonialism and consumerism, De Vries's chapter deals with the diamond industry within the context of Zionist nation-building in the period before the foundation of the

state of Israel. He recalls that up until the 1930s even those Jews who dominated the diamond business did not consider Zionist Palestine as an alternative
to the major diamond centers in Amsterdam and Antwerp. All this changed,
however, with the rise of Fascism, the strengthening of commercial ties between the British Empire and the De Beers diamond cartel, and finally the
outbreak of the Second World War. Hence, corporate and imperial economic
interests as well as international politics eventually introduced the diamond
business to the evolving Zionist polity. It is thus not surprising that the Zionist
movement reacted toward this development equivocally. While liberal Zionists
welcomed the decision to develop a diamond industry in Palestine and saw it as
an opportunity to enhance and legitimize entrepreneurship and capitalism in
the Jewish polity, leading Zionist organizations at the time were initially much
less receptive to this development. Labor Zionism especially saw the diamond
industry as an example of exploitative capitalism, reminiscent of the worst in
Jewish history. Yet, as De Vries notes, the more the Zionist establishment realized the economic significance of this industry the closer it came to embracing
its achievements. Finally, De Vries points to the nationalization or "Zionization" of the diamond industry, by which it became an integral part of Zionist
state-building in Palestine.

No discussion of Jewish economic history can forgo the question of perception and the way Jews are represented as economic actors by Jews and non-
Jews alike. Two essays in particular in this volume explore the different ways
in which Jews are imagined as *Homo economicus*. Looking at economic metaphors in narratives of Jews and Jewishness, Kirill Postoutenko discusses what
we might call the theology of Jewish economic distinctiveness. Specifically, he
analyzes the use of wandering as a type of circulation in the writings of Karl
Marx and Fyodor Dostoevsky. Both, following different Hegelian traditions,
describe the Jewish god in abstract terms—as money represents an abstraction
of actual wealth—and equate the historical teleology of Judaism (wandering)
with the economic teleology of capitalism (circulation). Yet while Dostoevsky's
religious antisemitism privileged a kind of anti-modern nativism and extolled
the virtues of rootedness to the soil, Marx's economical anti-Semitism emphasized universalism and the value of human labor. Thus, Postoutenko notes that
for both thinkers the spatial metaphor of the Jew (wandering/circulation) presents a new dialectic notion of evil.

Anthony Kauders's contribution explores the image of the "money-Jew" in a
period in which the decision to reside in Germany was tantamount to breaking
a taboo. For Jews living in Israel and elsewhere, the only reason that could account for the persistence of a Jewish presence in postwar Germany was material
gain. Interestingly, in Kauders's account, the self-perception of many of those
Jews residing in the Federal Republic was not far from the view that saw them
as merely pursuing "Egypt's pot of meat." Kauders claims that many of these

Jews seem to have chosen portable vocations and designed their lives in such a way as to facilitate a swift relocation, if suddenly needed or desired. Moreover, Kauders indicates that even the desire for rapid accumulation of wealth should be interpreted as an upshot of the situation of the Jews in the Federal Republic. He argues that money facilitated flexibility and a sense of control over their destiny as well as symbolizing recovery and empowerment in the midst of the perpetrators' society. Not surprisingly, in the eyes of non-Jews this declarative use of money to demonstrate power and to display belonging served as a pretext to conjure up long-standing anti-Semitic images of the greedy and dodgy "capitalist Jew." Kauders, however, suggests that by the 1980s, once Jews started accepting their own presence in Germany as given, there was no need to ascribe a distinct social meaning to money, and consequently the relations between Jews and their non-Jewish environment entered a new phase.

Interestingly, up until recently the discourse on Jewish economics was carried out primarily from the perspective of the producers and even the capitalists, that is, from the perspective of Jews as moneymakers.[55] One can only wonder why it took scholars of Jewish culture so long to appreciate the significance of consumption, not least because of the weight Judaism ascribes to consumption. Indeed, the question of spending gained much more attention within Judaism than that of earning. The Kashrut laws that up to today comprise an important part of Jewish life are a profound example of the significance of consumption in traditional Jewish life. What one is allowed to eat, how one should dress, or even how one should spend his or her free time are only some of the issues that belong to the régimes of consumerism that are strictly regulated in Judaism. As opposed to the intervention and rigidity in the realm of consumption, the issue of earning a living within Judaism seems to reveal a great deal more pragmatism and flexibility.[56] Two essays in particular in this volume address the question of how the emerging consumer culture interplayed with the lives of European Jews. In her chapter, Sarah Wobick-Segev discusses coffeehouses as sites of consumption and display in three nineteenth-century German cities. She shows how consumption provided new venues to imagine cultural belonging beyond the existing structure of religious, political, and cultural differences. In Wobick-Segev's narrative, the coffeehouse becomes a spectacle of German-Jewish selfhood, revealing how Jews sought to maintain a separate identity while at the same time developing a sense of belonging to the majority society. Thus, for Jews, visiting coffeehouses was not simply a leisure activity. Purchasing coffee at a coffeehouse is interpreted here as the purchase of social place. Wobick-Segev notes that this declarative use of social space to profess and display belonging was precisely the conduct that evoked the bile of many non-Jewish coffeehouse guests and owners.

The department store, no doubt one of the hallmarks of modern consumer culture, is the focus of Paul Lerner's chapter. He explores representations and images of department stores in Germany around the turn of the twentieth century, showing how at that time the construction of the power of consumer culture and the economic power of Jews were represented as overlapping and even identical forces. Thus, for example, the allegedly manipulative power of the new cathedrals of consumption was equated with long-standing stereotypes of Jewish shady business practices, as well as Jews' sexual depravity. According to Lerner, the link between the opposition to mass consumption and the rise of new forms of anti-Semitism is not coincidental, and should be understood as part of the struggle to organize and tame the social space and time in which modernity is acted out.

The cumulative effect of the essays presented in this volume reinforces the argument of the impressive multiplicity of meanings embedded in the conjunction of culture, the economy, and Jewish history. This point might seem obvious to some readers, but until recently scholarship has done relatively little to address the multifaceted dominations of these interrelationships. It is our hope that this volume will invite scholars to explore further this threefold conjunction so that the economy as a cultural field will receive its worthy place in Jewish studies.

NOTES

1. Michael Brenner and Gideon Reuveni, eds., *Emancipation Through Muscles: Jews and Sports in Europe* (Lincoln: University of Nebraska Press, 2006). Further recent publications in this area include Jack Kugelmass, ed., *Jews, Sports, and the Rites of Citizenship* (Chicago: University of Illinois, 2007); Ezra Mendelsohn, ed., *Jews and the Sporting Life* (New York: Oxford University Press, 2008).
2. See for example Nachum Gross et al., eds., *Economic History of the Jews* (New York: Schocken Books, 1975); Nachum Gross, ed., *Jews in Economic Life* [in Hebrew] (Jerusalem: Shazar Centre, 1985); Menahem Ben Sasson, ed., *Economy and Religion* [in Hebrew] (Jerusalem: Shazar Centre, 1995); W. D. Rubinstein, "Jews in the Economic Elites of Western Nations and Antisemitism," *The Jewish Journal of Sociology* 42, nos. 1 and 2 (2000), 5–36.
3. Maurice Godelier, *Rationality and Irrationality in Economics* (New York: Monthly Review Press, 1972), 263.
4. For further discussion on this approach to culture and the economy see Paul du Gay and Michael Preke, eds., *Cultural Economy* (London: Sage, 2002), as well as in the newly founded *Journal of Cultural Economy*.
5. Leopold Zunz, *Etwas über die rabbinische Literatur* (Berlin: In der Maurerschen Buchhandlung, 1818), 24.

6. On this approach see Gershom Scholem, "Wissenschaft vom Judentum einst und jetzt," in Gershom Scholem, *Judaica I* (Frankfurt a.M.: Suhrkamp Verlag, 1963), 147–164.

7. On Dubnow and his concept of Jewish history see Anke Hilbrenner, *Diaspora-Nationalismus: Zur Geschichtskonstruktion Simon Dubnows* (Göttingen: Vandenhoeck & Ruprecht, 2006). For a useful overview of the Jewish political landscape of the time see Ezra Mendelsohn, *On Modern Jewish Politics* (New York: Oxford University Press, 1993).

8. Simon Dubnow, *Weltgeschichte des jüdischen Volkes*, vol. 1 (Berlin: Jüdischer Verlag, 1928).

9. On this idea of a total Jewish history see also Eugen Täubler's notion of an all encompassing German Jewish history as an integral part of German history: Eugen Täubler, *Aufsätze zur Problematik jüdischer Geschichtsschreibung 1908–1950* (Tübingen: Mohr, 1977).

10. Guido Kisch, "The Jews' Function in the Medieval Evolution of Economic Life: In Commemoration of a Great Scholar and his Theory," *Historia Judaica* 6 (1944): 1–12; Toni Oelsen, "Wilhelm Roscher's Theory of the Economic and Social Position of the Jews in the Middle Ages," *Yivo Annual of Jewish Social Science* 12 (1958/59), 176–195.

11. Wilhelm Georg Friedrich Roscher, "Die Stellung der Juden im Mittelalter, betrachtet vom Standpunkte der allgemeinen Handelspolitik," *Zeitschrift für die gesamte Staatswissenschaft* 21 (1875): 503–526. Parts of this article were published in English translation as Wilhelm Georg Friedrich Roscher, "The Status of the Jews in the Middle Ages Considered from the Standpoint of Commercial Policy," *Historia Judaica* 6 (1944), 13–26.

12. Roscher, "The Status of the Jews," 26. Reflecting on Roscher's model of explaining the economic function of the Jews, historian Raphael Strauss, writing at the beginning of the Second World War, interestingly observed: "Down to the to the complete collapse of 1933 there was no period in Central European history in which the rulers did not support the Jews and protected them against the shortsighted pressure of special interests and nationalist prejudice, strong rulers successfully and weak ones unsuccessfully. Hence the vacillating policy pursued against the Jews throughout the centuries with alternations of privileges, toleration, and expulsion." Raphael Strauss, "Jews in the Economic Evolution of Central Europe," *Jewish Social Studies* 3 (1941), 15–40, here 38.

13. On this debate see, for example, Elmar Waibl, *Ökonomie und Ethik* (Stuttgart: Frommann-Holzboog, 1985).

14. Shionoya Yuichi, ed., *The German Historical School: The Historical and Ethical Approach to Economics* (London: Routledge, 2001).

15. Max Weber, *The Protestant Ethic and the Spirit of Capitalism* (London: Routledge, 2005). On Weber's approach to the Jews see Gary A. Abraham, *Max Weber and the Jewish Question: A Study of the Social Outlook of his Sociology* (Urbana: University of Illinois Press, 1992).

16. Werner Sombart, *The Jews and Modern Capitalism*, translated by M. Epstein (New Brunswick: Transaction Books, 1997). On Sombart and Max Weber see for example: Arthur Mitzman, *Sociology and Estrangement: Three Sociologists of Imperial*

Germany (New York: Knopf, 1973); Freddy Raphael, *Judaisme et Capitalisme: essai sur la controverse entre Max Weber et Werner Sombart* (Paris: Presses Univ. de France, 1982); Avraham Barkai, "Judentum, Juden und Kapitalismus. Ákonomische Vorstellungen von Max Weber und Werner Sombart," *Menora* 5 (1994), 25–38.

17. Lujo Brentano, *Die Anfänge des modernen Kapitalismus* (Munich: Verl. der K.B. Akademie der Wissenschaft, 1916), 159. On the debate surrounding Sombart's work see Alfred Philipp, "Die Juden und das Wirtschaftsleben. Eine antikritisch-bibliographische Studie zu Werner Sombart: 'Die Juden und das Wirtschaftsleben,'" PhD diss., University of Berlin, 1929; Toni Oelson, "The Place of the Jews in Economic History as Viewed by German Scholars," *Leo Baeck Institute Year Book* (1962), 183–212; S. David Landes, "The Jewish Merchant: Typology and Stereotypology in Germany," *Leo Baeck Institute Year Book* (1974), 11–30; Paul Mendes-Flohr, "Werner Sombart's *The Jews and Modern Capitalism*: An Analysis of Its Ideological Premises," *Leo Baeck Institute Year Book* (1976), 87–107.

18. Ignaz Schipper, "Anfänge des Kapitalismus bei den abendländischen Juden im frühen Mittelalter," *Zeitschrift für Volkswirtschaft, Sozialpolitik und Verwaltung* 15 (1906): 501–564. On Schipper: Jacob Litman, *The Economic Role of Jews in Medieval Poland: The Contribution of Yitzhak Schipper* (Lanham: University Press of America, 1984).

19. Schipper, "Anfänge des Kapitalismus," 564.

20. Dubnow, *Weltgeschichte des jüdischen Volkes*, xv.

21. Georg Caro, *Sozial- und Wirtschaftsgeschichte der Juden im Mittelalter und der Neuzeit* (Hildesheim: G. Olms, 1964, first published in 1908).

22. Ibid., 9.

23. Werner Sombart, *The Jews and their Participation in the Creation of the Present-Day Economy*, translated into Hebrew by Israel Shalom Bauhauslauwizsky (Kiev: Globermann Print, 1912), 1.

24. On these institutes see Michael Brenner, *The Renaissance of Jewish Culture in Weimar Germany* (New Haven: Yale University Press, 1996); Mitchell B. Hart, *Social Science and the Politics of Modern Jewish Identity* (Stanford: Stanford University Press, 2000).

25. On this aspect see Hart, *Social Science*.

26. Ibid.

27. Salo W. Baron, *A Social and Religious History of the Jews*, vol. 2 (New York: Columbia University Press, 1937), 187. For a critical view on Baron's work: Yitzchak Baer, "A Social and Religious History of the Jews (Comments on S. Baron's New Book)" [in Hebrew], *Zion* (1938), 277–299.

28. Salo W. Baron, "Modern Capitalism and Jewish Fate," in Salo W. Baron, *History and Historians* (Philadelphia: The Jewish Publication Society, 1964), 43–64.

29. Bernard D. Weinryb, "Jewish Economy" [in Hebrew], *Moznayim* 7 (1938), 336–344.

30. Bernard D. Weinryb, "Prolegomena to an Economic History of the Jews in Germany in Modern Times," *Leo Baeck Institute Yearbook* 1 (1956), 279–306.

31. Cecil Roth, "The Economic History of the Jews," *Economic History Review* 14 (1961), 131–135, 131.

32. Weinryb, "Prolegomena," 284.

33. Ibid., 295–296.

34. Ibid., 285.

35. Martin Goodman, Jeremy Cohen, and David Sorkin, eds., *The Oxford Handbook of Jewish Studies* (Oxford: Oxford University Press, 2002).

36. Gary Martin Levine, *The Merchant of Modernism: The Economic Jew in Anglo-American Literature, 1864–1939* (New York: Routledge, 2003).

37. On the notion of trust in the economy: Tanja Ripperger, *Ökonomik des Vertrauen* (Tübingen: Mohr Siebeck Verlag 1998); Ute Frevert, ed., *Vertrauen: Historische Annäherungen* (Göttingen: Vandenhoeck & Ruprecht, 2003).

38. Christian Fuchs, "Transnational Space and 'Network Society,'" *21st Century Society* 2, no. 1 (2007), 49–78.

39. For some recent attempts to employ economic theories to explain economic aspects of Jewish life in the past see Maristella Botticini and Zvi Eckstein, *From Farmers to Merchants: A Human Capital Interpretation of Jewish Economic History* (London: Center for Economic Policies, 2002); Avner Greif, *Institutions and the Path to the Modern Economy: Lessons from Medieval Trade* (Cambridge: Cambridge University Press, 2006); Adam Teller, *Money, Power, and Influence: The Jews on the Radziwill Estates in 18th Century Lithuania* [in Hebrew] (Jerusalem: Shazar Centre, 2005).

40. Bjorn Wittrock, "Modernity: One, None, or Many?" *Daedalus* 129, no. 1 (2000), 31–60.

41. Richard Sennett, *The Culture of the New Capitalism* (New Haven: Yale University Press, 2006).

42. Karl Marx, *The Jewish Question*, available on http://www.marxists.org/archive/marx/works/1844/jewish-question/ (accessed on August 16, 2010).

43. Cited in Nathan Weinstock's introduction to Abrahm Leon, *The Jewish Question: A Marxist Interpretation* (New York: Pathfinder Press, 1970), 38.

44. Leon, *The Jewish Question*, 80.

45. Ibid., 249.

46. Ibid.

47. Ellis Rivkin, *The Shaping of Jewish History: A Radical New Interpretation* (New York: Charles Scribner's Sons, 1971), 329.

48. Simon Kuznets, "Economic Structure and Life of the Jews," in *The Jews: Their History, Culture and Religion*, ed. Louis Finkelstein (New York: Schocken, 1960), 1601.

49. For more on this see Jonathan Karp, *The Politics of Jewish Commerce: Economic Thought and Emancipation in Europe, 1638–1848* (Cambridge: Cambridge University Press, 2008).

50. Derek J. Penslar, *Shylock's Children: Economics and Jewish Identity in Modern Europe* (Berkeley: University of California Press, 2001).

51. In this context Penslar cites Edna Bonacich and John Modell's study on the economic basis of ethnic solidarity, claiming that "when minorities become like majority economically, it is difficult to preserve their distinctiveness." Penslar, *Shylock's Children*, 261.

52. On this see especially Alfred Marcus, *Die wirtschaftliche Krise des deutschen Juden: Eine soziologische Untersuchung* (Berlin: Georg Stilke, 1931); Jacob Lestschinsky, *Das wirtschaftliche Schicksal des deutschen Judentums: Aufstieg, Wandlung, Krise, Aus-*

blick (Berlin: Zentralwohlfahrtsstelle der Deutschen Juden, 1932). More generally on this discourse see Martin Liepach, "Das Krisenbewusstsein des jüdischen Bürgertums in den Goldenen Zwanzigern," in *Juden, Bürger, Deutsche: Zur Geschichte von Vielfalt und Differenz 1800–1933*, ed. Andreas Gotzmann, Rainer Liedtke, and Till van Rahden (Tübingen: Mohr, 2001), 395–418; Moshe Zimmermann, *Die deutschen Juden 1914–1945* (Munich: Oldenbourg, 1997).

53. Jacob Neusner, *Why Does Judaism Have an Economics?* (New London: Connecticut College, 1988), 22.

54. David Biale, "Preface," in David Biale, ed., *Cultures of the Jews: A New History* (New York: Schocken, 2002), xxx.

55. Most work on Jews as consumers deals with the American experience; see especially Andrew Heinze, *Adapting to Abundance: Jewish Immigrants, Mass Consumption, and the Search for American Identity* (New York: Columbia University Press, 1990); Marilyn Halter, *Shopping for Identity: The Marketing of Ethnicity* (New York: Schocken Books, 2000); Elizabeth Hafkin Pleck, *Celebrating the Family: Ethnicity, Consumer Culture, and Family Rituals* (Cambridge, MA: Harvard University Press, 2000). On the European context see Leora Auslander, "'Jewish Taste'? Jews, and the Aesthetics of Everyday Life in Paris and Berlin, 1933–1942," in *Histories of Leisure*, ed. Rudy Koshar (Oxford: Berg, 2002), 299–331; Auslander, "Beyond Words," *The American Historical Review* 110 (2005), 1015–1045.

56. David Biale, "Jewish Consumer Culture in Historical and Contemporary Perspective," in *Longing, Belonging, and the Making of Jewish Consumer Culture*, ed. Gideon Reuveni and Nils Roemer (Leiden: Brill Publications, 2010); Mordechai Levin, *Social and Economic Values: The Idea of Professional Modernization in the Ideology of the Haskalah Movement* [in Hebrew] (Jerusalem: Byalik Institute, 1975); Meir Tamari, *The Challenge of Wealth: A Jewish Perspective on Earning and Spending Money* (Nothvale, NJ: J. Aronson, 1995), Meir Tamari, *"With all Your Possessions": Jewish Ethics and Economic Life* (New York: Free Press, 1987).

❧ I ❧

RETHINKING THE ECONOMY
IN JEWISH HISTORY

1

CAN ECONOMIC HISTORY DATE THE INCEPTION OF JEWISH MODERNITY?

Jonathan Karp

Two questions arise when we combine the terms Jews, modernity, and economics: first, "When do Jews enter the modern economic age?" and second, "Is there something characteristically *Jewish* about modern economic life?" In juxtaposition, these questions appear to be mutually exclusive. The first assumes the prior existence of economic modernity and the Jews' eventual incorporation into it, while the second presumes that Jews are the actual agents of this modernity. In the one case the Jews are backward, in the other ahead of their time.

Though these views are contradictory, each is in its own way also logical. The rationale behind the depictions of Jews as harbingers of modern capitalism, for instance, appears clear enough. Their stereotypical (exaggerated but not fabricated) profile as quintessential middlemen, merchants, brokers, peddlers, hucksters, moneylenders, and bankers (all distinct but functionally related activities) would seem to anticipate definite trends in modern economic life: the decline of once numerically predominant peasantries, vastly increased urbanization, expanded commercial liberalization, the growth of credit institutions, and an ever more globalized trade. The fact that Jews acquired their middleman profile in the late medieval and early modern periods suggests that they were "modern" before modernity, or capitalist before capitalism. Yet evidence for the opposite conclusion is equally powerful. Many of the core movements of modern Jewish history—the Haskalah, the rise of secular Jewish philanthropy, not to mention many strands within Zionism and the Jewish left—reflect an image of Jews as backward, divorced from productive labor and primary production, alienated from their physical bodies as well as from the land and soil,

---

Notes for this chapter begin on page 37.

overrepresented in their "traditional" outmoded occupations and woefully un-
derrepresented in the "productive" activity of agriculture and heavy industry.[1]

Whereas these critiques originated in Western and Central Europe during
the eighteenth century, they would become equally prominent decades later in
Eastern Europe, despite the major structural differences between the economic
lives of Jews in these two regions (specifically, the far greater proportion in the
East of Jewish artisans and laborers but crucially not of Jewish farmers and
peasants).[2] Nor were such criticisms of Jewish economy confined to the Ashkenazic world. We find adumbrations of the theme of economic regeneration
in prominent Sephardic communities of the seventeenth and eighteenth centuries. It was the celebrated Sephardic merchants and brokers of Amsterdam
who in 1642 developed one of the first Jewish vocational schools, the Avodat
Hesed Society. While the society initially directed its activities at poor Tudesco
(Central European Ashkenazic) and Polish Jews, Sephardic Atlantic merchants
and their spokesmen did not ignore the mounting poverty afflicting their own
Nação, as the Portuguese community termed itself.[3] Indeed, Sephardi leaders
played a double game, penning eloquent apologia proclaiming the enormous advantages to wealth and trade derived from granting settlement privileges to Jews
while simultaneously hatching grandiose schemes to establish New World agricultural colonies for the occupational regeneration of their fellow Sephardim.[4]

If the paradox cannot not resolved by distinguishing Ashkenazic from Sephardic, or Western from Eastern European Jews, perhaps it can be resolved by
juxtaposing rich and poor ones. One might posit that rich and successful Jews
were modern and poor ones backward. But this solution is also more apparent than real. In terms of their functional positions in the larger economy, as
opposed to their class positions in the Jewish one, wealthy Jews did not differ
fundamentally from their impoverished coreligionists. If we choose a date of
around 1800, then most European Jews could be described, broadly speaking,
as "middlemen" of one kind or another. True, Jewish artisans existed everywhere, were prominent in Amsterdam and a number of Italian, Greek, and
Balkan settlements, and flourished in significant proportions throughout many
parts of Eastern Europe. Yet even artisans would come to be regarded as backward, once industrialization appeared as the wave of the future.

In the meanwhile, the stereotypical Jewish identity was defined by the world
of commerce and exchange, whether it referred to a wealthy broker like the
eighteenth-century Londoner Samson Gideon or a Jewish old-clothes man of
London's "Duke's Place."[5] No doubt the former was usually more acculturated
and less despised than the petty trader, but in terms of the functional nature of
their activities they represented two sides of the same coin, so to speak. Indeed,
the historian Jonathan Israel has argued that Jews at both top and bottom of
the economic "pyramid" comprised a kind of vertical network in the early modern period by which goods and resources (principally metals and money) were

absorbed through retail activities and funneled up into the large-scale financial operations of court Jews.[6] Was this Jewish middleman orientation, functioning both horizontally, via the global trade networks of seventeenth-century Sephardim, and vertically, through the structural interdependence of Ashkenazic Jews at all social levels, a precursor of capitalist approaches and a symbol of things to come, or was it emblematic of outmoded and premodern methods of doing business?

Fitting the Jews into European Economic History

There may be a way of reframing this question so as to evade the cul-de-sac that resulted from Werner Sombart's parallelism between the Jews and modern capitalism. Sombart's 1911 book, in which he argued that the rationality manifested since ancient times in the Jewish religion led Jews to pioneer modern commercial life, inspired a raft of rejoinders and generally contributed to the emergence of a new historical and theoretical discourse on the nature of Jewish economy.[7] But the book's anti-Semitic overtones and overly broad characterizations also had the effect of hindering discussion by sharpening the polemical and apologetic tone of the debate.[8] To avoid such pitfalls, we should formulate the question in a more neutral way, i.e., "Can economic history date the inception of Jewish modernity?"

The body of work that comes closest to addressing this question is that produced during the last two decades by the aforementioned Jonathan Israel. In a major overview in *European Jewry in the Age of Mercantilism (1550–1750)* and a large number of detailed articles addressing specific aspects of Jewish commercial life, Israel has provided a meticulous re-creation of early modern Jewry's commercial networks. These included principally: (1) Balkan overland spice and textile traders linking the Levant with northern Italy as well as northern Europe; (2) Levantine (eastern) and "Ponentine" (western) Sephardic merchants operating out of the Adriatic ports of Venice and Ancona as well as the Ligurian free port of Livorno to extend commercial exchange between Ottoman, Italian, and Iberian domains; (3) Atlantic trade connecting Bordeaux, Le Havre, and Antwerp, and later Amsterdam, Hamburg, and London, with New World ports; and (4) Polish overland commerce through the network of German fairs at Leipzig and Frankfurt and through the river trade toward the Baltic ports of Danzig and Riga. This, Israel repeatedly affirms, was a truly global commerce, if not the first of its kind then among the most extensive to date. Although in Israel's rendering the Sephardim occupy center stage, the Ashkenazim (as central European court Jews and military provisioners, or as Polish-Jewish *arendators*, shippers of grain, timber, and fur) play a key supporting role.[9]

While no synopsis can do justice to Israel's intricate mise-en-scène, like Sombart he appears to view Jews as pioneers of economic modernity, insisting they are a neglected but key force within the later phases of the West's commercial revolution.[10] In this sense, his work serves as a sort of Jewish companion piece to Braudel's *The Wheels of Commerce*. It provides an account of the rise of Jewish trade networks and their contribution to the commercial revolution of early modern Europe.[11] But there is also a difference. While Braudel seeks to analyze the genesis of a system, capitalism, whose origins he locates in the Mediterranean commercial crucible of the fifteenth and sixteenth centuries, Israel is effectively telling the story of a Jewish "moment" in the emergence of that system, one whose further development through the consolidation of national economies and the rise of industrialization essentially leaves Jews behind. With the Treaty of Utrecht in 1713, ensuring reactionary Bourbon rule in Spain, the exhaustion of New Christian migration from Iberia, and a short eighteenth century of relative peace in Northern Europe, Jews could no longer remain at or near the commercial forefront.[12] As modern bureaucracies succeeded in performing the tasks once required of middleman minority groups, the Sephardic trading diaspora took on the character, says Israel, of a "self-eroding system."[13] Even the emergence of a new generation of cutting-edge bankers like the Rothschilds at the end of the Napoleonic Wars could not revive or resume this epoch. In fact, Israel's account of the Jewish age of mercantilism appears devoid of any connective tissue with preceding and succeeding eras.[14] We find no narrative of or analytical continuity between Jewish economic life in the Middle Ages, whose precise relation to the "early modern" Israel never makes clear, and the age of mercantilism, or for that matter between the "early modern" and "modern," except insofar as Israel implies that where Jews had been ahead they now fell behind, and where they had been economically modern they were now outmoded.[15] The age of Menasseh ben Israel and Penso de la Vega (the Sephardic author of the first treatise on the stock exchange, *Confusion de confusions*[16]) is less the true beginning of Jewish modernity than a false dawn, a glorious chapter presaging not triumph but decline. Alas, for Israel there would be no future "Jewish Century."

In some respects Israel's portrait fits into to recent scholarly efforts to revise the image of the early modern period in Jewish historiography, which an earlier generation had tended to describe in terms of deepening crisis, messianic debacle, renewed sectarianism, growing social division and oligarchic control of Jewish communities, heresy hunting obscurantism, and the like.[17] In place of this gloomy assessment, Israel presents a coherent, plausible, and attractive account of a pioneering Jewish commerce, an economic counterpart to various endeavors to rehabilitate the retrospective image of post-expulsion Sephardic cultural vitality.[18] But in other ways his is an orthodox view, not so much within the traditions of Jewish historiography as within those of European economic thought, which insists that trading diasporas are a characteristically premodern and protocapitalist phenomenon. It is in this literature of political economy that we witness an elaborate playing out of the paradox formulated at the start of this article: the image of Jews as simultaneously avant-garde and retrograde.

The Image of the Jews as Economically Avant-Garde

The earliest economists, so-called mercantilist authors, occasionally said laudatory things about the potential contributions of Jewish commerce to national treasure, reflecting the phenomenon of "mercantile philo-Semitism" that Israel describes and sometimes himself epitomizes. In some cases these authors built directly upon the literature of seventeenth-century Jewish apologetics, particularly the highly influential work of the Venetian rabbi Simone Luzzatto. Luzzatto's 1638 *Discorso circa il stato de gl'Hebrei et in particolare dimoranti nell'inclita Città di Venetia* (Discourse on the Condition of the Jews and Particularly Those Residing in the City of Venice) helped to shape the economic arguments (though not just the economic ones) employed by Menasseh ben Israel in 1655 for Jewish readmission to England and by John Toland in 1714 for the Jews' naturalization in Great Britain and Ireland. His influence probably extended to the mercantilist writer Josiah Child, the journalist Joseph Addison, and later in the century to Moses Mendelssohn and others.[19] Utilizing contemporary Italian political and economic thought, Luzzatto enthusiastically praised the civic and moral benefits of commerce, the utility of money and credit, and not least of all the unique mercantile qualifications of Jews.[20] What was most pointed in his formulation was the argument that Jews are ideally suited to perform the role of a nation's commercial agents since, beyond the trading skills they have honed over centuries, they possess neither the desire nor the capacity to translate their earnings from mercantile service into landed power and political authority:

> They possess no stable properties, exercise no mechanical arts, are far from being able to profit from positions in the courts and other municipal offices, and are burdened with large families because their religious obligations do not permit them celibacy. They must therefore earn their livelihoods through diligent industry and make their way by painstaking determination and assiduity. Consequently, it is evident that wherever the Hebrews reside there traffic and commerce flourish.[21]

Despite its undertone of protest at the plight of the Jews, Luzzatto's argument for Jewish tolerance depended on maintaining the Jews' disabilities, since it was precisely these that rendered Jews less threatening and more trustworthy than other foreign merchant groups, such as the Genoese. In his appeal for Jewish readmission to England, Menasseh ben Israel later pithily and pointedly reformulated Luzzatto's rationale in lobbying for Jewish readmission to England. "[T]hey aspire at nothing," insisted Menasseh, "but to preferre themselves in their way of Marchandize."[22]

Parallel rationales probably underlay official documents granting Jews and New Christians specific economic privileges by princes and statesmen in Italy, France, the Netherlands, and elsewhere, as well as in various European colonies in the western hemisphere. But these governmental documents, such as the remarkable "Livornina" of 1593, tended to present matter-of-fact statements promoting Jews' privileges and economic opportunities, long on concrete details but short on economic arguments and rationales.[23] Wholly different were the exuberant pronouncements of writers like Toland and Addison, which occasionally took on theological overtones. Menasseh ben Israel, for instance, insisted that Jewish commerce reflected a providential plan: God had implanted a commercial talent in the Jews in order to render them indispensable to the gentile nations that must host and protect them during their long exile.[24]

Such a theory is not surprising in the case of a rabbi like Menasseh, but even the deist Toland appeared to echo Genesis 12:3 in his observation that Jews bring bounty where they are welcomed but leave desolation where they are forced to depart. "What a paltry fisher town was Livorno before the admission of the Jews?," remarked Toland, and "[w]hat a loser is Lisbon since they have been lost to it?"[25] Toland is usually taken to be the epitome of the scientific-minded freethinker, and indeed, following Luzzatto, he emphasized that the Jews have no distinct nature but "visibly partake of the Nature of those Nations among which they live." Yet Toland also believed that the gifts of the Jews, deriving from their scriptural inheritance, render special blessings to those nations that treat them well.[26]

Joseph Addison's praise of Jews likewise possessed theological overtones, describing them as "the Instruments by which the most distant Nations converse with one another, and by which Mankind are knit together in a general Correspondence: They are like the Pegs and Nails in a great Building, which, though they are but little valued in themselves, are absolutely necessary to keep the whole Frame together."[27] The image evokes the idea of a great chain of being, or a social cosmos of seemingly disparate and incompatible parts that in reality is perfectly interwoven by the agency of an all-seeing and benevolent providence. Such admixtures of religious and utilitarian thinking were not uncommon in the economic thought of the eighteenth century and sometimes took on a philo-Semitic flavor as well.[28] An advocate of the Jewish Naturalization Act of 1753, for example, insisted that while Scripture obligates Christians "to behave with love and tenderness to all men upon the earth," they must love "the *Jews* [emphasis in original] in preference to those of any other kingdom, nation, or religion," since "those people are known all over the world to be all merchants and traders, from the highest to the lowest."[29]

The Image of the Jews as Economically Retrograde

It was one thing to express admiration of Jewish merchants but quite another to proclaim them harbingers of a new commercial age. In the literature of "mercantile philo-Semitism" one encounters numerous encomiums to the economic benefits of the Jews but little notion that mankind has entered into a new economic age, one for which the Jews appear as symbols or agents. It is true that in the works of conservatives like Lord Bolingbroke, "stockjobbers," sometimes synonymous with Jews, figure prominently among the *novi homines* who are sweeping away the traditional agrarian order of gentlemanly honor and propriety.[30] But such nostalgia is not to be confused with the detailed articulation of the workings of a market system. This awareness of the rise of a new economic order characterized by abstract and universal rules could be found in the writings of the Physiocrats in France and David Hume and Josiah Tucker (and later Smith) in Great Britain. But of these only Tucker commented extensively on the commerce of the Jews. An Anglican divine and noted economist who anticipated many of the progressive liberal doctrines of Hume and Smith, Tucker was the first to draw a connection between these new rules of markets and the merchant activities of the Jews.

Like the mercantile philo-Semites, Tucker admired the Jews as a trading nation. But his interest in them, piqued by the clamorous popular reaction against the 1753 Naturalization Act ("Jew Bill"), was largely symbolic.[31] An irascible debunker of the myth of Britons' ancient feudal rights (the "ancient constitution"), Tucker contrasted Jews as a modern commercial people with the outmoded monopolistic trading companies of his own day, such as the Levant and Hudson Bay Companies. Whereas medieval Anglo-Jewry had once been forced by tyrannical governments to fulfill all of England's monetary functions, thereby incurring the hatred of the mob, nowadays it was these exclusive companies, Tucker lamented, that acted the part of exploitative Jews. Ironically, as Tucker saw it, the naturalization promised by the Jew Bill represented an advance for the kind of liberal government and free trading system that would dissolve privileged monopolies of old. The naturalization of a maligned commercial people, such as the Jews, would help seal the triumph of what Tucker labeled the "New System of Civil and Commercial Government" that had been inaugurated by the Glorious Revolution of 1688.[32] In this sense, the Jews were both the emblems and beneficiaries of a new order, one to which we might apply the term "modern" and "capitalist," even if Tucker himself did not.

Tucker's writings on the Jew Bill mark a turning point in the attitude of political economy toward Jews. Mercantile philo-Semitism would soon be eclipsed by new approaches to Jewish commerce associated with the laissez-faire doctrines of classical economics—particularly as these were interpreted in Continental Europe. In Britain itself, no major economist after Josiah Tucker paid much attention to the Jews. Despite the encyclopedic quality of Adam Smith's works, this great prophet of liberal policy and free trade barely referenced them. David Hume's occasional positive remarks were balanced by the smattering of Edmund Burke's nasty ones.[33] Neither Thomas Malthus nor David Ricardo, regardless of the latter's own Jewish ancestry, accorded Jews any special role as economic actors (nor for that matter did later British economists like William Stanley Jevons and Alfred Marshall).[34] While it is hard to account for silences, this one likely reflects the Jews' diminishing commercial importance in the West, as Israel has detailed—or, equally important, their diminishing economic distinctiveness in an increasingly commercial British society. But the decline of mercantile philo-Semitism also reflects the shifting position of the middleman in contemporary economic thought.

As Tucker put it: "Money without Industry, is an Hurt, not a Blessing."[35] In their efforts to contravene the (to them) erroneous doctrines of earlier economic schools, writers like Tucker, Hume, and Adam Smith insisted that money was not at all the cause of wealth. Policies and regulations designed to enhance the importation and reduce the exportation of specie were at best futile and at worse harmful. Such policies could be inflationary. Worse, they tended to benefit only idle and parasitic segments of the population and result in what Hume, no doubt thinking of the Scottish financial adventurer John Law, referred to as "dangerous and ill-concerted projects" at the expense of "the industry, morals, and numbers" of a [nation's] people.[36]

At a more structural level such policies, according to these critics, reflect a fundamental misconception about the nature of wealth. The subdivision of labor, the classical economists believed, had already revolutionized productivity and would continue to do so in the future. *The Wealth of Nations* is replete with the Smith's protestations that, popular impressions notwithstanding, Britain at the time was demonstrably better off it than it had been half a century ago, let alone during the "rude" centuries of baronial rule so celebrated by champions of the "ancient constitution." Yet Smith is equally adamant that this remarkable progress did not derive from the mere presence of merchants, at least not directly, but rather from investment in agriculture and industry. While Smith included merchants in his catalogue of "productive labour," he also formulated a hierarchy of productive occupations that placed farmers at the top, manufacturers in the middle, and merchants toward the bottom (though still well above soldiers, actors, and bureaucrats, all of whom he claimed were not productive at all!). By "productive" Smith meant labor that creates commodities—such as food, raiment, shelter, etc.—necessary for their own reproduction and expansion.[37] Value is equivalent to or associated with productive labor, while exchange is merely the means through which commodities (embodying productive labor) are circulated. Smith draws a key distinction between capital and money. Capital (or "stock"), according to Smith, is wealth engaged in or available for productive investment, whereas money is a convenience (albeit a substantial one) that facilitates production by simplifying the process of exchange. Similarly, agricultural and industrial labor constitutes the human corollary of capital, whereas the merchant's activities correspond to money.[38]

In formulating his ideas in this manner, Smith aimed to dismantle what he called "the mercantile system," or at least to demolish its justifications in the earlier literature of political economy.[39] The term "mercantilism" has lately come under criticism from historians of political economy, both because of its vagueness and because authors like Smith sometimes overstressed the differences between his own doctrines and those of his predecessors. When it comes to the relative value placed on merchants versus artisans and agriculturalists, however, the distinction between Smith and the "mercantilists" remains useful.[40] It was the "mercantile system" that had elevated the merchant to a top echelon, and this system, it so happened, that had sometimes championed Jews and other trading nations. Smith was not necessarily opposed to trading nations and indeed argued that under certain circumstances they were entirely beneficial.[41] But Smith foresaw a society (and in Holland had already glimpsed it) in which every man "lives by exchanging, or becomes in some measure a merchant."[42] When this occurs, a historical stage has been reached, for "the society itself grows to be what is properly a commercial society."[43]

Although Smith did not employ the term modernity, he regarded a commercial society as the most advanced and modern possible.[44] And since it was achieved when "every man … becomes in some measure a merchant," a commercial society was one in which the idea of exchange had become so deeply rooted in public psychology and institutions that special classes of merchants, particularly ones based on corporate or ethnic restrictions, were no longer required. Of course, for Smith the division of labor still applied (indeed, now more than ever); professional merchants were still required. But the kind of mercantilist arrangements whereby merchants were corporately defined in law and privileged in policy were no longer justifiable. Consequently, ethnic mercantile monopolies got dissolved through market mechanisms that rewarded individual rather than group performance. It is in this sense that one can infer from Smith (or more accurately from Smith's general approach to political economy) that a specifically *Jewish commerce* in the manner projected by Luzzatto is not modern but rather premodern in nature.

Ideological Change and Economic Continuity

In the "dismal science" of economics, perhaps being talked about is the only thing worse than not being talked about. In the late Enlightenment period and in the subsequent era of revolution and romanticism, Jews again became a focus of economic analysis, this time not as the heroic commercial pioneers of mercantilist thought but as symbols of the discredited fiscal order of the *ancien régime*. It should be reiterated that this occurred not in Britain but particularly in France and Germany, among writers and political thinkers who came under the influence of Adam Smith, David Hume, and the Physiocrats. Although late eighteenth-century British reformers worried about the pronounced commercial orientation of lower-class Jews and sought to "productivize" them through vocational education, discussion of Jewish commerce there tended to be confined to philanthropists such as Joshua Van Oven on the one hand, and conservative anti-Semites such as William Cobbett on the other. For the most part, as noted, the more respectable British political economists now tended to ignore the Jews.[45]

This was not at all the case on the continent, where, compared with Britain, the corporatist character of the *ancien régime* was much less well-integrated with emerging market mechanisms. A concomitant of the French Revolution's "abolition of feudalism, or dissolution of the corporate order, was the critique within much classical economic theory of the privileged corporations and state-authorized monopolies favored by mercantilist writers, already apparent, as noted, even in the otherwise philo-Semitic writings of Josiah Tucker. In Continental Europe, with its often reified application of classical economic doctrine, the full erection of a liberal economic order—one that professed to find no place for an corporate division of labor—seemed to require that the Jews' occupational profile come to resemble that of the society as a whole. As part of the process of forging a general commercial society, Jews needed to be divested of their particular and deeply engrained commercial identity. Channeling them into agriculture and crafts would help better align the Jews' occupational profile with that of contemporary society as a whole. Besides, in light of their long overrepresentation in trade, engagement in physical labor and contact with the soil would help root the Jews in more solid virtues associated with primary production. This was essentially the formula of Christian Wilhelm von Dohm, the Prussian bureaucrat and economist who in 1781 wrote famously in favor of the civic emancipation of the Jews, as well as of the Abbé Grégoire, Mirabeau, and other advocates of Jewish integration, including numerous Enlightened Jews themselves.[46]

While Jews would not produce a full-fledged political economy of their own, representatives of the Jewish Enlightenment did reflect current economic attitudes in many of their writings. Ironically, the figure traditionally touted as the founder of Jewish modernity, Moses Mendelssohn, employed arguments that harkened back to the apologetics and economic philo-Semitism of Luzzatto and Addison. To our ears Mendelssohn certainly sounds progressive when he insists, in a rejoinder to critics of Jewish commercial life, that even the activities of "the pettiest trafficking Jew" are productive.[47] But the fact that he made this assertion in a defensive and apologetic context is telling. He suspected (not without justification) that critiques of Jews' social ills were motivated by anti-Jewish prejudice and missionary agendas as much as solicitousness for the their welfare. And while Mendelssohn favored Jewish emancipation, he sometimes professed to prefer the older philo-Semitic model, in which the Jews were at least appreciated for their commercial services, to the critical tone of the Enlightened, in which they were often broadly derided for their backwardness.[48] That said, Mendelssohn also seems to have misunderstood (or misrepresented) the views of some of his opponents. He did not appear to acknowledge, for instance, the distinction drawn by Dohm (borrowing from the Physiocrats and likely also from Smith) between professions that were merely useful and those that were genuinely "productive" in the sense described above.[49]

Far more in keeping with the spirit of the times was Mendelssohn's colleague, Naftali Herz Wesseley, who in his *Yein Levanon* (The Wine of Lebanon)—more so than in his better-known reformist manifesto *Divre' Shalom ve-Emet* (Words of Peace and Truth)—attempted to translate and adapt the new economic ideals of agricultural engagement and occupational productivization for a traditional Hebrew reading audience. These would become stock themes of the Haskalah, particularly as it spread into East Central and then Eastern Europe during the first several decades of the nineteenth century. Mendelssohn's disciple Herz Homberg and later Mendel Lefin and Yosef Perl in Galicia, and Isaac Ber Levinson in Russia, were veritable tribunes of the new ideology.[50] While their ideas were not uniform or facile, they concurred on the major point that in its present condition Jewish society was economically backward, and that while wealthy merchants might embody proper middle-class values and propriety, the overproduction of petty traders was a plague that must be stemmed through vocational training and, where possible, agricultural colonization.

By this point we have said enough to suggest an answer to our earlier question of whether economic history can date the inception of Jewish modernity. The late Enlightenment and Haskalah periods, at least among a segment of the educated elite, clearly viewed Jewish economic life more pessimistically than Jewish spokesmen and some Christian thinkers and statesmen during the sixteenth and seventeenth centuries. But this suggests that the key change was far more one of subjective mentality and ideology than of objective behavior and social structure, occurring more in the domain of economic thought than economic history. And indeed, despite the mountain of maskilic rhetoric, admonition, and exhortation, Jews' economic behaviors, as opposed to doctrines and attitudes, did not fundamentally change in the late eighteenth and early nineteenth centuries. Jewish economic life continued to be overwhelmingly commercial and financial, with relatively few Jews shifting on a long-term basis into agriculture and crafts. In fact, surveying the *longue durée* of modern Jewish history, we can see that while Jews experienced many shifts in economic fortune (notably urbanization, population growth, and in the West an often striking degree of upward mobility), outside of Palestine they did not become peasants or farmers in significant percentages (say, 15 percent or greater). Many of the trends they followed into modernity were already in place and continuous with the Jews' premodern economic profile. The partial proletarianization of Russian Jews in the late nineteenth century, although it appears to contradict this statement, was in fact relatively short-lived—to be succeeded by a return to more traditional middleman occupations even within the peculiar non-capitalist framework of Soviet Russia. While a demographic "transformation of the Jews" did occur in the modern era, it was not the fundamental economic reorientation proposed by their would-be "modernizers."[51] Consequently, a more detailed examination of the modern economic history of the Jews, while essential for other purposes, will not help us to address the question of periodization. Economic history cannot date the inception of Jewish modernity, although the history of economic attitudes by and about Jews possibly might.

What is Modern, (Jewish) Commerce or (Gentile) Industrialization?

We therefore have little choice but to return in the concluding section of this essay to the field of political economy, that is, to the history of economic thought and ideologies. In doing so we discover that the entire emphasis on "productivization" that so animated Jewish movements such as the Haskalah, Jewish socialism, and labor Zionism, was rooted in an error from the standpoint of current economic thought. Most economists no longer accept the labor theory of value, either in the version formulated by Adam Smith, or by David Ricardo, or eventually by Karl Marx. For over a century, value has been understood by non-Marxist economists as a property rooted in subjective attributions of utility rather than in objective categories of labor input or quantities of labor-power.[52] The consequences of this conceptual error (at least from the point of view of modern economics) have not been confined to the technical question of the nature and location of value but also to the historical question of how economic development or even economic history as a whole should be periodized. This is clear from the fact that the fateful concept of an industrial revolution, which is rooted in classical economists' focus on productive labor, is now being challenged by historians who employ different assumptions about the nature of value, as will be discussed below.

When Smith wrote that "the labour of the manufacturer fixes and realizes itself in some particular subject or vendible commodity," which endures "for some time at least after that labour is past" and constitutes "a certain quantity of labour stocked and stored up to be employed" on some future occasion, he was already anticipating the later theory of industrialization.[53] Smith regarded agriculture as the apex of productiveness, in part because, he insisted, it was only in agriculture that nature plays a considerable role in performing the necessary work. This applied not only to crops but to livestock as well, since the farmer's "labouring cattle, are productive labourers" too. Contrastingly, in manufacturing "nature does nothing; man does all."[54] While this might be true in a narrow technical sense, Smith appears to have underestimated the degree to which "nature" also plays a role in manufacturing and the functioning of machinery and did so even in his own day. Surely the burning of fuel in smelting, the use of steam power for generating energy for transport, and the operation of principles of chemistry and physics in the creation and operation of machinery all entail the work of nature just as much as do the grazing of cattle and raising of crops. Had Smith applied his doctrine of commodities as embodiments of natural and human productivity to manufacturing as fully as to agriculture, he might have recognized the potential of the former to outstrip the latter.

As it happened, it was not Adam Smith but Karl Marx who fully developed a theory of industry and factory production as the apotheosis of "commercial society," Smith's final stage of historical development. Marx took over Smith's distinction between productive and unproductive labor and applied it to his class analysis. The proletariat embodied society's collective labor power; hence it was the ultimate productive class. The bourgeoisie, on the other hand, played a role that was initially productive through its organization of the means of production and its undermining of feudalism. But having completed the tasks of reorganizing labor on a market basis and destroying the political power of the nobility, the bourgeoisie no longer served any beneficial purpose. Indeed, its manner of exploiting productive labor had now become an obstacle to the further dramatic expansion of industry.[55]

In Marx's scenario even more than in Smith's, Jews had no real role to play. Following his early speculations in "On the Jewish Question," Marx essentially excluded Jews from his analysis because despite their commercial and financial orientation, they lacked the characteristics of a class, which for him was a social rather than an ethnic or religious category. In Marx's *Capital* the Jews barely make an appearance; they are not even to be confused or combined with the modern bourgeoisie but are at best made to symbolize an antiquated form of early medieval commerce, a "trading nation," to employ his term. According to Marx, trading nations like the Jews did not and could not innovate economically or socially; on the contrary, their activity was fully compatible only with the feudal economic mode. "In the precapitalist stages of society," wrote Marx, "commerce rules industry. The reverse is true of modern society." Thus Marx viewed the Jews of his own day—leaving aside a handful of Western Jewish financiers—as a throwback to a primitive and outmoded form of bourgeoisie, fit only for the most backward societies, such as Poland.[56]

Marx's emphasis on industrialization as the characteristically modern economic process exerted a decisive influence on subsequent historical periodization schemes. "Capitalism" came to define the modern age. And while capitalism might be seen to possess a prehistory going back to the commercial revolution of the Italian city-states, or at least to the Dutch and English maritime empires, its *telos* was clearly the industrial revolution that began in late eighteenth-century Britain and moved to mid nineteenth-century Germany and the United States. The fact that this revolution somehow skipped nineteenth-century Italy and Holland, where the entire process had supposedly begun, and France, where the "bourgeois revolution" had first taken place, was never adequately explained. It is only recently that these major anomalies have caused historians to question how universal, uniform, necessary, or inevitable a process industrialization truly was.[57] Moreover, postindustrialization in the West and the intensified process of globalization have reminded scholars that finance and trade possess a significance that is not merely subordinate to that of industry. There may in fact be many roads to economic modernization. Industrialization is surely one but perhaps not the singular driving force that Marx and later Max Weber claimed it to be.

This questioning of the role of classical-type industrial revolutions in the process of economic modernization brings us back to the dilemmas of Jewish political economy. Did the adoption of the labor theory of value by classical economists misdirect them into a historical schema that privileged industry (making things) over commerce (exchanging them) as the pivot of development? If so it would suggest that the dissenters to the industrialization theory, such as Werner Sombart, Georg Simmel, or more recently Yuri Slezkine, have been more right than wrong about the role of Jews as economic modernizers. All three authors have argued that the middleman more than the industrialist has been the fulcrum of modern economy (and in Slezkine's case, of modern culture as well). Such a premise has led these authors to emphasize the essentially modern character of the Jews and the Jewish character of modernity, a thesis that possesses a certain inescapable truth, even if it appears troublingly ahistorical, if not essentialist.[58] Sombart and Slezkine, for instance, assume that commerce is a distinguishing mark of modern economy, even though commerce (even of a rather extensive and intricate kind) is in fact ancient, as they themselves in their unguarded moments admit.[59] Similarly, both authors unhelpfully characterize the Jews as an ancient-modern people, as if the Jewish nature were constant and non-Jewish history variable, continuously morphing until it is finally able to catch up.[60] In presenting matters this way the authors call into question the very coherence of the concept of modernity. And so the paradox persists.[61]

Broadly speaking, the Jews suffered heavy but momentary dislocation from industrialization, yet in its wake they resumed much of their former commercial character, often accompanied by dramatic upward mobility. In other words, the presumed watershed event of modern economic history, the Industrial Revolution, only ended up making them more so what they already had been long before. For this reason, their story—or rather, the stories of what actually happened to them, what they told themselves, and what others told about them—must be seen as illuminating in its capacity to subvert the paradigms of modernity, economic or otherwise.

NOTES

This essay is a slightly revised and updated version of an article originally entitled "Economic History and Jewish Modernity: Ideological Versus Structural Change," published in the *Jahrbuch des Simon-Dubnow-Instituts* 4 (2007): 249–266. I would like to thank the Simon Dubnow Institut and the publisher, Vandenhoeck & Ruprecht, for their kind permission to republish it here. I would also like to thank Professor Vicki Caron for her careful reading and helpful comments on a draft of the original version of this essay.

1. There still exists no comprehensive study of modern Jews' perceptions of their own economic backwardness. In addition to Penslar, *Shylock's Children*, see Mordecai Levin, *'Erkhe hevrah ve-kalkalah ba-'ideologyah shel tekufat ha-Haskalah* [Social and Economic Values: The Idea of Professional Modernization in the Ideology of the Haskalah Movement] (Jerusalem: Bialik Institute, 1975); Jonathan Frankel, *Prophecy and Politics: Socialism, Nationalism, and the Russian Jews, 1862–1917* (Cambridge: Cambridge University Press, 1981).

2. On this structure in the second half of the nineteenth century, the essential work remains Arkadius Kahan, *Essays in Jewish Social and Economic History* (Chicago: University of Chicago Press, 1986).

3. See Yosef Kaplan, "The Self-Definition of the Sephardic Jews of Western Europe and Their Relation to the Alien and the Stranger," in *Crisis and Creativity in the Sephardic World, 1391–1648*, ed. B. R. Gampel (New York: Columbia University Press, 1997), 121–145, here 139.

4. Isaac de Pinto, *Reflexoëns Politicas, Tocante à Constitutiçam da Naçam Judaica, Exposiçam do Estado de suas Finanças, Causeas dos Atrasos, e Desordens que se experimentam, e Meyos de os prevenir* ([Political Reflections on the Constitution of the Jewish Nation, Revealing the State of its Finances, the Causes of its Delinquencies, the Disorders it has Experienced, and to Prevent them] Amsterdam, 1748); Robert Cohen, "Passage to the New World: The Sephardi Poor of Eighteenth-Century Amsterdam," in *Neveh Ya'akov: Jubilee Volume Presented to Dr. Jaap Meijer*, ed. L. Dasberg and J. N. Cohen (Assen: Van Gorcum, 1982), 31–42; Robert Cohen, "The Edgerton Manuscript," *American Jewish Historical Quarterly* 62 (1973): 333–347; Tirtsah Levie Bernfeld, "Financing Poor Relief in the Spanish-Portuguese Jewish

Community in Amsterdam in the Seventeenth and Eighteenth Centuries," in *Dutch Jewry: Its History and Secular Culture (1500–2000)*, ed. Jonathan Israel and Reiner Salverda (Leiden: Brill, 2002), 62–102; Mordechai Arbell, "Jewish Settlements in the French Colonies in the Caribbean (Martinique, Guadeloupe, Haiti, Cayenne) and the 'Black Code,'" in *Jews and Expansion to the West*, ed. Norman Fiering and Paolo Bernardini (New York: Berghahn Books, 2001), 291–308.

5. See Lucy Stuart Sutherland, "Samson Gideon: Eighteenth Century Jewish Financier," *Transactions of the Jewish Historical Society of England* 17 (1951–52): 78–92. On Duke's Place, the hawking center for London's poor, see Henry Mayhew, *London Labour and the London Poor* (London, 1851).

6. Jonathan Israel, *European Jewry in the Age of Mercantilism, 1550–1750* (Oxford: Clarendon Press 1985); Jonathan Israel, *Diasporas within a Diaspora: Jews, Crypto-Jews and the World Maritime Empires (1540–1740)* (Leiden: Brill, 2002), 132, 171.

7. Werner Sombart, *Die Juden und das Wirtschaftsleben* (Leipzig: Dunkler & Humblot, 1911), usually translated as *The Jews and Modern Capitalism*. On the reception of Sombart, see Derek J. Penslar, *Shylock's Children: Economics and Jewish Identity in Modern Europe* (Berkeley: University of California Press, 2001), 163–173.

8. See the introduction by Bert F. Hoselitz to Sombart, *The Jews and Modern Capitalism* (Glencoe, IL: Free Press, 1951). For an overview and discussion of the subsequent literature, see Walter P. Zenner, *Minority in the Middle: A Cross-Cultural Analysis* (Albany: State University of New York Press, 1991).

9. In his *European Jewry in the Age of Mercantilism*, Israel implies that Ashkenazic and Sephardic trade was interrelated, and that there existed a kind of grand nexus of Jewish networks. However, in his *Diasporas Within a Diaspora: Jews, Crypto-Jews and the World Maritime Empires (1540–1740)* (Brill: Leiden and Boston, 2002), he appears to back off from such an implication. The latter work focuses almost entirely on Sephardim.

10. Israel, *Diasporas Within a Diaspora*, vii and 4.

11. Fernand Braudel, *Civilization and Capitalism, 15th–18th Century*. 3 vols. (New York: Harper & Row, 1982–1984), vol. 2: *The Wheels of Commerce*. In fact, Braudel helped pioneer the study of the activities of Jewish and other merchant diasporas in late sixteenth- and seventeenth-century Mediterranean trade. See his *The Mediterranean and the Mediterranean World in the Age of Philip II*, vol. 2 (New York: Harper & Row, 1973), p. 728. For comments about and criticisms of his approach to these diaspora groups, see Francesca Trivellato, *The Familiarity of Strangers: The Sephardic Diaspora, Livorno, and Cross-Cultural Trade in the Early Modern Period* (New Haven: Yale University Press, 2009), 102–103.

12. On the reasons for eighteenth-century economic decline, see Israel, *European Jewry in the Age of Mercantilism*, 237–254; idem., *Diasporas Within a Diaspora*, 563–571.

13. Israel, *Diasporas within a Diaspora*, 568.

14. Israel underscores the highly time-bound character of his topic: "there existed certain highly specialized Jewish diasporas within the wider Jewish diaspora of a kind which had not really existed before and which ceased to exist—at least with anything like the important scope they attained in those two centuries—after around 1740." *Diasporas within a Diaspora*, vi.

15. Israel does briefly explain why he believes early modern Sephardi merchants differed from their medieval Jewish predecessors. As he notes, the former's "was a

new type of Jewish commercial system which while showing some affinities with medieval Jewish patterns of trade and finance, differed in that it chiefly used maritime rather than overland routes and was principally based not on local markets and dealings in agricultural produce but rather on importing non-European products over long distances." Israel, *Diasporas Within a Diaspora*, v. But this statement hardly does justice to the nature of medieval Jewish economy or explores its causative relationship to the post-medieval era.

16. Joseph Penso de la Vega, *Confusion de confusiones; dialogos curiosos entre un philosopho agudo, un mercador discreto, y un accionista erudito descriviendo el negocio de las acciones, su origen, su ethimologia, su realidad, su juego, y su enredo* (Amsterdam, 1688). A partial English translation by Herman Kellenbenz was published under the title *Confusion de confusiones, 1688: Portions Descriptive of the Amsterdam Stock Exchange* (Boston: Kress Library of Business and Economics, 1957).

17. The view goes back to Heinrich Graetz, *Geschichte der Juden von den altesten Zeiten bis auf die Gegenwart* (Leipzig: O. Leiner, 1897–1911), vol. 9.

18. Some representative examples are Yosef Hayim Yerushalmi, *From Spanish Court to Italian Ghetto* (New York: Columbia University Press, 1971); David B. Ruderman, *Kabbalah, Magic, and Science: The Cultural Universe of a Sixteenth-Century Jewish Physician* (Cambridge: Harvard University Press, 1988); Yosef Kaplan, *An Alternative Path to Modernity: The Sephardi Diaspora in Western Europe* (Leiden: Brill, 2000).

19. See Benjamin Ravid, *Economics and Toleration in Seventeenth Century Venice: The Background and Context of the Discorso of Simone Luzzatto* (Jerusalem: American Academy for Jewish Research, 1978); Guiseppe Veltri, *Renaissance Philosophy in Jewish Garb: Foundations and Challenges in Judaism on the Eve of Modernity* (Leiden: Brill, 2009), chap. 9; Guiseppe Veltri, "Alcune considerazioni sugli Ebrei e Venezia nel pensiero politico di Simone Luzzatto ("Some Reflections on the Jews of Venice in the Political Thought of Simone Luzzatto")," in *Percorsi di storia ebraica. Atti del XVIII convegno internazionale dell'AISG, Cividale del Friuli-Gorizia, 7/9 settembre 2004* [Pathways in Jewish History. Proceedings of the 18th International Convention of the Italian Association for the Study of Judaism], ed. Cesare Ioly Zorattini (Udine: Forum, 2005): pp. 247–266; Isaac E. Barzilay, "John Toland's Borrowings from Simone Luzzatto: Luzzatto's *Discourse on the Jews of Venice* (1638) the Major Source of Toland's Writing on the *Naturalization of the Jews in Great Britain and Ireland* (1714)," *Jewish Social Studies* 31 (1969): 75–81; Jonathan Karp, "The Mosaic Republic in Augustan England: John Toland's 'Reasons for Naturalizing the Jews,'" *Hebraic Political Studies* 1, no. 4 (Summer, 2006), 462–492.

20. As Veltri notes, Luzzatto was influenced by the Neopolitan economist Antonio Serra, author of *Breve trattato delle cause che possono far abbondare li regni d'oro e d'argento dove non sono miniere* [A Brief Treatise on the Causes that Can Make Gold and Silver Abundant Where There are No Mines] (Naples, 1613, reprint edited by Leonardo Granata, San Giovanni in Fiore, 1998). See Veltri, "Alcune considerazioni," 5. On Machiavelli's influence on Serra, see Theodore A. Sumberg, "Antonio Serra, A Neglected Herald of the Acquisitive System," *American Journal of Economics and Sociology* 50, no. 3 (July, 1991), 365–373.

21. Simone Luzzatto, *Discorso circa il stato de gl'Hebrei in particolar dimoranti nell' inclita Citta di Venetia, di Simone Luzzatto, Rabbino Hebreo* (Venice, 1638), Consideratione

IV, p. 19. See Jonathan Karp, *The Politics of Jewish Commerce: Economic Thought and Emancipation in Europe, 1638–1848* (Cambridge: Cambridge University Press, 2008), 25.

22. Lucien Wolf, ed., *Menasseh ben Israel's Mission to Oliver Cromwell* (London, 1901), 89.

23. See Bernard Dov Cooperman, *Trade and Settlement: The Establishment of the Jewish Communities of Leghorn and Pisa,* unpublished PhD diss., Cambridge, MA: Harvard University, 1976; Trivellato, *The Familiarity of Strangers,* 76–81.

24. Wolf, *Menasseh ben Israel's Mission to Oliver Cromwell,* 79.

25. John Toland, *Reasons for Naturalizing the Jews of Great Britain and Ireland on the Same Foot as All Other Nations* (London, 1714), 42.

26. See Karp, "The Mosaic Republic in Augustan England," 480–485.

27. Joseph Addison and Richard Steele, *The Spectator,* vol. 3, edited by Henry Morley (London, 1891), number 495.

28. On religious themes in early economic thought, see Richard C. Wiles, "Mercantilism and the Idea of Progress," *Eighteenth-Century Studies* 18, no. 1 (Autumn, 1974), 56–74, here 67–68.

29. From an anonymous pamphlet appended to *A Letter to the Right Honorable Sir Thomas Chitty, Knt. Lord Mayor of London* (London, 1759), 4 (emphasis in original).

30. On this topic see Isaac Kramnick, *Bolingbroke and his Circle: The Politics of Nostalgia in the Age of Walpole* (Ithaca, New York, and London: Cornell University Press, 1992), passim. Karp, *Politics of Jewish Commerce,* chap. 3.

31. On Tucker, see George Shelton, *Dean Tucker and Eighteenth-Century Economic and Political Thought* (London: St. Martin's Press, 1981).

32. Josiah Tucker, *A Second Letter to a Friend Concerning Naturalizations* (London, 1753), 14–15, 36–37.

33. On Hume, see Adam Sutcliffe, "Can a Jew Be a Philosophe? Isaac de Pinto, Voltaire, and Jewish Participation in the European Enlightenment," *Jewish Social Studies* 6, no. 3 (Spring/Summer 2000), 31–51. On Burke, see Jerry Z. Muller, *The Mind and the Market: Capitalism in Modern European Thought* (New York: Knopf, 2002), 129–130.

34. That is not to claim that British economists such as J. A. Hobson and J. M. Keynes were immune from the traditional anti-Jewish prejudices and snobbery. It is simply that Jews were incidental to their economic theories. See Colin Holmes, "J.A. Hobson and the Jews," in *Immigrants and Minorities in British Society,* ed. Colin Holmes (Boston: Allen & Unwin, 1978), 125–157.

35. Tucker, *The Elements of Commerce* (London, 1754), 103.

36. David Hume, *Essays Moral, Political and Literary,* edited by Eugene F. Miller (Indianapolis: Liberty Classics, 1985), 305, 321.

37. Adam Smith, *The Wealth of Nations,* edited by Edwin Cannan (Chicago: University of Chicago Press, 1976), 351

38. Smith, *The Wealth of Nations,* 309.

39. Smith addresses the mercantile system in Book IV of *The Wealth of Nations.*

40. See Wiles, "Mercantilism and the Idea of Progress," 56–58 and the sources cited there.

41. Smith, *The Wealth of Nations*, 386.

42. Ibid., 108.

43. Ibid., 26.

44. See Andrew S. Skinner, "Adam Smith: An Economic Interpretation of History," in *Essays on Adam Smith*, edited by Andrew Skinner and Thomas Wilson (Oxford: Clarendon Press, 1975), 154–178.

45. See Todd Endelman, *The Jews of Georgian England, 1714–1830: Tradition and Change in a Liberal Society* (Philadelphia: Jewish Publication Society of America, 1979), 102–104, 227–247.

46. See Karp, *The Politics of Jewish Commerce*, chap. 4.

47. Paul Mendes-Flohr and Jehudah Reinharz, eds., *The Jew in the Modern World: A Documentary History*, 2nd ed. (New York: Oxford University Press, 1995), 47. Mendelssohn's arguments strike us today as more "modern" than Dohm's, but this fact merely underscores the need to define "modern" in historically contextual terms.

48. Moses Mendelssohn, *Schriften zum Judentum* [Writings on Judaism], II, Volume 8, edited by Alexander Altmann (Stuttgart: Mohr, 1971), 3–25.

49. E.g., Smith, *The Wealth of Nations*, 352. On the distinction in Physiocratic doctrine, see Jean-Claude Perrot, *Une histoire intellectuelle de l'économie politique* (Paris, 1992), 220–236.

50. See Karp, *The Politics of Jewish Commerce*, chap. 7; Levin, *'Erkhe hevrah ve-kalkalah*, 39–73; Derek J. Penslar, "The Origins of Jewish Political Economy," *Jewish Social Studies* 3 (1997): 26–60; Nancy Beth Sinkoff, *Out of the Shtetl: Making Jews Modern in the Polish Borderlands* (Providence: Brown University Press, 2003), passim.

51. Calvin Goldscheider and Alan S. Zuckerman, *The Transformation of the Jews* (Chicago: University of Chicago Press, 1984), 47–48, 88–89; for the United States, see Daniel Soyer, "Class Conscious Workers as Immigrant Entrepreneurs: The Ambiguity of Class among Eastern European Jewish Immigrants to the United States at the Turn of the Century," *Labor History* 42, no. 1 (2001), 45–59. This is not the place to take up the important challenge issued by Eli Lederhendler in his powerfully argued *Jewish Immigrants and American Capitalism, 1880–1920* (New York: Cambridge University Press, 2009). Suffice it to say that Lederhendler acknowledges that at some point well prior to their pauperization in the late nineteenth century, Eastern European Jews did constitute a kind of middleman minority. He also readily concedes that by the middle of the twentieth century the American descendents of these Jews experienced a far-reaching *embourgeoisement*. What Lederhendler disputes, however, is that any causative connection links these two facts.

52. For an early and influential critique, see Eugen von Böhm-Bawerk, *Karl Marx and the Close of His System*, trans. Alice M. McDonald (London: T.F. Unwin, 1898).

53. Smith, *The Wealth of Nations*, 351.

54. Ibid., 385.

55. Karl Marx and Friedrich Engels, *The Communist Manifesto* (London and New York: Penguin Books, 1998), passim.

56. Karl Marx, *Capital: A Critique of Political Economy*, vol. 3, trans. Ernest Untermann (Chicago: Charles H. Kerr and Co., 1909), iv.xx.23. Jerry Z. Muller has argued convincingly that at a symbolic level Marx's analysis of the exploitative nature

of industrial capitalism resembles or even borrows from traditional Aristotelian condemnations of usury, so often associated with Jews in medieval Europe. Jerry Z. Muller, *The Mind and the Market*, 189.

57. See generally, Roy Porter and Mikulás Teich, eds., *The Industrial Revolution in National Context: Europe and the U.S.A.* (Cambridge: Cambridge University Press, 1996); Leonard R. Berlanstein, ed., *The Industrialization and Work in Nineteenth-Century Europe* (New York: Routledge, 1992); Peter Musgrave, *The Early Modern European Economy* (New York: St. Martins, 1998), 197–200.

58. Yuri Slezkine, *The Jewish Century* (Princeton: Princeton University Press, 2002).

59. See Slezkine, *The Jewish Century*, chap. 1. See also Jean Andreau, *Banking and Business in the Roman World* (New York: Cambridge University Press, 1999), 11–14; Keith Hopkins, "Taxes and Trade in the Roman Empire (200 B.C.–A.D. 400)," *The Journal of Roman Studies* 70 (1980): 101–125, esp. 105–106. It is one thing to emphasize the role of commerce, another to stress the presence of a market system as the characteristically modern system of economic organization. It seems that Slezkine cannot do so since he is committed to presenting as equally modern the role played by Jews in the Soviet Union, where no market system existed, and the role they played in the United States.

60. See Slezkine's introduction to *The Jewish Century*, 1, where he writes: "It is by being exemplary ancients that the Jews have become model moderns."

61. Simmel, in contrast, viewed modern capitalism as merely the intensification of a process that had begun well prior the Industrial Revolution. As Jerry Z. Muller has argued, for Simmel economic modernity is more an acceleration than a revolution, a gradual takeoff rather than a sudden leap. Outsider trading diasporas like Jews, Huguenots, and Armenians, Simmel argues, often facilitate the coalescence of commerce and finance, rendering them full participants in the modern market order rather than throwbacks to an earlier one. I am grateful to Jerry Z. Muller for sharing with me a draft of his article, "Capitalism, Rationalization, and the Jews: Simmel, Weber, and Sombart," which will appear in a forthcoming volume of the *Simon Dubnow Institute Yearbook*. See also see Amos Morris-Reich, "The Beautiful Jew Is a Moneylender: Money and Individuality in Simmel's Rehabilitation of the the 'Jew'" *Theory, Culture and Society* 20, no. 4 (2003): 127–142.

⤳ 2 ⤳

WANDERING AS CIRCULATION

Dostoevsky and Marx on the "Jewish Question"

Kirill Postoutenko

The proposition of putting side by side a Russian religious writer and a German political economist unacquainted with each other and seemingly uninfluenced by one another appears unviable. Prominent cultural figures as they were, Dostoevsky and Marx were not silent on such nineteenth-century hot topics as monetary economy or the Jewish religion. However, their preferred social milieus, intellectual habits, and discursive modes were quite disparate, and the two contemporaries' narrative references to Jews and money appear different in all but the most general cultural clichés. Even these clichés, discernible in Dostoevsky's essay sequel *The Writer's Diary* (1873–1881) and Marx's pamphlet *On the Jewish Question* (1843) resist translation into a common language:

> Even in childhood I read and heard the legend about the Jews that told how they were all faithfully awaiting the Messiah, every one of them, from the lowest Yid to the very highest and most learned among them, the philosopher and cabbalist-rabbi; that they all believe the Messiah will gather them together in Jerusalem once more and will use his sword to bring down all the other people to sit at their feet; that for some reason for Jews, at least the overwhelming majority for them, prefer but one profession—the trade in gold or, at least, the working of that metal; and they do this, supposedly, so that when Messiah appears they will not have a new fatherland and not be attached to an alien land which they would own, but will possess everything only in form of gold and jewels that will be easier to take away.[1]

> Money is the jealous God of Israel, in face of which no other God may exist ... money is the alienated essence of man's work and man's existence, and this alien essence dominates him, and he worships it. ... The exchange is the real God of the Jew. His God is only an illusory exchange.[2]

Notes for this chapter begin on page 58.

The differences between the fuzzy logic of a mystical parable and the polished dialectics of an economic pamphlet are obvious. And yet it would be hasty to view Dostoevsky and Marx as incomparable. Indeed, as we shall see, the two thinkers follow strikingly similar paths in their attempts to discern and counter the workings of absolute evil in history. What engendered this similarity in such disparate contexts? What could account for their development? These are questions that necessitate the examination of the rhetorical nature of the narratives in question.

Wandering Jews, the "Messiah" before the Second Coming, and the Narrative of Self-Doubt

Translated into abstract categories, the major concepts of Dostoevsky's text may read respectively as false deities ("Deities"), false humans ("Humans") and false values ("Values"); the sequence of these unmasking references is used by the narrator to describe absolute evil in terms of Christian cosmology. While this cosmology surfaces only through the factual language of sacred history, it retains its own argumentative power throughout the narrative.

Thus, "Deity" is a false deity for two reasons. Firstly, it makes a parody of sacred history because its usual (for Christians) synecdoche—the Messiah—appears on earth before the time of the Second Coming, pretending to be the real Messiah and thus trying to end the historical time before the arrival of Jesus Christ. In a similar vein, the precise teleological function of the pretender—to prevent the Kingdom of God on Earth—cannot be fulfilled without the imposture of Christ ("Christ" = Antichrist) and the falsification of the future: the restoration of Jerusalem to its global power effectively means preventing the real Kingdom of God on Earth. Accordingly, "Humans" are not humans at all as soon as they lack attachment to the homeland and roam around the world for no apparent purpose ("Humans" = wandering humans). And yet the exact role of "Humans" in Christian history—to assist the Antichrist in conquering other peoples—stems not so much from their unconstrained mobility as from their belief in the Jewish God ("Humans" = wandering humans = Jews). As for "Values," Dostoevsky describes them in the legend as an attribute of "Humans," so we may provisionally hold that their semantics is subject to the same double interpretation. In this vein, "Values" are fake values because they are not immovable ("Values" = wandering values). However, the specific properties of "wandering" values—durability, capaciousness, and universal exchangeability (wandering values = money) acquire significance only in the light of their cosmological purpose: handed by Jews to the Antichrist at his first summons, "Values" would bring unparalleled wealth to Jerusalem and secure its global domination ("Values" = wandering values = money).

The narrator draws the three simulacra—Antichrist, Jews and money—into an ostensibly neat formula of absolute evil. But the superficial tidiness of this equation does not explain the choice of variables in it and sheds little light on the standpoint from which the proposition is uttered.

Given that the existence of the Antichrist is implied in the Gospels (Matthew 24:5; John 2:18), the centrality of his image for the Christian view of absolute evil is hardly surprising.[3] The materialization of the Christ's archenemy in the form of the Jewish Messiah is also quite common in legends, plays, and other fictional references to the Antichrist starting in the thirteenth century (see below). However, the equally significant human and monetary movements in Dostoevsky's eschatology are not commonplace in canonic Christian narratives and may be incomprehensible without some genealogical reconstruction, historical contextualization, and rhetorical analysis.

To begin with, the ceaseless wandering of moneyed Jews has never been an indispensable part of the Christian doctrine of evil.[4] The internal rhetorical structure of this doctrine is not normally complicated by the dialectical interplay of meaningless substance and meaningful appearance, as construed by Dostoevsky. Indeed, the complex correlation between the Jewish jewelers' movement in a real environment in devoted expectation of their proper fate and their imaginary Master single-handedly directing this activity from the glorious future is nowhere to be found in Christian demonology. Hence, both the causality and dialectics of Dostoevsky's version of absolute evil hint at the extra-ecclesiastic sources of his writing that may span from isolated folklore motives to the overarching conditions of nineteenth-century European discourse. It could be instructive to begin this investigation with the least general elements of Dostoevsky's formula ("Humans" and "Values"), proceed then to its focal point ("Messiah") and conclude with authorship, disclosed in the text only *ex negativo* but ultimately successfully subordinating the essential difference between good and evil to the author's everlasting attempts at self-definition.[5]

At first glance, the "wandering Humans" of Dostoevsky have much less to do with the Christian construction of the ontological other than with the Jewish tradition of religious self, but in reality his version of Judaic Messianism is a rationalistic hyperbole almost certainly unrelated to the self-perception of Israelites. Indeed, the expectation of the Messiah was neither a particularly early nor a continuous trend in Judaism, and only a handful of Jews in each generation possessed a real experience of the displacement Dostoevsky attributes to all Jews.[6] As for the Holy Scripture, it contains rather vague references to traitors, murderers, or even devoted disciples of Jesus Christ left on earth until the Second Coming, and none of them emphasizes wandering.

The ontological rationale for the extremely long earthly existence of a mortal usually conflates two motives. The first, created by Christian apologetics for its own purposes, focuses on the necessity of providing the firsthand account of Christ to as many doubters as possible (the case of the apostle St. John).[7] The second, going back to such famous allegories as Prometheus, Sisyphus, and Tantalus, treats abnormally long life on earth as a just punishment for such ungodly deeds as Cain's murder of his brother Abel or the hypothetical treason mentioned by Jesus and quoted in St. John's Gospel. It is within this tradition that eternally restless sinners such as the Wild Huntsman or the lying Dutchman sneak into Christian doctrine, able to appear at any time and in any place, always moving in circles, chasing people in dark forests and (fortunately) defenseless against a good prayer.[8]

The relative harmonization of the two genealogically unconnected and semantically incongruent forms began around the thirteenth century. In popular consciousness, the story of a Wild Huntsman was *post factum* added to the Passion of Christ to indicate the supernatural power of the Savior at the moment of his utmost physical exhaustion: the Jew who prevented Christ—"the enemy of Moses"—from drinking out of a trough on his way to Golgotha turned into an eternal wanderer with the head of a deer (or an Old Testament prophet), flames bursting from his mouth, often followed on his never-ending journey by witches, courtesans, apostates, tradesmen, and unbaptized children.[9] On a doctrinal level, the Fourth Ecumenical Council lowered the barriers between learned Christology and popular imagination, having sanctioned the distribution of all stories, Christian and non-Christian, that glorified the Almighty.[10]

To be sure, neither mass creativity nor papal politics streamlined the development of the legend: the torments of Prometheus reverberate in the fifteenth-century Greek (and later Slavic) folklore account in which the Old Testament conception of reciprocal justice completely overshadows its Christian framework: here a certain Phalas, cured of anemia by Christ, slaps him in the face—only to find himself later torn apart by wild animals three times a day, year after year.[11] However, in the later versions of the legend, Jesus Christ appears not only morally victorious but rhetorically invincible: the sole function of the Wandering Jew in the narrative becomes the negative affirmation of the eternally Divine. Condemned in an influential chronicle, *Ignoti Monachi Cistersiensis S. Mariae de Ferraria* (1228), to compulsive rejuvenation every one hundred years, the sinner is effectively pushed out of Christian history and is yet utterly dependent on it. As in other versions of the legend, death—the longed-for release from timelessness—can be granted to the Wandering Jew only at the time of the Second Coming.[12] In a similar vein, the vagabond, unable to sit down at a tavern or to stay more than three days in one village, is more often than not oblivious to the moral purpose of his restlessness. So, for instance, a certain Malchus from Judas's army—the most popular Wandering Jew in the thirteenth to the sixteenth centuries—does not repent for his assault on Christ, although the readers, of course, must have drawn their own conclusions linking Malchus's eternal punishment and his heinous crime.[13] Starting

in the seventeenth century, the offender is given a chance at moral regeneration—in the *Dudulaeus Pamphlets* (1602) he undergoes a metamorphosis from a
fierce enemy of the Savior to his loyal follower—but the belated transformation
does not alter his slavish position in a Christian narrative.

The normative preconditions of the discourse in which the Wandering Jew,
his striking of Jesus, his restlessness, and his immortality appeared include the
divinity of Christ, the criminality of wandering, and the profanity of worldly existence.[14] Whereas in the figure of Christ the miracle of resurrection produces
time in its dialectics of earthly and heavenly, human and divine, the role of his
alter ego is reduced to a purely passive voice. Stripped of his name, Buttadeos
(the one who punched God), also known as Vottadeo (the one who believed in
God), is shown acting without being active, living out a miracle he refuses to
accept, and utterly depending on the history from which he has been thrown
away.[15] As a manifestation of pure negativity within Christian discourse, the
Wandering Jew conforms to the perception of evil, created by God to complete
the moral dichotomy of the world.[16] If anything, the resigned outcast is too tame
for such a grandiose role, and little by little the Wandering Jew fuses with other,
more menacing, Christian figurations of vice, loses his bleak one-dimensionality,
and develops into a colorful shadow (if not a potent contender) of absolute
good.

The legend of the Antichrist was only a small element in the late medieval tendency to see Jewish disbelief in the Christian God as a service to the
devil. In the fifteenth-century German play *The Duke of Burgundy*, the rival
of Christ was entrusted by Jews to eradicate Christianity through poisoning,
massacres, black magic, witchcraft, and ritual murders.[17] The success of the
play was no doubt aided by incipient economic and religious disturbances in
Europe, which coincided with the arrival of Jews from the Mediterranean and
were immediately associated with it.[18] Three centuries later, Martin Luther reversed the internal hierarchy of evil by equating the Antichrist with the Jewish
Messiah.[19] It is not unimportant that the firmly established blood relationship
between Satan, Jews, and the Antichrist came to the surface in the legend of
the Wandering Jew after another three centuries' time—precisely in the time of
Dostoevsky and Marx. For instance, in Jean Paul's *Plan to Comets* (1820–1822)
the Wandering Jew, Cain, Satan, and the Antichrist merge into a single being;
this example was followed by many novelists and poets of the mid-nineteenth
century.[20]

But an even more significant consequence of this amalgamation is the gradual transformation of the Wandering Jew into a grandiose superhuman being.
The Wandering Jew's forsakenness in boundless time and space, which had
earlier indicated the weakness of the humble vagrant before the Christian god,
suddenly becomes a colorful testament to his supernatural abilities. Thus, in
Spanish and Portuguese tales "Juan de Espera en Dios" is said to know the

whole of history, and indeed in the popular book *Kurtze Beschreibung und Erzehlung von einem Juden mit namen Ahasverus* (1602) the main hero knows more about Christ than all church historians and evangelists combined (!) and may recollect every minute of the saints' and apostles' lives, passions, and deaths.[21] A similar metamorphosis of random individual experience into a universal awareness transcending the boundaries of human perception occurs with the spatial orientation of the wanderer. Thus, in Giovanni Maranas's *Chronicle of the Wandering Jew* (1692–1693) the Wandering Jew has been to all places in the world and can effortlessly speak their languages.[22] Not infrequently the magical omniscience and omnipresence were combined with the traditional diabolic skill of being able to change one's substance and appearance: Dostoevsky's contemporary David Hoffman, in his *Chronicles Selected From the Origins of Cartaphilus, the Wandering Jew, Embracing a Period of Nearly XIX Centuries* (1842), shows his protagonist assuming and then rejecting a myriad of names, characteristics, and intellectual and philosophical positions (from the prophet Mohammad to the Wandering Jew himself).[23] Capable of speaking any language, reaching out to every corner of the globe, and wearing any mask, by the late eighteenth century the Wandering Jew achieves a truly universal equivalence that clearly surpasses his function in the legend (to serve as a backdrop to the historical triumph of Christ and his religion) but still falls short of a separate teleological alternative to Christianity. The Wandering Jew is still hard to imagine without his exemplary loneliness and arresting peculiarity, but gradually his forlorn tread becomes an allegory for whole trades, religions, and nations.

To be sure, the allegorical reading of a legend does not necessarily emphasize the religious discord: in an Estonian tale, a shoemaker who does not let Christ rest in his courtyard on the road to Calvary brings disgrace to all of his colleagues.[24] Still, the distinctive feature of the Wandering Jew in a legend is his offensive behavior toward Jesus, and therefore he is most typically associated with other enemies of the Savior. The temporal and spatial closeness of an accident at the Jew's house to his compatriots' far more serious crime against Christ (in calling for the crucifixion) directs the legend's allegorical extension and proportionally sharpens its tone. While the lonesome globetrotting of a single apostate was usually—especially before the eighteenth century—considered to be an adequate punishment for the contempt of Jesus Christ, the restlessness of the whole confession could only be justified by its collective guilt dating back to the beginnings of Christian history: this is the message of Johann Jacob Schudt's compendium *Jüdische Merkwürdigkeiten* (1718), reiterated (with increasing ferocity) in Slavic tales (possibly known to Dostoevsky) and works by contemporaries such as Michal Broch (*Na piaskakh*, 1845) or Karl Gutzkow (*Plan eines Ahasverus*, 1842).[25] Anti-Semitic cartoons in the German magazine *Kladderadatsch* (1867–1870) that featured the Wandering Jew as a summary manifestation of "Judaism" solidified the association between two negatives of

Christology—"Jewish people" as a global tribe of God-killers who are "wandering" in the aftermath of their expulsion from Christian history. Nevertheless, the positive causal correlation between Jews and their wandering was simply not to be found in a discourse that pictured Christ as the only source of all causality.

The rise of anti-Semitism in Europe in the 1850s shows the limits of Christian belief in the purely "instrumental" role of Jews in Christianity. As in the Middle Ages, when the "great rumors" about a Jewish army lead by the Antichrist came to fill the void between the multiple appearances of the Devil and his heinous crimes, in the first capitalist century the newer scenarios of social domination were mobilized to explain the function of "wandering Humans" in Christian history. The void between the innumerable appearances of the Devil and his unchanging substance was still filled with ad hoc dialectics of the abstract and the concrete, but with the growing popularity of secular reasoning this dialectical image of absolute evil grew more complex. With fewer and fewer people believing in the authenticity of the legend (Pierre de l'Estoile in the early seventeenth century plainly called it "stupid" and "improbable"), the search for its modern Christian interpretation gained strength: Jewish wandering was now construed not as a simple iconic representation of the quest for global supremacy, but rather as a cover for the more sophisticated interplay of diabolic essence and its worldly manifestations.[26] This is where universal equivalence became the semantic framework of new allegory; this is when James de Rothschild took the place of the Wild Huntsman.

One of the earliest versions of the legend, penned by Antonio di Francesco di Andrea around 1450, featured a certain Giovanni Bottadio, whose raison d'être (to be the living witness of the divine power) and mode of existence (unable ever to stay in one place for more than three days) remained the most distinctive features of the Wandering Jew for many centuries.[27] "The One Who Punched God" was also said to have some supernatural attributes both widespread in mythological tradition (he could become invisible) and directly associated with his movement (he could speak all languages and tell world history from any point of time, and he had always enough of anything he needed but never more money than necessary for a particular situation).[28] In this context, the magical ability of the Jew to secretly balance supply and demand for his benefit seems to be a simple extension of his individual irregularity, caused by immediate contact with the Divine, abnormally long life, and prolonged estrangement from Christian society. However, in many later references to the Wandering Jew (for instance, the recourse to the popular motive of an inexhaustible purse) his unfailing attachment to money is seen as a mystical constant of Jewish identity that may well have a deep teleological significance but cannot be fully elucidated within the discursive framework of the legend.

The intricacy of tying the association between the Wandering Jew and money to the figure of Christ is conspicuous in a confused Italian fable (popular also in Malta): here the angry Jesus promises his offender no rest on earth or in the sea, but predicts that the coin the Wandering Jew is holding in his hand will return back to him to prove his separation from the world.[29] Small wonder that the relation between *wandering* humans and *wandering* values has rarely been rationalized to the point of systemic interaction of two independent processes with a common teleological significance. As time went on, the second, derivative, movement (wandering money) relegated the first—the original—to the shadows and became directly associated with the common cause of the Wandering Jew, the Devil, and the Antichrist. A case in point is the conversion of the inexhaustible purse—a relatively harmless feature of Jewish self-sufficiency—into a cover for a wider exchange conspiracy of Wandering Jews in which Christians are always on the losing side. Thus the hero of Josef Jaroslav Kalina's ballade *Jidašův peniz* (1852)—a synthesis of Wandering Jew and Judas—pays an old man for his hospitality with three of a total thirty silver coins, but the transaction quickly erupts into a deadly quarrel between the three sons of the privileged host, and the "benefactor" cold-bloodedly reclaims the money from their dead bodies.[30]

In this respect, Dostoevsky's version of the legend is decidedly old-fashioned: "Values" follow the same routes as "Humans." What makes his image of the Wandering Jew special, though, is the complete overturning of its negative semantics: rather than being the mere consequence of spontaneous apostasy, the outwardly limitless traveling of a hero in time and space becomes the prerequisite for its logical completion—the comprehensive invalidation of the Christ's message. In other words, the clueless groping of a single pariah in the dark in search of his lost identity, prescribed by the major figure of Christian history, gives way to a highly self-conscious movement of the deniers' tribe toward an alternative realization of history under the guidance of the Christ's formidable opponent. To be sure, such an ambitious refurbishment of a rather conservative tale required splitting its center of gravity in two: no more a feeble plaything of Christian eschatology, the Wandering Jew in Dostoevsky's interpretation stakes a claim to his teleological antithesis and aligns himself with the alter ego (and most formidable enemy) of absolute good.

But *The Writer's Diary* displays a much more radical absorption of Jewish historical teleology with this modern, rational, semantically positive interpretation of the Wandering Jew: the dispersion of Jews, filled with a contemplative expectation of the Messiah, is retold here as an active preparation for the global triumph of Israel, which will be largely based on the dialectical overcoming of gold's transient economical value by its eternal religious value. For Dostoevsky, the fall of the Wandering Jew from Christian teleology threatens to implode this history under the leadership of the premature Messiah—i.e., the "Deity," whose falsity is as much a function of his "shorting" of Christianity, shared by other Jews, as it is an allegorical summation of Jewish adherence to negative actions and values, meaningful only in a context of their hijacking of sacred history. It becomes apparent that the second—and more explicit—focal point of the modified story, the figure of the "Messiah," is aimed at synthesizing the dichotomies engendered by the representations of historical negativity ("Humans" and "Values") in the process of their progressive emancipation from the clutches imposed by the original fable. But the hierarchy of these syntheses is of principal importance for defining the semantics of the "Messiah" in Dostoevsky's text, and it deserves to be followed more closely.

In H. von Levischnigg's work *Ahasver* (1842), the Wandering Jew is shown through the fictionalization of James de Rothschild—the veritable symbol of developed European capitalism.[31] The name of the Austrian banker, residing in France, was in Dostoevsky's time one of the most common allegories for topics as broad as "Judaism," "money," and "power." The self-evident sociopolitical factors that contributed to the formation of this peculiar figuration were the obvious economical and emerging political leadership of Jews in general and the Rothschilds in particular in nineteenth-century Europe. After all, no fewer than three of the members of the Rothschild dynasty were elected in 1842 to the French National Assembly.[32] A handful of witnesses to the rise of the financial empire of the Rothschilds commented specifically on the paradox of the supreme political power of the traditional outcasts—with the economic background of this success as its default basis. Following the catchy slogan penned by Alphonse Tousenel in 1845 ("Jews are Kings of the Epoch"), the wife of the Russian chancellor Nesselrhode observed wryly that the house of Rothschild was more important in France than the heads of the governments, and Ludwig Boerne ironically suggested making the world happy by giving the Rothschilds the thrones of European monarchs.[33] However, for a sizeable number of observers (Dostoevsky included) the financial and political power of the Rothschilds and other moneyed Jews was only a preparatory stage of their future religious power: a Christian utopian, Pierre Leroux, compared the contemporary financial and stock exchange activity to the Crucifixion, and Charles Fourier, one of the idols of Dostoevsky's socialist past, envisioned the dynasty of Rothschild leading Jews to Jerusalem to take up the restored throne of David and Solomon and conquer the world.[34]

Given the common roots of Christian and socialist aversion to money, the closeness of French communist thinkers of the nineteenth century to the thoughts of the devoted monarchist is hardly unexpected. What is surprising, though, is Dostoevsky's, manifest inability for all his obsession with the religious significance of the Jewish economical triumph, to move beyond the sketchy and disjointed image of the "Messiah," remembered, perhaps, from his socialist past. Indeed, the other prefigurations of Jewish global dominance in *The Writer's Diary* cling to the standard dialectics of substance and appearance, only slightly complicated by a new layer where it is claimed that European

politics was a mere façade for domination by the Jew and his bank, from behind yet another mask—socialism—to cause chaos, wipe out Christianity, and
set the stage for the return of the Antichrist.[35] Even more puzzlingly, the two
disparate hypostases of the false "Deity"—an economical being and a politico-
religious abstraction—never join together or even sufficiently develop in their
respective contexts. "Rothschild" is frequently mentioned in *The Insulted and
the Injured* (1861), *The Gambler* (1866), *The Idiot* (1869), and *The Adolescent*
(1875), but remains a bare symbol of the raw power procured by unlimited
wealth, whereas "The King of Jews" survives in frantic, elaborate, partly incomprehensible sketches on the margins of *The Idiot* and *The Brothers Karamazov*
but is almost entirely excised from the final versions of both texts.[36]

The natural explanation for this startling incoherence right in the center
of Dostoevsky's demonology might be the shift in the synthesis between the
opposite facets of absolute evil. Apparently, the internal dichotomies abstract/
concrete, natural/supernatural, essential/superficial, which allow the Devil to
emanate the comprehensiveness essential for rising to the challenge of his creator and rival in a cosmological drama, are lacking in Dostoevsky's texts' integrated embodiment on the figural level (personages).[37] Their coordination is
relegated then to the authorial level, so that the narrator's discursive acts (such
as choices of narrative modes, semantics of the first-person moral statements,
or groupings of personages and events) can be the only differentiators between
absolute evil and the rest. Contrary to expectations, though, the writer's extraordinary attention to the form and substance of cosmological negativity does
not engender a single rhetorical entity within his text, be it a balanced constellation of voices and masks or a coherent set of summary postulates.

On the face of it, many of Dostoevsky's figural representations of Judaism
may serve as a cornerstone for the future consolidation of the scattered facets
under the diabolic banner. Thus a favorite character among Dostoevsky scholars, Isai Fomich Bumstein—from Dostoevsky's autobiographical novel, *Notes
from the Dead House* (1862)—responds to an empty threat by his fellow pris-
oner to send him from Siberia "still farther": "With God's help and money life
is good everywhere."[38] The perfect mood of Bumstein is telling. The journey to
the remotest corner of the world is perfectly tolerable for one of the "Humans"
as long as he can at any moment relate himself to his false "Deity" and his false
"Values." As in the legend told by Dostoevsky in *The Writer's Diary*, the restlessness of the Jew turns to its opposite as long as the offender, punished by the
Christian god, secures links with its transcendental antipodes. But the firmness
of Isai Fomich Bumstein, who in a hostile environment endows his exile to
Siberia with cosmological meaning, does not turn him into the new Antichrist.
On the contrary, the exchange, crowned by the rhetorical victory of a Jew over
his Russian opponent, is inscribed in a familiar framework where the lifeless
other has no other purpose than to serve as a moral and narrative antithesis

to the narrating Christian self. Isai is no more than a lifeless sequence of witticisms, a purely formal refutation of Orthodox rhetoric, aimed at displaying his petty-mindedness and pseudo-religious mercantilism.[39]

It is only in Dostoevsky's attempts to put the introspective scenarios of self-definition into words that the struggle between deity and "Deity" opens up in its real complexity. If the truth be told, in his last novel, *The Brothers Karamazov* (1881), the writer does succeed in shaping the image of a human soul as a battlefield of God and the Devil (Ivan Fedorovich), and even empowers Ivan's son Alesha with fictitious comments upon this duplicity.[40] But the Herculean task of managing the throngs of fleeting demarcations between absolute good and its opposite always falls on the narrator's shoulders, and it proves to be a heavy burden to bear. Bogged down in the Sisyphean toil of getting over its own incompleteness and reversibility, the reflecting subject is unable to maintain the difference between its objectified consciousness (as the automatic replication of observer in the process of self-observation) and the negative principle of Christian teleology (as the obligatory mirroring of the Creator in a dualistic cosmology).

Obviously the writer did not invent the philosophical model of self-alienated spirit, brought to perfection in German transcendental idealism and known to Dostoevsky from his well-read friend and ally Apollon Grigoriev.[41] Nor did he create the fictional device of the hero's double presence in the text, which allows his hidden thoughts and repressed feelings to surface: doubles already played a central role in E. T. A. Hoffman's fantastic tales (which Dostoevsky admired and imitated) and were an object of Carl Gustav Carus's philosophical criticism (which Dostoevsky wanted to translate into Russian).[42] But Dostoevsky was possibly the first author of fiction who tied to his own narrating self its negative determination both in terms of default (Christian) teleology and in terms of default (reflexive) psychology. As the main hero of *Double* (1846) cannot decide whether his double is his enemy, his alienated part, or his self-alienated self, so Dostoevsky in *The Writer's Diary* is torn between the feelings of the historical and moral otherness of Jews, their dialectical opposition to Christians' longing for post-historical synthesis, and their frightening rationalization of his personal doubts in God.[43] Indeed, throughout the text we can register not only the narrator's oscillations between open anti-Semitism and defense of individual Jews, but also his alternating appeals to the Russian readership.[44] Hence, in one chapter Dostoevsky calls for resistance to Jews alienated from real, immovable values (native soil) by means of their double self-alienation (wandering with money); in another, aptly called "The Isolated Case," we encounter Jews and Christians waiting for a common Messiah; and in a third Russians are called upon to fulfill the mission of Israelites by becoming the rulers of Jerusalem.

Paradoxically, this set of contradictions supports not only the narrative integrity of *The Writer's Diary*, but also the unity of Dostoevsky's worldview as a whole. As an adept of a Christian double-valued moral system, the writer attributes to Jews the traits of absolute evil, and he incorporates this negative absoluteness in his narrative. The Jews in his legend are not a bunch of purposeless vagabonds, banned from Christian history for their sins against Jesus Christ, but an almost complete negative of the Supreme in all its infinite diversity and magnitude, including the false "Deity" ready to impose upon Christians a false history, and false "Humans" prepared to furnish this "Deity" with false "Values." As a believer in Christian teleology, though, Dostoevsky recognizes the value of absolute evil as a dialectical presupposition of the universal (post-historical) good: this is why he crowns "The Isolated Case" with a happy ending, showing Christians and Jews mourning, praying, and waiting together at the funeral of Gindenburg.[45] At the same time, as both a human really living in history and a narrator actually narrating his text, Dostoevsky is bound to witness and describe the dissolution of his religious and narrative self. Indeed, his dream of universal happiness spells doom for his own default Christian perspective, from which the figures of Jewish evil could only be construed: both extremes are to be dialectically overcome by the universal fulfillment of the Christian ideal after the arrival of a common Messiah and the end of history.

It is perhaps at this crucial point that the despairing writer attempts to regain ground by placing himself after Christian history and beyond the synthesis of dialectical opposites. Proclaiming in his later works his belief in the "Russian God" and "native soil," Dostoevsky de facto became a post-Christian (earthly) Messiah, a glorifier of his own non-reflective self, and a proponent of the post-synthetic cult of bare matter.[46] The "Jewish" egoism and materialism that the Russian writer lamented together with countless other anti-Semites boomeranged against him toward the end of his life. What remains to be seen are what chances Dostoevsky had to avoid this trap. The answer to this question demands a comparative study.

Circulating "God," Jews Expelled from "History," and the Spectacle of self-Denial

Let us look again at the excerpt from the article *On the Jewish Question* quoted in the introduction.[47] Like Dostoevsky, Marx speaks of false "Deities," false "Humans," and false "Values," but the rhetoric of exposure is somewhat more intricate. For Dostoevsky the falsity of the first element of absolute evil stems from the untimely appearance of its customary synecdoche in Christian history; this haste is, in principle, sufficient to relegate the "Messiah" to the realm of the Devil. For Marx, Christian history is of little immediate concern. Rather, the deceitfulness of "Deity" stems from its encroachment upon human wholeness, which senselessly breaks humans into alienated substance and incomplete appearance. The agency that prevents humans from returning to the natural status quo (their unity) is exchange, the specific modifier of "self-alienated Humans" that sets them in perpetual motion according to laws contrary to human existence per se (circulation). The resulting unbridgeable gap between the "Humans" (mortals robbed of their self-alienated essence), and their estranged and modified part (circulating "self-alienated Humans") forms a basis for religious (self-) adoration. The phenomenal realization of this total exchangeability of the estranged human self, for Marx, is the medium of economic exchange, whereas the major historical manifestation of human disintegration is the Jewish religion. Dostoevsky's tripartite evil (the Antichrist, Jews, and money) shrinks in Marx's pamphlet to a dyad (Jews and money), and the respective semantics of its parts is adjusted to the needs of monist teleology. Thus the fatal rupture of Jewish identity takes place not between its bearers and the absolute value, but within human beings as such: in other words, Jews (and other "Humans," as Marx implies) forgo their humanness not by estranging themselves from the repository of absolute good (native soil), but by destroying their own absolute goodness in a process of self-estrangement. Accordingly, the second part of the dyad—money—not only retains its customary attributes (capacities of unlimited movement and unreserved exchange) but simultaneously takes in the major function of Antichrist—to head the historical realization of the alternative to absolute good.

Obviously, Marx adheres to the same general conventions of linear writing as Dostoevsky, and the summation of the components of absolute evil in his nonfictional text is entrusted to the narrator—the economist's alter ego. However, the particular relations between the two narrators and their narratives are somewhat different. On the one hand, Marx's textual self seems to have a more coherent semantics because his set of assertions pertaining to the absolute evil is better coordinated. Indeed, the falsity of "Humans" in his text is inversely proportional to the spuriousness of "Deity": the more people indulge in self-alienation, the stronger is the power of money and the further is the society from the ideal of absolute good. On the other hand, Dostoevsky's narrative stance is less dependent on its purely negative articulation in a portrait of absolute evil. His worst-case scenario of Christian history ends with its eclipse from within, with the messianic impostor interrupting the historical transition from the First to the Second Coming through his mock-up of the Kingdom of God on earth. Consequently, in his defense of absolute good, the narrator in *The Writer's Diary* does not have to go beyond the historical and teleological framework of Christianity, and his narrative association with absolute good is negatively affirmed by his critique of the Antichrist, Jews, and money in categories of Christian double-valued morality. Marx, by contrast, employs the traditional Christian allegories of evil—Jews and money—outside their historical and teleological frame, so his references to absolute evil, consistent with each other, shed little light on the positive meaning of Marx's narrative self beyond his purely discursive (and totally self-referential) first-person authority.[48] Unlike the Russian Christian, the German atheist had neither a binary moral template nor a canonic historical narrative at his disposal. Consequently, the search for an exhaustive meaning of absolute evil in Marx's negative teleology is unthinkable without a purely textual reconstruction of its cosmological opposite.

Notwithstanding its purely secular character, Marx's economic anti-Semitism shares its allegorical beginnings with Dostoevsky's religious anti-Semitism. While Dostoevsky took the Christian parable of the Wandering Jew to explain Jewish estrangement from Christian history, Marx utilized the notion of monetary "circulation" to show the irreversibility of Jewish self-alienation.[49] As we can see, the fictionalization of Jews as the true antithesis of the divine required not only their breakdown into dialectical oppositions normally associated with absolute good, but also a direct subordination of the Jewish distinctive feature (restlessness) to absolute evil. Marx was confronted by the similar necessity of inscribing Jewish self-alienation into a reliable negative teleology, and his changes in the semantics of the word "circulation" were no less sweeping than Dostoevsky's revision of "wandering."

The classical concept of circulation as it appeared in seventeenth century physiology was firmly embedded in the homeostatic perception of harmony: the absolute repetitiveness of the blood movement in human organism attested to its stable equilibrium, whereas the acceleration of blood circulation was a symptom of madness.[50] Even after the migration of the word "circulation" into economics a century after, its semantics remained beholden to the teleology of "eternal return": in Raymond Quesnay's *Tableau Économique* (1758) the self-regulating autonomy of the market was understood as the uniform velocity of exchanges between money and products, which kept prices unchanged.[51] As was the case with Dostoevsky, Marx's radical break with the circularity of circulation furnished Jewish movement with a semantically positive (albeit historically negative) temporality: in Marx's own words, his breakthrough in monetary theory turned the "circle" of monetary flow into a "spiral."[52] And in a way similar to his Russian contemporary, Marx endowed his version of absolute evil with the signature diabolic interplay of substance and appearance (rationalized as the dialectics of the abstract and the concrete): in the *Outline of the Critique of Political Economy* (1858) he masterly displays the devilish elusiveness of money, bouncing back and forth between money as a "general form of wealth," which is a "pure abstraction," and money in its "material, accessible [*handgreiflicher*] form," which is a pure "fantasy." Naturally, it is only in a state of perpetual exchange between its chimerical hypostases ("circulation") that money becomes a reality.[53]

Conclusion

The internal semantic structure of a false "Deity" was quite different in Marx and Dostoevsky, and the roots of this discrepancy lay in the teleological incompatibility of the two discourses. In Dostoevsky's representation of absolute evil, its substantial diversity was organized into a tripartite hierarchy where the supernatural agency regulated human wandering (directly) and economic movement (indirectly); consequently, of all the incarnations of the Devil on earth, only the highest authority (Antichrist) could exercise decisive influence upon Christian teleology, whereas Jewish restlessness was meaningless except in conjunction with this influence, and monetary movement was nothing but the mimetic echo of this restlessness. Marx's approach to the "jealous God of Israel," on the contrary, stressed the independence, individuality, and indivisibility of its semantics: the growth of monetary capital in each capitalist transaction and the progressive self-alienation of workers in the process of historical transition from early feudalism to developed capitalism seemed to be one and the same autonomous process observed at different distances.[54] This complete absorption of Jewish "pseudo"-religion by a more general negative teleology—economic history—was not simply a dialectical opposite of Dostoevsky's religious reductionism. Marx radically broke with the Stoic perception of money as a morally indifferent (i.e., teleologically irrelevant) phenomenon, which until then had reigned supreme in European socialism: one could recall, for instance, that Pierre-Joseph Proudhon combined his loathing of Jews as a manifestation of absolute evil with the elaborate dreams of a "just" credit system.[55]

But Marx's materialistic monism and economic determinism did not fully disabuse the radical philosopher from the traditional Christian dialectics of history. For all his tendency to read the religious essence of Judaism as the shadow of its economical appearance, Marx often sided with other Young Hegelians identifying Jews as a negative principle of world history or even a negative pole of human development—the hyperbole of human materialism and egoism.[56] Small wonder that anti-Christian Marx found it difficult to avoid the rhetorical posture of the proto-Christian narrator with all its unsolvable contradictions. Like Dostoevsky, Marx strove for a post-historical completion of his historical teleology—the overcoming of human self-alienation in the process of production—but was unable to fully detach himself from his personal humanness and his generic historicity. Indeed, the image of the harmonious post-historical superhuman in Marx's dreams was characteristically vague and paradoxically indebted to just one extreme of his historical dialectics (a proletarian Messiah).[57] Inversely, the narrative identity of Marx was largely shaped by instantaneous negation (rather than dialectical overcoming) of his own Jewish past, made from the standpoint of his actual presence in German political struggle.[58]

It turns out that both Dostoevsky's religious anti-Semitism and Marx's economical anti-Semitism are based on the same spatial metaphor ("wandering Jew"/"circulating money") aimed at enriching (Dostoevsky) or surpassing (Marx) Christian teleology and philosophy of history with a new, dynamic, dialectical notion of absolute evil. The trouble both thinkers had in spelling out the comprehensive and coherent idea of good attests to the unruly power of this negative notion of universal equivalence, formed in accordance with mutually incompatible conventions of Judeo-Christian writing pertaining to authorship (as the ultimate source of harmony in narrative) and otherness (as the necessity of the opposite for self-definition). For all the good intentions of Marx and Dostoevsky, invented "Vice" is determined to dominate their narratives devoted to the historical triumph of virtue and truth.

NOTES

The work on this article was supported by the Academic Fellowship Program of the Open Society Foundation and the Alexander von Humboldt Foundation.

1. Fyodor M. Dostoevsky, *The Diary of a Writer*, trans. Boris Brasol [1873–1881] (New York: Charles Scribner's Sons, 1949), 90.
2. Karl Marx, "On the Jewish Question," trans. Richard Dixon and Clement Dutts [1843], in Karl Marx and Friedrich Engels, *Collected Works*, vol. 3 (New York: International Publishers, 1975), 172.
3. See Gregory C. Jenks, *The Origins and Early Development of the Antichrist Myth* (Berlin and New York: Walter de Gruyter, 1991).
4. See, for instance, Robert Chazan, *Medieval Stereotypes and Modern Antisemitism* (Berkeley and Los Angeles: University of California Press, 1997).
5. In terms of authorship, the storyteller's abhorrence of the Jewish Messiah, Jews, and money exposes him as a passionate anti-Semite and anti-capitalist.
6. See Joachim Becker, *Messiaserwartung im Alten Testament* [Expectation of the Messiah in the Old Testament] (Stuttgart: Verlag Katholisches Bibelwerk, 1977); Jacob Neusner, *Self-Fulfilling Prophecy: Exile and Return in the History of Judaism* (Boston: Beacon, 1987), 31.
7. George K. Anderson, *The Legend of the Wandering Jew* (Providence: Brown University Press, 1965), 14.
8. See Josephus J. Gielen, *De Wandelende Jood in volkskunde en letterkunde* (Amsterdam: De Spieghel, 1961), 138.
9. Anderson, *Wandering Jew*, 2.
10. Ibid., 619–620.
11. In Russia, the legend was known at least as of the seventeenth century; see Avrahm Yarmolinsky, "The Wandering Jew: A Contribution Toward the Slavonic Bibliogra-

phy of the Legend," in *Studies in Jewish Bibliography and Related Subjects In Memory of Abraham Solomon Freidus* (New York: Alexander Kohut Memorial Foundation, 1929), 323.

12. Anderson, *Wandering Jew*, 18.

13. Ibid., 12

14. Ibid., 5–6.

15. Gaston Paris, *Légendes du Moyen Age* (Paris: Hachette, 1904), 187–221.

16. Roland Auguet, *Le juif errant: Genése d'une légende* (Paris: Payot, 1977), 73–74.

17. See Joshua Trachtenberg, *The Devil and the Jews: The Medieval Conception of the Jew and Its Relation to Modern Antisemitism* (New Haven: Yale University Press, 1943), 36–37.

18. See David N. Smith, "The Social Construction of Enemies: Jews and the Representation of Evil," *Sociological Theory* 14, no. 3 (1996): 212.

19. See Trachtenberg, *The Devil and the Jews*, 54.

20. Anderson, *Wandering Jew*, 199.

21. Ibid., 41.

22. Ibid., 129.

23. Ibid., 160.

24. Ibid., 98.

25. Ibid., 216–165.

26. Ibid., 648.

27. Gaston, *Légendes du Moyen Age*, 205.

28. Ibid., 89.

29. Anderson, *Wandering Jew*, 26.

30. Ibid., 246.

31. Ibid., 225.

32. Léon Poliakov, *Histoire de l'antisémitisme: L'âge de la science* (Paris: du Seuil, 1955), 218.

33. Ibid., 158–159.

34. Ibid., 157, 174.

35. See the summary and discussion in Hans Kohn, "Dostoevsky's Nationalism," *Journal of the History of Ideas* 6 (1945): 412.

36. See Robert Chappl, "Materialy iz 'Slovaria iazyka Dostoevskogo' (realii kul'tury, istorii i byta Germanii)" [From a 'Dictionary of Dostoevsky's Language': The Realia of German Culture, History and Everyday Life], in *Dostoevsky: Materialy i issledovaniia* (Saint-Petersburg: Nauka, 1992), 252; Kirill Postoutenko, "Ne-otchuzhdenie u Dostoevskogo. Politiko-ekonomicheskii rakurs" [Non-Alienation in Dostoevsky: On the Crossroads of Politics and Economics], *Wiener Slawistischer Almanach, Sonderband* 54 (2001): 142.

37. This technique is analyzed in G. Belzer, *Hegel en Dostoievsky* (Leiden: E.J. Brill, 1953), 92.

38. Fyodor Dostoevsky, *Notes from the Dead House*, trans. Guy and Elena Cook [1862] (Moscow: Raduga Publishers, 1989), 89.

39. Michael R. Katz, "Once more on the Subject of Dostoevsky and Jews," in *People Of the Book: Thirty Scholars Reflect On Their Jewish Identity*, ed. Jeffrey Rubin-Dorsky and Shelley Fisher Fishkin (Madison: University of Wisconsin Press, 1996), 134;

Felix Ph. Ingold, *Dostoewskij und das Judentum* (Frankfurt am Main: Suhrkamp, 1981), 149.

40. See Iakov E. Golosovker, *Dostoevsky i Kant* (Moscow: Nauka, 1963), 77.

41. See V. N. Belopol'sky, "Dostoevsky i Shelling," in *Dostoevsky: Materialy i issledovaniia* (Leningrad: Nauka, 1988), 39; Wayne Dowler, *Dostoevsky, Grigor'ev and Native Soil Conservatism* (Toronto, Buffalo, and London: University of Toronto Press, 1982), 34–36; Heinrich Stammler, "Dostoevsky's Aesthetics and Schelling's Philosophy of Art," *Comparative Literature* 7 (1955), 322. Dostoevsky's most painstaking inquiry into the depth of self-alienated consciousness is to be found in his *Notes from Underground* (1864); see Roger Anderson, *Dostoevsky: Myths of Duality* (Gainesville: University of Florida Press, 1986); J. R. Hill, "Abstraction in Dostoevsky's *Notes from Underground*," *Modern Language Review* 76 (1981): 129–137; Temira Pachmuss, "Dostoevskii and Rainer Maria Rilke: The Alienated Man," *Canadian-American Slavic Studies* 12 (1978), 392–401.

42. R. C. Williams, "The Russian Soul: A Study in European Thought and Non-European Nationalism," *Journal of the History of Ideas* 31 (1970), 576.

43. On gentlemen Goliadkin's ambivalent relation to his double see René Girard, *Dostoïevski du double à l'unité* (Paris: Plon, 1963), 17; J. Rolland, *Dostoievski: La Question de l'autre* (Paris: Editions Verdier, 1983), 121; Igor P. Smirnov, "Otchuzhdenie v otchuzhdenii (o 'Zapiskakh iz mertvogo doma')" ['Alienation in Alienation' in *Notes from the Dead House*], *Wiener Slawistischer Almanach* 7 (1981): 37–48.

44. Gabriela Vassena, "The Jewish Question in the Genre System of Dostoevsky's *Diary of a Writer* and the Problem of the Authorial Image," *Slavic Review* 65 (2006): 58.

45. See Aaron Z. Shteinberg, "Dostoevsky i evreistvo," *Versty* 2 (1927): 106; Gary Rosenshield, "Dostoevskii's "The Funeral of the Universal Man" and "An Isolated Case" and Chekhov's "Rothschild's Fiddle": The Jewish Question," *Russian Review* 56 (1997): 490.

46. On Dostoevsky's messianic self-interpretation see Pamela Davidson, "The Validation of the Writer's Prophetic Status in the Russian Literary Tradition: From Pushkin and Iazykov through Gogol and Dostoevsky," *Russian Review* 62 (2003), 534–536.

47. Due to the space restrictions (natural for a collective monograph) Marx's teleological interpretation of Judaism is presented here in brief.

48. On the first-person authority, which is always present but has no real bearing on the speaker's social identity, see Donald Davidson, *Subjective, Intersubjective, Objective* (Oxford: Oxford University Press, 2001), 202–203.

49. For discussion of interpenetration between religious and economic alienation in Marx and Dostoevsky see Bohdan Urbankowski, *Dostojewski—dramat humanizmów* [Dostoevsky: The Drama of Humanisms] (Warsaw: KAW, 1978), 176; Ingold, *Dostojewskij und das Judentum*, 156.

50. Joseph Vogt, "Ökonomie und Zirkulation um 1800," *Weimarer Beiträge* 43 (1997): 69; Roland Borgards, "Blutkreislauf und Nervenbahnen: Zum physiologischen Zusammenhang von Zirkulation und Kommunikation im 18. Jahrhundert," in *Gedächtnis und Zirkulation: Der Diskurs des Kreislaufs im 18. und frühen 19. Jahrhundert,*

ed. Harald Schmidt and Marcus Sandl (Göttingen: Vandenhoeck & Ruprecht, 2002), 25–38.

51. Harry Schmidtgall, "Zur Rezeption von Harvey's Blutkreislaufmodell in der englischen Wirtschaftstheorie des 17. Jahrhunderts," *Sudhoffs Archiv: Zeitschrift für Wissenschaftsgeschichte* 57 (1973): 429.

52. On the teleological significance of this change see Louis Althusser and Étienne Balibar, *Lire le Capital I* (Paris: Presses Universitaires de France, 1971), 155.

53. Karl Marx, "A Contribution to the Critique of Political Economy," trans. Richard Dixon [1843], in Karl Marx and Friedrich Engels, *Collected Works*, vol. 30 (New York, International Publishers, 1975), 20.

54. G. A. Cohen, "Marx's Dialectics of Labor," *Philosophy and Public Affairs* 3 (1974), 250–251.

55. On Proudhon's Judeophobia see Poliakov, *Histoire de l'antisémitisme*, 176–177.

56. Allan Arkush, "Judaism as Egoism: From Spinoza to Feuerbach to Marx," *Modern Judaism* 11 (1991): 211–223.

57. Edward Andrew, "Work and Freedom in Marcuse and Marx," *Canadian Journal of Political Science / Revue canadienne de science politique* 3 (1970), 245.

58. See, for instance, Lewis S. Feuer, "The Conversion of Karl Marx's Father," *The Jewish Journal of Sociology* 14, no. 2 (1972), 157; Julius Carlebach, *Karl Marx and the Radical Critique of Judaism* (Boston: Routledge and Kegan Paul, 1978), 330–332; Sander L. Gilman, "Karl Marx and the Secret Language of Jews," *Modern Judaism* 4, no. 3 (1984), 275–294.

⊱ 3 ⊰

MONEY MAKES THE JEW GO ROUND
West German Jewry and the Search for Flexibility
Anthony D. Kauders

Jews who decided to remain in West Germany after the Holocaust were confronted with a Jewish public in Israel, the United States, and throughout the world that regarded a Jewish presence in Germany as sacrilegious. Hannah Arendt's comment to Gertrud Jaspers, the Jewish wife of the famous Heidelberg philosopher, was a rather restrained example of this attitude, but its thrust was nonetheless unmistakable: "How one actually can bear to live there as a Jew, in an environment that doesn't even deem it necessary to talk about 'our problem,' and that today means our dead, is beyond me."[1] Other voices were less tactful. Gershom Scholem, the eminent historian of Jewish mysticism, expressed his dismay that the German-Jewish theologian Hans-Joachim Schoeps could dare to breathe in the country.[2] Another prominent immigrant to Israel, the publisher Gershom Schocken, called upon the Jewish state to dissociate itself from Germany's Jews, while members of the Israeli Knesset (parliament) declared that the latter "weakened and devalued the honor of our people."[3]

Jews in West Germany not only faced feelings of guilt in the late 1940s or early 1950s, but continued to do so well into the 1970s and 1980s. These sentiments, initially occasioned on account of their decision to stay, were compounded by the many injunctions to abandon the "God-forsaken" land.[4] Jews who publicly reacted to their predicament at first opted for a "Zionist" solution—and identified with Israel unconditionally. But when the accusations did not abate, German-Jewish responses became ever more defiant, often commencing with the argument that Jews had a right to choose their abode, then moving on to denounce the notion of German collective guilt, and finally ap-

Notes for this chapter begin on page 73.

propriating the view that the presence of Jews in the FRG was a litmus test for German democratization.[5]

These responses were reflective in spirit—and often emanated from Jewish officials. A less cerebral way of addressing one's bad conscience was related to money. Many Jews appreciated the abstract nature of money, for it allowed them not only to make a living in the country, but also to leave it as quickly as possible. In the first decades after the Shoah, few Jews had the intention of staying in Germany permanently. Many therefore preferred to rent rather than to buy real estate, and many favored work in import-export businesses over jobs in the civil service sector. Stores that could be sold swiftly and professions that could be pursued elsewhere were more in line with "Jewish" objectives than occupations that possibly precluded emigration. "Liquid" money, numerous Jews believed, would enable them to be in control of their destiny—and make it easier to come to terms with their bad conscience. In some extreme instances, the pursuit of money was indicative of how certain Jews—in this case men who worked in Frankfurt's real estate sector in the early 1970s—paid little heed to the concerns of society at large precisely because they did not intend to become part of that society in the foreseeable future. These developments are the subject of this chapter.

Bonn's Pot of Meat

When the biblical children of Israel arrived at the wilderness of Sinai on the fifteenth day of the second month after their departure from the land of Egypt, they must have felt exhausted. The entire assembly complained to Moses and Aaron: "If only we had died by the hands of God in the land of Egypt, as we sat by the pot of meat, when we ate bread to satiety, for you have taken us out to this Wilderness to kill this entire congregation by famine."[6] Ever since this story was first related to the world, exegetes have interpreted it as an example of how human beings can relinquish their (spiritual) freedom for (base) material goods. Not surprisingly, Jews in Israel and elsewhere decided that the only reason why Jews continued to live in the Federal Republic was that they had forsaken the freedom of Zion for West Germany's riches.

The Israeli Consul in Munich, for example, was convinced that these Jews were "an element that was far removed from an idealistic stance." In a letter to the Israeli foreign office in November 1949, Eliahu Livneh surmised that Jewish concerns in Germany centered on "money and profit," and that the "sole bases" of Jewish existence in the country were "insensitivity and the credit balance."[7] The head of the Jewish Agency in Munich, one Amos, advanced similar thoughts in August 1950. Addressing Livneh, he summarized his feelings on the matter as follows: "The moral degeneracy that has been spreading among the Jews of Germany, especially among its businesspeople, makes its necessary to dissociate the Zionist movement and its institutions from the Jewish community in Germany, as we are not in the position to guarantee a continuation of an honorable Jewish existence" in the country.[8] One year later, the New York–based newspaper *Aufbau* maintained that a swift emigration of Germany's "opportunistic" Jews would be in the best interest of Germans and Jews alike.[9] The extent to which this opinion took hold of the imagination was remarkable. As late as 1998, the cofounder of Germany's Central Council of Jews (*Zentralrat der Juden in Deutschland*), Norbert Wollheim, repeated the same story in an interview with the well-known German-Jewish journalist Richard Chaim Schneider. Showing no compunctions, he asserted that many Jews had remained in the Federal Republic because of "Egypt's pots of meat," which they "enjoyed."[10] For the emigré Wollheim, who had left West Germany for the United States in 1951, postwar Jewish life in Germany remained dubious.

Most of these commentaries appeared at a time when *Wiedergutmachung* (restitution) was still heavily contested and few Jews were actually benefiting from generous compensation payments. Indeed, in the 1950s many Jews in West Germany barely made a living and relied on welfare from both Jewish and German institutions. But this state of affairs did not interest Livneh or Amos. Especially in Zionist circles, the mere thought that Jews in Germany had refused to immigrate to Israel was anathema. Besides, Zionist ideology had always belittled if not condemned the quest for money. Max Nordau, the inventor of "Muscle Jewry" (*Muskeljudentum*), was only the most famous exponent of this position, having argued over a century ago that Germany's Jews would not fight anti-Semitism as long as it did not endanger their "stomach and their idleness (*Bequemlichkeit*)."[11] At the Seventh Zionist Congress in Basel (1905), Shmarya Levin castigated what he called "exchange Jews" (*Wechseljuden*), for whom the pursuit of happiness was the be all and end all of existence and for whom the future of the Jewish people was immaterial.[12] Zionists hoped that Jews would one day spurn "unproductive" occupations (trade) and embrace "productive" ones instead (crafts and agriculture). In expounding this position, they culled many of their ideas from romanticism, as well as from widespread (anti-Semitic) notions of what comprised proper masculinity.[13]

In the 1950s, however, another motive became paramount. At the time, Israel was suffering from numerous problems. On the psychological front, the constant fear of future wars produced unease within the population. Massive immigration from Arab countries worsened an already precarious situation. Various governments tried to curb inflation by rationing goods. Unemployment and a serious housing shortage made matters worse. When thousands of Jews decided to leave the country, many with the intention of returning to (West) Germany, Israelis felt betrayed—and could only imagine that the underlying aim of these people was to improve their financial situation.

In fact, 12,000 to 15,000 Jews remigrated to Germany, most of them from Israel. Economic considerations were often crucial in making the decision. Many Jews wished to retire, and many hoped that the process of *Wiedergutmachung* would be speeded up if they lived in the Federal Republic. Others anticipated that the chances of finding a job were better in Munich or Berlin than in Haifa or Tel Aviv—particularly at a time when Israel was undergoing one crisis after another while West Germany's economy was in full swing. Still others wished to oversee the restitution of their property and businesses in person. The decision of the Bonn parliament to grant financial help to immigrants in the order of DM 6,000 per person led to a further wave of immigration in 1956. Finally, a number of Jewish lawyers moved to West Germany, expecting to represent clients seeking recompense from the government.[14]

The decision to return was tantamount to breaking a taboo. Some Jews tried to deceive friends and relatives about their intention to remigrate, which they could do only for so long before friendships and family ties collapsed.[15] Numerous Jews would justify their presence in West Germany by suggesting that they could play an important mediatory role between the Federal Republic and Israel. An immediate, less reflective response, however, was to develop a particular relationship to money, one that would make it easier to deal with one's feelings of guilt for living in the "blood-soaked" land.

Remaining Aloof

Now, at first sight the Jewish approach to money or the economy in Germany was hardly extraordinary. To be sure, in the first postwar decades the number of Jewish *rentiers* was especially high. Furthermore, few Jews could be found in industry or agriculture, confirming trends of past centuries. Yet by and large, the economic situation of most Jews in the Federal Republic resembled that of most non-Jews in the country: at first they were destitute, then many managed to make ends meet, later a majority belonged to the middle classes, and finally a great number (of Russian Jews) relied on welfare. Aside from this last phase, the economic state of West German Jewry largely coincided with the country's economic development.

Let us look at further details. In the 1940s and 1950s, psychological traumata, language problems, and a hostile environment delayed the economic integration of many Jews. Few Jews could rely on business connections and most were excluded from informal networks.[16] Jewish industrialists were in short supply. Several members of the former business elite returned to Germany, such as Hermann Eisner of the Engelhardt brewery, Rudolf Hahn of Mannesmann, and Rudolf Ullstein of the eponymous publishing house. Some, such as the broadcasting pioneer Siegmund Loewe, came back sporadically or divided their

time between Germany and their new domiciles. But on the whole, their influence on the economy remained marginal.[17]

In the 1950s, numerous Jews worked in the textile and cleaning industry.
Only in the case of Frankfurt, where Jews were disproportionately employed
as skinners and furriers, is it possible to speak of continuity with the prewar
period.[18] In his annual report on 1961, the general secretary of the Central
Council, Hendrik van Dam, wrote that the Jewish population in the Federal
Republic predominantly comprised members of the free professions, white-
collar employees, and pensioners. Jews no longer figured in the banking system,
van Dam added.[19] The situation had not changed markedly some thirty years
later, even if the number of Jewish lawyers, doctors, and television personalities had risen in the meantime. Writing in 1993, the administrative director of
Düsseldorf's Jewish community wrote the following about "his" Jews: "Primarily they belong to the middle classes (*Mittelschicht*), and only very few are poor;
these receive social welfare from the community. The majority of members is
made up of self-employed physicians, businessmen, etc. as well as salaried employees; really wealthy members are … as absent as really poor."[20]

Beyond these dry facts, however, it is possible to detect at least two unusual aspects of West German–Jewish economic history: the tendency to regard
occupations as guarantees of mobility and the tendency to rent rather than
buy real estate. Owing to their bad conscience, many Jews in the Federal Republic sought to avoid occupations and lifestyles that would have entailed a
long-term commitment to Germany. As the sociologist Y. Michal Bodemann
has explained, "the preference for job qualifications that were relatively transferable, that is, not bound to the land or language" indicated that, initially
at least, most Jews did not intend to stay in the country.[21] These Jews therefore preferred firms that could be set up and dissolved quickly, avoiding companies that required time to be established and that could not be liquidated
overnight. Accordingly, many Jews worked in real estate, but very few owned
factories.[22]

Since we lack statistics or surveys that would substantiate this finding, I
would like to relate the stories of two families whose paths were fairly typical of
many Jews in West Germany.[23] Charlotte H.'s parents both survived Auschwitz
and later met in a DP (displaced persons) camp in southern Germany. Fairly
soon thereafter, they settled in a medium-sized city, where her father dealt in
tools, iron, and paints. His brothers moved into the nearby metropolis and
established a branch of the firm, which gradually came to specialize in textiles.
Charlotte's father became a successful businessman who imported textiles from
Italy and the Far East. Many of his Jewish friends were also involved in the
textile trade, while others owned furniture stores or supermarkets.

For Charlotte and her family, the Jewish community was an "extended living room." They kept kosher and had no Gentile friends. In the community

center, photos of Israeli politicians decorated the walls, while collection boxes for donations to the Jewish state were on prominent display. Charlotte's family kept a distance from their German surroundings. By contrast, their relationship to Israel was always close. The parents owned an apartment in Tel Aviv that they hoped would figure as proof of their Zionist commitment—and that they had given the country a chance. Repeatedly they told friends and relatives that their presence in West Germany was necessary in order to help the rest of the family in Israel with money and goods. Although Charlotte's mother wished to buy a house in Germany, her husband regularly refused to consider the option. Only after two decades did he purchase an apartment, which in the following years mainly served as a source of income.

Sammy J.'s parents were also Holocaust survivors. Both came from Lithuania, where they had known each other before the war. Sammy's father was liberated from Dachau, Sammy's mother from Stutthof. They met again in a southern German DP camp and married there in 1951. Early on, Sammy's father dealt in all kinds of wares, often as part of black market activities; in subsequent years he pursued other trades, including the production of sweets and the distribution of movies. In the late 1950s he became increasingly involved in real estate, owning up to fifty buildings. Many of his best Jewish friends could also be found in this profession.

Unlike Charlotte's family, Sammy's was not traditional. On the contrary, his parents often invited non-Jews to their home, a fact that made them "proud," according to Sammy. Although the family moved into ever larger apartments, they preferred to rent rather than buy real estate—even when the number of buildings in their possession increased considerably over the years. Only in Israel did the family live in their own house. In 1968, the family moved to the "Holy Land," which did not keep Sammy's father from spending three weeks a month in Germany to oversee his business interests. Only Sammy returned to the Federal Republic permanently. Following stints in the textile industry and in real estate, Sammy now works as a consultant for a large corporation.

Both Charlotte and Sammy agree that money was of paramount importance to their fathers. The reasons they proffer are similar: prosperity stood for "survival" and was somehow to "make up for the losses of the Holocaust." Charlotte refers to her father's "weakened self-esteem" (*angeknackstes Selbstwertgefühl*), whereby wealth served as a form of "narcissistic compensation." To be better off than the "perpetrators," she holds, could also be quite satisfying. The children, however, often suffered from a lack of empathy on the part of their parents—a fault they associate with the Holocaust. On this note, Charlotte and Sammy add that the traumata experienced during the Holocaust could account for the behavior of certain Jews in the real estate business. Making money—irrespective of how others responded to this behavior—was not so different from securing food in the face of death, they maintain.

Sammy's and Charlotte's stories are not unusual. By choosing particular occupations and forms of life, their parents remained aloof. Firms were supposed
to be transferable, families as well. It was imperative that too great a dependence on Germany be avoided. One's own bad conscience demanded such a
distance, as did the various voices from Israel and the Jewish world. Some men
displayed detachment is a very special way—they earned money ruthlessly and
thereby demonstrated that they could not be bothered about (German) public
opinion.

In March 1957, the press organ of the West German Jewish welfare organization (*Zentralwohlfahrtsstelle*) published a lengthy piece on welfare in Bavaria.
As part of its overview, it mentioned a group of survivors that was accustomed
to "see an enemy or an exploiter in every human being." As a result, it was
impossible for these people to accept something in good faith or to trust others; rather, they "worshiped money as the quintessence of any *joie de vivre*."
As "victims of brute force," they had made force a part of their own lives and
experienced "love mainly as a commodity."[24] One need not subscribe to each
and every aspect of this analysis to acknowledge its overwhelming message, to
wit: the accumulation of massive wealth was only possible where "at least in the
beginning all forms of investment in personal well-being or leisure were deemed
superfluous and all energy was put into the rapid accumulation of wealth."[25]
The goal was to leave Germany with as much capital as possible—and as
quickly as possible. Many Jews felt uncomfortable with these people "in their
midst." For non-Jews, the latter served as a pretext to conjure up anti-Semitic
images of the "greedy," "unscrupulous," "materialistic," and "selfish" Jew—part
of their desperate attempt to explain specific developments—capitalism, real
estate speculation, the rapid modernization of urban areas—that they feared
and rejected by resorting to age-old stereotypes.

The Wealthy Jew

In the mid 1960s, Frankfurt's municipal authorities decided to expand the city's
center to include the West End, a predominantly residential area bordering
the university, the main train station, and the financial district. The city had
been suffering from economic turmoil, selling all of its university holdings to
the state of Hesse in 1967, although it had spent the horrendous sum of DM
700 million to rebuild the institution not long before. It was therefore crucial,
the city elders believed, to attract major enterprises to Frankfurt so as to secure
badly needed trade taxes.[26] One way of establishing firms in the city was to find
private investors who would acquire properties with borrowed money and then,
upon securing entire blocks, resell these assets to national and international
firms.

The real estate magnates usually bought houses that were in perfectly good state. In order to tear down the buildings as soon as possible, they were not averse to employing uncompromising methods. First, they raised rents to astronomical heights. If that did not do the trick, they raised them even further. Next, they refused to have repairs made or refused to provide heating, electricity, and water. Sometimes they had radiators and water pipes dismantled. By renting apartments to very large groups of so-called "guest workers," the investors hoped to provoke bourgeois (*bürgerlich*) residents into moving out. Alternative methods included hiring gangs who would vandalize stairwells and backyards or physically threaten the remaining tenants.[27]

Who were these investors? Otto Fresenius, a leading official of the pressure group Aktionsgemeinschaft Westend, meticulously collected data on those who benefited most from the new plans for the neighborhood. Among the firms on his list were Allianz, Metallgesellschaft and Zürichversicherung. The list with the names of investors was much longer—and included Hershkowitz, Buchmann, Kaiser, Preisler, Eimer, A. Rosen, Markiewicz, Steinbüchl, Rubinstein, Semli, Bubis, Göbel, Schütz, Perel, Graumann, and Gruza.[28] A majority of these men were Jewish—and it would be possible to add further Jewish names to the inventory.

One might proffer several explanations for—or, perhaps, retorts to—this unusual fact. First, Jewish capitalists behaved like capitalists everywhere. Secondly, capitalism does not differentiate between Jews and Gentiles. Thirdly, speculation—by Jews and non-Jews alike—is part of capitalism. Fourthly, non-Jewish speculators behaved ruthlessly as well, at times even more ruthlessly.[29] All these clarifications are fair enough, but they do not account for the peculiarity of the situation. Many of these Jews went well beyond what was considered to be proper deportment even within their cutthroat business—and some were put on trial because of their actions.[30] The question, therefore, is not why Jews were speculators or why Jews were unscrupulous speculators, but rather why some Jews behaved the way they did in Frankfurt am Main in the early 1970s. After all, one of the unwritten laws of Jewish life in West Germany was to remain inconspicuous. Jews knew very well that anti-Semites used any (alleged) misconduct by individual Jews as an excuse to castigate the Jews as such. In the wake of the Holocaust, surrounded by people who in the 1930s and 1940s had not stood out for courageous resistance to anti-Jewish policy, most Jews followed this unwritten rule and kept to themselves as much as possible.

It seems more promising, then, to return to the above discussion on "remaining aloof" in order to explain the actions of certain Jews in Frankfurt's real estate sector. Their conduct, it can be argued, demonstrated their disinterest in the city and country, their indifference to the opinions of their critics and opponents, and their distance from the concerns and fears of the general population. For the most part, they had no sentimental ties to Frankfurt or Germany and did not intend to change that. The (rapid) accumulation of money thus served three purposes: it allowed for flexibility and independence, so that one could work and live elsewhere should the occasion arise; it symbolized economic success against the odds—the odds being near-death during the Shoah; and it came at the expense of people who belonged to the *Tätervolk*.[31]

Not surprisingly, the opponents of these developments did not care one way or the other. One group, the Aktionsgemeinschaft Westend, endeavored to retain the neighborhood as a residential area, repeatedly protesting against plans to build streets and erect skyscrapers. Founded in 1969, it attempted to cooperate with the municipality but was equally prepared to demonstrate on the street. In 1973 it received the Theodor Heuss Medal in recognition of its involvement.[32] Although the organization was not openly anti-Semitic, individual members, including prominent ones, occasionally evinced such sentiments.[33] Wilhelm K., for example, suggested that many people in the West End explained "Jewish" behavior with reference to restitution: because the Jews had suffered, they were now permitted to do whatever they saw fit.[34]

Another well-worn theme was to distinguish between German Jews (of an earlier era) and Eastern Jews. In an effort to dissociate the Aktionsgemeinschaft from anti-Semitism, the group published a newsletter in which it outlined the Jewish history of the West End—without, however, mentioning the period during which the city's Jews were ostracized, deported, and murdered. The reader was to infer that the Aktionsgemeinschaft repudiated any type of anti-Jewish prejudice because it appreciated the historical Jews of a previous age.[35] In 1973, Wilhelm K. wondered how the situation could have escalated the way it did, especially in a part of town whose texture and architecture had been the product of "peaceful coexistence" between Christians and Jews.[36] Sometimes members of the Aktionsgemeinschaft mentioned German Jews who actively opposed the real estate speculators as evidence of the real problem, namely the presence of Eastern Jews.[37] Years later, this distinction remained acute. Tilmann S., a well-known Social Democratic journalist and active member of the Aktionsgemeinschaft, could write in the mid 1980s that the postwar Jewish community did not adhere to the same "ideals of *Bildung* and *Besitz* [*Bildungs- und Besitzvorstellungen*]" as its pre-1933 predecessor.[38] While this view was not wrong, it perpetuated racist clichés about Eastern Jews. Similarly, another prominent member of the interest group maintained that the policy of the Jewish community "has for many years been determined and dominated by the Orthodox, Polish" immigrants, who lacked "any connection with the liberal traditions of the old Frankfurt Jewish community"—as if it was possible to differentiate plainly between German and Eastern Jews, as if all of Frankfurt's Jews had been liberal in the Weimar Republic, and as if non-Jews had appreciated, even adored these liberal Jews until a nasty little man from across the border decided to terminate the symbiosis in 1933.[39]

While the Aktionsgemeinschaft as an organization did not succumb to anti-Semitic agitation, numerous squatters, students, left-wing protesters, and Social Democrats were less hesitant in this respect.[40] To take three examples: late in February 1972 the local East End section of the SPD sent a letter to the Hessian Minister of the Interior Bielefeld, in which the party described a gift the city had received from the "economic criminal" Ignatz Bubis as "Judas's pay" (*Judaslohn*).[41] One does have to be a Bible exegete to appreciate the extent to which SPD politicians tried to appeal to the anti-Semitic stereotype of the Jewish traitor. At about the same time, an unnamed Social Democrat complained about a brochure that had been distributed by the housing council (*Häuserrat*) and the student union. According to the critical observer, the piece resembled Goebbels's paper *Der Angriff* both in its layout and in its content—and contained ample anti-Semitic propaganda.[42] Let us finally consider a poster that was reproduced several times in February 1974. "Wanted," the placard read, and on the bottom it was ostensibly signed by the "leading state prosecutor at the regional court Frankfurt." As for its content, the reader was introduced to a notorious gang, led by Ignaz (sic) Bubis, which "has been up to no good on the real estate market for some time." Next there followed a truly remarkable list of names. The makers of the poster had decided that non-Jewish names would only appear in combination with Jewish ones, creating the impression that non-Jewish speculators only acted as part of a Jewish setup. That not being enough, they added a picture of an evening dinner party scene, providing the following caption for the uninitiated: "They shun the public and mostly hide behind their wives and lawyers. What we have here is a cabal therefore, a conspiracy of men who operated behind the scenes and whose shady business deals ruined the city."[43]

It was in this kind of social climate that Gerhard Zwerenz's *Die Erde ist unbewohnbar wie der Mond* (The Earth Is as Inhospitable as the Moon) appeared. Though of dubious literary merit, the novel is an interesting contemporary document, not least because its vitriol combines anti-urbanism, anti-Semitism, and anti-capitalism. Zwerenz hates the new city of Frankfurt, with its "catacombs" housing destitute and alienated zombies. In his story, the protagonists identify Jews by their noses and eyes, and the Jews in turn not only speak a "careless Jews' German" (*nachlässiges Judendeutsch*) or "half-Yiddish," but also pursue their business interests Old Testament–style (*alttestamentarisch*)—an eye for an eye, a tooth for a tooth. Zwerenz's main character, the Jew Abraham Mauerstamm, is a speculator whose aspirations are far removed from those of his "great European predecessors." In other words, Abraham is not a cultivated German Jew, and on top of that he refuses to become one. On the contrary, he merely does whatever his demanding mother expects, which runs to something like the following: "The landscape full of Jewish cemeteries" is to be transformed into a "gigantic cemetery for Aryans buried alive."[44]

The novel might have attracted even less attention than it did had not the famous movie director Rainer Werner Fassbinder taken up the subject and turned it into a play some two years later. *Der Müll, die Stadt und der Tod* (The Garbage, the City, and Death), first published in 1975, equally sought to depict the transformation of urban spaces. Fassbinder, though, could not help but convey his anti-capitalist message with recourse to anti-Semitic imagery. In his case, there was no need to give the anti-hero a name; it was evidently sufficient to call him "the wealthy Jew." This man also acted in a ghastly environment, where human beings became smaller by the day, mutating into "living corpses" and "horror figures." "The wealthy Jew," however, wandered through the city "as if it weren't chaotic, inhospitable like the moon, as if it were open, honest, straightforward." He is helped by the police as well as by the lord mayor, who require his services in order to keep the system going. Yet the "wealthy Jew" despises these figures, and especially those who sweat while "building houses with their hands."[45]

A decade later Frankfurt's Jewish community protested against plans to stage the play in the city's main theater, dismissing popular arguments in favor of artistic freedom. Even Bubis's Jewish critics, such as Dan Diner and Micha Brumlik, showed solidarity with the real estate tycoon. To their minds, the struggle against land speculation had become the struggle against Jewish speculation.[46] They rightly accused Fassbinder of anti-Semitism, given that the dramatist had identified capitalism with the Jew—and with the Jew only. The incarnation had been completed; Jew and capitalism became one when the figure of the "wealthy Jew" was no longer able to say why he accumulated money in the first place. The Jew, in short, was a cipher for profit and capitalist exploitation.[47] It can be argued that this was the last spectacular manifestation of a well-known anti-Semitic topos in Germany: the Jew as the embodiment of rapacious (as opposed to creative), abstract (as opposed to concrete), equalizing (as opposed to individual), international (as opposed to national) capital.[48] We come across this theme one last time in several interventions on Fassbinder's behalf.[49]

Conclusion

By the early 1980s, many Jews in West Germany had largely accepted the fact that they would be staying in the country for good: poor and wealthy Jews alike realized that they would not be leaving the Federal Republic in the foreseeable future.[50] During the opening of Frankfurt's long-awaited Jewish community center in September 1986, Ignatz Bubis's friend Salomon Korn declared that the Jewish community had at long last become part of the city. In the architect's words: "Whoever builds a house wants to stay." In this case, Korn meant a house in which one intended to live. As such, the new center was a "historical turning point," symbolically ending the "liquidation community" of yester-year.[51] It was in the 1980s, then, that the special relationship to money that I have recounted in this essay came to an end. Money was no longer needed to be flexible, because the feelings of guilt had more or less vanished—at least to the extent that Jews in the past had felt compelled to remain aloof from the rest of German society. From now on, living as a Jew in the Federal Republic was not exceptional enough to warrant an exceptional approach to the economy.

NOTES

I would like to the German Research Council (DFG) for supporting my research with a grant. I am equally grateful to the Deutsche Verlagsanstalt (DVA) for allowing me to use material originally published in Anthony D. Kauders, *Unmögliche Heimat: Eine deutsch-jüdische Geschichte der Bundesrepublik* (Munich: Deutsche Verlagsanstalt, 2007).

 1. Hannah Arendt and Karl Jaspers, *Briefwechsel 1926–1969*, edited by Lotte Köhler and Hans Sahner (Munich: Piper 1993), 77. Letter written on 30 May 1946.
 2. Gershom Scholem, *Briefe II: 1948–1970*, edited by Thomas Sparr (Munich: C.H. Beck, 1995), 14. Letter written on 6 November 1949.
 3. Tamara Anthony, *Ins Land der Väter oder der Täter? Israel und die Juden in Deutsch-land nach der Schoah* (Berlin: Metropol, 2004), see respectively 96, 94.
 4. The *Allgemeine Wochenzeitung der Juden in Deutschland* (later *Allgemeine Jüdische Wochenzeitung*) regularly commented on the German-Jewish bad conscience. For examples from the 1970s, see "Wir, die deutschen Juden" (11 December 1970), 1; "25 Jahre Allgemeine. Gedanken zum Selbstverständnis einer jüdischen Zeitung in der Bundesrepublik (14 May 1971)," 1; "Zahlen statt Politik" (11 June 1971); "Thema: Jüdische Jugend in Deutschland" (26 November 1971), 1; "Gemeinsam für die Zukunft" (29 September 1972), 1; "Stabilität jüdischen Lebens" (21 March 1973), 1–2; "Makkabi-Europa-Exekutive in Berlin: Anerkennung für jüdische Gemeinschaft in Berlin" (3 September 1976), 3.
 5. For this development see chapter 4 in Kauders, *Unmögliche Heimat*.
 6. Exodus 16:1–16:3, quoted from the Stone Tanach.
 7. Anthony, *Ins Land der Väter*, 154. See also Meron Mendel, "The Policy for the Past in West Germany and Israel: The Case of Jewish Remigration," in *Leo Baeck Institute Year Book* (2004), 129.
 8. Anthony, *Ins Land der Väter*, 170.
 9. Ibid., 102, footnote 173.
10. Norbert Wollheim, "Wir haben Stellung bezogen," in Richard Chaim Schneider, *Wir sind da! Die Geschichte der Juden in Deutschland von 1945 bis heute* (Munich: Ullstein, 2000), 119.

11. Yehuda Eloni, *Zionismus in Deutschland: Von den Anfängen bis 1914* (Gerlingen: Bleicher, 1987), 207.

12. Michael Berkowitz, *Zionist Culture and West European Jewry before the First World War* (Cambridge: Cambridge University Press, 1993), 116.

13. Derek J. Penslar, *Shylock's Children: Economics and Jewish Identity in Modern Europe* (Berkeley: University of California Press, 2001), 205–216 and Moshe Zimmermann, "Muscle Jews versus Nervous Jews," in *Emancipation through Muscles: Jews and Sports in Europe*, ed. Michael Brenner and Gideon Reuveni (Lincoln and London: University of Nebraska Press, 2006), 13.

14. Tobias Winstel, "Über die Bedeutung der Wiedergutmachung im Leben der jüdischen NS-Verfolgten: Erfahrungsgeschichtliche Annäherungen," in *Nach der Verfolgung: Wiedergutmachung nationalsozialistischen Unrechts in Deutschland?* ed. Hans Günter Hockerts and Christiane Kuller (Göttingen: Wallstein, 2003), 199–227; Tobias Winstel, "'Healed Biographies?' Jewish Remigration and Indemnification for National Socialist Injustice," *Leo Baeck Institute Year Book* (2004): 137–152; Harry Maor, *Über den Wiederaufbau der jüdischen Gemeinden in Deutschland seit 1945* (unpublished dissertation, Mainz, 1961), 48.

15. Sammy Speier, "Von der Pubertät zum Erwachsensein. Bericht einer Bewußtwerdung," in *Jüdisches Leben in Deutschland seit 1945*, ed. Micha Brumlik, Doron Kiesel, Cilly Kugelmann, and Julius H. Schoeps (Frankfurt a.M.: Jüdischer Verlag, 1988), 182 and Martina Kliner-Fruck, *"Es ging ja ums Überleben." Jüdische Frauen zwischen Nazideutschland, Emigration und ihrer Rückkehr* (Frankfurt a.M. and New York: Campus, 1995), 284.

16. Maor, *Über den Wiederaufbau*, 6; Benno Nietzel, "Die jüdische Presse und die Debatte um die Rückerstattung entzogenen Eigentums 1945–1952," in *Zwischen Erinnerung und Neubeginn: Zur deutsch-jüdischen Geschichte nach 1945*, ed. Susanne Schönborn (Munich: Martin Meidenbauer, 2006), 137.

17. Martin Münzel, *Die jüdischen Mitglieder der deutschen Wirtschaftselite 1927–1955: Verdrängung—Emigration—Rückkehr* (Paderborn: Ferdinand Schöningh, 2005), 286, 291, 293, 324, 327, 369, 293, 405.

18. Maor, *Über den Wiederaufbau*, 81–85.

19. ZA (Zentralacrhiv zur Erforschung der Juden in Deutschland, Heidelberg), B. 1/15., 459, Juden in Deutschland. Jahresbericht 1961, 40–41.

20. Michael N. Szentei-Heise, "Jüdische Gemeindearbeit in der Bundesrepublik: Das Beispiel Düsseldorf," *Judaica* 49, no. 1 (1993): 11.

21. Y. Michael Bodemann, *In den Wogen der Erinnerung: Jüdische Existenz in Deutschland* (Munich: *Deutscher Taschenbuch Verlag*, 2002), 128.

22. Y. Michael Bodemann, *A Jewish Family in Germany Today: An Intimate Portrait* (Durham, NC: Duke University Press, 2005), 8.

23. The interviews took place on 11 February 2007 in a large German city. The interviewees wished to remain anonymous.

24. "Die Jüdische Wohlfahrstpflege in Bayern seit dem Ende des Krieges," *Jüdische Sozialarbeit* 2, no. 2 (1957): 12, in ZA B. 1/10., 381.

25. Bodemann, *In den Wogen*, 127. See also Micha Brumlik, *Kein Weg als Deutscher und Jude: Eine bundesdeutsche Erfahrung* (Munich: Ullstein, 2000), 29 and Hans Jacob Ginsburg, "Sitzen wir nicht mehr 'auf gepackten Koffern'?" *Judaica* 49, no. 1 (1993): 5.

26. Hans-Reiner Müller-Raemisch, *Frankfurt a.M.: Stadtentwicklung und Planungsgeschichte seit 1945* (Frankfurt a.M.: Campus, 1996), 200–230, here 206. Less helpful: Frolinde Basler, "Frankfurt in der Nachkriegszeit bis 1989," in *Frankfurt a.M.: Die Geschichte der Stadt in neun Beiträgen*, ed. Frankfurter Historische Kommission (Sigmaringen: Jan Thorbecke, 1991), 521–578.

27. Jürgen Roth, *z.B. Frankfurt: Die Zerstörung einer Stadt* (Gütersloh: Bertelsmann, 1975), 29–30 and Janusz Bodek, *Die Fassbinder-Kontroversen: Entstehung und Wirkung eines literarischen Textes. Zu Kontinuität und Wandel einiger Erscheinungsformen des Alltagsanti-Semitismus in Deutschland nach 1945, seinen künsterischen Weihen und seiner öffentlichen Inszenierung* (Frankfurt a.M.: Peter Lang, 1991), 30–31; Institut für Stadtgeschichte Frankfurt (ISG), Nachlass Loy, S1/264, No. 44, Flyer of Häuserrrat Westendgruppe and No. 51, Flyer Häuserrat, Hauskollektiv Kettenhofweg 109 and AStA of Frankfurt University.

28. ISG, Nachlass Loy, S1/264, No. 47, Lecture by Otto Fresenius at Technical University Darmstadt, 19 October 1970, 4.

29. This is Irene Dische's argument in her unusual article "Die Reichen Juden in Deutschland," *Transatlantik* 6 (1981): 16. See also Juliane Wetzel, "Neue Gemeinden—alte Bilder: Von den Schwierigkeiten der Deutung jüdischer Nachkriegsgeschichte in Deutschland," in *Shylock? Zinsverbot und Geldverleih in jüdischer und christlicher Tradition*, ed. Johannes Heil and Bernd Wacker (Munich: Wilhelm Fink, 1997), 253–260.

30. ISG, V66/56, Flyer of 23 October 1973, "Prozeß gegen Rosen!"

31. See also Dan Diner, "Man hat mit der Sache eigentlich nichts mehr zu tun," in Schneider, *Wir sind da!* 240–241.

32. *Frankfurter Neue Presse*, "Ein großes Lob von Heinemann," 12 February 1973.

33. Heiner Schäfer, "Muß das Frankfurter Westend sterben? Bericht über die Aktionsgemeinschaft Westend in Frankfurt," *Bauwelt* 44 (1970): 1684. See also the remarks by B. to Alfred Biolek in ISG, V66/70, letter of 4 February 1992. B. speaks of the sophisticated (*differenziert*) stance of many citizens.

34. ISG, s1-257, Wilhelm K. to Federal Minister for Housing Lauritz Lauritzen, 14 October 1968.

35. ISG, Nachlass Loy, S1/264, No. 48, "Rettet unsere Stadt," Informationsbrief 1.2, "Juden im Westend."

36. ISG, S1-257, Wilhelm K. to Hans-Werner Hübner, 23 August 1970.

37. ISG, V6/70, B. to Probst Dieter Trautwein, 14 March 1979.

38. ISG, S1-344, No. 3, "Frankfurt—eine Metropole?" no date.

39. ISG, V66/80, B. to Reinhard, 24 October 1986.

40. See, for example, Bodek, *Fassbinder-Kontroversen*, 40 and Dische, "Die Reichen Juden," 20.

41. ISG, Nachlass Rudi Arndt, S1-163/91, letter of 25 February 1974.

42. ISG, Nachlass Rudi Arndt, S1-163/91, "Entwurf." Evidently anti-Semitism had been a problem within the protest movement, so much so that the Hausgemeinschaft Eppsteinerstrasse 47 decided to distance itself publicly from anti-Semitism: ISG, V66/85, "Entwurf," no date.

43. ISG, V66 Plakatsammlung, "Gesucht."

44. Gerhard Zwerenz, *Die Erde ist unbewohnbar wie der Mond* (Frankfurt a.M.: Fischer, 1973), 7, 9, 11, 18, 103, 202, 223.

45. Rainer Werner Fassbinder, *Der Müll, die Stadt und der Tod* (Frankfurt: Verlag der Autoren, 1984), 67, 69, 71–73, 84, 88, 93, 97.

46. Brumlik, *Kein Weg*, 117; Micha Brumlik, "Warum ich mit Ignatz Bubis solidarisch bin: Ein Bekenntnis" as well as Dan Diner, "Verheddert im Stacheldraht der Geschichte: Aus einem Gespräch über Normalität und antijüdische Ressentiments," both in *Deutsch-jüdische Normalität... Fassbinders Sprengsätze*, ed. Elisabeth Kiderlin (Frankfurt a.M.: Pflasterstrand, 1985), 61–65, 74–80; Hans Jakob Ginsburg, "Juden auf der Bühne: Eine Minderheit empört sich," in *Die Fassbinder-Kontroverse oder Das Ende der Schonzeit*, ed. Heiner Lichtenstein (Königstein/Ts.: Athenäum, 1986), 128.

47. Gehart Scheit, *Verborgener Staat, lebendiges Geld: Zur Dramaturgie des Antisemitismus* (Freiburg: Caira, 1999), 528.

48. Joachim Schlör, *Das Ich der Stadt: Debatten über Judentum und Urbanität, 1822–1938* (Göttingen: Vandenhoeck & Rupprecht, 2005), 221–222; Jeffrey Herf, *Reactionary Modernism: Technology, Culture, and Politics in Weimar and the Third Reich* (Cambridge: Cambridge University Press, 1984), 135–138, 151; Moishe Postone, "Nationalsozialismus und Antisemitismus: Ein theoretischer Versuch," in *Zivilisationsbruch: Denken nach Auschwitz*, ed. Dan Diner (Frankfurt a.M.: Fischer, 1988), 242–252; Lars Rensmann, *Demokratie und Judenbild: Antisemitismus in der politischen Kultur der Bundesrepublik Deutschland* (Wiesbaden: VS Verlag für Sozialwissenschaft, 2004), 107–108; Klaus Holz, *Nationaler Antisemitismus: Wissenssoziologie einer Weltanschauung* (Hamburg: Hamburger Edition, 2001), 219–220, 223.

49. See, for example, Peter Iden, "Das muß jetzt sichtbar werden für alle," in Lichtenstein, *Die Fassbinder-Kontroverse*, 100.

50. I analyze this development in the fifth chapter of *Unmögliche Heimat*.

51. Salomon Korn, *Die fragile Grundlage: Auf der Suche nach der deutsch-jüdischen "Normalität"* (Berlin and Vienna: Pendo, 2003), 35, 48–49. The phrase became part of the title of a museum catalogue: Georg Heuberger, ed., *Wer ein Haus baut, will bleiben. 50 Jahre Jüdische Gemeinde Frankfurt a.M.: Anfänge und Gegenwart* (Frankfurt a.M.: Societaets-Verlag, 1998).

II

JEWS IN THE MARKETPLACE

≈ᶠ **4** ᶠᷓ

ALL TALK OR BUSINESS AS USUAL?

Brokerage and Schmoozing in a Swiss Urban Society in the Early Nineteenth Century

Susanne Bennewitz

In nineteenth-century Germany and Switzerland, a small-scale trade agent was often called a "Schmuser." This term of Yiddish origin was used by everyone in daily conversation, thus qualifying brokerage as a typically Jewish occupation regardless of the actual ethnic background of the businessman. Although the banker, the merchant, and the trading middleman are very well-recognized figures and functions within Jewish history, and are clearly seen as Jewish domains in the economic field, brokerage as a distinct Jewish livelihood has not yet been the focus of Jewish historiography. Studies on Jewish brokerage in the early modern time and pre-emancipation era are preoccupied with the rare instances of official accreditation of Jewish agents, a form of registered brokerage.[1] In contrast, the documentation on small-scale trade agents and independent brokers is as scanty and incidental as on other non-regular livelihoods; hence the state of interpretation for Jewish or non-Jewish outside brokerage remains very sketchy. But only slightly more attention has been paid to the subject of registered brokerage at the end of the nineteenth century.[2]

This chapter presents a micro-historical case study on schmoozing and informal brokerage in the early nineteenth century in the Swiss town of Basel, where schmoozers were primarily Jews. Its aim is to explore the social and cultural significance of schmoozing as an economic activity. Most noteworthy is the fact that brokerage had been a ubiquitous and accepted service in manifold business relations well before any formalized definition of the profession. Only in historical perspective, due to their low-scale profit and intermediary position, have schmoozers remained in the shadows of entrepreneurs, their more prominent clients.

I will start my discussion by clarifying the economic position of the informal broker and characterizing the social and legal setting that led to this new phenomenon in nineteenth-century Swiss cities. Then I will move to explore, on a micro-historical level, different aspects of the schmoozer's work. This investigation will not only reveal the unique nature of informal brokerage as a distinct subtype of middleman activities but will also demonstrate how schmoozing impacted the interaction between non-Jews and Jews in a Swiss city.

Jews in the Swiss Market

Since it is representative of many marketplaces in Switzerland in the Revolution and Restoration periods, the city of Basel will serve as a case study.[3] Except for the short interval of the Helvetic Republic (1798–1803), urban and provincial territories were still protected by provincial policies. No unified Swiss citizenship existed, and political rights, such as residential and professional permits, were privileges of the municipal community members. In most of the Swiss provinces, Jews were not members of the municipalities and did not qualify as legal residents until the 1860s. It was still rare to find Jewish entrepreneurs and families in Swiss cities in the first half of the nineteenth century. The Jews accredited in Swiss cities were, with few exceptions, French burghers protected by international treaties, who had inherited their French citizenship over generations. Jewish immigration was a consequence of the emancipation of Jews in France (1791) and took place despite the lack of equal rights for Jews in Switzerland.

The Jewish community of Basel was one of the first Jewish resettlements in Switzerland in the modern era. With the French occupation and the erection of the Helvetic Republic, Switzerland became a near de facto satellite of Napoleonic France. In this overall context, the Alsatian-Jewish elite moved to urban communities in Switzerland following emancipation and the extension of freedom of residency, as did the merchants and bankers from Alsatian villages close to Basel. These Jewish entrepreneurs had already been partners in the Swiss market despite certain restrictions and exclusions. During the Revolutionary and Napoleonic wars, they were especially needed for the horse trade and troop supply, and they took part in the textile trade, the most important commercial business between France and Switzerland. By far the largest numbers of Jewish youth and elders in the rural settlements worked as small-scale traders, as second-hand dealers, as peddlers, as servants, or in community-related professions.

Within the group of Jewish immigrants in Basel, we also find a diverse range of livelihoods. Only tailoring, shoemaking, and other craftsmanship had been forbidden to Jews and other foreigners following the short Revolutionary era. Most of the Jews who managed to stay in the town during the discriminatory, anti-Jewish rule of the Restoration period belonged to the upper class of entrepreneurs, traders in luxury items, and international merchant bankers. They fostered close business relations with the few merchant and banker families of the patrician class, who handled large sums of capital even by Swiss standards. Yet the capital base in Basel was much too large to be absorbed by the local or Swiss economy. The municipality of Basel took a very protective position in favor of the craft guilds, prohibiting industrial innovation. This caused an even greater flow of capital into foreign investment options, especially the evolving French and Alsatian industry.

Considering the Jewish participants in the urban market, we are concerned here with more than just the residential families and their unmarried employees, who never totaled more than two hundred individuals between the years 1800 and 1850. Instead, I am speaking of a larger regional population group. Even very successful French Jewish businessmen with offices and depots in the town could not obtain residential permits to live within the fortified city. But they checked in at the town gates daily. The attraction of the city for less-defined purposes and as a center of a makeshift economy had even increased since the French Revolution, because the heavy head tax on Jews entering the city had been lifted by 1797. Thus, the majority of Jewish partners in the Basel market and banking centers around 1826 were daily commuters, on foot or by carriage, and not inhabitants of the city.[4] Alsatian villagers—Jews and Christians alike—visited the town daily, crossing the borders of countries and, even more complicated, the city walls. They brought fruit and vegetables, cattle and horses, leather and hides, watches and handkerchiefs, bales of cotton, linen, and wool. They came to visit the markets and taverns or to offer their services.

Variations of the Social Profile of the Middleman

In one form or another most of the Jewish participants in the Basel market and banking centers might be called middlemen. Yet it is misleading to view this group as a model of a middleman minority or to apply other patterns of outsider minorities to this population. The Jews from Alsace were no strangers to the region, nor did all the Jewish entrepreneurs and middlemen form a closely-knit network based on kinship, common interest, or solidarity, as theories of middlemen minority groups have contended.[5]

Rather, although Jewish and Christian families were clearly distinguished by religious and ethnic attachment, which also holds true for the different Christian denominations, they lived in close social and physical contact with each other. From an economic perspective, production, trade, and consumption had necessitated interaction between members of both groups for many years. Jews had settled on the French side of the border for more than a century, and in some of the Alsatian villages close to Basel they formed 30 to 50 percent of the population, hardly a minority in a demographic sense. By 1815, one could no longer distinguish Jewish socio-dialects in day-to-day conversations on the street, in the taverns, or at the market. It is also a false assumption that a Jewish middleman from an upper-Alsatian village was more eloquent in French than was a Swiss merchant. Although these Jewish middlemen crossed national borders as part of their daily business, most of them were not international or long-distance travelers and traders. Furthermore, in contrast to the characteristics of a "middleman minority," they did not share in economic success and wealth.

The middleman minority theory is even more inappropriate for our current focus on informal brokerage, because in this particular case we are investigating only the subtype, a middleman who was not a trader between the producer and the retailer but a go-between, an intermediary, or a broker. The merchant middlemen and the go-between middlemen formed different interest groups and different social spheres within an extended ethnic group. The religious and cultural ties between those interest groups were always present, but the groups did not generally share common ground in their economic networks and alliances.

From Mendicant to Regular Services: Linguistic Notes

I do not intend to depict brokerage as a new invention of the emancipation era. I think it is more appropriate to characterize the development of independent brokerage out of the even older but more informal practices of trading, and to characterize the new recognition of the independent Jewish broker as a process of professionalizing. It was a new service in trade that encountered the typical allegations and difficulties of a new profession or a new group of service providers, but at the same time, it seems to have been an already common practice. The changes can be perceived as a transformation from optional and ritual relations to mandatory and binding relations or services. Looking at the social form and place as well as at the ritual forms of market interactions makes it obvious: the independent broker took part in a deal where the beggar and witness used to be part of the ritual. The beggar, or the individual who lived on voluntary donations and charity, used to witness a deal, to bless the fortune of the business partners. In return, he received a tiny lump sum, which made the bargain officially valid. The use and change in terminology between 1798 and 1850 is telling. Several denotations for a broker's commission that were in use in Basel in the early nineteenth century refer to ceremonial or ritual donations as part of a business deal.[6] In fact, the struggle for recognition took place partly in the realm of occupational titles, as it can be traced even in authoritative documentation like the courts' files.

According to the different social and economic fields, and according to the legal empowerment of brokerage, the agents were addressed differently. The usage of the general German terms *Makler* or *Unterhändler* is rarely found in formal or informal speech. By far the most honorable reference was made with the Italian term *Sensal*. The state-official agents were addressed as *Sensalen*, no matter what their economic specialization was. The term referred to a respectable service and a remarkable turnover and it can hardly be found in the case of Jewish brokerage.[7] Most of the time brokers were addressed as *Courtier*, and this was used for licensed brokers and outside brokers alike. The connotation was very broad, ranging across all kinds of market branches, types of formalization, and fields of business. Even the Jewish marriage broker was called *Courtier* in the city court, coming close to the primary meaning of *Courtier* in French. In contrast to *Courtier*, the term *Schmauser* or *Schmuser* pointed toward low-income service and Jewish service providers. This term was never used to refer to inside brokers, but to informal brokerage and short-range interaction.

The epithet "Jew" was also used for someone offering middlemen services, so that *Handelsjud*, *Pferdjud*, or simply *Jud* became a descriptor for brokers or at least occasional brokers, in contrast to the Jewish *Handelsmann* in the same sources.[8] While the reimbursement for a *Sensal* or *Courtier*'s service was clearly remuneration for work, called *Courtagelohn* or simply *Courtage*, the payment for schmoozers' and less formalized services was called *Gottespfennig*, *Schmausgeld*, or *Trinkgeld* by the clients. All those later terms refer to the concept of alms and of voluntary donations.

The Jewish brokers themselves tried to implement a different terminology for their service fees; they asked for *Lohn* or *Courtage*. The reports on court decisions testify that brokers and business partners argued not only about the amount of the reimbursement, but also about the label. The demand for *Lohn* on the part of unregistered brokers was clearly part of their professionalization. Their role in the trading business had once been a mendicant service; now they asked for recognition of their work. By the middle of the nineteenth century, the Jewish broker in town had clearly achieved the honorable status of the *Courtier*, leaving the term schmoozer for a pejorative usage and for the intermediaries on the cattle market.

Private Brokerage

More practically, the go-between middleman was an agent who was not involved legally in the business transaction itself. He was not the owner of the object or commodities for sale, he had no legal title to finalize the purchase, and he had no responsibility for the actual transaction and payment. Legally, he was an independent third party in a deal, a witness rather than an assessor. Even if he commented on the quality of goods as part of his intermediary services, he could not be held legally responsible for the quality of goods. In contrast to a salesman or hired agent, the broker held no binding mandate from the seller or the buyer. Instead of a salary or commission paid by one party, he received his payment in equal share from both parties. These legal characteristics can be confirmed by the general picture gleaned from legal proceedings concerning outside brokerage in the city of Basel in the early nineteenth century.

The historiography on brokerage has been shaped by the contrast and rivalry between state-licensed and unregulated brokerage. Normative sources naturally draw a distinct line between accredited livelihood on one side and informal livelihood on the other, most of the time discrediting or even banning unregulated work and business. This has also become the starting point for addressing private brokerage. In the historical picture of nineteenth-century Germany and Switzerland, private brokerage developed slowly from an illegal livelihood to a livelihood that, by the end of the century, had been legally instituted.[9] The lack of regulations and professional corporations for independent brokers has led to the assumption that private brokerage was illicit. Although this was true for some territories and cities, it was not true in general and was not the case in Basel.

To avoid the normative narrative and the typology of regulated versus unregulated business, I will focus instead on occupation and interaction rather than on existing or non-existing professional regulations in a narrow sense. If we describe schmoozing and brokerage as a form of social interaction and culturally embedded communication, then we find this occupation in a variety of economic and non-economic fields by the beginning of the nineteenth century. For example, marriage arrangements were organized by middlemen, a traditional service that was rewarded by both parties according to the amount of the dowry.[10] The same terms were applied to the brokerage at the weekly livestock market, where Jewish brokers triggered deals and provided expertise. If two parties finally agreed on a deal, they paid the broker or a number of intermediaries a flat rate per head of cattle. We find Jewish brokers in the wholesale business, arranging deals on iron, wool, porcelain, fabrics, or transportation. We find them even as intermediaries in the retail business in town, or we find them carrying around sugar and glue, almost like errand boys. All these intermediaries and negotiators were called *Schmausers,* and they were used to being paid equally by both the vendor and the buyer.

A more rigid set of obligations and legal responsibilities was placed on inside brokers, who were nominated and licensed by the local government itself. These official brokers held a highly acclaimed and profitable office comparable to that of notaries. The few positions for official brokers in Basel were available only to members of the patrician elite. As part of their sovereignty, they ensured and controlled the local market in goods, real estate, bonds, and assignments, both on individual demand and on a regular basis in public places like the merchant house. Reference to Jewish brokerage in Switzerland in the early nineteenth century is strictly confined to private brokerage. Jewish inside brokers, officially accredited for the stock exchange and the commodity market in the pre-emancipation era, are mentioned only for certain trading places in Europe, such as Amsterdam, Frankfurt, and London.

For the private broker the charges for transactions in the different sectors were more or less fixed. Thus, a horse sold on the market brought a return of two to four *Neue Thaler* for the broker. Real estate agents were paid according to the value of the contract. Between the years 1803 and 1812, an average commission for the broker was a reimbursement of half a percent of the contract. The reimbursement for informal brokerage in the trade in bills and obligations, in debts and credits, is not so easy to determine from the documented incidents, but clearly existed as part of the daily banking business in Basel. Jewish middlemen informed local investors and bankers on immovable goods in Alsace, on the liquidation of bills, on cases of inheritance or bankruptcy in the region. Closely related to the activity in the real estate market, the broker knew what property, what plot of land, vineyard, or house was about to be sold, and he knew on the other hand who was in need of an investment or of accommodation.

All of these intermediary services are described in the local court files for the period between 1800 and 1825. Private brokers, sometimes alongside licensed brokers, provided these services and reflected what appears to have been a Jewish sector. In most of the hearings, the service of a private broker was only incidentally mentioned, but in some cases the service itself was at the heart of the trial, for example when the broker himself had to appeal to the courts in order to be reimbursed. Since the turnaround for schmoozing on the cattle market was not a notable sum, most of the claims were documented only on the lowest level of jurisdiction by the town magistrate. Only brokerage in bills and credits, real estate, and the wholesale business was profitable enough to meet the prerequisites for a civil suit tried before the regular city court. Overall, the judges approved the service of private brokers in a variety of settings. Only marriage brokering was not accepted as a matter of civil obligations and jurisdiction. In this case, the middleman services were deemed religious matters, and the petitioners were advised to appeal to a Jewish board.[11] Everything else seemed to be in the realm of custom and customary law. The cases reported before the courts tell us about the difficulties and problems of an evolving business, but we must keep in mind that they show a certain degree of informal and formal acceptance of private brokerage from the start of Jewish business in Switzerland.

The schmoozer brought the wholesalers and the retailers together, as well as connecting the consumer with a singular opportunity for a strong horse or a spacious apartment. Some negotiators lived in town: one resident specialized in the horse trade, one family in real estate, and the tavern keeper offered at least services in bills and transport. Other schmoozers came from out of town. The available evidence suggests that independent brokers in Basel were Jewish, but they were interconnected with Jewish partners or Christian business partners or members of both ethno-religious groups.

The work of the private broker consisted in walking and talking. He went back and forth between two parties, between the shop and the tavern, between the property in the countryside and the banker in the city. He acquired information on the goods and objects, details and figures; he mediated for clients who wanted to remain anonymous as long as possible; he haggled about the value and the price. Sometimes he brought in several clients, to pit one against the other and hasten the procedures of bargaining and negotiating.

Overall, what was typical in these services was the independence of the agent, who acted according to his own input and targets. The broker not only mediated between two or more parties; he actually brought them together on a contract or deal, either by introducing them in person or by distributing the relevant information to them. This initiative on the part of the private broker was a notably new experience for clients, who complained before the courts that they never wanted to become clients and that it was only incidentally that they garnered useful information from the schmoozer, which finally led to a contract. This fact points to new features of private brokerage: it affected more fields of economic exchange as well as new groups of consumers or traders. Further, an absolute increase or even evolution of informal brokerage in town at the turn of the nineteenth century is also plausible. As previously mentioned, the head tax on Jews had been lifted so that a visit to town on a market day was less of a financial risk than before. More Jews from the countryside could put their best foot forward and explore the urban market. Yet at the same time, peddling—a traditional livelihood of many Alsatian Jews—increasingly became a matter of concern and regulation for Swiss authorities. In the year 1797 and again in 1803 it was essentially banned throughout the province of Basel, except in cases of certain types of goods that needed to be imported. For Jews, schmoozing became an alternative to actual peddling, thus lowering the capital investment and the business risk and offering occasional and marginal income in return. It was a relatively accessible occupation because it did not interfere with the state policies on the import and export of goods or with the authorities of guilds for professions and products. The occupations of peddlers and brokers may seem very closely related in terms of their economic function, but in looking at legal and social conditions, we find that they were quite distinct alternatives. It is necessary to carefully differentiate between peddling and brokerage in the social-historical analysis of Jewish lower-class options in the emancipation era. Although both forms of trade services could also work on commission, as a rule the peddler needed more start-up capital than the negotiator. Documentation exists on one case where the switch from itinerant trade to brokerage shows a clear biographical change: after years of selling on credit and accumulating a shortfall in itinerant trade, the individual started all over again as a broker in real estate.[12]

A Jewish Prerequisite, or a Jewish Profession?

As we have seen, many of the sources on the early history of schmoozing come to us from legal documents. This naturally raises the question: What were the objections to private brokerage in the early stage of the business? As I have mentioned, the proactive character of the intermediary service caused surprise and opposition. We must realize that brokers could ask for remuneration as soon as they could prove that a deal or contract was based partly on their communication. A clear agreement on a broker's fee during the negotiation process was not mandatory.[13] Some customers claimed to have been involved involuntarily; others felt they had been harassed by the middleman. Fears of market deregulation were expressed; some patrons mentioned that the service of the broker seemed an unnecessary addition to the economy. These concerns from supposedly initial interactions with brokerage mirrored the complaints made by competitors and professionals in trading: neither all of the *Sensalen* nor the merchants and entrepreneurs agreed with the consolidation and legal approval of private brokerage.[14]

A trial in 1803 in which the wealthiest man in town, Christoph Merian, was found guilty and ordered to pay a regular commission to a Jewish real estate broker, was particularly significant. It proved in effect to be a litmus test of upper-class business habits. Members of the patrician class frequently made use of Jewish information services, though they hesitated to admit to this cooperation in public. It appears that for the patrician Merian the commission fee was more offensive than the official statement of a business relation with a *Schmauser*, meaning that a Jew could actually plead in court for a regular remuneration instead of a "granted" handout.[15] The fact that business cooperation and mutual financial interests between Jewish and Christian merchants existed was not hidden, however, and these interests were well known to the public in Basel.

Various reproaches against private brokerage came close to the arguments we know already from the discourse about trade and banking, namely that it was a useless addition to the necessities of production and consumption. Brokerage did not match the criteria of productive labor and its righteous reward that had been shaped by the Christian work ethic. Yet in contrast to the intervention of the trader, pawnbroker, or creditor, the function of the intermediary was even more intangible and indiscernible. The broker was not even in possession of goods or financial means: the sole goods he had to offer were information, knowledge, negotiating skills, and social contacts.

Indeed, the question of work and service became a recurring topic in the litigations. While the broker spent his time and effort building up a social network, investigating markets, traveling frequently, and negotiating products and prices, the customer appraised the service not as the fruit of work, but as a side effect of "natural" Jewish habits: arguing, haggling, curiosity, mobility. Even in the case where a middleman had gone back and forth repeatedly between distant parties, his behavior was appraised as part of his itinerant lifestyle, not as an intentional effort and investment. But the criteria for the provision of a service and the basis for a service charge by jurisdiction were quite adequate. Rather than asking for the chargeable time for work or for the additional errands for a single transaction, the judges were interested in the effect of the mediation for the client. If communication or information by the broker provided ascertainable input to the deal, the benefit and therefore righteousness of the service was given.[16] We may observe here the recognition of a new kind of service industry, fostered by the legal authorities in town.

Yet, needless to say, legal backing for an ethnic niche in terms of livelihood was not a sign of overall social acceptance. On the contrary, brokerage shaped the image of the ethnic group instead of evolving as a specialized profession among Jews. Brokerage as a legally recognized service may have even endangered the informal relationships between ethnic groups. It had an impact on direct contact and face-to-face communication: for example, one individual who casually conversed with a middleman claimed he feared that he could not distinguish anymore between talking and trading, between personal and business relations. The implicit allegation was that one was never sure with whom one interacted while chatting with a Jew, never knew whether he was a neighbor or whether he was a middleman. Thus, human interaction at its most basic—direct communication—seemed to be permeated by business relations. And indeed, the essential approach and skill of the middleman was that he did not distinguish between business and informal talk, between important and less important hints, between useful and useless information. The secrets of the middleman's job partly lay in this fuzzy logic of decision-making, in the openness to unseen opportunities and unexpected alliances.[17] Even while rejecting the underlying assumption that other social relations were more clearly associated with either an economic or a personal need, the specific interaction of brokers was seen clearly to blur conventions in communication. A number of libel suits dealt with confrontations built on this stereotype of a Jew: not the powerful oppressor, but the pure businessperson, a character that turns everything—even nothing—into an object of economic meaning. On one occasion, such a confrontation took place in the street leading out of the town toward France. At the end of one day, young servants in front of the tavern picked a fight with a Jew, mocking a villager who was heading home and had no burden or bag, asking him what he had in mind to sell, and whether he wanted to sell his walking stick.[18]

Insider Information as Advantage in Jewish Society

So far my remarks have concerned the cultural effects of a specialized economic practice that was associated with a minority, though it more precisely concerned a sub-entity of this ethnic minority. I will conclude with a further contextualization of the informal brokerage, this time concerning inner Jewish networks and their effect on the Jewish economy. It is most probable that the go-between, the low-income private broker, was a typical Jewish profession in the early emancipation era. It has generally been underestimated for several reasons. Principally, in some territories, it was a hidden business because of its illicitness; in other territories it was an informal and ritualized service, but one with such a small turnaround that it hardly gained the attention of the authorities. The low-scale livelihood had a low prevalence in court, and it became a registered business only decades after the liberalization of the market.

On the other hand, the essential feature of brokerage—the flow of information—has been the focus for explaining a Jewish advantage or predestination in the evolving liberal market. Cultural conditions and religious structures help to explain a closer network and a more intensive communication and information exchange in the Jewish diaspora.[19] The strong bonds on the grounds of kinship, religion, Jewish law, and economy provided close contact inside Jewish society and facilitated the bridging of space and borders. But while this explanation is derived from the flow of information from an overall ethnic unity (the circuit of closeness) and from the solidarity in networks, I would prefer an explanation that gives credit to a special effort in communication and transfer of knowledge. The actual profession or makeshift livelihood of go-betweens seems to be the missing link. It sets the effort and skills of a specialized group as the source of information exchange. It would probably be useful in future research to distinguish more clearly between merchants and their informers, who could make a living out of their service but never gained the remarkable profit and attention which high-risk investors made. Putting the private brokers into perspective as an explanation of the Jewish economic "success story" in the early-modern and liberal era gives the secret an ordinary face, the daily work of a lower-class group.

As I noted above, Jewish negotiators worked for Jewish and for Christian partners alike. Jewish brokerage was not at all confined to kinship or the benefit of kinship. But it is probable that this typically Jewish activity, overall, more often served Jewish than Christian investors. The greater number of inner Jewish broker-merchant contacts was not reflected in the court records, because conflicts inside the Jewish community could still draw on other procedures and mechanisms to be settled, while Jewish-Christian conflicts were almost always brought before the state authorities.

For instance, the following conflict between an agent and a financial merchant within the Jewish community, both residents in Basel, came to court only because a series of informal arrangements did not reach a settlement. The disagreement started when the agent, Simon Wolf, informed Samuel Wahl, a financial speculator, about the possibility of buying Alsatian obligations out of the liquidation of an inheritance in Basel. Instead of paying the commissioner, the investor Wahl allegedly forced him to take a risk in the deal as an investment partner, which meant that the agent Wolf, who had no funds, signed up for the stocks and simultaneously signed a certificate of debt to his partner for half of the purchasing price. Shortly after, the investor Wahl began to press and then to prosecute the debtors of the original obligations, thus beating down the market value of the titles. Most of the Alsatian debtors were insolvent, so the obligations were expropriated by court order and Wahl himself became the unchallenged bidder for the real estate itself. The revenue from the compulsory action was far from meeting the former asset value of the stocks, of which the agent Wolf still owed 50 percent to Wahl, his former partner and now the sole holder of the properties. The young agent decided to take revenge and ceded his certificate of debt to a well-known Jewish beggar along with a lump sum. Although the problem was not legally solved by the unconventional move of the agent, he had the laughter of the Jewish community on his side.[20] This example gives us an idea of the additional set of social regulations and power games surrounding brokerage in the Jewish institutions that settled frequent conflicts.

There was no strong backing for the interests of the informal broker either in Jewish-Christian business contacts or in inner Jewish networks before the nineteenth century. Yet the broker's conventional presence and economic function may be even more neglected by historiography. At least the legal and social recognition of this Jewish livelihood in a Swiss town prior to the emancipation in 1866 is surprising and calls for comparative study.

NOTES

1. Jews admitted as official brokers, mainly for trading in the stock exchange, are already reported for the seventeenth and eighteenth century, for example in Lon-

don, Amsterdam, and Frankfurt. This is not the case for Switzerland or the city of Basel; therefore I refer in this chapter only to outside brokerage by Jews. For approaches to Jewish brokerage that focus on the official profession, I refer to the recent study on Frankfurt by Gabriele Schlick, "Eine jüdische Elite in Frankfurt am Main im Spannungsfeld von ständischer und bürgerlicher Gesellschaft: Das Beispiel des Wechselmaklers Süskind Isaak Hirschhorn," in: Anja Victorine, ed., *Eliten um 1800: Erfahrungshorizonte, Verhaltensweisen, Handlungsmöglichkeiten* (Mainz: Philipp von Zabern, 2000), 19–34; Gabriele Schlick, "Jüdische Wechselmakler am Börsenplatz Frankfurt am Main und die Wirtschaftspolitik des reichsstädtischen Rates," in *Hoffuden—Ökonomie und Interkulturalität: Die jüdische Wirtschaftselite im 18. Jahrhundert*, ed. Rotraud Ries and J. Friedrich Battenberg (Hamburg: Institut für die Geschichte der deutschen Juden, 2002), 102–114.

2. The phenomenon of Jewish brokerage in German-speaking countries is mostly discussed in the realm of the rural Jewish economy and in the context of Jewish participation in the cattle market. See for example Monika Richarz, "Die soziale Stellung der jüdischen Händler auf dem Lande am Beispiel Südwestdeutschlands," in *Jüdische Unternehmer in Deutschland im 19. und 20. Jahrhundert*, ed. Werner E. Mosse and Hans Pohl (Stuttgart: Steiner, 1992), 271–283; Monika Richarz, "Emancipation and Continuity: German Jews in the Rural Economy," in *Revolution and Evolution 1848 in German-Jewish History*, ed. Werner E. Mossse and Arnold Paucker (Tübingen: Mohr, 1981), 95–115; Ulrich Baumann, *Zerstörte Nachbarschaften: Christen und Juden in badischen Landgemeinden 1862–1940* (Hamburg: Dölling und Galitz, 2000); Uri Kaufmann, *Jüdische und christliche Viehhändler in der Schweiz 1780–1930* (Zürich: Chronos, 1988); Karl Heinz Burmeister, *Der jüdische Pferdehandel in Hohenems und Sulz im 17. und 18. Jahrhundert* (Wiesbaden: Reichert, 1989). A different context of discussion provides the specific function of brokers in international and long-distance trade: see Niall Ferguson, *The House of Rothschild: Money's Prophets 1708–1848* (London: Viking, 1998), esp. chap. 10; Margit Schulte Beerbühl and Jörg Vögele, eds., *Spinning the Commercial Web* (Frankfurt: Peter Lang, 2004), chap. 2. Yet this socioeconomic figuration of an agent differs in part from the one I am presenting here, because most of those agents in the international market were hired and not independent agents, if not inside brokers.

3. For an in-depth investigation on the Jewish community in Basel, see Susanne Bennewitz, *Basler Juden—französische Bürger: Migration und Alltag einer jüdischen Gemeinde im frühen 19. Jahrhundert* (Basel: Schwabe, 2008).

4. Adressbuch der Stadt Basel, Basel 1826, Appendix, list of "täglich hiesige Stadt besuchende Handelsjuden."

5. The limits of middleman minority theory have been discussed before. The assumption of unity, exclusivity, and homogeneity in particular has been called into question: see Walter Zenner, *Minorities in the Middle: A Cross-cultural Analysis* (Albany: State University of New York Press, 1991). On the other hand, a recent contribution to the field by Yuri Slezkine draws heavily on the assumption of cohesive forces in a tribe of strangers even for the modern period: see *The Jewish Century* (Princeton: Princeton University Press, 2004), chaps. 1 and 3.

6. The English term *broker* derives from the Spanish *al boroque*, which is a ceremonial gift to finalize a business deal; this in turn refers to the Arabic *al barka* (variant of *al*

baraka), the blessing. *The American Heritage Dictionary of the English Language*, 4th ed. (New York: Bartleby, 2001).

7. The term *Judensensal* is found though in a tax register on residents from 1806. In this context the taxable profit of a *Sensal* was probably the motivation for the clergy to choose the term. Staatsarchiv Basel-Stadt, Steuerakten M 1, Handels-, Gewerbs- und Capitalistenabgabe 1803–1840.

8. The professional titles for Jews in address books and branch registers from Basel are modeled along a fine distinction between a Jewish *Handelsmann* and a pejorative *Handelsjud*. The *Handelsjud* individual was active in the same branch as his *Handelsmann* colleague and held the same license for trade, but he had a different social status. Business success, style and habit in commerce, and the difference between a merchant and a broker determined professional title.

9. Mario Axmann, *Maklerrecht und Maklerwesen bis 1900: Eine rechtshistorische Untersuchung insbesondere der bürgerlich-rechtlichen Quellen* (Stuttgart: Boorberg, 2004).

10. The terms for the Jewish middleman for marriages, as they appear in the court files of Basel, were *Schmauser* and *Courtier*, a term of French origin.

11. The Jewish community in Basel was not officially recognized until the 1860s and did not belong to either the Swiss rabbinate in canton Aargau or the French rabbinate. In practice, the rabbi in Hegenheim in Alsace ministered in Basel, and people settled their claims before this or other Alsatian rabbinates. To my knowledge, we lack any records for rabbinical jurisdiction over the upper-Rhine district in the early period of the French consistory, and I have no idea whether Jewish business matters were sometimes settled with the mediation of a rabbi or a rabbinical court. There is evidence that Jews from Basel approached Alsatian rabbis in matters of marriage law and the right of succession. The rabbinical ruling was not binding or officially enforced, so that an agreement before the rabbi had to be reassessed in the public courts if one party disobeyed it. None of the litigations between two Jewish parties in business matters that were brought to the Basel civil court refer to a previous meeting with a rabbi or Jewish court.

12. Account book of Nathan Lauf from Hegenheim, ca. 1838–1881, private collection, Basel.

13. Private brokers sometimes even had their payment approved by officials, even though the deal had not been finalized. In other cases, the broker's claim for a fee was turned down because the business partners had not agreed on a brokerage fee while fixing the price of the goods.

14. For other residential merchants the benefit of the Jewish trade service was appealing: for example, Basel merchants helped inside brokers with petitions and testimonies or provided them with office space in their own business.

15. Staatsarchiv Basel-Stadt, Gerichtsarchiv A 227, Wolf Felix Levy von Hagenthal contra Christoff Merian, March–May 1803.

16. Effort put in without any business deal being realized had also been given a chance for reward in court decisions.

17. It is noteworthy that reports about deals mediated by a broker do not mention the assets of acquaintance, trust, and honor. On the contrary, the broker acted deliberately against the binding forces of networks and established relations.

18. Staatsarchiv Basel-Stadt, Gerichtsarchiv DD (Korrektionelles Gericht) 11, 14. Sept. 1836, Schlägerei in der Spahlen.

19. Natalie Zemon Davis, "Religion and Capitalism Once Again? Jewish Merchant Culture in the Seventeenth Century," *Representations* 59 (1997): 56–84.

20. Staatsarchiv Basel-Stadt, Gerichtsarchiv A 236, Samuel Wahl contra Simon Wolf, 13 February 1821; 27 February 1821; 17 April 1821. Samuel Wahl contested the last move of the agent Wolf before the civil court and the court had to decide whether the agent was out of the game and the financial speculator left with a beggar. Because of bribery of a witness for the prosecution, Wahl disqualified himself in this case and was turned down by the civil court.

≈ 5 ≈

SOCIALISTS, BANKERS, AND SEPHARDIC JEWS

The Pereire Brothers and the Crédit Mobilier

Helen M. Davies

Within the multifaceted and contested historiography on the Jews in nine-teenth-century France, the bankers and financiers Emile Pereire (1800–1875) and his brother Isaac (1806–1880) are significant figures in the discourse. They were first-generation post-emancipation Jews, Jewish Saint-Simonians, early "socialists," leading personalities among the Second Empire *grande bourgeoisie*, prime examples of assimilation, and targets of anti-Semitism.[1] This chapter looks at the Pereires as children of Bordeaux, an eighteenth-century port city and mer-cantile powerhouse, and of the community of Sephardic Jews, regarded by some as the first such community to "encounter the requirements of an emerging nation-state" and to be granted full and equal citizenship in return for the con-tribution they made to it.[2] First, I will deal with the Pereires in the context of the Sephardic community of southwestern France with its tradition of self-reliance, financial utility to, and integration within, the Bordeaux economy. Secondly, I will examine the philosophy that nurtured them when they moved to Paris, i.e., Saint-Simonianism—a philosophy that changed but also reinforced their ideas and formed a base from which they launched their business activities.

From Traders to Citizens

The Pereires' history is woven into the Sephardic fabric of Bordeaux. This city, comparatively close to the Spanish border and accessible by sea, was one of the first refuges of the Sephardic merchants and their families who were expelled from Spain in 1492 by Ferdinand and Isabella in their quest for Catholic supremacy, or who fled the Inquisition and auto da fé in Portugal after 1497. The first formal acknowledgement of their right to live and work in Bordeaux was through Letters Patent issued by Henry II in 1550, in which they were addressed as "nouveaulx [sic] Chrétiens" and not as Jews, for their entry to France had depended on their assumed status as *conversos*, converted Catholics.[3] Their utility to the monarch was thus as merchants whose networks spread as far as the Levant, and whose "great zeal and affection" for the king and capacity to increase trade in local commodities had been amply demonstrated. Over the next two centuries, however, in successive Letters Patent the term "Nouveau Chrétien" ceased to be used as a serious denomination of the Sephardim in favor of that of "Juif Portugais."[4]

During this period, the situation of the Sephardim in the southwest of France was dictated by a combination of circumstances. These included their financial acumen, their financial resources built up judiciously over a century or more, their commercial networks throughout the Sephardic diaspora, their utility to the Bordeaux economy in providing financial and banking services, and their sound community structure, all of which in turn had contributed to the maintenance of their legal status. Not that this had been a smooth progression, for the monarch had from time to time wished to rid the kingdom of these newcomers, and the merchants of Bordeaux had occasionally harbored similar ambitions, protective of their own commercial interests.[5] But the Bordeaux parliament, recognizing the difficulties that the loss of the Sephardim would present for the city, frequently used its influence to maintain the Jewish presence there. For example, in the first years of the eighteenth century when, at various times, there were shortages of grain, the Jews were able to loan the city a total of 230,000 livres to purchase wheat.[6]

A measure of the Jews' confidence and successful integration within the economic and political structures of Bordeaux can be seen in the evolving organization of their own community. Writing at the beginning of the nineteenth century, the Jewish historian and lawyer Francia de Beaufleury described how for the first time in 1699 the Sephardim instituted Tzedaka, a voluntary tax to support their poorest members, to which forty families contributed.[7] Out of this emerged the Mahamad, the council of the Sephardic *nation* in Bordeaux, which rapidly took over all the *nation*'s affairs.[8] These included the management of religious life, maintaining the synagogues and cemeteries, the funding and eventually the supervision of the Talmud Torah, supervising food- and wine-making, providing welfare for the needy, paying imposts levied by the king, raising taxes to pay for the expenses of the *nation*, and maintaining a watchful eye over the privileges contained in the Letters Patent.[9] In 1760, the Sephardim were granted the status of a corporation, charged with regulating their own religious and commercial affairs, and directed by an oligarchy that stipulated the personal qualities and financial stability of its leaders.[10] The oligarchy governed virtually every aspect of the lives of its people efficiently and well. The Pereires' paternal ancestors, the Rodrigues Pereire family, who had arrived from Spain in 1741, thus found themselves in a Catholic city that welcomed their contribution to its economic vitality and well-being and, in turn, had begun to tolerate Jewish religious observance.

The Letters Patent of 1776, signed by Louis XVI, are significant on two counts. First, it was the Pereires' grandfather, Jacob Rodrigues Pereire, who negotiated them as the official representative of the Jews of the southwest of France at the courts of Louis XV and Louis XVI, and second, they were written in terms that advanced the situation of the Jews considerably compared with those promulgated earlier.[11] The Jews were accorded liberty to buy and sell property and to live anywhere in France, liberties granted equally to those residing in the kingdom and to those who might wish to do so, on the same terms as other subjects born in France.[12] Thus, even before the French Revolution and the decree of the National Assembly in January 1790 granting emancipation to the Sephardic Jews of southwestern France and equality with other citizens of France, they had already been granted considerable liberties within the kingdom in recognition of their commercial and financial skills, their utility, and the degree to which they had integrated effectively into the Bordeaux merchant community.[13] During the French Revolution in 1789, when the question of their admissibility as citizens was first posed before the new National Assembly, the Sephardim were able to argue confidently that they had as much right to citizenship as anybody else.[14]

Networks, Global and Local

The Revolution—which brought formal recognition of the Sephardic Jews' equal status—also brought disaster to the city of Bordeaux, ending its economic supremacy. Ongoing uncertainty about the slave trade, on which much of Bordeaux's commercial interests depended, and the unrest and rebellion of the slaves in Sainte-Domingue, led ultimately to Sainte-Domingue's secession from France and the formation in 1804 of the free and independent republic of Haiti. The adverse consequences for the city from the resulting loss of sugar and tobacco revenues were exacerbated by the continued blockade of the port by the British. Into the next century, the constant state of war waged by Napoleon during the period of the Consulate and Empire wrought further havoc on the trade of Bordeaux. Emile Pereire was to recall years later how, with France deprived of its most important colony, Sainte-Domingue, Bordeaux was paralyzed, unable to use its port, its shipping, its arsenals, or even its people, who lived from commerce.[15]

By the time of the Pereires' birth—Jacob-Emile in 1800 and Isaac in 1806—Bordeaux was in a state of severe economic depression from which it was not to recover for decades. Upon the death of their father in 1806, the Rodrigues Pereire family, now comprising a widowed mother with three small boys, found itself thrown upon the stretched resources of the close-knit Sephardic community.[16] Thus, the young Rodrigues Pereires were to be materially affected by the misfortunes of Bordeaux during the chaotic period of the Consulate, Empire, and the Bourbon Restoration, dependent on the goodwill of family friends and on Sephardic charitable organizations. The Bordeaux Consistory, a measure introduced by Napoleon in 1808 to regulate the affairs of the Jews, kept its flock alive.[17]

The pattern followed by the Bordeaux economy bore witness to its dependence on the Atlantic sea-trade and on colonial produce, the hinterland being home to only one export industry, wine, and sugar refining having collapsed almost totally. This lack of diversity contributed to a disparity in economic growth, between the north and east on the one hand and the southwest of France on the other, a trend exacerbated by the extent of taxes imposed even on wine. Arguments on the benefits of free trade within France, and between France and its customers abroad, had been aired during the Revolution, but in the changed circumstances of the early nineteenth century, they developed greater urgency.[18] As a result, Bordeaux became a center and focus of the free trade movement in France. The Bank of France, instituted by Napoleon in January 1800, was of no assistance, being risk-averse and defining its role narrowly. Its focus was on Paris, the only city where its bills circulated. Factory owners in other cities and towns seeking credit, investment capital, relied for the most part on the usurious practices of notaries.

The Sephardic community of Bordeaux lived for the most part in a self-determined quarter to the south of the city, described by one historian as "a voluntary ghetto."[19] The Rodrigues Pereire home was at its very center within the densely populated Rue Bouhaut, where 25 percent of Bordeaux's 2000 Jews lived, and where four synagogues provided places of worship until Napoleon in 1810 approved a public synagogue (the first in France), which was constructed in 1812. Their mother had opened a small haberdashery shop to support them, but on the failure of her business in 1813, she was unable to provide her sons with the level of education she considered worthy of the grandsons of Jacob Rodrigues Pereire or of their abilities. Both boys, who showed promise, thus found low-level jobs with Sephardic businesses, Jacob-Emile eventually working in 1815 with Nunes and Hardel, and Isaac in 1820 with David Gradis.[20] Emile and Isaac Pereire were thus drawn to Paris by expectations of employment no longer conceivable in Bordeaux.

When the Pereire brothers left for Paris in the early 1820s, then, they took with them a potent mix of religious, cultural, and economic attitudes and values that endured in one form or another for the rest of their lives. They were practicing Jews, acculturated in the Judaism of the Sephardim, who had perforce accommodated themselves with the prevailing culture in the countries in which they had lived, first in Spain and Portugal, then in France. They were heirs to the particular culture of the Bordeaux Jews, who were successful, self-reliant, disciplined, oligarchic, integrated within the Catholic merchant economy, fulfilling essential roles in banking and financial services while maintaining order and discipline within their community. In this tradition, a boy was likely to find his first employment either within the family business or, as with the Rodrigues Pereires, with others in the Sephardic business community.[21] While the universalist terms of Emancipation demanded that the Sephardic Mahamad be abandoned, the Jewish welfare societies that replaced it and the Bordeaux Consistory fulfilled a similar function and continued the same path in managing the community.

The memories of Bordeaux's golden era remained sufficiently vivid to feed the imagination of the Rodrigues Pereires, but the causes underlying the city's decline became salutary lessons to be studied and learned. The benefits of free trade and of an economy unfettered by unnecessary taxes became axiomatic in this environment. So too did the need for adequate transport linkages and a banking system that gave egalitarian access to credit, all ideas that were to become central to the Pereires' economic philosophy.

Bankers, Saint-Simonians, and Jews

Jews flocked to Paris in the 1820s. The five hundred or so living there in 1789 had grown to an estimated 6,000 by 1821, the greater number by far being Ashkenazim from Alsace-Lorraine.[22] The influx of young people, Jews and non-Jews alike, hopeful and ambitious, captured in the characters of Balzac's Lucien Rubempré and Stendhal's Julien Sorel, created a ferment of ideas, partly in response to the repressive measures of the Bourbon Restoration.[23] The Pereires moved to Paris at the instigation of their uncle, Isaac Rodrigues Henriques, known as Rodrigues *fils*, with whose family they lived. This Paris household included seven children in a family setting that had increasingly moved away from the traditional religious life practiced in Bordeaux, ceasing to be known as "Rodrigues Henriques" in favor of the simpler "Rodrigues," and neglecting both attendance at the synagogue and strict observance of the requirements of the Sabbath. The Pereire brothers eventually followed the pattern of simplifying their names, which they changed to "Pereire," possibly to avoid confusion with their cousins, and Jacob-Emile became known simply as "Emile."[24] On their part, this also signaled a gradual accommodation with non-Jewish society.

In any case, they confronted complex and profound differences in Parisian Jewish life compared with the society they had left behind. Soon after they arrived, Emile in 1822 and Isaac in 1823, competitions were held in Rouen and Strasbourg with the aim of establishing whether Jews were capable of entering fully into French society.[25] French Jewish writers themselves called for changes within their faith that would render the rituals of Judaism more acceptable to "civilization."[26] In the banking world, Protestants of French and Swiss origin— such as the Delessert, Mallet, and Hottinguer families—had begun to make inroads against Catholic domination. And so too had the Jews, the d'Eichthal, Cahen d'Anvers, and Fould family banks having gained ground, and James de Rothschild, who had moved to Paris in 1812, having set up a branch of Rothschild *frères* in 1817. While the admissibility of Jews to French society was being questioned in some circles, Jews were starting to take advantage of the business opportunities that arose.

The Pereires' uncle, who held a position with the Fould bank, was a financier and accountant who passed on his knowledge to his young nephews, arranging positions for them both. Emile was initially placed at the Bourse and Isaac with the banker Vital-Roux et Cie. Rodrigues *fils* was also, remarkably, at the center of a salon of influential bankers and politicians. Several were or had been regents of the Bank of France, such as the *bayonnais* Jacques Laffitte, and the economist Vital-Roux, men at the center of France's financial world. There were other bankers, Benoît Fould and the Hottinguer brothers, Jacques Ardoin and Halphen. Rodrigues *fils* was also close to the Mendelssohn family and its scion, the banker Abraham Mendelssohn.[27] Thus, the Pereires found themselves strategically placed within, and benefiting from, an already established network in banking and financial circles, consisting largely of Jews and Protestants.

At the same time, the Rodrigues brothers, Olinde and the younger Eugène, introduced them to a somewhat different, though interrelated social group. In 1823, Olinde Rodrigues had become secretary to the philosopher Claude-Henri Rouvroy, the comte de Saint-Simon (1760–1825), who over the last twenty years or so of his life and in a fairly inchoate manner had developed a plethora of ideas about the nature of society and the significance to it of finance and industry, engineering, and science. He wrote of the need for cooperation, or "association" among society's components, elaborating the concept that only human endeavor should be rewarded, according to need and to effort. He had come to believe that '*l'industriel*,' by which he meant an individual who made a positive contribution to the economy, epitomized the hope of the bourgeois world, not only in providing businesses and employment, and thus maintaining the economic fabric of society, but as the political force whose expert administration would maintain an effectively functioning society. Saint-Simon's last work, *Le Nouveau Christianisme*, was on a different theme, however, positing a belief that Christianity as it had been practiced was a failure, that society must move beyond Catholicism and reassert the primacy of the commandment to love one's neighbor as oneself, and in so doing improve the position of the poorest and most numerous class.[28]

When they met Saint-Simon at the home of the banker Jacques Ardoin, Emile Pereire was not yet twenty-five years of age, and Isaac was only eighteen.[29] All the philosopher's ideas struck an immediate chord, and when, after Saint-Simon's death, Olinde Rodrigues undertook to continue the work of the late philosopher, they were among his most ardent supporters. The earliest publication of this new group, *Le Producteur*, contained articles on many of the themes familiar to the followers of Saint-Simon, which would continue to occupy them until the end: banking and improved access to credit, the structure and organization of industry, political economy, the uses of technology—steam, railways, canals—and the necessity of lowering indirect taxes and import duties. The elder Pereire himself contributed a short piece on a report to the Chamber of Commerce in Paris concerning the provision of coal to the capital and arranged for the journal to be circulated in Bordeaux.[30] The direction taken by the group, which now became loosely associated as the "Saint-Simonians," spoke directly to the background and life experiences of the Bordeaux Sephardim, particularly those ideas that focused on the primacy of '*l'industriel*' as the key figure in society, and on the bank, both as the central source of credit, investment in enterprises, and technological advancement, and as a force for good. At the core was a concept of society in which the "*spirit of conquest* is gradually substituted by *the spirit of association* in social relationships [ital. as in original]," in which members of "the poorest and most numerous class" become the beneficiaries of industrial development.[31]

What attracted the Pereires to Saint-Simonianism? Clearly, as I have already noted, there was congruence between the evolving doctrine, to which they themselves contributed, and their circumstances and experiences to that point. For the first twenty or so years of their lives they had been immersed in the mercantile culture of Bordeaux, and while Bordeaux was not the city it had once been, young Sephardic boys nevertheless learned the language of business from an early age, knowing their future lay somewhere within its repertoire. The Pereires learned the language of money in particular, for that was where their closest family members and friends were employed, and the Saint-Simonian emphasis on new, radical approaches to banking and finance was readily acceptable to young men who had been on the receiving end of a depressed economy.[32] The Pereires were sympathetic also to the proposition that a council of bankers and industrialists would be best placed to direct an equitable society, a measure they knew from their own experience of the Bordeaux Consistory and one that had been a constant presence in the history of the

Jewish community through the Sephardic Mahamad. Further, the underlying priority within Saint-Simonian doctrine—to ensure improvement in society's poorest and most numerous class—was immediately comprehensible to men for whom Tzedaka was a central theme in Judaism.

As Jews, they found social ease and acceptance in Saint-Simonian circles that was not so evident in Parisian society at large. Saint-Simonian doctrine was respectful of Judaism as the precursor to Christianity and of Mosaic law as the foundation of the system of justice. The Pereires' cousin, Eugène Rodrigues, crystallized these ideas in his *Lettres sur la religion et la politique*, which was predicated on equality between Judaism and Christianity and on the need to move beyond Catholicism.[33] Lisa Moses Leff has also written persuasively of the impact Saint-Simonianism had on its Jewish adherents in forging a Jewish identity independent of religious observance, and it is clear that in Saint-Simonianism the Pereires indeed found confidence and reassurance in being Jewish, "an assertion of the right to difference," while becoming increasingly distanced from the practice of Judaism.[34]

In the late 1820s, the Saint-Simonians responded to worsening economic circumstances, which, under the government of the Bourbon Charles X and sparked by an acute shortage of food, brought misery throughout the country. High tariff protection against basic raw materials coupled with prohibitive costs in importing heavy machinery, equipment, and skilled labor from Britain stifled growth of any scale in manufacturing. Investment in industry was not among the Bank of France's priorities, and access to credit was limited. Between 1815 and 1830 the urban workforce suffered a decline in wages of nearly 30 percent alongside a 60 percent increase in the cost of living, all of which exacerbated already overcrowded, unsanitary, unhygienic living conditions. Hundreds of thousands of factory workers received welfare in some form. And despite anti-strike laws still in force from the Revolution, as many as thirty strikes occurred in Paris in 1830. The Saint-Simonians committed themselves to practical engagement with the working class, forming workers' associations in each of the twelve *arrondissements* to provide support and emergency services, doctors, and pharmacists, establishing communal houses for workers, and educating them in the teachings of Saint-Simonianism.[35] The priority that Saint-Simon and his followers accorded the "poorest and most numerous class" was significant for the Jewish Saint-Simonians, and in the case of the Pereires we should recall their own poverty in the depressed city of Bordeaux and the role the Sephardim had played in sustaining their community. All of these experiences had an impact, as Isaac recalled many years later when he wrote of his preoccupation from his "extrême jeunesse" with improving the situation of poor.[36]

The first public exposition of the new doctrine of the Saint-Simonians, which took place in December 1828, was a collaborative effort in which the Pereires almost certainly played some part.[37] It painted a revolutionary picture of a society centered on "association" rather than on competition, on universal education, and on the abolition of property rights. This vision depended on industry, and at the core of industry a centralized banking system that would regulate and fuel its needs through the wise provision of credit. The bank's purpose was as much social as financial, for it would also unify, direct and classify workers according to their capacities, with an oligarchy of bankers central to the task.[38]

Over the next several years, further public meetings exposed the doctrine to large, enthusiastic audiences, testing the developing ideology. Young Saint-Simonians ventured to the provinces to proselytize, with varying degrees of success, while Saint-Simonian journals brought the ideas to an even greater audience. One of these journals, *Le Globe*, received as many as twelve hundred letters monthly from the provinces.[39] The Pereires themselves played a role in this burgeoning movement, helping with production of the journals and assuming positions in the formal structures that developed—Emile as a member in the second tier around the leadership, which included Olinde Rodrigues and Isaac as the letters' editor for *Le Globe*. Both also contributed to developing the industrial content of Saint-Simonian doctrine.[40]

By 1830, the government of Charles X and his prime minister, the Prince de Polignac, was in crisis. Fresh elections held in June and July saw the National Assembly gain opposition liberals, who then moved a vote of no confidence in the government. Charles X and Polignac prorogued the parliament, gagging the liberal press and dismissing the National Assembly. The liberal newspapers, ignoring the gag, called for Polignac's resignation, but it was the rioting of Paris's artisans that triggered a more drastic and permanent solution to the impasse. After three days of bloodshed in July, during which two thousand people were killed, Louis-Philippe, Duc d'Orléans, was installed as France's first avowedly constitutional monarch.[41]

The advent of the July monarchy gave the Pereires an opportunity also, for this event fortuitously saw the brief appearance of the banker Jacques Laffitte as Louis-Philippe's chief minister. A Saint-Simonian ally, Laffitte had attempted to persuade Restoration governments to support a bank that would provide investment capital to industry, a Caisse Générale pour le Commerce et l'Industrie. This time it was Emile and Isaac Pereire who, probably with Laffitte's encouragement since they were known to him, put a comparable idea before a government commission of inquiry set up in September 1830 to investigate the causes underlying the general malaise in industry and commerce being felt throughout France, causes whose effects had been signaled first by Bordeaux.[42] The central idea in the Pereires' proposal was the establishment of a bank to invest in commerce and industry against solid guarantees, based on principles of mutuality and on the emission of interest-bearing banknotes. Government was to provide guarantees of up to 50 million francs, thus ensuring stability in times of downturn. A council of bankers, merchants, manufacturers, and members of government would provide advice and experience in assessing the creditworthiness of borrowers, bearing some resemblance, indeed, to the role and composition of the governance of the Bordeaux Sephardim. As significant as the proposal was in the Pereires' careers, both in the elaboration of a concrete financial structure that sought to make practical sense of Saint-Simonian debate and in the beginning of their business partnership, its rationale also gives an idea of the philosophical position they had reached: "An entirely new order is to be to be established, founded on liberty; an order which must give each day a greater importance to work."[43] In the event, the proposal was unsuccessful.

Still, Saint-Simonianism offered the brothers an opportunity to publish their ideas, which they did prolifically, in *Le Globe* and *L'Organisateur*, in articles that concentrated largely on economic and financial issues while integrating the Saint-Simonian social and political agenda.[44] Later, Emile also contributed to Jacques Laffitte's own journal *Le National* and to the *Revue encyclopédique* established by other Saint-Simonians, Pierre Leroux and Hippolyte Carnot.[45] All the Pereires' writings were consistent, starting from the premise that the political and societal problems of France could only be resolved through economic and financial reform and restructure on a major scale. The means of achieving these reforms were consistent also. On the one hand, they proposed eliminating government spending that they saw as impeding development, including provisions in the national budget for war, the navy, and the military. Further, they would expunge amortization, the sinking fund allocated in the state budget to offset future debt. They argued for the progressive diminution of indirect taxes, especially those on salt and wine, which eroded basic living standards and which they considered ineffective and punitive sources of funding. In the same vein, they argued for the lowering of tariffs, especially those on raw materials such as coal. They would eliminate the "*octroi*," the physical barrier that ensured taxes were paid on merchandise entering Paris and other towns. These measures, they argued, would clear the way for industrial development on a scale hitherto unknown in France and create employment, particularly in major infrastructure projects. However, the central element in their policies, and the most important, was the establishment of a central banking system as the principal source of credit for the necessary developments in industry and commerce.[46]

These writings were replete with motifs and ideas drawn from Saint-Simonianism, concepts of "association," of the "*prolétaire*." They commented on political news and events in a forthright manner, castigating the July government for its betrayal of the "*prolétariat*," a new word that Emile Pereire used to identify the "*prolétaires*" as a class.[47] The young Isaac gave four public lectures to a large audience in Paris in 1831, which were published in *L'Organisateur* as "Lessons on Industry and Finance."[48] He described the class struggle between the workers and "the idle" ("*l'oisif*," interpreted as those whose income derived from property), predicting a future when the universal association of workers would have at its disposal the instruments of production, and when reward would be determined not by money, but by morality, ability, and effort, thus transferring the right to property from the idle to the workers.[49] In identifying property as the basis of the struggle between the worker and the "idle," he looked to a new system of banking as the solution, a *"caisse de prêt et d'emprunt,"* directed by captains of industry who would personally guarantee credit borrowed by industry, and issuing its own interest-bearing banknotes.[50]

Emile Pereire made his name through a single article contributed to the *Revue encyclopédique* in October 1831, a critical review of the budget of 1832 in the context of the events of Lyon, where 100,000 workers rebelled against their wages and working conditions amid scenes of violence and bloodshed. Highlighting areas in which budget provisions actively weighed on the living conditions of workers and their families, he then argued for the elimination of indirect taxes on salt, drink, tobacco, and the lottery, to increase consumption and production. In their place, he proposed construction of a vast system of communications, of canals, roads, railways, swelling the number of jobs available. Here as elsewhere, he referred to the possibilities inherent in encouraging the savings of workers in the form of life insurance companies, and the establishment of savings banks.[51]

Through this intense period of writing and reflection, the Pereires had learned the art of propaganda, and they continued to publish in furtherance of their interests for the rest of their lives. In 1838, Isaac commenced a regular column for the *Journal des Débats*, an innovation in which he followed movements on the stock market: the "Revue de la Bourse," written anonymously and not averse to promoting the viability and prospects of Pereire companies.[52] Either individually or together over the period after 1835, they produced more than a score of pamphlets, including nine on the Bank of France.

Saint-Simonians in Business

The Pereires' initial business success, in 1837, was the opening of the first passenger railway line in France, carrying passengers the comparatively short distance of 19 kilometers from Paris to St Germain-en-Laye and back. As a model demonstrating the uses and profitability of rail, it succeeded in leading eventually to other, larger projects. All these depended on finance, and it was through the Saint-Simonian network, which had also provided the technological expertise, that Emile Pereire was able to persuade James de Rothschild to invest in the Paris-St Germain and similar ventures. This led ultimately to the construction in 1846 of the great Chemin de Fer du Nord, of which Emile was director and Isaac the loyal deputy.[53] Over time, however, the Pereires found

the tutelage of Rothschild constraining. On the collapse of the July government in 1848 they were now in a position to profit from the coming to power of
Louis-Napoleon Bonaparte and his coup d'état in 1851, which paved the way
for his installation as the Emperor Napoleon III. The Pereires finally launched
their own joint stock investment bank, the Crédit Mobilier, in 1852, with investment capital of sixty million francs.

The Crédit Mobilier was listed on the Bourse on 23 November 1852 under
the presidency of the banker Benoît Fould, brother of Napoleon III's minister
of state, Achille. The roster of its principal backers' names is instructive, replete
with bankers and financiers, a significant number of them Jewish or Protestant—Adolphe d'Eichthal of Louis d'Eichthal et fils, the younger brother of
the Saint-Simonian Gustave; Ernest André, a Protestant banker of the house
André et Cottier; the Swiss Charles Mallet of Mallet frères; Abraham Oppenheim of the Cologne bank Salomon Oppenheim et Cie; and Salomon Heine
of Hamburg.[54] The bank became the source of investment for many Pereire
companies, whose scale and variety were remarkable, including in France the
Société Immobilière, established to reap the rewards of Haussmann's redevelop-
ment of Paris; a number of rail companies, of which the most significant was the
Compagnie du Midi; the shipping Compagnie Générale Transatlantique with
its associated shipbuilding yards at Saint-Nazaire; the Compagnie Générale du
Gaz de Paris; two insurance companies; and a vast industrial laundry. In Spain,
they created the Crédit Mobilier Espagnol, the Compagnie du Gaz de Madrid,
and the Compagnie des Chemins de Fer du Nord de l'Espagne. Elsewhere in
Europe, in Austria, Italy, Switzerland, Russia, and the Ottoman Empire as well,
there were railway, banking, and finance companies.[55] By 1867, the Crédit Mobilier had invested somewhere in the vicinity of four billion francs.[56]

What influence did Saint-Simonianism have on their businesses practices?
Saint-Simonian concepts clearly lay at the heart of their principal enterprises.
The Paris-St Germain was the direct result of discussion and debate in Saint-
Simonian circles, and Michel Chevalier's description of the "Mediterranean
System," a vast railway network linking Paris with Marseille and thence across
the Mediterranean to North Africa, was the basis for the development of much
of the Pereires' own network. The Crédit Mobilier, at least in theory, owed much
to evolving Saint-Simonian ideas of a central banking system, and Isaac Pereire
described its purpose to shareholders in 1854 in those terms. It would provide
new sources of capital to contribute to the development of public and industrial
credit, to develop national industries and establish major companies, acting as
a new fiduciary agent that would help grow the savings of the most humble.[57]
A recent discussion of the Crédit Mobilier, in which its ideological links with
Isaac Pereire's early "Lessons on Industry and Finance" are highlighted, credits the Pereires with the conception and implementation of an enterprise that
aimed at nothing less than the reorganization of industrial society.[58]

As former Saint-Simonians and employers, did they actually attempt to alleviate the difficulties of the poorest and most numerous class? They certainly appear to have remunerated their staff well. In the Compagnie Générale Transatlantique a complex system of rewards for loyalty existed—including profit-sharing, shares and bonuses, and an extra month's salary.[59] From 1838, starting with the Paris-St. Germain, they provided their workforce with centers for the sale of discounted goods, food, wine, clothing, coal, linen, the basics of life.[60] They were among the first to institute sick leave and sick pay—including recuperation for tuberculosis sufferers in a special health center—superannuation, and long service leave.[61] For the children of railway employees they founded schools, providing free tuition and transport, and subsequent employment was found within the company.[62] These rewards and benefits were not entirely uncommon among the largest of the Second Empire industrial enterprises whose proprietors, motivated by religious virtues of charity and compassion on the one hand, also knew that social stability and political harmony came at some cost. In this reading, the Pereires' employment practices can be interpreted as authoritarian and paternalistic, intended to dampen the socialist and revolutionary elements that threatened the Bonapartist regime from the outset. Nevertheless, there was continuity in the way they dealt with this issue and the priority they gave to it, extending from their articles in the 1830s up to Isaac Pereire's late work, La Question Religieuse, in 1878.[63] It is at least arguable that the Pereires were guided as much by religious precepts engrained through their childhood and the lessons learned within the Saint-Simonian movement, as they were by any perceived need to gain the quiescence of their workforce.

Despite the considerable funds under management, the Crédit Mobilier did not fulfill its ambitions, nor, given the primacy the Saint-Simonians attached to the development of heavy industry, was its investment in manufacturing remarkable. Great industrialists like the Schneider family of the Le Creusot iron foundry, for example, who owed their initial success to the Pereires' Paris-St Germain, later steered clear of the Pereires, believing they dabbled in risky finance. Indeed, a lack of overall consistency characterized the nature of Crédit Mobilier investments, which, though impressive enough in aggregate, appear to have been driven by a restless energy, or mere opportunism. Napoleon III's support of the Pereires, which turned out to be a two-edged sword, may partially explain this lack of clear direction.

The Pereires versus the Rothschilds

The Pereires' rivalry with the Rothschilds, a product of the launch of the Crédit Mobilier, was a continuing irritant. David Landes has recently pointed out that when James de Rothschild's former employees asserted their independence, this insubordination provoked more than a little pique on the part of Rothschild, but in this instance, Rothschild had misread the signs.[64] On the very eve of the announcement of the Crédit Mobilier's creation, he had written to Louis-Napoleon Bonaparte to dissuade him from expressing approval.[65] Later, Rothschild was to attempt a venture similar to the Crédit Mobilier, with mixed results. He worked increasingly with a loose coalition of the more conservative Jewish and Protestant bankers, the Haute Banque, representing largely family-owned concerns, to protect their interests against the Pereires. At the outset there actually remained considerable interchange among the banking fraternity: members of the Haute Banque sat on the board of, and held shares in, the Crédit Mobilier, and Emile Pereire remained on the board of the Nord railway until 1855.[66] However, it was the Pereires' forays out of France that caused the Rothschilds particular concern, especially the Pereires' involvement in the Darmstädter Bank für Handel und Industrie, which was run along the lines of the Crédit Mobilier and located close to the family headquarters in Frankfurt.[67]

It was the Société Immobilière, the vehicle established with the overt support of the Baron Haussmann, the prefect of the Seine, to redevelop Paris, along with its counterpart in Marseille, that brought about the Pereires' undoing. As of the mid 1860s, new properties remained vacant, causing a major shortfall in cash flow. The Crédit Mobilier, which had borrowed massively from the state-owned Crédit Foncier to save the Société Immobilière, could not extinguish the debt. The Rothschilds were infinitely the more powerfully placed, with Alphonse de Rothschild, a regent of the Bank of France, thus preventing the Pereires from returning to the market to raise further capital. The share price, which in 1852 had opened at 2,100 francs, plummeted, with James de Rothschild's active support, to 140 francs. The Crédit Mobilier actually survived the crash, but its survival was conditional upon the resignation of the Pereires and their making substantial reparation to shareholders, 10 million francs out of a total 36 million francs.[68] While the Pereires were not ruined financially by their bank's failure, they responded differently to it: Emile increasingly retired from public life while Isaac fought back, retaining control of the Spanish companies and regaining that of the Compagnie du Midi and the Compagnie Générale Transatlantique.

Conclusion

The remarkable careers of Emile and Isaac Pereire owed much to personal characteristics, for they possessed above all high intelligence, a capacity for hard, intensive work sustained over long periods, and a talent for organization and implementation. It was a mix of historical circumstances that enabled these traits to come to fruition in the way that they did. In a passage referring directly to the Pereires, the writer Ernest Feydeau once described Bordeaux as the great nursery ("pépinière") that fed the Paris Bourse with the sons of Israel.[69] Despite Feydeau's evident anti-Semitism, it is clear that both Emile and Isaac Pereire owed something of their careers as bankers and industrialists to their experiences in Bordeaux's Sephardic community. The Sephardim had built their lives in France around their financial resources, their capacities with finance, and their utility to the Catholic mercantile community. As Jews, they had survived because of the orderly manner in which they governed their own people, structuring organizational life in a way that enabled their members to prosper, ensuring the welfare of their poor, and providing for the public practice of Judaism after a long period as *conversos*. The Sephardim were also part of a wider community, an extensive diaspora trading north from Spain and Portugal—despite impediments in those countries—to Bayonne, Bordeaux, Amsterdam, and London, east as far as the Ottoman Empire, and west to the Americas. Their worldview was international. Here we may also recall the significance to the Pereires of Bordeaux, the city itself, which exemplified many of the difficult issues needing to be addressed in the French economy, issues whose resolution they pursued actively from the time they arrived in Paris, both in their writings and their businesses.

The Pereires matured in a community for which money was the lingua franca.[70] Any alternative career to the one they pursued was unlikely. Isaac Pereire in particular developed innovative ways of managing finance and of raising capital—interest-bearing banknotes, debenture bonds, annuities, an "omnium" of international bonds among them.[71] I have dealt with the significance of the Sephardic oligarchy of businessmen in the Pereires' conception of good governance, but this also flowed in some senses to the management of the Pereires' businesses and their private lives. The Pereires demanded trust and confidence derived from a circle of family and friends who had known each other well over a long period. The two brothers depended on and trusted each other implicitly, and they and their families either shared the same living arrangements or lived in close proximity throughout their lives. Beyond, a small network that included Bordeaux and Bayonne Sephardim provided the necessary basis of trust and mutual comprehension.[72]

Their encounter with Saint-Simonianism was fortuitous in drawing together elements already embryonic in their Sephardic heritage. The Saint-Simonian emphasis on banking and credit as the way forward used a language in which the Pereires were already conversant. They understood and accepted the central role the bank would play in the future of industry and in the provision of employment. The primacy attaching to the direction of society by a business oligarchy was an idea of which they had practical experience. And, as I have noted, the Saint-Simonian acceptance of Judaism as historically significant, as the forerunner of Christianity and as the foundation of justice and law, reso-nated for the Pereires and other Jewish followers.

Emile and Isaac Pereire, in both their businesses and their ideas, were inter-nationalists. They were receptive to, and realized, business opportunities in Eu-rope, the Levant, Central and North America, Africa, and the Far East. Having been raised in a port city within the Sephardic Diaspora, this element in their careers is not surprising. They were also protagonists of free trade, Emile having been, with Michel Chevalier, one of those who persuaded Napoleon III to sign the Anglo-French Commercial Treaty of 1860, extending free trade between England and France.[73] The Saint-Simonians were international in their out-look also. Beneath the overtones of the "civilizing mission" about their ideas, the sense that France had a duty to spread its virtues, they also believed in a peaceful Europe in which free trade played a role in redefining industry and the organization of work.[74] This aspect of the Pereires' association with Saint-Simonianism could be explored further as a powerful illustration of their own influence on the movement.

The failure of the Crédit Mobilier was catastrophic for the Pereires and its shareholders alike, yet its historical significance is apparent on several levels. In finance, it can be seen as the forerunner to modern banking, spawning a score of imitators.[75] It was a major player in the industrial revolution that ac-celerated during the Second Empire, despite the constraints on its activities and the competition from its rivals.[76] Perhaps most interestingly, however, it may be interpreted as a flawed attempt to combine the early socialist ideals of Saint-Simonianism—concern with the organization of work and offering the means of production to the working class—with the concept of a centralized investment banking system.

NOTES

1. This chapter is based on Helen M. Davies, "Jewish Identity, Social Justice, and Capitalism: The Making of the Pereire Brothers," PhD dissertation, University of Melbourne, 2005. There have been three biographies written about the Pereires: Jean Autin, *Les frères Pereire: Le bonheur d'entreprendre* (Paris: Perrin, 1984); Guy Fargette, *Émile et Isaac Pereire: L'esprit d'entreprise au XIXe siècle* (Paris: Harmattan, 2001); Maurice-Édouard Berthon, *Émile et Isaac Pereire: La passion d'entreprendre* (Paris: Presses Universitaires Françaises, 2007). A number of excellent articles have been written about them, notably by Barrie M. Ratcliffe. See for instance his "Les Péreire et le saint-simonisme," *Saint-Simonisme et pari pour l'industrie, No. de*

Économies et sociétés v, no. 7 (1971): 1215–1256; "Some Banking Ideas in France in the 1830s: The Writings of Emile and Isaac Pereire, 1830–1835," *Revue internationale d'histoire de la banque* 6 (1973), 23–46; "Some Jewish Problems in the Early Careers of Emile and Isaac Pereire," *Jewish Social Studies* 34, no. 3 (1972), 189–206.

2. I have found most useful in this context Lois C. Dubin, *The Port Jews of Habsburg Trieste: Absolutist Politics and Enlightenment Culture* (Stanford, CA: Stanford University Press, 1999) and Frances Malino, *The Sephardic Jews of Bordeaux: Assimilation and Emancipation in Revolutionary and Napoleonic France* (Tuscaloosa: University of Alabama Press, 1978). For another approach to the history of the Sephardic Diaspora in Europe see Yosef Kaplan, *An Alternative Path to Modernity: The Sephardi Diaspora in Western Europe* (Leiden: Brill, 2000).

3. Letters Patent were royal commands having the force of law. See Gérard Nahon, ed., *Les "nations" juives portugaises du sud-ouest de la France (1684–1791)*, (Paris: Fondação Calouste Gulbenkian, Centro Cultural Português, 1981), 21.

4. Ibid., 26–39; see for instance X, "1574, 11 Novembre: Privilèges octroiés par le Roy aulz Espaignols et Portugais de la Ville de Bordeaux," and XII, "1723, juin : Lettres Patentes du Roy, pour les Portugais des généralités de Bordeaux et Auch." Jacques Blamont notes that the description "Portugais" became synonymous with the word "Juif" in Spain and soon after in France and Western Europe: Jacques Blamont, *Le lion et le moucheron: histoire des marranes de Toulouse* (Paris: Odile Jacob 2000), 25.

5. Nahon, *Les "nations" juives portugaises*, doc. I, 3–7, "Arrêt du Conseil qui expulse quatrevingt-treize familles de Juifs de Guienne," 20 November 1684.

6. Malino, *Sephardic Jews*, 9.

7. Louis Francia de Beaufleury, *L'établissement des juifs à Bordeaux et à Bayonne, depuis 1550* (l'an VIII; reprint, Bayonne: Jean Curutchet, Éditions Harriet, 1985), 29.

8. The term *nation* was used to refer to individuals having "a specific collectivity," the term "nation portugaise" being employed for the first time in Angers in 1511. See Jean-Paul Léon, "Autour de quelques familles juives de Bordeaux," Diplôme dissertation, L'École des Hautes Études en Sciences Sociales, 2005, 6.

9. My understanding of the affairs of this Sephardic community has benefited from several works, including the "Introduction" to Simon Schwarzfuchs, ed., *Le registre des délibérations de la nation juive portugaise de Bordeaux (1711–1787)* (Paris: Fundação Calouste Gulbenkian, Centro Cultural Português, 1981), 5–51 and Gérard Nahon, *Juifs et judaïsme à Bordeaux* (Bordeaux: Mollat, 2003), 61–92.

10. Malino, *Sephardic Jews*, 12–13.

11. Nahon, *Les "nations" juives portugaises*, 41–44, XIV, "1776, juin, Versailles: Lettres Patentes portant confirmation des privilèges des Juifs Portugais."

12. Ibid.

13. Ibid. 45–46, XV, "1790, Paris : Lettres Patentes du Roi, sur un décret de l'Assemblée Nationale, portant que les Juifs … y jouiront des droits de citoyen actif." This decree accorded citizenship to the Sephardic and Avignon Jews, but not to the Ashkenazim, who waited another eighteen months for the provisions to be extended to them.

14. Granting citizenship to Sephardim and Ashkenazim in two separate decisions was contentious. I will not touch here on the struggle that preceded granting emancipation to the Ashkenazim.

15. Emile et Isaac Pereire, *Écrits de…*, (Paris: Gustave Pereire, 1900), t. IV, fasc., 4, 1943, "Enquête Commerciale," *Le National de 1834*, 15 October 1834.
16. A son born in 1803, Mardochée Télèphe, died in 1820.
17. Jean Cavignac, *Les israélites bordelais de 1780 à 1850: autour de l'émancipation* (Paris: Éditions Publisud 1991), 320–326.
18. See for instance Marcel Dorigny, "Recherches sur les idées économiques des Girondins," in *Girondins et Montagnards: Actes du Colloque, Sorbonne 14 décembre 1975*, ed. Albert Soboul (Paris: Société des Études Robespierristes, 1980), 79–102.
19. Cavignac, *Israélites bordelais*, 15 and 302–304.
20. Autin, *Frères Pereire*, 22.
21. Cavignac, *Israélites bordelais*, 267 and passim.
22. Michel Roblin, *Les juifs de Paris: démographie-économie-culture* (Paris, Éditions A. et J. Picard & Cie, 1952). Roblin reckoned the Sephardic population at about 300. Ibid., 51–53.
23. One of the most interesting analyses of the Restoration is in Sheryl Kroen, *Politics and Theater: The Crisis of Legitimacy in Restoration France, 1815–1830* (Berkeley: University of California Press, 2000).
24. Autin, *Frères Pereire*, 22.
25. These competitions, held in 1823 and 1824 respectively, are described in both Jay Berkovitz, *The Shaping of Jewish Identity* (Detroit: Wayne State University Press, 1989), 46–47; and Julie Kalman, "Evolutions in Hatred: Anti-Jewish Sentiment in Restoration and July Monarchy France," PhD diss., University of Melbourne, 2004, 106ff.
26. One of these, Joseph Salvador, was known to Emile Pereire, who promoted his work, *Loi de Moyse ou système religieux et politique des Hébreux*, to Sephardic friends in Bordeaux and Bayonne. See Henri Léon, *Histoire des juifs de Bayonne* (1893; reprint, Marseille: Laffitte Reprints, 1976), 428.
27. This milieu was described in Alfred Pereire, *Autour de Saint-Simon: Documents originaux* (Paris: Honoré Champion 1912), 101. Alfred was a grandson of Isaac Pereire.
28. For an introduction to Saint-Simon's life and ideas see Nathalie Coilly and Philippe Régnier, eds, *Le siècle des saint-simoniens: du nouveau christianisme au Canal de Suez* (Paris: Bibliothèque Nationale de France, 2006), 26–32 and Juliette Grange, *Saint-Simon: Écrits politiques et économiques, Anthologie critique* (Paris: Pocket, 2005).
29. Alfred Pereire, *Je suis diléttante* (Paris: Conquistador, 1955).
30. Henri Fournel, *Bibliographie Saint-Simonienne* (Paris: Jihanneau, 1831), 51. See also letters from Bordeaux friends of Emile in the Archives de la famille Pereire Paris.
31. Fournel, *Bibliographie*, 34.
32. Aside from Rodrigues *fils*, their other mentor was the Bordeaux banker Samuel Alexandre. See Davies, *Jewish Identity*, passim.
33. Eugène Rodrigues, *Lettres sur la religion et la politique, 1829: Suivies de l'éducation du genre humain de Lessing* (Paris, 1831). Rodrigues translated the work by Lessing from the German.
34. Lisa Moses Leff, *Sacred Bonds of Solidarity: The Rise of Jewish Internationalism in Nineteenth-Century France* (Stanford: Stanford University Press, 2006), especially 95–102.

35. Roger Magraw, A History of the French Working Class: Volume 1, The Age of Artisan Revolution (Oxford: Blackwell 1992); and Guillaume de Bertier de Sauvigny, The Bourbon Restoration, trans. Lynn M. Case (Philadelphia: University of Pennsylvania Press, 1966), 254–255. Some 163,000 workers in the Nord department (over 70 percent), 80,000 in the Pas-de-Calais, and 63,000 in the department of the Seine received assistance. See also Robert B Carlisle, The Proffered Crown: Saint-Simonianism and the Doctrine of Hope (Baltimore: Johns Hopkins University, 1987), 137–140.
36. Écrits, t. III, fasc., 1 Écrits divers, 516, "Députation (Septième Partie): Élection de M. Isaac Pereire au Corps Législatif (1869)."
37. The leadership of three, St.-Amand Bazard, Prosper Enfantin, and Olinde Rodrigues, was joined by Hippolyte Carnot, Henri Fournel, Charles Duveyrier, and Abel Transon in preparing the lectures that became known as the "Exposition." Bazard presented them initially. See Jean-Pierre Alem [J. P. Caillot], Enfantin: le prophète aux sept visages (Paris: Jean-Jacques Pauvert, 1963), 36.
38. Doctrine de Saint Simon: première année, exposition 1829 (Paris: Au Bureau de l'Organisateur, 1830), xxxviii, 128–133.
39. See for instance Carlisle, Proffered Crown, 135.
40. This was recorded in Le Globe on 11 January 1831. See also Bibliothèque nationale de France, Arsenal, Fonds Enfantin, 7822/29, "Classement des membres de la famille Saint-Simonienne par Fonctions"; and L'Organisateur 375, no. 48 of 9 July 1831.
41. P. M. Pilbeam, The 1830 Revolution in France (London: Macmillan, 1991). See also John M. Merriman, ed., 1830 in France (New York: New Viewpoints, 1975); Jill Harsin, Barricades: The War of the Streets in Revolutionary Paris, 1830–1848 (New York: Palgrave, 2002).
42. The responses to this inquiry from the Chambers of Commerce have been comprehensively explored in Christopher H. Johnson, "The Revolution of 1830 in French Economic History," in Merriman, 1830 in France, 147–158.
43. Pereire, Écrits, t. V, fasc., 2, Première Partie, 1. Laffitte's term ended in March 1831. But it was he who started the first investment bank, in 1837.
44. Isaac Pereire published a "Letter to a Jewish Woman" in l'Organisateur, in which he defended his increasing adherence to the "Nouveau Christianisme." See L'Organisateur, 246ff.
45. From 1831.
46. The writings were collected as t. I, fasc., 1-2, and t. IV, fasc., 1–4 of the Écrits de Emile et Isaac Pereire.
47. Écrits, t. IV, fasc., 2, "Variétés : mélanges d'économie sociale," Le National, 20 January 1833.
48. Ibid., t. I, [fasc., 1], "Leçons sur l'industrie et les finances," 1–61.
49. Ibid., 14, "Deuxième leçon : transformation de la valeur, de l'échange, de l'argent dans l'organisation matérielle de l'avenir."
50. Ibid. Barrie Ratcliffe has given an excellent account of the Lessons in his article "Les Péreires," 1242–1244.
51. Écrits, t. I, fasc., 2, "Examen du budget de 1832," 1–38.

52. These are to be found in Ibid., t. II, fasc., I and II. In his old age, Isaac bought the journal *La Liberté*, which he used to publicize his philosophy and comment on current events.

53. Archive de la famille Pereire.

54. M. Aycard, *Histoire du Crédit Mobilier* (Paris, Librairie Internationale, 1867), 18.

55. Autin, *Frères Pereire*, 364, Annexe No. 7.

56. Franck Yonnet, "La structuration de l'économie et de la banque sous le Second Empire : le rôle du Crédit Mobilier des Pereire," in Coilly and Régnier, *Le siècle des saint-simonians*, 125. Yonnet has made good use of Jean-Baptiste Vergeot, "Le crédit comme stimulant et régulateur de l'industrie : La conception saint-simonienne, ses réalisations, son application au problème bancaire d'après guerre," Thèse de droit, Paris, 1918.

57. Société Générale du Crédit Mobilier, *Rapports du conseil d'administration et résolutions des actionnaires dans leurs assemblées générales : exercices de 1853 à 1864* (Paris, 1865), "Rapport présenté par le Conseil d'Administration dans l'Assemblée Générale Ordinaire et Extraordinaire des Actionnaires, du 29 avril 1854." Isaac Pereire had replaced Benoît Fould as president in 1854.

58. Yonnet, "La structuration de l'économie," 125–129.

59. The chief of traffic, for instance, earned 11,000 francs per annum, and his deputy 4,300 francs. See Marthe Barbance, *Histoire de la Compagnie Générale Transatlantique: un siècle d'exploitation maritime* (Paris: Arts et Métiers Graphiques, 1955), 99.

60. Centre des Archives du Monde du Travail, Compagnie des Chemins de Fer du Midi, 78 Q 7, *Assemblée Génerale Ordinaire des Actionnaires, Rapport du Conseil d'Administration* (Paris: Imprimerie Poidevant, 1864), 44–48.

61. Ibid. See also Barbance, *Compagnie Générale Transatlantique*, 99–100.

62. *Écrits*, t. IV, fasc., 4, 2225–2230, "Écoles de Morcenx."

63. Isaac Pereire, *La Question Religieuse* (Paris: Motteroz, 1878).

64. David Landes, *Dynasties: Fortunes and Misfortunes of the World's Great Family Businesses* (New York: Viking Adult, 2006), 60–64.

65. Niall Ferguson, *The World's Banker: The History of the House of Rothschild* (London: Weidenfeld and Nicolson, 1998), 570.

66. David S. Landes, "The Old and the New: The Financial Revolution of the 19th century," in François Crouzet, W. H. Challoner, and W. M. Stern, eds., *Essays in European Economic History, 1789–1914* (London: Edward Arnold, 1969), 122–123.

67. According to Isaac's son Gustave, it was the entry of the Pereires into Austria, challenging the domination of the Rothschild family firm, that sealed the rivalry between the two. See *Écrits*, t. IV, fasc., 4, xxix. A letter Isaac wrote to Emile from Paris in September 1858 confirmed this. See also Ferguson, *The World's Banker*, 572.

68. Centre des Archives du Monde du Travail Crédit Mobilier 25/AQ/3.

69. Ernest Feydeau, *Mémoires d'un coulissier*, 2nd ed. (Paris: Librairie Nouvelle, 1873), 165–166.

70. Jacob Rodrigues Pereire won prizes awarded by the French Academy of Sciences and became a member of the Royal Society of London.

71. Ratcliffe, "Some Banking Ideas," 33–36, has an excellent account of these.

72. Correspondence in the Archives de la famille Pereire attests to the strength and permanence of these attachments.
73. Davies, *Jewish Identity*, 271–272. Emile Pereire worked in conjunction with Michel Chevalier, who has received the major credit on the French side for engineering the treaty. Documents in the Archives de la famille Pereire also verify the conclusion that Emile Pereire played a significant role.
74. This "civilizing mission" was evident, for example, in Chevalier's "Système de la méditerranée"; see *Le Globe*, 12 February 1832. See also Francis Démier, "Les Europe des saint-simoniens," in Coilly et Régnier, *Le siècle des saint-simoniens*, 158–167.
75. See for instance Yonnet, "L'age d'or," 129; and Landes, *Dynasties*, 60–64.
76. Yonnet, "L'age d'or," 129.

✑ 6 ✑

Buying, Selling, Being, Drinking

Jewish Coffeehouse Consumption in the Long Nineteenth Century

Sarah Wobick-Segev

Dr. Friedrich Löwenberg sat in a deep melancholy at the round marble table of his coffeehouse. It was one of those old, *gemütlich* Viennese cafés on the *Alsergrunde*. He had been coming there for years, since his days as a student. With the regularity of a bureaucrat he would arrive at five in the afternoon. The pale, sickly waiter greeted him with resignation. Löwenberg made a polite bow toward the equally pale cashier, with whom he never spoke. Then he sat himself down at the round reading table, drank his coffee, read through all the newspapers, which the waiter officiously brought. And after he was done with the daily and weekly newspapers, the funnies and the scholarly journals, which never took less than one and a half hours, then came the conversations with friends or the lonely dreams.[1]

By the early twentieth century, when Theodor Herzl penned the novel *Altneuland*, the coffeehouse had become a well-established institution in the social, economic, and cultural fabric of German-Jewish life. Thus engrained in the landscape of the time, it could even serve Herzl as a literary device: an old, stale, aging venue—symbol of Europe—that Dr. Löwenberg had to leave in order to begin his adventure. Yet the café was nevertheless also an integral part of Herzl's daily and imaginary life, such that it was almost natural that he elsewhere envisioned a Jewish homeland in Palestine complete with Viennese-style cafés.[2] The café has been recognized for some time as a space that served more than tasty treats and a variety of beverages. For instance, it could serve as a site for associational meetings of smaller groups that could not afford to rent out their own space, for informal business meetings, and for journalists at

---

Notes for this chapter begin on page 131.

work. As a consumptive site—not only literally—it was a venue where access to social, political, and cultural space could be purchased.[3] Despite these facts, it may not appear altogether obvious why the café gained such importance as a space for consumption and sociability in Jewish life during the long nineteenth century.

Though the above excerpt from Herzl's novel does not by any means offer a flattering picture of a coffeehouse (at least with regard to the sickly-looking service staff), it does highlight some of the main reasons why the coffeehouse was a popular and central site of consumption. The café was relatively inexpensive; one could sit undisturbed for hours nursing a single cup of coffee or other beverage, allowing individuals of different socioeconomic categories a chance to partake in this social space. Coffeehouses were also known for making a variety of newspapers available to all those who visited. Some cafés even boasted an assortment of over a hundred periodicals, allowing patrons to catch up on the local, regional, national, and international news, often in more than one language. Finally, since it was possible to spend significant amounts of time in the cafés while spending, relatively speaking, very little money, coffeehouses were ideal gathering places for friends and colleagues, for meetings and for business. In short, the coffeehouse was more than a physical place. It was a space in which one could not only buy information (through the form of newspapers and discussions with other guests) but also purchase sociability or access thereto, i.e., access to a place in European society, religiously mixed or homogenous. As such, the complicated relationship for Jews as a minority group within the larger, German-speaking, Christian society, and the concomitant tensions related to being at once an outsider and insider, are reflected in the equally intricate relationship to the coffeehouse itself.

Spanning the long nineteenth century—the century of the café—we will examine in this chapter the Jewish coffeehouse experience in three separate German cities: Hamburg, Frankfurt, and Berlin. Though these three cities and their Jewish communities differed substantially in terms of their historical development and geopolitical location within the German Empire, they were nonetheless three very central and vital Jewish communities throughout the period under discussion. Moreover, the communities shared a broader cultural framework, which despite variations was common across German-speaking lands. This included a flourishing urban, bourgeois culture, a strong intellectual and professional milieu, and a variety of consumptive venues. Comparing these three major Jewish communities provides us an opportunity to explore the different ways in which Jews used the coffeehouse to create, display, and consume modes of Jewish belonging. That said, I do not intend to offer a comprehensive survey of coffeehouse life in the cities under study. The history of the Jewish experience in German-speaking countries will be presented in this chapter through a series of stories about the ways in which Jews used the social space of the coffeehouse to make claims to various guises of belonging and to a place in urban society. As well, we will explore in part how non-Jews reacted to the growth of a religiously mixed urban society over the course of the nineteenth century.

Here I would like to offer examples of how Jews employed the coffeehouse to display and consume two models of belonging. The first model reflects the consumption of a specifically Jewish sense of belonging—in other words, we could characterize this model through the notion of "insider" consumption. I do not mean to suggest unified or homogenous Jewish identity, but rather that the coffeehouse offered a place for a variety of Jewish senses of belonging—Zionist, Yiddishist, religious, professional, cultural—to be displayed and consumed. The second model can be viewed as "outsider" consumption, according to which Jews attempted to gain access to and play a part in a larger, non-Jewish social environment through their consumption of beverages and social space in specific cafés. In cases of both insider and outsider consumption, Jews employed space to display either their distinctive self-identification (their Jewishness) or their integrated selves. The case of Hamburg will be used to illustrate outsider consumption, where the café stood in for civic life more broadly and the Jews' place in the former was representative of their desired inclusion in the latter. The cases of Frankfurt and Berlin, on the other hand, will exemplify insider consumption whereby cafés—Jewish-owned and not—became sites for the consumption of a variety of guises of Jewish belonging. Clearly, both models can be found in the various cafés of each city over the years. I have merely chosen to take several illustrative examples to make the examination clearer. It should be borne in mind that according to both models Jews were integral components of European society. As insiders and as outsiders, their place within the café reflected their position within society, and whereas they were often in liminal positions, the Jews of the German-speaking lands were nevertheless intrinsically European. Yet my focus here is less on the decision of certain Jews to leave the European coffeehouse, and Europe as well, than it is on their attempts to enter these institutions and then employ them as social space, in so doing engaging in a culture of consumption.

Scholarship on consumption has stressed the purchase-elements of identity in modern, consumer-oriented societies.[4] These studies, focusing primarily on Western Europe in the nineteenth and twentieth centuries, have examined how products and the spaces in which they are consumed and displayed are employed to express modern, fluid identities. Yet, far from reflecting upon merely superficial activities or notions of self, the history of consumption has unearthed the political and cultural layers of such everyday activity. These day-to-day habits represent the everyday rituals that both express and reinforce selfhood.[5] Meanings—in the terms of this study, senses of selfhood and belonging—are "social products, ... creations that are formed in and through the defining activities of people as they interact."[6] By entering a coffeehouse and purchasing victuals, individuals purchased entry into a social space that held meaning for them. As a commodity, the meaning of this social space was determined by the owners as well as by the clientele, and the diversity of the latter became apparent in the variety of meanings given to the locale. We will see that for the Jewish residents of Hamburg, Frankfurt, and Berlin, purchasing a space in a coffeehouse could imply the customer's desire to be accepted into general civic life; it could reflect the customer's religious leanings or political orientation; it could serve as a site of professional networking. In all cases, each customer chose to purchase access to a space and participate in it. This participation served to further reinforce the meaning and importance of the site itself. The more Jews came to coffeehouses for business or out of a desire to participate in the larger civic life, the more the site represented their interests and needs. We will begin by examining the case of Hamburg, where Jews used the coffeehouse for outsider consumption. There the coffeehouses became exemplary sites for the general Jewish quest for a place in the city's civic world. Thereafter we will turn to the cases of Frankfurt and Berlin, both examples of insider consumption.

Hamburg and the Coffeehouse Riots

Cafés in Hamburg in the early nineteenth century played the unlikely role of staging ground for a debate over Jewish emancipation and the place of Jews in the city's civic spaces. In a sense, Jewish "conspicuous consumption" in the cafés was understood by all participants as an attempt to buy a place in Hamburg's public. Jewish sociability and consumption in coffeehouses was, thus, intrinsically connected to a world of discourse—both spoken and written (through the many periodicals available),[7] and sometimes, though more rarely, violent.

In 1819, 1830, and 1835 the city of Hamburg witnessed anti-Jewish riots, all of which first erupted in cafés on the Jungfernstieg (a prominent downtown street on the *Binnenalster*). In all three cases, these expressions of anti-Jewish resentment emerged out of an ongoing debate over the place of Jews in Hamburg's social and political life. The larger intellectual and political debate about Jewish civil rights—which in the late eighteenth century played itself out according to the emancipation quid pro quo—focused on the Jews' collective and individual worthiness of civil rights and was eventually manifested within coffeehouses and in other public spaces.[8] As early as the late eighteenth century, young Jews had begun to frequent coffeehouses; their presence in these spaces had become emblematic of Jewish social amelioration for the Jews who chose to frequent these sites, and further was tied to the larger question of Jewish emancipation at the end of the eighteenth and beginning of the nineteenth centuries.[9] This symbolic meaning was, moreover, not lost on many of the non-Jewish Germans who frequented the same coffeehouses. Jews' entrance into the coffeehouse and their conspicuous consumption in these sites were understood by both Jews and non-Jews alike as an attempt to buy access to Hamburg's public world.

Indeed, prior to the outbursts of violence in 1819, the very presence of Jews in the popular cafés of the city had been subject to public argument. Officially, Jews had not been permitted to enter public spaces of recreation and leisure in Hamburg, though this was repeatedly ignored by coffeehouse owners and their Jewish clientele alike. This general taboo and the breaking of it thus provoked, in 1798 and in 1810, a flurry of pamphlets and writings that equated, ultimately, the place of Jews in Hamburg's cafés with their place in civic society.[10] In addition to being spaces of refreshment, coffeehouses became sites of conspicuous consumption,[11] which further highlighted the Jews' "intrusion" into a largely Christian civic stage. Indeed, the pamphlet debate that took place in 1798 was precipitated by the decision of a coffeehouse owner, a Mr. Heus, in the nearby suburb of Eimsbüttel, to refuse service to Jewish clients. Defenders and critics alike took up their pens to justify or, conversely, deride his decision. One of his supporters, K. Niemann, cited the preexisting regulations preventing Jews from entering such sites and argued that their large numbers discouraged Christians from Hamburg from visiting the café. For Niemann, only when Jews became active and useful citizens (*Staatsbürger*) should they enjoy all the advantages of civil society (*bürgerliche Gesellschaft*), including, apparently, the enjoyment of the social world of the café.[12] The nature and content of this particular debate would repeat itself, though with physical violence, in the coffeehouse riots of 1819 and after.

The violence in Hamburg in 1819 was immediately preceded by an outbreak of riots across parts of the German-speaking lands, the first of which occurred in Würzburg in early August of the same year. Stefan Rohrbacher has argued that the three major anti-Jewish riots in Germany in 1819, those in Würzburg, Frankfurt, and Hamburg, centered on the "symbols of Jewish aspirations for emancipation and Christian unwillingness to accept profound changes in the status of the Jews."[13] The public presence of Jews seemed to correspond to their increased role in society. In this sense the "Hep, Hep! Riots" can be seen as a reaction to the question of Jewish emancipation not only in Hamburg, but more broadly.[14] This thesis is even indirectly corroborated by the Hamburg city senate's report on the causes of the riots: while the Jews were not directly held responsible for the outbreak of the riots, they were considered to have indirectly provoked them by peddling, and by their relatively recent appearance in public spaces, such as coffeehouses, where they were said to visit in groups, speak loudly, dominate the venue, and drive out the other guests.[15] In other words, the perceived conspicuous place of Jews in coffeehouses and other public sites was at the heart of the unrest. By frequenting the prominent coffeehouses in the city center, Jews of Hamburg stressed and displayed the new, more integrated role they desired to play.

The young Jews who frequented these cafés were thus the targets of violence aimed at preventing this consumption. In fact, the first signs of unrest in Hamburg began on Thursday, 19 August 1819, when a young Jewish man was injured as he was forcibly pushed out of a coffeehouse in downtown Hamburg.[16] On the following Sunday (a day when young Jews traditionally visited coffeehouses in Hamburg) a group of young men entered the Elb-Pavillon and accosted various Jewish guests with the cry "Hep, Hep!"[17] One of the assailants even asked a Jewish coffeehouse guest whether the latter was Jewish and what his opinion about recent events was.[18] This case is particularly interesting because it shows that in terms of physical appearance (i.e., clothing, head coverings, and shaving habits), some Hamburg Jews had begun to fashion themselves along non-Jewish norms and were thus "invisible" as Jews in public. In other cases, several Jews who filed police reports were able to name their assailant (though somewhat incorrectly, Rudolphi instead of Ludolphi), suggesting that they had a passing acquaintance with their attackers, who likewise probably knew at least some of the Jewish coffeehouse guests.[19] As such, we cannot assume that those who attacked Jews in coffeehouses or other public spaces were able to identify who was Jewish based on external markers such as dress. This further confirms that Jews, by attending these coffeehouses, desired to purchase, along with their coffee, a place in religiously mixed society and attempted, at least partially, to join in this social space not only through their presence but also through their dress.

A further example illustrating the use of the coffeehouse for outsider consumption can be seen in the case of three young Jewish men and colleagues from East Prussia who were accosted in the Schweitzer Pavillon (another coffeehouse on the Jungfernstieg) on that same Sunday in late August of 1819. In the ensuing altercation, according to the police report, one of the Jewish men, Wilhelm Kalmer, lost a medal he had worn to the coffeehouse. The medal, he added, had been awarded to him by the King of Prussia.[20] It might seem curious that he chose to wear this medal to the coffeehouse; his reasons for this choice are left to speculation. From one perspective, this act can be seen as an attempt to further stress an integrated identification into German culture and society. By this point in late August, anti-Jewish unrest had swept across German-speaking lands. The debate over Jewish emancipation and Jewish "worthiness" of emancipation had taken on a physical dimension, and within this context Kalmer may have thought that in wearing a medal given to him by the King of Prussia he would demonstrate that he had fulfilled his obligations to a German state and thus was worthy of civil rights. From another perspective, his decision to wear a Prussian medal in Hamburg might have been a provocation, pitting one regional identity against another. The medal, especially as a symbol of the state of Prussia and allegiance to the King of Prussia, might have been

particularly galling to the "free" citizens of Hamburg.[21] In any event, by wearing the medal and attending the coffeehouse, Kalmer was intent on displaying
a very clearly integrated sense of belonging—to either a German state or to
German national aspirations.

All of these incidents, however, were merely the prelude to the actual riots.
Le Moniteur Universel reported on 3 September 1819 in an article from Hamburg dated 24 August 1819 that quarrels and fights erupted nearly every night.
If a Jew dared to be seen on a public walkway or enter a coffeehouse frequented
largely by Christians, he would certainly meet violent opposition.[22] The next
day, the same paper published another article from Hamburg arguing that "the
Jews" were to blame for the violence, since they had reportedly instigated the
fighting by attacking Christians in a coffeehouse (Jews were said to have had
a 10–1 advantage). The coffeehouse, according to the report, was very close
to an area of Hamburg where a high concentration of Jews lived.[23] *The Times*
(London) reported: "The persecution of the unhappy Jews does not seem to
have relaxed among the people of Germany. At Hamburg, they were driven on
the … evening of their Sabbath, out of the coffee-houses, and away from the
public walks, to the cry of the dark ages, 'Hep, hep'!"[24]

In the aftermath of the first days of violence, the owner of the Schweitzer
Pavillon decided to ban Jewish guests from entering his coffeehouse—rejecting
Jews both as customers and as members of the social world of the coffeehouse
and Hamburg's public. Blaming the Jews for the violence, Donat Ruben placed
signs in and around his coffeehouse, which read:

> Since the owner of the Pavilion has been made responsible for order and peace
> in this establishment by the local authorities, the owner sees the necessity—in
> order to restore the earlier order and peace—to entirely forbid the entrance
> to this establishment of all Jews—as the only instigators of these incidents of
> unpleasantness.[25]

The case came to the attention of the authorities because of a complaint lodged
by a Jewish customer, Martin Steinthal, who was refused service as a result of
the new policy. According to his testimony (dated 28 August 1819), Steinthal
had gone on the preceding afternoon to the Schweitzer Pavillon. He ordered a
drink but received no reply, so he sat down at a table and was then approached
by one of the coffeehouse workers, who showed him one of the notes. After he
had finished reading the note, the coffeehouse worker said ironically "*Adieu
partez*" and the other customers broke out into laughter; Steinthal left without
another word.[26] By being forced out so, he was told that as a Jew there was no
place for him in this coffeehouse or in the larger society (at least in the opinion
of the coffeehouse owner, his employees, and some of his other guests).

The coffeehouse worker's choice of words, "*Adieu partez*," to oust this Jewish
customer was not coincidental. By speaking to him in French, the coffeehouse
worker inverted Hamburg's recent history and used French as a symbol not of

universal belonging but of exclusion. After all, Hamburg had been occupied and then annexed by France under Napoleon, and during this time the Jews of Hamburg had been granted equal civic and political rights. After the defeat of Napoleonic France, however, this emancipation was reversed. The citizens of Hamburg had, as a result of this defeat and occupation, no great affection for the French, and by telling Steinthal to leave in French, the coffeehouse worker at the Schweitzer Pavillon was playing with the connection between the French occupation and Jewish emancipation, though, as already stated, inverting the connection and using French as a tool to exclude Jewish coffeehouse guests.

In 1830 and 1835, as in 1819, the coffeehouse continued to hold a central place in Christian-Jewish relations, as a focal point in the struggle for civic emancipation and as the nexus for larger political debates more generally. The first element of the context of the 1830 tumult lay in Christian-Jewish relations. Namely, in Hamburg a new angle was emerging in the debate on emancipation, based on a redefined understanding of emancipation. Previously, coffeehouse attendance was used as a sign of one's improvement (amelioration in exchange for civil rights); in the 1830s, coffeehouse attendance had come to be viewed by many Jews in Hamburg as a right they deserved on the basis of their common humanity, a right they did not need to prove by a specific set of behaviors.[27]

O. C. Gaedechens, a contemporary and son of a wealthy merchant family of the city,[28] noted that prior to the unrest young, Jewish men had apparently made themselves unpopular through their supposedly rude behavior in two coffeehouses on the Jungfernstieg. The young Jewish men were said to have been generally loud; on Saturdays, when a larger number of young Jewish men came to the coffeehouses, they were said to have read and practically monopolized French newspapers for hours at a time (much longer than was actually necessary to read the newspapers); further, Gaedechens suggests that these young men provoked the public at one coffeehouse by lighting their cigars before 10:30 PM, which was apparently considered neither customary nor polite; finally, when the Marseilles was played, some of the Jewish guests were said to have whistled and hissed.[29] Naturally, we must take this information with a proverbial grain of salt. Less relevant than the veracity of these claims is the perception of the Jewish presence in the popular coffeehouses on the Jungfernstieg. Again, as before, the coffeehouses in Hamburg remained exemplary places in civic life for public debate and discussion. The Jews' "conspicuous" consumption and attempts to participate in the civil realm challenged forcefully those who would exclude them.

Despite the experience of two previous riots and a total of sixteen years since the first riot to at least hypothetically ease the palpable tension surrounding the issue of the place of Jews in Hamburg public spaces, violence erupted anew in Hamburg in 1835. This time the unrest was precipitated by the attempt of two coffeehouse owners on the Jungfernstieg to close their doors to Jewish customers. First, they dramatically increased the price of coffee for Jewish customers. This did not have its desired outcome, because the young Jews were willing to pay heavily in order to keep visiting the coffeehouse and assert their symbolic rights to a place in Hamburg society.[30] Therefore, on 1 August 1835 the attempt was made to remove the Jews with force. When the young Jews returned the next day, a fight ensued, provoking an anti-Jewish demonstration the day thereafter during which windows of Jewish homes were broken.[31]

This experience of the Jews in Hamburg illustrates the contentious attempts young Jewish men of the city made to participate in the city's coffeehouse and civic life in the early nineteenth century. Though they might have desired to socialize with other Jews or to sit alone, they wanted to do so in the mixed environment of the city's famous coffeehouses and, thus, to be treated as any other Hamburg coffeehouse guest. The Jews involved in the coffeehouse debates in Hamburg used the coffeehouse in order to buy refreshments and purchase social space, as well as to stake a claim to a place in Hamburg and German social and political life through a quest for civic emancipation. Initially, coffeehouse attendance seems to have been linked with the display of civic improvement. Yet by the 1830s Jews argued for a place in public life on the grounds of common human rights. They were quite literally willing to pay any price, returning to cafés where the owners had increased prices for Jewish guests, and then resorting to violence to protect what they believed to be their right to frequent coffeehouses. Their consumption of this space and sense of belonging was precisely the behavior that raised the ire of many non-Jewish coffeehouse guests and owners.

Frankfurt and the Coffeehouse-*gasse*

Jewish coffeehouse attendance in Frankfurt was rarely as fraught or as violent as it was in Hamburg. In this section, we will explore how coffeehouses in Frankfurt became sites for insider consumption. In the following examples, we will see how coffeehouses in the city served a specifically Jewish clientele that sought to socialize together. Attendance in these cafés permitted Jews to display and consume a variety of Jewish senses of belonging with other Jews through conversation and access to the Jewish press. Though Jewish coffeehouse consumption in Frankfurt did not arouse rioting, exclusion did play a role in the creation of the first Jewish-owned coffeehouses in Frankfurt am Main.

According to Paul Arnsberg, the impetus for the establishment of a coffeehouse owned and operated by a Jewish Frankfurter resulted from the unpleasant experiences of a French Jew by the name of Singer who was asked to leave a café in Frankfurt in the very early years of the nineteenth century. Not willing to take the insult lightly, he and a friend decided that they should invest in the opening of a Jewish-owned café. By 1811 Frankfurt was home to not one but three Jewish-owned coffeehouses.[32] Thus, for the better part of the nineteenth century, Jewish coffeehouse life in Frankfurt am Main centered around these three cafés, which were located in or immediately adjacent to the *Judengasse* (or old ghetto). As we will see, on account of their ownership, clientele, and geographic location, these three coffeehouses clearly exemplify insider consumption. Café Hecht, the first to open, was originally owned by Abraham Hecht; the next to open was Café Gundersheim (as of 1855 Café Goldschmidt), owned by two brothers: Moses and Joseph Gundersheim. Finally, Abraham Salomon Sichel opened Café Sichel (later Café Levy) as a kosher coffeehouse.[33] All three were located very close to the synagogue: Café Hecht was located directly across from it;[34] Café Gundersheim was situated two houses down (west) from it;[35] and Café Sichel was right next to the synagogue, but on its east side.[36] In other words, upon leaving the synagogue Frankfurt Jews only had to turn left and walk to the next building, or alternatively walk across the street, or turn right and walk two houses down, in order to visit a café. Helga Krohn and Rachel Heuberger note that even in the last third of the nineteenth century, many observant Jews still frequented the coffeehouses before morning prayers.[37]

Yet despite their location and proximity to the synagogue, from the beginning the three cafés had very different relationships to traditional religious observance. Only Café Sichel (later Café Levy) was kosher; Café Hecht was open on Saturdays; and Café Gundersheim raised the ire of the conservative members of the Jewish community and Rabbi Hirsch Halevi Horowitz in 1813 when the owners decided that the café would stay open on Tisha B'av (a fast day commemorating the destruction of the first and second temple).[38] Clearly, not all forms of insider, Jewish consumption, then, had to follow the same level of observance. These cafés offered their clientele the ability to purchase access to sites where Jewishness—in a number of different guises—was displayed. In these sites, the owners as well as the majority of the clientele subscribed to a religious (though at various levels of observance), cultural, historical, and even, later, national understanding of Jewishness. By attending such coffeehouses they stressed their belonging within the Jewish community, but they also stressed their apart-ness from other, non-Jewish cafés and thus from parts of non-Jewish society, at least during the early years of the Jewish coffeehouses in Frankfurt.

With the opening of the ghetto walls in 1808 and the granting of residential freedom to Jews in 1811, the Jewish population slowly moved out of the *Judengasse* and into other sections of the city. This broadened the geographical scope of the coffeehouse experience for the Jews of Frankfurt. Nevertheless, in 1895, for instance, 44.4 percent of the population of Ostend (the region between Anlagenring and Tiergarten, and between Sandweg and Hanauer Landstrasse) was Jewish.[39] Since the western border of the Ostend is not far from the old Jewish ghetto, the geographic displacement was not necessarily particularly great. As such, it should come as no surprise that Café Goldschmidt (earlier Café Gundersheim) remained popular among Frankfurt Jews.

In fact, of the three previously mentioned coffeehouses, only one, Café Goldschmidt, survived into the twentieth century. After changing ownership in 1855, the new owners began a series of renovation projects that resulted in the expansion of the coffeehouse to three times its original size.[40] We can surmise that the owners of Café Goldschmidt were able to effectively out-compete the neighboring cafés and eventually monopolize Jewish coffeehouse life near the old ghetto. And despite the gradual demographic shift out of the ghetto and toward other sections of the city, until 1925 Café Goldschmidt had a reputation for serving a predominantly Jewish clientele. Known by locals as Café Jonteff (*Yom Tov*), it became the meeting place of Jewish small businessmen, traders, and merchants.[41] The continued Jewish character of this coffeehouse—characterized by both its ownership and by the majority of those who frequented the café and self-consciously consumed both coffee and sociability in a relatively homogenous milieu—is perhaps less surprising given its geographical location (downtown) and historical connection to pre-emancipation Jewish life in Frankfurt.

Yet other evidence suggests that Café Goldschmidt was not entirely exceptional and that Jews tended to frequent certain cafés over others long after the ghetto walls had been destroyed and civic emancipation had been achieved. In doing so, they created de facto Jewish cafés (Jewish because of their clientele, not ownership) in traditionally non-Jewish areas. Café Bauer on Schillerstrasse (in the downtown area), for instance, had the reputation of catering to a Jewish clientele. Opening on 19 September 1884, the café had 120 newspapers in numerous languages, including Russian and Polish. It was considered, as a result, a central gathering place for foreigners. In addition, the café subscribed to *Der Israelit* and the *Israelitisches Familienblatt*, both of which appealed specifically to the German-Jewish reading public.[42] Even observant Jews came to the café on Saturday because credit was extended so that Jewish guests did not need to pay on Shabbat.[43] Finally, the café was also home to the Zionist *Stammtisch* after 1897.[44] Thus, both Café Goldschmidt and Café Bauer are examples of coffeehouses that catered to and were frequented by a predominantly Jewish clientele—but these were Jews of different self-identifications: religious and observant, national, and liberal. The extension of credit on Shabbat permitted observant Jews to consume a warm and fresh cup of coffee while remaining observant in the company of others of the same faith. Yet for Jews who were not particularly (or at all) religious, this same space still offered something special—a very specifically Jewish milieu, defined according to changing parameters of what it meant to be Jewish. Going to such a coffeehouse involved a very different sense of and quest for belonging than going to a coffeehouse where the majority of those in attendance were not Jewish.

Whereas a number of young Jews in Hamburg in the early nineteenth century seemingly sought out religiously mixed cafés where they could purchase a space in this mixed sociability and, with it, a place in larger Hamburg society, a significant proportion of Jews in Frankfurt appear to have opted for a more homogenous social environment, made varied and heterogeneous only by the multiple forms of Jewishness on display in each café. Instead of moving further apart, both literally and figuratively, Jews in Frankfurt remained bound to one another through the coffeehouse, even after they abandoned the more stringent aspects of religious observance.

Performing Jewishness in Berlin

Berlin, though not nearly as synonymous with cafés as Vienna, is nonetheless famous for the coffeehouse life it offered. Here, too, examples can be easily found of Jews who visited certain coffeehouses over others and displayed in these coffeehouses a particularly Jewish sense of belonging. As in Frankfurt, the coffeehouse in Berlin was an ideal institution for Jews to meet with like-minded coreligionists for ideological, professional, or social reasons. It was also even literally a stage on which Jewish belonging could be displayed to other coffeehouse guests. Unlike in Frankfurt, though, all the coffeehouses under discussion were owned by non-Jews (though it should be noted that Berlin offered numerous Jewish-owned cafés and restaurants, some of which were also, unsurprisingly, kosher).

By the late eighteenth and early nineteenth centuries, the beginnings of the local café culture had begun to take shape in the city.[45] Yet the cafés and coffeehouse life that gained fame and interest in Berlin rose to prominence only in the late nineteenth century and flourished in the 1920s. Of special interest have been the so-called literary coffeehouses, where intellectuals, writers and *bohèmes*—both Jewish and non-Jewish—gathered to meet, write, and while away entire days in the often smoky confines of the coffeehouse, Jewish artists among them. Nevertheless, the bohemian coffeehouse model did not monopolize the café culture of the city.

Café Bauer in Berlin (owned by Matthias Bauer, also the proprietor of the Café Bauer in Frankfurt am Main, mentioned above) was a very popular, bourgeois, religiously mixed, Viennese-style café on the corner of Unter den Linden and Friedrichstrasse.[46] The latter was a boulevard with more than 250 "places to drink and eat, guesthouses, restaurants, [and] stores selling victuals. Certain buildings, in fact, [bring] together up to three businesses of these kinds: a hotel, a café and beer hall, under one and the same roof."[47] As such, this important street was nearly synonymous with consumption and leisure in late nineteenth-century Berlin. Additionally, the Café Bauer was popular among the Jewish population of Berlin and served as the subject for a series of oil paintings done by the Jewish artist Lesser Ury. The paintings depicted the bourgeois setting of the café, often at night.[48]

Location, as we have seen in Frankfurt, played a role in the choice of cafés. Café Bauer, as we saw, was situated at the heart of imperial Berlin and offered a space both cosmopolitan and bourgeois. As such, it allowed guests to buy a sense of belonging into a culturally heterogeneous milieu that was, nevertheless, socially and economically much more homogenous (i.e., bourgeois). At the same time, it was only two kilometers away from the Scheunenviertel, where many Jews lived (predominantly poorer Jews who had left Eastern Europe in response to the growing turmoil at the tail end of the nineteenth century) and several important synagogues were located.[49]

Café Bauer provided an excellent work space. Cafés in general offered excellent sites where small groups and associations could meet, informal business transactions be performed, and journalists and writers write. The vast array of newspapers often present in coffeehouses and definitely available at Café Bauer was also a decisive pull factor for a number of coffeehouse patrons. Hirsch Hildesheimer, son of the rabbi for the Orthodox community of Berlin (Adass Jisroel) and himself an instructor at the Orthodox *Rabbinerseminar*, went to Café Bauer every afternoon. Even on Shabbat he would go to the café, taking one of his children with him. The only time, in fact, that Hirsch Hildesheimer did not go to Café Bauer was during Passover.[50] Hildesheimer's choice of *Stammcafé* appears to have been based less on its relative proximity to *Gipsstrasse* where the Hildesheimer family lived and the Orthodox synagogue was located, than on what could be purchased there for a cup of coffee. For him, the coffeehouse was not only a comfortable social space. As the editor of the *Jüdische Presse* and a man dedicated to both neo-Orthodoxy and Jewish nationalism, he was known to go daily to Café Bauer, where he would sit "surrounded by a giant mountain of all the authoritative newspapers that came out in Germany in order to write down or cut out all that could interest his readership."

> Everyone knew him there, of course; often he was the focal point of a large circle, since everyone knew that one could meet him up on the second floor, to the right, at his particular table in the late morning, around 12 PM. How often he would be sought out, badgered, bothered by one person or another, distracted from his work, which was so important to him.[51]

It did not, it appears, matter that the establishment was not kosher. We may presume, on the basis that the Frankfurt Café Bauer provided credit for Jews who came on Shabbat, that similar arrangements were made in Berlin and Hildesheimer did not pay on Saturday. For Hirsch Hildesheimer, the café's importance came in its massive collection of newspapers; Café Bauer, after all, boasted a newspaper directory unsurpassed in Berlin, carrying over 300 periodicals.[52] Hildesheimer's consumption of the coffeehouse space at Café Bauer allowed him to meet with colleagues and also merge the physical space of the café with the virtual space of the Jewish press. For Hildesheimer, Café Bauer was as much a site for socialization and business as it was a site for inner Jewish consumption.

One of the key ingredients of Café Bauer's success among its Jewish clientele was that the owner offered his guests a cosmopolitan space. The wide variety of newspapers appealed to a broad and educated public, and the willingness to accommodate the differing needs of the clientele in the end resulted in the creation of an ideal place of leisure for Jewish guests, a place where Jews could feel comfortable being openly Jewish—asking for credit on Shabbat or reading Jewish newspapers (among other publications). Matthias Bauer, a non-Jew, desired to create a cosmopolitan space and enabled this through his choice of location (in the heart of the capital city), the variety of reading material, and his eagerness to serve all clients. For this reason, Hildesheimer and his children were naturally not the only Jewish customers at Café Bauer.

The coffeehouse's potential openness, as it was exemplified in Café Bauer, could also be a cause for anxiety among more traditional members of the Jewish community. In the early years of the twentieth century, prior to the First World War, a joke circulated suggesting that Café Loy, situated on *Oranienburgerstrasse* and very near the liberal Neue Synagoge, was frequented by liberal Jews on Yom Kippur. These customers, again according to the joke, could find a sign pointing them to table in the back room that was supposedly set for those individuals who were "fasting."[53] According to a version told by Gershom Scholem, who did not mention the venue by name, "[m]alicious souls used to say in the years before World War I that a headwaiter stood at the entrance to the well-known restaurant next to the Grosse Synagogue on Oranienburger Strasse (corner of Artilleriestrasse) and addressed the guests in their holiday finery as follows: 'the gentlemen who are fasting [for Yom Kippur] will be served in the back room.'"[54] Jokes often exaggerate or distort reality, yet they also suggest larger social and cultural anxieties. In the case of this particular joke, one of the many divisions within the Jewish population of Berlin is exposed and ridiculed, namely that between the liberal and neo-Orthodox. Thus, even though one can speak of an internal Jewish coffeehouse model, it should be stated that this model does not reflect a homogenously Jewish coffeehouse experience.

A further example of the variety of the insider consumption can be seen in the case of Café Monopol. A short walk north from Café Bauer on Friedrichstrasse, one arrived at Café Monopol (at the Friedrichstrasse train station), the *Stammcafé* of actors, literary figures, and Zionists in the late nineteenth century.[55] With the increased number of Eastern European Jewish immigrants to Germany and more specifically to Berlin, the internal dynamic of coffeehouse life mirrored this demographic shift in Berlin more broadly. Café Monopol was the home to the Eastern European Zionist *Stammtisch*, attended by Menachem

Ussishkin, Shalom Aleichem, and Shalom Asch.[56] Occasionally German-Jewish Zionists came to visit, but the two groups did not tend to interact much with one another.[57] This fact thus points again to a fault line within the Jewish community—this time based on country of origin—and within the internal model of Jewish interaction. After all, while both groups certainly represented examples of the internal Jewish model of coffeehouse use, the fact that both groups remained distinct and divided also demonstrates that even within this bifurcated model (internal versus external coffeehouse interaction) subdivisions could and did exist. As further evidence of these subdivisions, we can point to the later existence, still prior to the First World War, of a Yiddish table at the Café Monopol, which stood in full view of the Hebraist table.[58] Yet Zionists and Yiddishists were not the only Jewish participants in the life of Café Monopol. Itamar Ben-Avi, son of Eliezer ben-Yehuda, observed that this café was frequented by intellectuals, actors and actresses, and, "in short, German-Jewry in its entirety," as well as Jews from abroad.[59]

However, the (Eastern European) Zionist *Stammtisch* at Café Monopol most clearly exemplified the use of coffeehouses as sites for the consumption of access to inner-Jewish belonging. First, in spite of the fact that the guests sat in a café in Berlin, the participants of the "Israeli corner" spoke only Hebrew with one another. And though the café was not owned or run by Jews, the non-Jewish waiters greeted the Zionists with "Shalom," thereby recognizing the distinctly Jewish, nationalist self-identification of these particular coffeehouse guests.[60] Finally, the members of this *Stammtisch* even staged a Purim *spiel* at the Monopol, literally performing their Jewishness for each other and anyone else in the coffeehouse.[61]

During the Weimar Republic, the site of the Zionist *Stammtisch* moved to the Romanisches Café, this de facto literary salon frequented by Else Lasker-Schüler, Leah Goldberg, Erich Kestner, and Joseph Roth. At the same time, this café also was home to regular tables for Yiddishists and Bundists as well as the aforementioned Zionists.[62] In then end, like Frankfurt am Main, Berlin at the end of the nineteenth century and into the twentieth offered Jewish coffeehouse guests multiple venues to consume, display, and exhibit the various guises of Jewish belonging.

Conclusion

By exploring the Jewish experience in cafés in Frankfurt, Berlin, and Hamburg, this article has demonstrated how everyday consumptive practices, such as drinking coffee and thereby buying access to a social and civic world, were part of a dialogue within and outside the Jewish community on the place of Jews in the society. It illustrates the Jews' self-identification and senses of belonging to a number of guises of Jewishness over the long nineteenth century. In addition, it has highlighted Jewish attempts and negotiations to be an integral part of the wider, German society. The examples of Frankfurt and Berlin suggest that being Jewish in Germany, even as late as the 1920s, did not necessarily imply the complete assimilation assumed by so many narratives of German-Jewish history, but even in instances of dissimilation or the rejection of integration, the examples still show how embedded Jews of Germany were in their European homes. We can see here that coffeehouse life afforded the customers the opportunity to buy into a particular form of Jewish belonging—religious, business, or nationalist—and display it for others to see. This element of display—conspicuous consumption as it were—was also important for the Hamburg case. Yet the coffeehouse in Hamburg was used by Jews to display a modern, emancipated sense of belonging and make claims to German civil equality, while at the same time displaying a vocal and pronounced adherence to their Jewishness. After all, the Jews who attended the coffeehouses in Hamburg did so as Jews. They remained Jews and desired a place in the coffeehouse and Hamburg society as Jews.

I have argued here that the coffeehouse served as a site for the display and consumption of two broadly defined forms of Jewish selfhood: one that was specifically Jewish—religiously, nationally, or culturally—and consumed at times even in relatively homogenous social environments, and another posited on the self-conscious drive toward integration into the social and political community of nineteenth-century Germany. While I have argued that the meaning of their conspicuous consumption can be found in a quest for emancipation and the recognition of their civic improvement or human rights—and I still maintain that this argument is relevant and applicable—we should also ask what this meant for Jews at the time on a practical, social level. The quest for emancipation does not seem to have altered the positive interaction between Jews and non-Jews, and it even encouraged, at least in the short run, a rapprochement. And conversely, Jews who visited coffeehouses owned and frequented by non-Jews but who at the same time chose to openly display their Jewishness by reading Jewish newspapers, speaking in Hebrew or Yiddish, requesting credit on Shabbat, and meeting with other Jewish guests did not necessarily merely represent an inner-Jewish coffeehouse experience; rather, the degree of comfort and belonging they felt within the wider society by attending these coffeehouses was reflected in their ease at expressing a part of themselves that certain modern Jewish thinkers had suggested be left in the private world of the home (or tent, as the case may be). In other words, in a sense, the Jews of Hamburg succeeded, as seen in the later examples of Frankfurt and Berlin: Jews did become integrated in at least some public venues, even though the form of integration was not necessarily what the Jews of Hamburg had anticipated. Being Jewish and integrated in the coffeehouse in the late nineteenth century meant, in a sense, that one was able to be openly Jewish.

Notes

1. Theodor Herzl, *Altneuland* (Vienna, Basel, and Stuttgart: Hans Deutsch Verlag, 1962), 6. My translation.
2. Michael Burri, "Theodor Herzl and Richard von Schaukal: Self-Styled Nobility and the Sources of Bourgeois Belligerence in Prewar Vienna," in *Rethinking Vienna 1900*, ed. Steven Beller (New York and London: Berghahn Books, 2001), 122.
3. For some time now, the coffeehouse has gained attention from historians of Europe, especially from scholars of early modern England. See Markman Ellis, *The Coffee House: A Cultural History* (London: Weidenfeld and Nicolson, 2004) and Brian Cowan, *The Social Life of Coffee: The Emergence of the British Coffeehouse* (New Haven and London: Yale University Press, 2005). Most recently, scholars of Jewish history have turned their attention to the role of cafés in Jewish life. For instance, see the volume of *Cahiers du Judaïsme* 26 (2009) dedicated entirely to the topic of Jewish life in cafés. Also consider the recent conference, the Viennese Café as an Urban Site of Cultural Exchange (October, 2008), whose articles are published in a forthcoming volume from Berghahn Books (2010).
4. Earlier works on the subject include Alon Confino and Rudy Koshar, "Régimes of Consumer Culture: New Narratives in Twentieth-Century German History" *German History* 19, no. 2 (2001): 135–161 and Marion A. Kaplan, "Redefining Judaism in Imperial Germany: Practices, Mentalities, and Community" *Jewish Social Studies* 9, no. 1 (2002): 1–33. More recently, see Marline Otte, *Jewish Identities in German Popular Entertainment, 1890–1933* (Cambridge: Cambridge University Press, 2006) and Leora Auslander, "The Boundaries of Jewishness, or When is a Cultural Practice Jewish?" *Journal of Modern Jewish Studies* 8, no. 1 (2009), 47–64.
5. In this vein, Michel de Certeau has proposed that buying and selling are not simply economic activities: while the producer and advertiser create meaning for a given product, the consumer too imbues a commodity with his or her own meaning, often against the original intent of the advertiser, producer, or distributor. Michel de Certeau, *L'invention du Quotidien, Vol. 1: Arts de faire* (Paris: Union Générale d'Éditions, 1980).
6. Herbert Blumer, *Symbolic Interactionism: Perspective and Method* (Berkeley, Los Angeles, and London: University of California Press, 1969), 5.
7. Katherine Aaslestad, *Place and Politics: Local Identity, Civic Culture and German Nationalism in North Germany during the Revolutionary Era* (Leiden and Boston: Brill, 2005), 107; Ellis, *The Coffee House*; Cowan, *The Social Life of Coffee*.
8. David Sorkin, *The Transformation of German Jewry, 1780–1840* (New York and Oxford: Oxford University Press, 1987); Christian Wilhelm von Dohm, *Ueber die bürgerliche Verbesserung der Juden*, parts I and II (Berlin and Stettin: Friedrich Nicolai, 1781 and 1783).
9. Moshe Zimmermann, "Antijüdischer Sozialprotest? Proteste von Unter- und Mittelschichten 1819–1935," in *Arbeiter in Hamburg: Unterschichten, Arbeiter und Arbeiterbewegung seit dem ausgehenden 18. Jahrhundert*, ed. Arno Herzig, Dieter Langewiesche, and Arnold Sywottek (Hamburg: Verlag Erziehung und Wissenschaft, 1983), 90; Azriel Schochet, *Der Ursprung der jüdischen Aufklärung in Deutschland*, trans. Wolfgang Jeremias (Frankfurt and New York: Campus Verlag, 2000), 65–69, 86–94.

10. Stefan Rohrbacher, "The 'Hep Hep' Riots of 1819: Anti-Jewish Ideology, Agitation and Violence," in *Exclusionary Violence: Antisemitic Riots in Modern German History*, ed. Werner Bergmann, Christhard Hoffmann, and Helmut Walser Smith (Ann Arbor: The University of Michigan Press, 2002), 33.

11. Aaslestad, *Place and Politics*, 174–175.

12. K. Niemann, "Etwas zur Berichtigung der Urtheile des Publikums, über die bekannte öffentliche Anziege des Herrn Heus in Eimsbüttel" (Hamburg, 1798), 7–9, 31; Rohrbacher, "The 'Hep Hep' Riots," 33; Franklin Kopitzsch, *Grundzüge einer Sozialgeschichte der Aufklärung in Hamburg und Altona 2. Ergänzte Auflage* (Hamburg: Verein für Hamburgische Geschichte, 1990), 510–511.

13. Rohrbacher, "The 'Hep Hep' Riots," 31; Stefan Rohrbacher, *Gewalt im Biedermeier: Antijüdische Ausschreitungen in Vormärz und Revolution (1815–1848/49)* (Frankfurt and New York: Campus, 1993), 136, 145, 146–147. The Jewish homes that were attacked during the riots were outside of the traditional Jewish area.

14. This is the thesis of Katz's and Rohrbacher's work: see Jacob Katz, *Die Hep-Hep-Verfolgungen des Jahres 1819* (Berlin: Metropol Verlag, 1994) and Rohrbacher, *Gewalt* and "The 'Hep Hep' Riots."

15. Katz, *Die Hep-Hep-Verfolgungen*, 69.

16. Ibid., 60.

17. Staatsarchiv Hamburg, Polizeibehörde-Kriminalw. C, Jg. 1819, No. 108: Bl. 1 and 2. The term Hep, Hep has various possible etymologies; see Katz, *Die Hep-Hep-Verfolgungen*, 29, note 63.

18. Staatsarchiv Hamburg, Polizeibehörde-Kriminalw. C, Jg. 1819, No. 108: Extractus Protocolli Senatus Hamburgensis, dated Friday, 27 August 1819.

19. Staatsarchiv Hamburg, Polizeibehörde-Kriminalw. C, Jg. 1819, No. 108: Bl. 1.

20. Staatsarchiv Hamburg, Polizeibehörde-Kriminalwesen C Jahrgang 1819, No. 199, 1–4.

21. Katherine Aaslestad has pointed to the growth of regional identity in the wake of the anti-Napoleonic wars in Hamburg; see Aaslestad, *Place and Politics*.

22. *Le Moniteur Universel* (Paris), Friday, 3 September 1819.

23. *Le Moniteur Universel* (Paris), Saturday, 4 September 1819.

24. *The Times* (London), 2 September 1819.

25. "Da der Besitzer der Pavillons, von Seiten der hiesigen Behörde, für Ordnung und Ruhe in diese [sic] Locals verantwortlich gemacht; so sieht derselbe sich genöthigt; um die frühere Ordnung und Ruhe wieder herzustellen der sämtlichen Judenschaft, als einzige Uhrheber [sic] aller diese Unannehmlichkeiten, hiemit den Zutritt in diese Locals, gänzlich zu verbieten." Hamburg Staatsarchiv, Polizeibehörde-Kriminalw. C Jahrgang 1819 No. 120.

26. Staatsarchiv Hamburg, Polizeibehörde-Kriminalw. C, Jg. 1819, No. 120.

27. This view was promoted and found expression in the work of Gabriel Riesser—lawyer, Jew, and coffeehouse guest. Riesser wrote several pamphlets on the question of Jewish civic emancipation, worked in coordination with the Hamburg city Senate on a commission for the discussion of the conditions of the local Jews, and ultimately participated in the Frankfurt National Assembly in 1848. In his *Vertheidigung der bürgerlichen Gleichstellung der Juden gegen die Einwürfe des Herrn Dr. H. E. G. Paulus*, Riesser argued that Jews should be accorded equality unconditionally (that

is, without further civic or religious improvement). Gabriel Riesser, *Vertheidigung der bürgerlichen Gleichstellung der Juden gegen die Einwürfe des Herrn Dr. H. E. G. Paulus* (Alton: Johann Friedrich Hammerich, 1831).

28. Mosche Zimmermann, *Hamburgischer Patriotismus und deutscher Nationalismus: Die Emanzipation der Juden in Hamburg, 1830–1865* (Hamburg: Hans Christian Verlag, 1979), 32.

29. Gaedechens, *Unpartheyische Darstellung*, 1–2.

30. Zimmermann, *Hamburgischer Patriotismus*, 48; Zimmermann, "Antijüdischer Sozialprotest," 92–93; Helga Krohn, *Die Juden in Hamburg, 1800–1850: Ihre soziale, kulturelle und politische Entwicklung während der Emanzipationszeit* (Frankfurt am Main: Europäische Verlagsanstalt, 1967), 62.

31. Zimmermann, *Hamburgischer Patriotismus*, 48–49; Arno Herzig, "Die Juden in Hamburg, 1780–1860," in *Die Juden in Hamburg, 1590 bis 1990*, ed. Arno Herzig with Saskia Rohde (Hamburg: Dölling and Galitz, 1991), 71.

32. Paul Arnsberg, *Bilder aus dem jüdischen Leben im alten Frankfurt* (Frankfurt am Main: Waldemar Kramer, 1970), 171–172. Arnsberg provides an overview of many Frankfurt coffeehouses, which Jews visited from the early nineteenth century to the mid twentieth; see pp. 165–195.

33. Arnsberg, *Bilder aus dem jüdischen Leben*, 172.

34. Institut für Stadtgeschichte Frankfurt am Main, S3 / R9743.

35. Jüdisches Museum Frankfurt am Main archive, A 156.

36. Jüdisches Museum Frankfurt am Main archive, A 850, D305.

37. Rachel Heuberger and Helga Krohn, *Hinaus aus dem Ghetto… Juden in Frankfurt am Main, 1800–1950* (Frankfurt am Main: S. Fischer, 1988), 93–95.

38. Arnsberg, *Bilder aus dem jüdischen Leben*, 173–174.

39. Heuberger and Krohn, *Hinaus aus dem Ghetto*, 92.

40. Café Gundersheim was located on Bornheimerstrasse 5r from around 1837 to 1856, at which point the street was renumbered; its new address became Bornheimerstrasse 8: *Frankfurter Adress-Buch 1837* (Frankfurt am Main: Georg Friedrich Krug, 1837), 45; *Staats- und Adress-Handbuch der freien Stadt Frankfurt 1856: Dritten Theils erster Abschnitt: Handlungs-Adressbuch* (Frankfurt am Main: Georg Friedrich Krug, 1856), 27. The property on Allerheiligenstrasse was added ca. 1868/69: *Adress- und Geschäfts-Handbuch von Frankfurt am Main 1868/69 2. Theil* (Frankfurt am Main: Mahlau and Waldschmidt, 1868), 158.

41. Wolfgang Klötzer, *Zu Gast im alten Frankfurt* (Munich: Hugendubel, 1990), 136; Arnsberg, *Bilder aus dem jüdischen Leben*, 175; Institut für Stadtgeschichte Frankfurt am Main, S 3 / R 4000: Paul Arnsberg, "Von morgens sechs bis nachts um fünf," *Frankfurter Allgemeine Zeitung*, no. 301, Wednesday, 28 December 1966, 24.

42. *Der Israelit* was a neo-Orthodox weekly newspaper, and the *Israelitisches Familienblatt* was also a weekly that, though religiously more liberal, still tried to cater to Jews of all religious expressions and ultimately became "the most widely circulated Jewish periodical of Imperial and Weimar Germany." David A. Brenner, *Marketing Identities: The Invention of Jewish Ethnicity in Ost und West* (Detroit: Wayne State University Press, 1998), 31.

43. Institut für Stadtgeschichte Frankfurt am Main, S 3 / R 4000: Arnsberg (1966), 24.

44. Arnsberg, *Bilder aus dem jüdischen Leben*, 182.
45. Renate Petras, *Das Café Bauer in Berlin* (Berlin: Verlag für Bauwesen, 1994), 22, 26–29. The first café in Berlin opened in 1721. It was a Café-Konditorei, an establishment that sold coffee as well as pastries and cakes. Alfred Rath, "Berliner Caféhäuser (1890–1933)" in *Literarische Kaffeehäuser, Kaffeehausliteraten*, ed. Michael Rössner (Vienna, Cologne, and Weimar: Böhlau, 1999), 109.
46. Arnsberg , *Bilder aus dem jüdischen Leben*, 181.
47. Jules Huret, *Berlin um Neunzehnhundert*, trans. Nina Knoblich (reprint of 1909 edition, Berlin: Tasbach, 1997).
48. One reproduction was printed in the journal *Ost und West*; the original was owned by the Jewish gynecologist Dr. Leopold Landau. *Ost und West*, January 1905, Heft 1, 25–26.
49. Carolin Hilker-Siebenhaar, ed., *Wegweiser durch das jüdische Berlin* (Berlin: Nicolai, 1987), 59.
50. Henriette Hirsch, *Erinnergungen an Meine Jugend* (Leo Baeck Institute Memoir Collection, Jüdisches Museum Berlin, Reel 38).
51. Ibid., 32.
52. The newspaper directory from 1889 listed 348 titles from Africa, America, Asia, Australia, and, naturally, many from Europe. Apparently, at any given moment the café had up to 600 publications and staff responsible specifically for providing guests with desired reading materials. Petras, *Café Bauer*, 52; Christopher Grafe, "Café Bauer," *Cafés and Bars: The Architecture of Public Display*, ed. Christopher Grafe and Franziska Bollery (New York and London: Routledge, 2006), 119.
53. Sammy Gronemann, *Sammy Gronemann: Erinnerungen* (Berlin and Vienna: Philo, 2002), 210–211.
54. Gershom Scholem, *From Berlin to Jerusalem: Memories of my Youth* (New York: Schocken Books, 1980), 11.
55. Ibid., 141.
56. Steven E. Aschheim, *Brothers and Strangers: The East European Jew in German and German Jewish Consciousness, 1800–1923* (Madison: University of Wisconsin Press, 1982), 93–94; Stanley Nash, *In Search of Hebraism: Shai Hurwitz and His Polemics in the Hebrew Press* (Leiden: E.J. Brill, 1980), 171.
57. Aschheim, *Brothers and Strangers*, 93–94.
58. Nash, *In Search of Hebraism*, 172.
59. Itamar Ben-Avi, translated and quoted in ibid., 173.
60. Aschheim, *Brothers and Strangers*, 94; Stanley Nash, "Temunot Mi-hug Soharei Ha-Ivrit be'Berlin (1900–1914)," *Association of Jewish Studies Review* 3 (1978): 6.
61. Aschheim, *Brothers and Strangers*, 94; Nash, *In Search of Hebraism*, 172.
62. Nash, "Temunot"; Schachar Pinsker, "Ahavnu meod shaot ha'ashan b'batai ha'kafe…" *Ha'aretz*, 23 May 2008, Tarbut, p. 2.

⤜ 7 ⤛

CONSUMING POWERS

The "Jewish Department Store" in German Politics and Culture

Paul Lerner

The 1908 book *Berliner Warenhäuser* (Berlin Department Stores), by Leo Colze, is liberally quoted in many accounts of the history of department stores in Germany for its vivid descriptions of the early twentieth-century stores' size and splendor, their technological and business innovations, and their novelty and modernity.[1] The book focuses above all on the Kaufhaus des Westens or KaDeWe, according to Colze the most spectacular, most elegant, and most American of the city's "modern store palaces," whose opening in 1907 was accompanied by much fanfare and excitement. Colze evokes this sense of excitement and wonderment in passages like the following:

> An abundance of light streams by us. To the right and left are display windows, one after the other, full of masculine and feminine elegance. A spruced up human stream flows along the street, laughing and flirting, full of life, taking their time. Strollers, people with hats. Further ahead at Wittenberg Platz [site of the KaDeWe] magical rays of light, glistening treasures, silk fabrics, gold brocades, bronzes, bouquets of feathers, window displays like jewelry boxes: the new department store.[2]

Because of its occasionally rhapsodic prose and its paeans to the store's glamour and splendor, Colze's volume is a beloved primary source, a testament to the excitement and fascination generated by the early department stores. In fact, the text was republished in 1989 in a handsome new edition and is proudly displayed in the book section at the KaDeWe today.[3] Yet Colze's book is more than just a celebration of the grandeur of the store and the splendid cornucopia of goods that it offered. Upon closer scrutiny, beneath the celebratory rhetoric, readers may notice Colze's ambivalence about the department store phenomenon and the tensions that run through his characterizations.

Like many other contemporary observers Colze was clearly impressed, even awed, by the department stores' architectural beauty, their feats of engineering and design, their modern commercial methods, and perhaps most of all their appeal to the magical and fantastical. But his book also pays heed to their more ambiguous consequences. For example, he describes the stores as somehow pathological, using metaphors of illness and contagion to characterize their rapid spread and growth. He refers uncritically to a widely circulated cartoon depicting the department store as a giant fan sucking all of Berlin out through its blades. Furthermore, he bemoans that blocks of apartment houses had to be leveled for the construction of the KaDeWe on the Kurfürstendamm, the nascent retail and entertainment center in the western part of the city. Colze also notes that the new department stores were squeezing out smaller merchants and displacing indigenous German businesses with large companies backed by foreign, especially American, capital. He muses, rather sardonically, about the department stores' role in bringing luxury goods to the "little man," calling Wertheim the "master of Berlin's working class." Finally, Colze unsentimentally reports his conclusion that department stores' tremendous profits will soon wane and that their great era has already begun to run its course.

Underlying both his celebrations and his more sober and critical observations is Colze's assumption that department stores represented a powerful force. "There are four rulers in Berlin," he writes, "uncrowned Kaisers, whose iron dominion is heeded as widely as [Wilhelm II's] ... These uncrowned Kaisers are the department stores: Jandorf, Tietz, Wertheim, and since roughly the beginning of the year, the Kaufhaus des Westens."[4] Significantly, he compares the power of the stores, not their owners, to that of the Kaiser. Indeed, Colze stresses the stores' imposing size and scale, and also their power to transform Berlin's urban fabric and to change the lives and habits of its residents, as in the way the KaDeWe turned a previously residential section of Western Berlin into a bustling new commercial district.

Of course Colze was not unique in viewing the department stores and their owners as the source of tremendous economic and also social and cultural power: these types of depictions course through the abundant contemporary literature on department stores by the stores' critics and opponents. A great many of those accounts, as we will see, were motivated by anti-Semitism, and their authors portrayed the department stores as a manifestation of Jewish capitalism, as the latest example of pervasive and nefarious, but often hidden, Jewish economic power.

The proprietors of the three major Berlin department store chains at this time, Jandorf, Tietz, and Wertheim, were in fact of Jewish origin, and Jews owned the great majority, perhaps some 80 percent, of department stores throughout Germany before the Nazi assumption of power in 1933.[5] Colze's readers would have certainly known this: the rich Jewish department store owner had become a literary trope, a political stereotype, even a cultural cliché by this period, and the department store itself was widely perceived as a Jewish phenomenon. But while Colze's treatment shares representational themes with many of the harshest department store critics, his text exhibits a peculiar relationship to anti-Semitic stereotypes. His way of exposing the stores' hidden powers, indeed his portrayal of international capital and big banking as threats to traditional German small business, evokes a whole series of motifs that—often intertwined with anti-Semitic smears—informed most of the contemporary department store critiques. His description of the stores' power to entice throngs of (female) customers—"in thick packs and ceaselessly they stream in: the ruler calls, they follow gladly"—and of their manipulation, even exploitation, of the gullible masses through advertising and spectacle brings to mind salacious rumors of Jews' mysterious hypnotic powers over vulnerable gentiles, particularly gentile women.[6]

A reference to Rabbi Akiva in the middle of the book, however, is one sign that Colze's critique differs from the standard anti-Semitic caricatures. And any questions about Colze's own Jewish background are put to rest by his later discussion of his maternal grandfather, whom he calls the Marshall Field of the 1860s, the "department store king" of his *shtetl*—and indeed by the fact that Colze is actually a pseudonym for Cohn. Colze's critique, and the language he uses, suggest that assumptions about the "Jewish department store" were so deeply ingrained in German culture that they informed the writings of gentiles and Jews alike. It also begins to shed light on the resentment of small Jewish storekeepers toward the Jewish economic elite, a dimension that has been thus far completely overlooked in the historiography of German Jews and department stores. Finally, and most importantly for this essay, Colze's text shows that a belief in the department stores' formidable powers was shared across a broad cultural and political spectrum.

Like the department store itself, significant historical commentary on department stores came to Germany relatively late, and only after it had already appeared in the French, British, and American contexts in the 1980s.[7] Over the last decade or so, though, the historical and sociological literature on consumer culture and consumer society in Germany has grown rapidly and developed into an established field. Nevertheless, scholars have yet to adequately address either the role of Jews in Germany's nascent mass consumerist economy or the political and cultural resonance of the "Jewish department store" in late nineteenth- and early twentieth-century Germany.[8] While Nazi propaganda about department stores has become familiar, and the boycotting and ultimate "Aryanization" of Jewish-owned businesses has received its fair share of historical attention, the existing historiography has little to offer on wider perceptions of the "Jewishness" of department stores and other vehicles of mass consumerism in pre-Nazi Germany.[9]

This historiographic lacuna can be explained in part by the taboos surrounding the idea of "the Jewish department store," as historians are understandably reluctant to sound like they are recapitulating or giving any credence to Nazi and anti-Semitic slurs. It may also have deeper roots in the history of social and economic thought. That is, while the relationship between Jews and capitalism has been theorized from a variety of perspectives from Marx through Werner Sombart and beyond, no equivalent body of thought exists for consumer culture, for assessing the place of Jews not in mechanisms of production or in the circulation and distribution of goods and capital, but rather in marketing, in influencing notions of taste and fashion, and indeed in consumption.[10] These areas of cultural-historical inquiry offer new terrain for a meeting of Jewish history and the history of economy.

This essay takes steps toward filling these historiographic gaps by bringing Jews into the foreground in the history of department stores and mass consumerism in Germany. Specifically, it explores the cultural codes and representational strategies surrounding department stores in early twentieth-century Germany and focuses on the idea and motif that the stores embodied a kind of Jewish economic power. Through a variety of sources, including fiction, economic writings, and anti-Semitic propaganda, I analyze German projections and fantasies around modern consumer society, the upheavals and the possibilities of it, and the place of Jews within those images.

According to most accounts, the 1890s, the time when department stores began appearing in most major German cities and towns, represented the beginning of the German encounter with modern mass culture and emergent mass consumerism, which were experienced by many people as a powerful, almost unstoppable force. This force, the power of nascent consumerism, was seen by twentieth-century regimes and movements alternately as a threat or opportunity, a power that they could try to steer, shape, and modify according to their particular ideological priorities, but that they were unable to curtail.[11] The department store itself was often described in such terms. Enthusiasts and detractors alike stressed the might, power, and scale of both individual stores and of the department store phenomenon as a whole. Or as Herr Griebner, the director of advertising at a fictionalized KaDeWe, says in Erich Köhrer's 1909 novel *Warenhaus Berlin*, "the department store is like a fire whose flames, once ignited, devour ever more."[12]

My hypothesis is that concerns and anxieties about this force, about its impact on "traditional" German life and mores, were to a great extent displaced onto Jews, so that the power of emerging consumer culture and the economic power of Jews were often construed as overlapping or even identical forces. In the years between the turn of the century and the Nazi assumption of power, a period where the department stores—which because of their high volume could set prices low and thanks to their spectacular attractions (and free entry without obligation) could pull in throngs of shoppers and curious observers— appeared to sound the death knell for the German specialty shop. "Appeared" is a key word here because, as historians Uwe Spiekermann and Robert Gellately have both convincingly shown, these specialty shops (*Spezialgeschäfte*) in fact suffered no loss of profits and proved that they could adapt to modern retail culture. Indeed, the period between 1890 and 1914 actually saw a growth in their numbers, while department store proceeds never exceeded 5 percent of total retail activity.[13]

Nevertheless, shopkeeper organizations, precariously positioned between big capital and growing working-class movements, agitated for state protection from the department stores—seeking to enlist the state's powers of taxation and of regulating building and zoning against the apparent powers of the department stores—and in the process drew on and recast old anti-Semitic representations.[14] As such, small merchant associations revived an older discourse of calling on the state to protect its citizens from Jewish capital and then condemning the corrupt state's apparent unwillingness to deprive itself of the benefits of cooperating with the rich Jews.

The would-be historian of the "Jewish department store" is faced with the problem of disentangling discourse from economic reality, of separating the actual economic and cultural power held by Jewish-owned businesses from the hyperbolic claims about Jewish power made by anti-Semites and other contemporary observers. How, furthermore, can historians speak of the "Jewishness" of the department store? Beyond statistical determinations of how many stores were owned by Jews, was there something Jewish about the stores that was experienced, perceived, and communicated by contemporaries? My approach views the department store as a space in which various larger—economic, social, cultural, or "real" and "discursive"—forces and phenomena intersected. I trace the ways that these forces were identified and connected with Jews by both sympathetic and hostile observers and chroniclers of the department store phenomenon.

In some ways these connections still resonate. For example, in 1997 historian Helmut Frei commented that not only were the owners of most major German department stores Jews, but their families actually came from the same area. In fact, the Tietzes, Schockens, Urys, Wronkers, and others, proprietors of leading department store chains in different parts of Germany, hailed from the region around Birnbaum, a *shtetl* in Posen, which for Frei seemed too remarkable to be dismissed as coincidence. "However," he writes, "the exact circumstances in which the department store idea circulated among the Birnbaum Jews is unknown, nor do we know whether the translation of this idea into an innovative act followed a concerted and controlled strategy."[15] Frei, at least, acknowledges in his footnotes that much of his material comes from the work of Nazi economic propagandist Hans Buchner, but he still shows no awareness of how closely his language resembles early twentieth-century notions of a Jewish economic conspiracy.

Frei's claims indicate that the representation of department stores as "Jewish phenomena" still exists and remains intertwined with images of Jewish economic power and economic conquest. In the sizable body of early twentieth-century writings on department stores across a wide variety of media, several themes or representational motifs concerning the Jewish department store recur again and again. The remaining sections of this essay explore four of those recurring themes: the shoddiness of the goods for sale and the chaos of their presentation, the disturbed gender and sexual order that allegedly existed in the stores, the parasitic quality of these so-called "economic vampires," and finally, the motif of violence, fires, and explosions in the department stores.

Critiques of the Jewish department store pointed to the excessive luxury of the stores on the one hand, but simultaneously derided them as cheap or shoddy on the other. Historian Derek Penslar's treatment of the economic position of Jews around the Enlightenment helps explain the roots of this dichotomy, by which Jews were portrayed as either too wealthy or too poor, reflecting their status as "both marginal and empowered within the European economy."[16] In this context, then, Jewish economic power lay on the extremes of a spectrum reaching from the indigent rag trader to the rich department store baron.

The term most often used to denote Jewish-owned department stores in the anti-Semitic press was "Ramschbasare" (junk/rummage bazaar or market). Along with similar expressions like "Schleuderbasare" and "Großbasare," this label condemned the goods for sale as junky or cheap and characterized their presentation as chaotic.[17] It also implied that department store sales methods were underhanded. Essentially identical stores that did not happen to be owned by Jews—the Hertzog Department Store in Berlin, for example—were generally called "Kaufhäuser," a term that carried more dignified, elegant connotations, by the anti-Semitic press.[18] Use of the word "Ramsch," with its Yiddish resonance, further emphasized the Jewishness of the stores and the association of Jews with peddled goods and rummage. Connecting "Ramsch" with the word "bazaar" also served to orientalize the Jewish department store, evoking Middle Eastern or Asian market scenes of stalls crowded with wares and manned by haggling merchants purveying questionable goods at inflated prices.[19]

In the words of anti–department store zealot Paul Dehn in an 1897 work: "Dubious elements have immigrated here from the Orient, where different notions of business morals obtain."[20] Here Dehn conflates Poland, the actual place of origin of many department store entrepreneurs, with Turkey or the Levant, treating both as the East or the Orient. According to F. Roderich

Stoltheim, in his contribution to Theodor Fritzsch's anti-Semitic, series the *Hammer-Schriften* (Hammer-Writings), in which he set out to explain "the riddle of Jewish economic success": "The prototype of the department store is the oriental 'bazaar.'"[21] Dehn and Stoltheim, although separated by three decades, make many of the same arguments. Both contrast the self-serving, corrupt economics of the East with authentic, community-oriented business practices based on German traditions that valued honor and the public good, and both see the department store as an "eastern" phenomenon.[22] Werner Sombart, a far more respectable economic thinker, lamented that the department store had replaced the direct personal interactions between merchant and customer with an abstract, anonymous relationship between faceless masses of customers and distant ownership.[23] Stoltheim made explicit what Sombart had only hinted at: the "Hebrews" (as he put it) subverted older economic principles whereby the quality of goods determines success, with a new, amoral economic ethic solely concerned with maximizing profit.[24]

Of course, this representation could not have been further from the truth. One of the key features of the new department stores, in contradistinction to the smaller specialty shops, was that prices were fixed and displayed. Unsatisfactory goods, furthermore, could often be returned and exchanged, and the wares were set out in an orderly, highly self-conscious fashion, in no way reminiscent of a market stall. But the attacks on Jewish department stores furthered the notion that like Jews themselves, Jewish businesses were trying to "pass": pry under the surface, and an apparently orderly, well-run department store can be revealed to be a debased market scene of fraud and corruption. Hence, the title of one of Dehn's works was "Behind the Scenes at the Modern Store" (*Hinter den Kulissen des modernen Geschäfts*), contributing to the genre of exposing the nefarious hidden workings beneath the glitzy surfaces.

Similarly, the anti-Semitic press delighted in exposing department store accounting errors or cases of extortion or in pointing out, for example, that there was literally a Jew behind the scenes, as in the newspaper *Die Wahrheit's* reporting that the owner of the Kaufhaus Sonntag was none other than a so-called "little Herr Cohn."[25] Likewise, anti-Semitic authors persisted in referring to Adolf Jandorf by his original name, Abraham, to call attention to his Jewishness, and continued to treat members of the Wertheim family as Jews even though they had converted to Christianity.[26]

The idea of the Jew behind the scenes, and indeed the ragged Jew behind the elegant department store facades, resonated far beyond the anti-Semitic public sphere. Take the 1926 novel by the Swedish-Jewish writer Sigfried Siwertz, which was published in German translation in 1928 as *Das Große Warenhaus* (The Great Department Store).[27] The novel tells the story of department store entrepreneur Jeremias Goldmann. Goldmann began life humbly, as a Polish-Jewish rag trader, but emigrated to Sweden and ascended to the heights of

Swedish economy and society by creating Stockholm's largest and most ornate department store. In the novel Goldmann confesses that he enjoys strolling through his store incognito, an activity that evokes legends of rulers passing unrecognized among their people to assess popular moods. Tellingly, Goldmann's appearance and comportment have remained unaltered despite his enormous fortune, and he finds it amusing that no one could take him, such an unassuming, even "shlumpy" figure, for the director of Stockholm's ritziest establishment. He delights in recounting the behavior of a salesgirl who, seeing him in the store, treats him like an undesirable, unserious customer and tries to get rid of him. "Did you leave your money at home, sir?" she asks him patronizingly. Then she tries to steer him to the soap counter. As Goldmann recounts: "The girl was new and couldn't even imagine that this miserable little Yid [kleine mieße Jied] was actually the director, ha, ha, ha."[28] Hence, the scene dramatizes the way in which Goldmann's rag trade, peddler origins lie hidden behind the scenes in the luxury department store. No matter how rich and powerful, the department store owner is still marked by his peddler past, and regardless how elegant and luxurious it might appear on the outside, the store itself still bears the marks of a thinly disguised rummage bazaar.

Related to this theme was the common accusation that the Jewish-owned department stores frequently engaged in unethical, deceptive practices and that their facades masked an underbelly of corruption and opportunism. Critics frequently denounced the stores for fraudulent pricing or unethical sales tricks, such as touting cheaply priced goods in the store windows or in newspaper advertisements, even selling some wares below cost, for the purpose of luring in shoppers and then persuading them to buy more costly items, "reprehensible methods to be sure, but the most effective weapons in bringing down the respectable competition," in the words of J. W. Hausschildt, an early department store opponent.[29] Whether or not these practices actually occurred—and historians should read such sources with a great deal of skepticism—these accusations reflect a salient fear of the stores' power. Indeed, Hausschildt and many other commentators imply that powerful forces radiate from the department store, forces that lure innocent citizens in and then compel them, once inside, to buy what they do not need and to feel a desire for more. Critics like Hausschildt, who condemned the stores for creating false desires and manipulating naïve consumers into buying what they did not need prefigured the critique of the media's and mass culture's manipulative power that gained traction among the postwar European and American left. But in this case, the manipulative power of advertising and consumer culture is equated squarely with the Jews and thus plays on older stereotypes of Jewish duplicity and fraud in business.

Numerous propaganda brochures appeared with the stated goal of protecting the innocent public from these powers and educating citizens about common department store tricks, such as placing high-quality items on the top of stacks of inferior or defective products, claiming to have sold out of the bargain goods promoted in advertisements or in the display windows, and otherwise deceiving through misleading techniques of advertising and display.[30] Department store opponents had to concede that these practices were strictly speaking not illegal, but they charged the stores with violating the spirit of fair competition by preying on naïve, loyal customers who, used to honest, "German" business ethics, were easily duped by such techniques. Simultaneously, the stores' critics repeatedly attempted to strengthen existing laws against unethical business practices (*unlauterer Wettbewerb*) to apply to these methods.

Some contemporaries associated advertising itself with the department stores, the Jews, America, or all three, and many contrasted acceptable forms of product display "Werbung" with crasser and cruder forms of promotion and advertising, which they labeled "Reklame."[31] Sombart, for example, characterized "Reklame" as the modern equivalent of old-fashioned sleeve pulling.[32] In other words, according to his vision of traditional retail, when a potential customer walked down a commercial street, the small shop owners, or their representatives, leaned outside and tried to persuade him to enter their stores. Hence, he imagines that a customer would be pulled, as he puts it, by a "Herr Levy on one sleeve and on the other by a Herr Cohn," each beseeching him to enter and buy in his shop.[33] Advertising of course operated less directly, and replaced the old form of physical intervention, the sleeve tug, with modern, psychological methods. Among its drawbacks, according to Sombart, were that it defaced the beauty of the city, contaminated the culture, and corrupted traditional business practices by seeking to incite consumer desire (*Kauflust*) and operate on the psyche of potential customers. Hausschildt also condemned "Reklame" as inherently deceptive and corrupt. He proposed that display windows only be permitted to show goods for sale—so consumers could judge their quality—and not their prices, to prevent confusion and trickery.[34]

The notion that Jewish stores were chaotic rummage bazaars was also reflected in a growing concern, almost hysteria, over department store fires at the beginning of the twentieth century. Much of this concern was catalyzed by a deadly fire at the Goldberg Brothers' "Paris" Department Store in Budapest in the summer of 1903. In response to the Budapest fire, along with others in such places as Braunschweig, Berlin-Rixdorf, and Karlsruhe, the shopkeeper movement pressed the various German states for stricter building regulations against department stores. They sought to restrict sales areas to the first floor and basement only, tried to limit the number of customers who could be inside the stores at any given time, especially around holidays like Christmas and Easter when the stores filled up with zealous shoppers, and wanted to ban the hiring of female sales employees, seeing women as more prone to panic and hysteria in crisis situations.[35] Many observers, including the leadership of the Department Store Owners Association (*Verband deutscher Waren- und Kaufhäuser*), pointing out that the proposed regulations in many cases only increased the danger of fire, understood that these measures were simply a pretext, an excuse to agitate against the department stores and to make it impossible for them to compete.[36] Within these campaigns, a common assumption was that Jewish stores represented a greater fire danger because of their chaotic heaps of flammable products, their general unruliness, and even their owners' indifference toward public safety, especially after it was alleged that the Goldbergs had disregarded government safety regulations.[37]

The second recurring theme, the notion of a distorted gender order, appeared conspicuously in critiques and even celebrations of the department stores. On one level, the department store was of course a highly gendered space, a place of mainly female consumption, where advertising and display were intended to attract and appeal to women. The relationship between the (Jewish) department store owner and German female sales personnel and customers was vexing to many observers. Various critics in fact complained about gender relations in the stores and warned of the seductive powers of advertising and product display on vulnerable women.

The act of purchasing, the fulfillment of *Kauflust*, was in many cases equated with a kind of sexual expression, an intoxicating rush (*Berauschung*) where passion and desire took over from reason. As a character in the Siwertz novel claims, "the great department stores are constructed for the seduction of women."[38] In the discussion of kleptomania, a problem that attracted a great deal of medical and psychological interest in the early 1900s, stealing was characterized as a cycle of building tension followed by a release.[39] Psychoanalyst Wilhelm Stekel, for one, noted the tendency of women to steal sharp, pointy objects like pencils, in a none-too-subtle Freudian analysis. He was one of many to link sexual desire with the desire for goods and followed in a long medical and psychological tradition in claiming that women were much more likely to steal during menstruation or pregnancy or at times of heightened sexual arousal.[40] In general, the psychiatric perspective saw the department store environment and the temptations of its many wares as often too much to resist, even for otherwise healthy and upstanding women. Although a little bit of *Kauflust* was considered necessary to keep the economy moving, too much female desire was destabilizing and culturally problematic.[41]

What did these discourses on female sexuality, "*Kauflust*," and stealing have to do with Jews? Anti-Semitic writings on department stores picked up on the eroticized encounter between customer and commodity, and the interplay between women as objects of desire and women as buyers, and emphasized the alleged sexual depravity of the department store milieu. The *völkisch* newspaper *Die Wahrheit* portrayed the tea salon in Wertheim's flagship Berlin store as a clandestine spot for sexual liaisons, from which lovers often disappeared into the store's underground tunnels, and chastised Georg Wertheim for exposing young employees, in one case a sixteen-year-old waitress, to such immoral influences.[42] A 1907 issue of the same newspaper accused the store of stocking pornographic literature next to the children's section in its book department. Here again, the discourse depicts the department store as a force of Jewish depravity that intentionally corrupts youthful German innocence.

During the great age of the department store, from around the turn of the century through perhaps the early 1960s, the salesgirl was an icon, a fetishized and sexualized figure. She became a central character in many of the dozens of department store novels that appeared in Germany in these years. Perhaps the prototypical department store girl was Denise, the protagonist of Émile Zola's *Au Bonheur des Dames* (1883), the quintessential department store novel, which clearly influenced works in the German genre. Like Denise, salesgirls in the German novels are described, without fail, as beautiful, young, and blonde, such as young Trude Schneider in Josef Wiener-Braunsberg's 1922 novel *Warenhausmädchen: Roman aus Berlin der Gegenwart* (Department Store Girls: Novel from Present-day Berlin) or Else Bodenstedt, in Oskar Schweriner's *Arbeit: Ein Warenhausroman* (Work: A Department Store Novel) of 1912.[43] Depending on the novel's tone and outcome, they are represented either as good-hearted and pure, or naïve and corruptible and ultimately fallen, as in the case of Marianne Werder in Alexander Sternberg's brutal *Ein Warenhaus-Mädchen: Schicksale einer Gefallenen* (A Department Store Girl: The Fates of a Fallen Woman), a serialized novel of 1909.[44]

Relationships between salesgirls and department store owners were, unsurprisingly, a major theme in the novels and in the yellow press. Some of these fictionalized relationships may have been based on actual scandals, as in the case of Adolf Jandorf, who was accused of having extramarital relations with a series of his employees.[45] Demonstrations against the newly opened KaDeWe were held in Berlin in 1907 and 1908, where Jandorf was condemned for overworking and exploiting his employees, especially around Christmastime, and underpaying and mistreating them.[46] As a result of their poor pay, according to a charge frequently leveled against Jandorf and also Wertheim and Tietz, salesgirls were forced to supplement their income through prostitution.[47] Paul Dehn even accused department store owners of supplying women, namely female employees to male business associates "following Galician customs," an obvious reference to allegations about Jews and the white slave trade.[48] In Hans Vogt's melodramatic one-act play, *Du Kommst zu Spät: Eine Szene aus dem Warenhaus* (You're Late: A Department Store Scene), the department store director, Krajewski, has the lovely salesgirl Klara transferred from the Frankfurt store so he can be near her.[49] The story unravels when he learns that she is engaged to the store's bookkeeper, and the scene ends in rape and murder in the director's office. Finally, in one of the most fantastical accusations, a Berlin department store owner was condemned for keeping a harem of salesgirls at his disposal, although the accusing scandal sheet reassured its readers that the girls found him repulsive.[50]

However, more frequent than these vilifications, at least in the more benign descriptions of several department store novels, are depictions of the store owner as too old and hideous—too dark, too stooped over, and with too big a nose—for the young *Verkäuferin*, and his lust has to be channeled into a kind of gentle paternity, as in the case of Heinrich Heimberg in the Schweriner novel, whose hideous appearance evaporated when he spoke to his employees in his kind, fatherly tones, at which times his true, benevolent self was apparent.[51] Crucially, the Jewish storeowner never gets the girl: his real love and lust object is the store itself. In such a way even Jewish authors kept old anti-Semitic stereotypes in circulation, according to which Jewish men can only love money and business; their erotic and emotional investments follow their capital investments. Romantic or erotic love is strictly for gentiles.

Hence, in *The Great Department Store*, Goldmann metaphorically has a child with his store. The child is conceived in the bedding department—a frequent site of foul play in department store fiction—by an amorous couple just before the man has to ship out to the First World War. The father is killed in the war and the mother dies in childbirth, so Goldmann adopts the child and raises him in the store. "Oh Goldmann, you and your department store are having a child!" snickers his amused decorator.[52]

Department store entrepreneur Friedrich Neulandt in Köhrer's *Warenhaus Berlin* is too unsightly and dispassionate and too obsessed with business to retain the romantic attentions of his beautiful and bored wife, who attempts to trade in her *shtetl* origins for Hollywood glamour by adopting the name "Jane" and whose interests are aroused by a plotting blond cad, a sort of degenerate noble. Neulandt, caught in an irresolvable love triangle between his wife and his store, consummates his love of the Warenhaus Berlin in an orgy of flame (on Easter Sunday, in fact) that engulfs much of the western part of the city.[53]

More sinister representations placed the Jewish capitalist, the department store owner, as the manipulator, the dark force luring naïve women to their downfall—hence the third type of representation, the image of the Jewish department store as a parasite on the German people. Depictions of department stores describe the shop windows, the point of access with the street and the innocently passing public, as "*Fangarme*" (tentacles), "*Bauernfänger*" (peasant catchers), "*Gimpelfang*" (sucker-traps), or "*Mausefälle des Todes*" (deadly mouse traps), denouncing their publicized low prices to bait customers and even their demonic magnetism (*dämonische Anziehungskraft*).[54] In a 1900 newspaper article on the Tietz and Wertheim stores in Berlin, a journalist wrote that the department store owner "has the woman caught in the trap. Now he can trust in the allure of a thousand ringed fingers tempting her to buy something, and he can be certain that even the most thrifty of housewives, who has come because of an unprecedented bargain, will go home weighed down with items she does not need."[55] Many critics charged that by luring in women and tricking them into buying so much, the Jewish department stores were achieving the destruction of the German *Mittelstand*. They expressed this concern in histrionic tones with language full of death imagery and pamphlet covers and cartoons that depicted department stores as mighty, fearsome, and deadly.

One writer, for example, on the occasion of the Kaiser's visit to Wertheim in 1910, even as he confessed admiration for Wertheim's business skills, asked "how many corpses, how many thousands and thousands of existences has he trampled?" in constructing this department store empire.[56] He continued by calling the department store the "gravedigger" of the "honorable middle classes who, standing in loyalty to the Kaiser and the Empire are being driven out of their businesses and their livelihoods in great numbers."[57] Or as a 1903 polemic put it: "Just how little right to existence these department stores have, which endanger the public in the most serious way, is shown by the fact that nearly all of the economic vampires lie in the hands of international Jewish families, whose goal it is to plunder the working classes, to grab Germany's national wealth for themselves and to take hold of the state of the future."[58]

While scholars have called attention to the cinematic theme of the zombie in department stores and malls, an apt metaphor for the mind-numbing and conformity-producing effects of postwar North American hyperconsumption, one might ask what cultural connections can be drawn between vampires and sites of mass consumption on the one hand, and images of the parasitic Jew on the other.[59] In both cases women are the victims, the initial point of contact as the depraved Jewish capitalist (an unwelcome presence from the East) brings the broader community to ruin through his greed and trickery. A 1928 article in the Nazi propaganda sheet *Der Stürmer* made this connection explicit: "The Jew carries out the despoiling of non-Jewish virginity not merely for the satisfaction of his animalistic desires; rather he carries out the violation of non-Jewish bodies according to plan (as [he did] centuries ago!) because he knows that only those peoples whose women-folk lie at the disposal of the Jews can be brought into line with the Jewish plan of world domination."[60] And in 1929 the *Völkischer Beobachter* called for a boycott of Jewish-owned department stores, blaming German women for spending their husbands' money at the stores and thus enabling the construction of "one Jew-palace after another." The Jews, the article continued, were using their profits to "forge the weapons with which to impale your sons."[61] Such discourses intensified and appeared with increasing frequency after the Nazi assumption of power in January 1933.

Wilhelm Stücklen's 1918 play *Purpus* tells the story of the entrepreneur T. T. Purpus, who constructs a grand and ornate department store solely to lure in the object of his obsession, a rather unremarkable woman whom he sees as the embodiment of eternal femininity.[62] This drama, in strong contrast to the passages from the Nazi press, involves no explicit or even implicit anti-Semitism, but it thematizes a similar point: the department store is a powerful vehicle for attracting and seducing German women. Indeed, Purpus knows neither the name nor the address of his beloved, but he (correctly) assumes that if he opens a department store she will have to come.

Purpus serves as an appropriate segue to the fourth and final theme, the motif of fires, violence, and explosions in the department store. In *Purpus*, romantic rejection and unrequited love lead to the department store's destruction at the hands of an "army" of desperate and greedy shoppers, attracted by a sale unprecedented in the size of its markdowns, and ultimately to its fiery end at the hands of Purpus himself. "Clear out the store," is the play's highly fraught concluding line, delivered by Purpus's second-in-command as he catches sight of the fire that Purpus has set.

Fires and other types of violent endings appear with near ubiquity in department store fiction. Here one could include Vicki Baum's 1931 story "Jape im Warenhaus" in which the unfortunate Jape Flint's scheme to wait overnight in a department store so that he can steal a necktie, which he has come to see as the key to winning over his love interest, results in the murder of the store guard and then in an all-consuming fire when Flint attempts to burn the corpse to hide his crime.[63] The fire that destroys Goldmann's store in the Siwertz novel is similarly the result of foul play, the revenge act of someone whose father was caught stealing from the department store. And then there is Manfred Georg's 1928 novel *Aufruhr im Warenhaus* (Uproar in the Department Store), in which the New York department store "Spring," the nest of a plot of Marxist, Bessarabian freedom fighters who have fled Europe after an unsuccessful assassination attempt against an imperial official, becomes an aerial battlefield.[64] Georg's novel, certainly the most outlandish of the genre, ends with aerial war against the rebels, who have taken over the skyscraper department store, eerily prefiguring the American bomber that fell onto the roof of the KaDeWe in 1945.

These fictional fires, together with the repetitious yet often disingenuous warnings about fires by anti–department store crusaders, demonstrate that the obsession was shared across a wide cultural and political spectrum. In the words of a conservative deputy in a 1908 debate in the Prussian Diet:

> Gentlemen, I would like to speak to the great danger to body and life to which visitors to the mighty department stores are subjected the moment they enter these huge spaces … our department stores are growing more and more into mighty, I can only say, enormous structures, and I think it's not an unreasonable assumption when I maintain that the larger a department store is, the more people it can contain, all the more dangerous it is for the residents and especially the shopping public.[65]

Every two or three years the issue resurfaced in the Prussian Diet, especially around Christmastime, when the department stores became particularly crowded. Each department store fire—Bremen in 1903, Halle in 1905, for example—was met with zealous newspaper coverage and new public safety campaigns. Indeed, in literary representations the fires often occurred around major Christian holidays, such as Christmas, and New Year's Eve, suggesting a concern with large numbers of shoppers during the holiday seasons but also, on a metaphorical level, the rapturous, purifying destruction of hubristic Jewish power. For example, in the novel *Warenhaus Berlin,* city officials are concerned that the immense new department store building will block the nearby Kaiser Wilhelm Memorial Church and besmirch its sanctity, perhaps expressing the fear that a temple of Jewish commerce—the description of the department store as a "cathedral of consumption" goes back at least to Zola, and the comparison of consumption and religion traces back at least to Marx—will eclipse a sacred German Christian site.[66]

The department store fire, a nearly ubiquitous motif, can be seen as a metaphor for the explosive power of the consumer society and the powerful changes in German daily life that new forms of consumption represented and helped further. That is, the theme of fires—along with the department stores' other potential hazards, like shoplifting, lascivious behavior, violence, and depravity—expressed both the excitements and dangers associated with these new forms of economic enterprise and leisure activity. As a largely female public space, a hotbed of desires for goods and people, and a station for the circulation of national and international goods and capital, the department store contained, indeed stimulated, highly combustible forces, which made it an ideologically laden and psychologically fraught part of modern life. To some—most pointedly, but not exclusively, Nazis and other *völkisch* elements—these changes were intertwined with the Jews, as the department store remained a highly visible symbol of Jewish economic power and its potentially dark consequences.

A range of political, economic, and literary discourses converged around the concern over fires. And actual cases of violence to and in department stores can be traced from demonstrations against Tietz's Munich store in the 1890s, through countless attacks by SA thugs in the 1930s, and even after the war to the April 1968 department store bombings by Red Army Faktion members in Frankfurt.[67] Striking a violent blow at the department store, then, appears as an attack at the heart of modern society, an attempt to meet the violence and power (and destructiveness) of modern consumer culture with a violent counterattack. What was at stake here was the provocation of Jewish economic power in modern urban centers. These texts staged the struggle between different movements, groups, and ideologies not only over economy and urban space, but also over Germans' imagination and fantasies.

NOTES

1. Leo Colze, *Berliner Warenhäuser* (Berlin and Leipzig: Hermann Seemann Nachfolger, 1908).

2. Ibid., 11–12.

3. Leo Colze, *Berliner Warenhäuser*, vol. 11 of *Berliner Texte* (Berlin: Fannei und Walz, 1989). All references to this text are to the 1908 edition, unless otherwise indicated.

4. Colze, *Berliner Warenhäuser*, 9. The KaDeWe was owned by Jandorf and sold, along with the rest of Jandorf's holdings, to Tietz in 1926.

5. See above all Siegfried Gerlach, *Das Warenhaus in Deutschland: Seine Entwicklung bis zum Ersten Weltkrieg in historisch-geographischer Sicht.* (Stuttgart: Steiner, 1988).

6. Colze, *Berliner Warenhäuser*, 11. See Paul Lerner, "Consuming Pathologies: Kleptomania, Magazinitis, and the Problem of Female Consumption in Wilhelmine and Weimar Germany," *Werkstattgeschichte* 42 (Summer 2006): 45–56 for a detailed discussion of this point.

7. Major works include: Rosalind H. Williams, *Dream Worlds: Mass Consumption in Late Nineteenth-Century France* (Berkeley: University of California Press, 1982); Michael Miller, *The Bon Marché: Bourgeois Culture and the Department Store, 1869–1920* (Princeton: Princeton University Press, 1981); William Leach, *Land of Desire: Merchants, Power, and the Rise of a New American Culture* (New York: Vintage, 1993); Victoria de Grazia, ed., with Ellen Furlough, *The Sex of Things: Gender and Consumption in Historical Perspective* (Berkeley: University of California Press, 1996); Erika Diane Rappaport, *Shopping for Pleasure: Women in the Making of London's West End* (Princeton: Princeton University Press, 2000); Jeffrey Crossick and Serge Jaumain, eds., *Cathedrals of Consumption: The European Department Store, 1850–1939* (Ashgate: Aldershot, 1999).

8. In their survey of "Regimes of Consumer Culture" in twentieth-century Germany, Alon Confino and Rudy Koshar call on historians to pay greater attention to the role of consumer practices in constructing religious, ethnic, and class-based identities, but their call has still scarcely been answered: Rudy Koshar and Alon Confino, eds., *Regimes of Consumer Culture*: Special Issue of *German History* 19, no. 2 (2001). Among the most significant recent works on consumer culture in Germany are David Crew, ed., *Consuming Germany in the Cold War: Consumption and National Identity in East and West Germany* (Oxford: Berg, 2003); Erica Carter, *How German Is She? Postwar Reconstruction and the Consuming Woman* (Ann Arbor: University of Michigan Press, 1997); Wolfgang König, *Volkswagen, Volksempfänger, Volksgemeinschaft: 'Volksprodukte' im Dritten Reich: vom Scheitern einer nationalsozialistischen Konsumgesellschaft* (Paderborn: Schöningh, 2004); Shelley Baranowski, *Strength through Joy: Consumerism and Mass Tourism in the Third Reich* (New York: Cambridge University Press, 2004); Gideon Reuveni, *Reading Germany: Literature and Consumer Culture in Germany before 1933* (New York: Berghahn, 2006). One article that does foreground the relationship between Jews and consumption in Germany is Leora Auslander, "'Jewish Taste?' Jews, and the Aesthetics of Everyday Life in Paris and Berlin, 1933–1942," in *Histories of Leisure*, ed. Rudy Koshar (Oxford: Berg Press,

2002), 299–318. And see Moishe Postone, "The Holocaust and the Trajectory of the Twentieth Century," in *Catastrophe and Meaning: The Holocaust and the Twentieth Century*, ed. Moishe Postone and Eric Santner (Chicago: University of Chicago Press, 2003), 81–116 for a fascinating use of Marx's commodity fetish in an analysis of Jews and capitalism.

9. See, for example, Simone Ladwig-Winters, *Wertheim—ein Warenhausunternehmen und seine Eigentümer: Beispiel der Entwicklung der Berliner Warenhäuser bis zur "Arisierung."* (Münster: Lit, 1997); Avraham Barkai, *From Boycott to Annihilation: The Economic Struggle of German Jews, 1933–1943*, trans. William Templer (Hanover, NH: Brandeis University Press, 1989).

10. This area of inquiry has been developed in other contexts, most notably on Jews in the United States. See, for example, Andrew Heinze, *Adapting to Abundance: Jewish Immigrants, Mass Consumption and the Search for American Identity* (New York: Columbia University Press, 1990).

11. For a full development of this idea, see Victoria de Grazia, *Irresistible Empire: America's Advance through Twentieth-Century Europe* (Cambridge, MA: Belknap, 2005).

12. Erich Köhrer, *Warenhaus Berlin: Ein Roman aus der Weltstadt* (Berlin: Wedekind, 1909), 32.

13. Robert Gellately, "An der Schwelle der Moderne: Warenhäuser und ihre Feinde in Deutschland," in *Im Banne der Metropole: Berlin und London in den Zwanziger Jahren*, ed. Peter Alter (Göttingen: Vandenhoeck & Ruprecht, 1993), 131–156; Uwe Spiekermann, *Warenhaussteuer in Deutschland: Mittlestandsbewegung, Kapitalismus und Rechtstaat im späten Kaiserreich* (Frankfurt: Peter Lang, 1994).

14. On these issues in the French context, see Philip Nord, *Paris Shopkeepers and the Politics of Resentment* (Princeton: Princeton University Press, 1986).

15. Helmut Frei, *Tempel der Kauflust: Eine Geschichte der Warenhauskultur* (Leipzig: Edition Leipzig, 1997), 67.

16. Derek Penslar, *Shylock's Children: Economics and Jewish Identity in Modern Europe* (Berkeley: University of California Press, 2001), 21.

17. Apparently, several Berlin department store owners sued newspapers that used this term for defamation. See Paul Dehn, *Die Großbasare und Massenzweiggeschäfte* (Berlin: Trowizsch & Sohn, 1899), especially 18.

18. In common speech, the two terms were often used interchangeably, although *"Kaufhaus"* did sound more elegant than *"Warenhaus."* Technically, a *"Warenhaus"* was a kind of store that sold goods from multiple categories, a designation that was established for tax reasons. See, for example, Jürgen Schwarz, "Architektur und Kommerz. Studien zur deutschen Kauf- und Warenhausarchitektur vor dem Ersten Weltkrieg am Beispiel der Frankfurter Zeil," PhD diss., Johann-Wolfgang-Goethe-Universität, Frankfurt, 1995, 48.

19. Historian Heinrich Uhlig argues that the department stores had to bear some responsibility for this representation since they often used "oriental" themes and styles like the Thousand and One Nights. Heinrich Uhlig, *Die Warenhäuser im Dritten Reich* (Cologne: Westdeutscher Verlag, 1956), 15. See also Dehn, *Die Großbasare*, 38 for a similar observation.

20. Paul Dehn, *Hinter den Kulissen des modernen Geschäfts* (Berlin: Trowitzsch & Sohn, 1897), 6.

21. F. Roderich Stoltheim, *Das Rätsel des Jüdischen Erfolges* (Leipzig: Hammer-Verlag, 1928), 109.

22. See also Hans Buchner, *Warenhauspolitik und Nationalsozialismus* (Munich: F. Eher Nachfolger, 1929) and J. W. Hauschildt, *Der Kampf gegen die Waarenhäuse: Praktische Vorschläge zur Beseitigung Derselben* (Friedeberg: A. Dressler, 1897).

23. Werner Sombart, "Das Warenhaus, ein Gebilde des Hochkapitalistischen Zeitalters," in *Probleme des Warenhauses: Beiträge zur Geschichte und Erkenntnis der Entwicklung des Warenhauses in Deutschland* (Berlin: Verband Deutscher Waren- und Kaufhäuser, 1928), 77–88.

24. Stoltheim, *Rätsel*, 128–129.

25. "Intimes aus dem Kaufhaus Franz Sonntag," *Die Wahrheit* 3, 16 November 1907, 2.

26. On the Wertheim family, see Erica Fischer and Simone Ladwig-Winters, *Die Wertheims: Geschichte einer Familie* (Berlin: Rowohlt, 2005).

27. Sigfrid Siwertz, *Das Große Warenhaus*, trans. Alfons Fedor Cohn (Berlin: Brandusche Verlag, 1928).

28. Siwertz, *Große Warenhaus*, 28.

29. Hauschildt, *Der Kampf gegen die Waarenhäuser*, 6.

30. See, for example, "Aus der Praxis der Ramschbazare und Warenhäuser," *Hammer* 9 (1910): 128–130; Hans Buchner, *Dämonen der Wirtschaft: Gestalten und dunkle Gewalten aus dem Leben unserer Tage* (Munich: F. Eher, 1928).

31. On the history of advertising in Germany, see Christiane Lamberty, *Reklame in Deutschland: Wahrnehmung, Professionalisierung und Kritik der Wirtschaftswerbung* (Berlin: Duncker & Humblot, 2000); Jonathan Wiesen, Pamela Swett, and Jonathan Zatlin, eds., *Selling Modernity: Advertising in Twentieth-Century Germany* (Durham, NC: Duke University Press, 2007), and Uwe Westphal, *Werbung im Dritten Reich* (Berlin: Transit, 1989).

32. Werner Sombart, "Die Reklame," *Morgen: Wochenschrift für Deutsche Kultur* 2 (6 March 1908): 281–286.

33. Ibid., 283.

34. Hauschildt, *Der Kampf gegen die Waarenhäuser*, 10.

35. See materials in Geheimes Staatsarchiv Preußischer Kulturbesitz (GehStA), Rep. 93B, 1437.

36. See, for example, "Petition from the Verband deutscher Waren- und Kaufhäuser," January 1906, in (GehStA), Rep. 93B, 1437.

37. Letter from Berlin Polizeipräsident Borries to the Prussian Minister of the Interior, Berlin, (1904) in GehStA Rep. 93B, 1436.

38. Siwertz, *Große Warenhaus*, 78.

39. See Lerner, "Consuming Pathologies"; Uwe Spiekermann, "Theft and Thieves in German Department Stores, 1895–1930: A Discourse on Morality, Crime and Gender," in Crossick and Jaumain, *Cathedrals of Consumption*, 135–160; Detlef Briesen, *Warenhaus, Massenkonsum und Sozialmoral: Zur Geschichte der Konsumkritik im 20. Jahrhundert* (Frankfurt: Campus, 2001), especially chap. 3.

40. Wilhelm Stekel, *Impulshandlungen: Wandertrieb, Dipsomanie, Kleptomanie, Pyromanie und verwandte Zustände* (Berlin: Urban & Schwarzenberg, 1922).

41. See Leora Auslander, "The Gendering of Consumer Practices in Nineteenth-Century France," in de Grazia with Furlough, *The Sex of Things*, 78–112.

42. Among other articles, see "Die Geheimnisse des Teesalons im Warenhaus Wertheim," *Die Wahrheit* 3, 19 January 1907, 1.

43. Josef Wiener-Braunsberg, *Warenhausmädchen: Roman aus Berlin der Gegenwart* (Berlin: Ehrlich, 1922); Oscar Schweriner, *Arbeit: Ein Warenhausroman* (Berlin: Dunkker, 1912).

44. Alexander Sternberg, *Ein Warenhaus-Mädchen: Schicksale einer Gefallenen* (Berlin: Verlag moderner Lektüre, 1909).

45. His alleged moral shortcomings were used against him when his application for the title of Kommerzienrat was considered by Prussian authorities, but I have found no evidence that these allegations were true. See, for example, letter from the Prussian Minister für Handel und Gewerbe to the Polizeipräsident Berlin, 28 March 1908, Landesarchiv Berlin (LAB) A Pr. Br. Rep. 30, Tit 94, Nr. 10937.

46. See, for example, *Die Freiheit*, 14 May 1907, clipping in LAB A Pr. Br. Rep. 30, Tit 94, Nr. 10937.

47. For one of many examples, see Hauschildt, *Der Kampf gegen die Waarenhäuser*, 2.

48. Dehn, *Großbazare*, 45.

49. Hans Vogt, *Du Kommst zu spät: Eine Szene aus dem Warenhaus* (Leipzig: Bruno Volger Verlag, 1914).

50. "Der Harem im Warenhaus am Andreasplatz," *Die Wahrheit* 4, 30 May 1908, 1–2.

51. Schweriner, *Arbeit*, 8.

52. Siwertz, *Große Warenhaus*, 102.

53. Köhrer, *Warenhaus Berlin*, 135.

54. See, for example, G. Gerber, *Warenhauspest* (Plauen: Kampfgemeinschaft gegen Warenhaus und Konsumgenossenschaften der NSDAP, 1932); Hauschildt, *Der Kampf gegen die Waarenhäuser*; "Der Warenhaus-Unfug," *Hammer* 11, 15 January 1912, 43–45; and "Wertheim Triumphator!" *Staatsbürger Zeitung*, 27 November 1906, clipping in LAB A Pr. Br. Rep. 30, Tit 94, Nr. 14311 (Wertheim).

55. Quoted in Spiekermann, "Theft and Thieves," 141.

56. *Die Wahrheit* 4, 21 March 1908, clipping in LAB A Pr. Br. Rep. 30, Tit 94, Nr. 14311.

57. Ibid. See also Gerber, *Warenhauspest*.

58. "Behördliche Reklame für Warenhäuser," *Staatsbürger-Zeitung* 39, 24 November 1903, clipping in GehStA Rep. 93 B, 1436.

59. Anne Friedberg, *Window Shopping: Cinema and the Postmodern* (Berkeley: University of California Press, 1993).

60. Quoted in Uhlig, *Die Warenhäuser im Dritten Reich*, 38.

61. Quoted in ibid., 36.

62. Wilhelm Stücklen, *Purpus: Ein Schauspiel in drei Akten* (Berlin: Drei Masken Verlag, 1919).

63. Vicki Baum, "Jape im Warenhaus," in *Die Anderen Tage: Novellen von Vicki Baum* (Berlin: Ullstein Verlag, 1931), 215–241.

64. Manfred Georg, *Aufruhr im Warenhaus* (Berlin-Friedenau: Weltbücher-Verlag, 1928).
65. In GehStA PK I HA Rep. 93 B (Ministerium für öffentlichen Arbeiten), Nr. 1439 Waren und Geschäftshäuser, Bd. 5, 1907–1913
66. Köhrer, *Warenhaus Berlin*, 39.
67. Uhlig, *Warenhäuser im Dritten Reich*; Simone Ladwig-Winters, "The Attack on Berlin Department Stores (Warenhäuser) after 1933," in *Probing the Depths of German Antisemitism: German Society and the Persecution of the Jews*, ed. David Bankier (New York and Jerusalem: Berghahn Books/Yad Vashem, 2000), 246–270.

III

JEWISH ECONOMIES IN NATIONAL AND TRANSNATIONAL CONTEXTS

⚜ **8** ⚝

GOING NATIVE

Moritz Jellinek and the Modernization
of the Hungarian Economy

Michael L. Miller

In 1883, on the twenty-fifth anniversary of the establishment of the First Hungarian Insurance Company, the celebrated Hungarian artist Gyula Benczúr (1844–1920) painted a group portrait of the founders of this institution. The portrait depicts twenty-eight mustachioed, middle-aged men who were present at the founding meeting on 15 July 1857, including Henrik Lévay, the first president of the company; Ferenc Deák, the liberal Hungarian politician; and Baron József Eötvös, the Hungarian reformer and statesman. At the far left of the portrait stands an earnest-looking, red-headed man in his early thirties, a recent arrival to the City of Pest, who in a matter of years had become a member of Pest's economic elite.[1]

Moritz Jellinek, who was thirty-three years old at the time, had arrived from Moravia only seven years earlier, but by 1857 he had already played a central role in many of the milestones in the economic modernization of Hungary, including the establishment of Pest's Cereal Exchange in 1855. In 1865, he helped found Hungary's first (horse-drawn) tramway company, a forerunner of the electric tramway, trolleybus, and subway that would provide the necessary infrastructure for Pest's economic and physical expansion in the last four decades of the nineteenth century. In this respect, he can be considered the unsung father of Budapest's mass transport system.[2] Moritz Jellinek's professional successes—and concomitant rapid social integration—are all the more noteworthy, since, as a Jew, his occupational opportunities remained restricted until 1867, when the Jews of the Habsburg Empire were finally emancipated.

Notes for this chapter begin on page 168.

The role of the Jews in the modernization of Hungary's economy has re-ceived considerable scholarly attention, most notably in a collection of essays, *Jews in the Hungarian Economy, 1760–1945*, published in 1992.[3] A number of other works have focused on the prominent Jewish wholesalers, manufacturers, and bankers who played commanding roles in the development of Hungary's in-dustrial and financial sectors throughout the nineteenth century.[4] These works share a common emphasis on the backwardness of the Hungarian economy, the absence of an indigenous middle class, and the expectation among many liberal Hungarian noblemen that "Jewish economic skills and capital might provide a shortcut to modernization in Hungary."[5] These factors created a favorable envi-ronment for recent immigrants, allowing Jews from Bohemia and Moravia, who were already engaged in petty commerce, to fill an important economic niche upon their arrival in Hungary. Many of these Jews found a hospitable political environment that not only valued the entrepreneurial skills and ramified fam-ily connections that these new immigrants brought with them, but also viewed Jewish wholesalers, manufacturers, entrepreneurs, and financiers as an integral part of the nation-building process. Perhaps no one illustrates this better than Moritz Jellinek, who considered his entrepreneurial activities as a consummate expression of Hungarian patriotism and who, in the words of the *Pesti Hírlap*, "had become a Magyar in body and soul" (*testestül-lélkestül magyarra lett*).[6]

The Jellinek Brothers: Adolf, Hermann, and Moritz

Born in 1824, Moritz Jellinek was the youngest of three highly accomplished sons born to Sara née Back and Isaak Löbl Jellinek (d. 1854), a Jewish leaseholder in the village of Drslawitz, near Ungarisch-Brod in southern Moravia (today Uherský Brod, Czech Republic). Moritz Jellinek has been overshadowed by his two older brothers, Adolf and Hermann, both of whom left a considerable mark on nineteenth-century European intellectual history.[7] Adolf Jellinek (1821–1893), three years Moritz's senior, was a highly prolific and highly esteemed ori-entalist and Jewish scholar who published widely in the Jewish periodicals of his day; a gifted orator as well, he achieved fame as a synagogue preacher in Leipzig before assuming the post of preacher and chief rabbi in Vienna.[8] Hermann Jell-inek (1823–1848), one year Moritz's senior, was a Young Hegelian philosopher and publicist whose complicated relationship to Judaism is best exemplified by his choice of Uriel da Costa (1585–1640) for his literary musings.[9] With the outbreak of the Viennese Revolution of 1848, Hermann dedicated himself to the radical democratic cause, writing articles for the *Allgemeine Österreichische Zeitung* and *Der Radikale*, sharply attacking the Habsburg regime. After the revolution was suppressed in October 1848, Hermann stood accused of "open incitement to armed insurrection" and was executed by firing squad a month later—a traitor to the Habsburg Empire and a martyr to the revolution.[10]

Moritz's relationship with his brothers had a considerable impact on his intellectual, professional, and personal development. Adolf Jellinek's connections with Dr. Julius Fürst, editor of the Leipzig-based German-Jewish weekly *Der Orient*, opened up journalistic opportunities for Hermann and Moritz alike. Moritz began writing articles for *Der Orient* in 1844 (at the age of twenty) and wrote extensive reports from Moravia during and after the Revolution of 1848.[11] The revolution drew Moritz particularly close to Hermann, who had moved to Vienna in March 1848 after being expelled from Berlin. Moritz traveled regularly from Ungarisch-Brod to Vienna to visit his brother and observe his "passionate activity."[12] As he later recalled: "My love for him was beyond expression, and his words were my oracle. ... My entire life centered around him."[13] Still, although Moritz evinced a deep attachment to Hermann (and even named his daughter Hermina), he remained quite aloof from radical politics after the Revolution of 1848. Perhaps the lesson he learned from his brother's death was to work within the system, not against it.

Hermann and Adolf, both men of letters, encouraged their younger brother to pursue a more practical (and more lucrative) career in business. While they were pursuing their studies in Leipzig in the early to mid 1840s, Moritz was living with his father, first in Napajedl, a small village outside of Ungarisch-Brod, where they leased a distillery, and then in Ungarisch-Brod itself. The father and three brothers corresponded regularly in this period, and their letters—written primarily in Judeo-German—shed light on Moritz's first years in the world of business.[14] In November 1844, Adolf praised twenty-year-old Moritz, then living in Napajedl, for helping out his father and finally becoming "a supporter of our house."[15] Then in May 1845, Hermann suggested that Moritz move "to town" (i.e., Ungarisch-Brod), where the connections with Vienna would enable him to begin trading in cereals or manufactured goods.[16] Adolf also pushed Moritz to leave Napajedl for Ungarisch-Brod or beyond so that he could set up "a sound and solid business" (*"ein tüchtiges und solides Geschäft"*).[17] In 1845 or 1846, Moritz and his father finally moved to Ungarisch-Brod, where Moritz used the opportunity to embark on his own business career. Hermann praised Moritz's skills and encouraged his father to provide the necessary capital.[18] He also admonished Moritz to focus on his business activities and not to be distracted—like his two brothers—by studies.[19] Oddly, the extensive correspondence never mentions the details of Moritz Jellinek's business activities, but it is likely that he, like many other Moravian Jews, was involved in the petty trade of grain and other commodities.[20]

Moritz's decision to leave Moravia was also influenced by his two brothers. As early as 1846 Hermann had encouraged Moritz to move to Hungary, where many Moravian Jews had migrated in the course of the eighteenth and nineteenth centuries.[21] The decisive moment, however, came after the Revolution of 1848, in the wake of Moritz's marriage to Johanna Fuchs (October 1849) and Adolf's marriage to Rosalie Bettelheim (May 1850).[22] In terms of Moritz's professional future, his brother's marriage appears to have been more significant than his own. Rosalie Bettelheim was the daughter of Markus Bettelheim, an affluent grain wholesaler in Pest, who owned a four-family house in Leopold-stadt (Lipótváros), one of Pest's most prestigious districts.[23] It is not clear how Adolf and Rosalie met, but this match certainly corresponds to the traditional Jewish pairing of wealth and learning. What is clear, however, is that Moritz benefited tremendously from his brother's marriage, since the new family connection in Pest opened up new economic vistas for him. In 1850, Moritz took his wife and daughter to Pest, where they moved into the so-called "Bettelheim House." Moritz became a grain wholesaler, with the help of his brother's well-connected father-in-law.

Moritz's most important new connection was the Bohemian-born David Fleischl (born 1801), who had settled in Pest in 1825. Fleischl, who pioneered Hungary's goose-feather industry, also owned a leather factory in Vienna, ran a trading company with branches in Pest, Vienna, and Leipzig, and served as director of the Hungarian branch of the Austrian Creditanstalt bank[24] As might be expected from a man of such stature, he was also a pillar of the Pest Jewish community, serving as its president in the 1850s, when the monumental Dohany Street Synagogue (1857–1859) was commissioned and built. A close friend of the Bettelheim family, David Fleischl took Moritz under his wing, put "great trust" in him, and asked this recent arrival from Ungarisch-Brod to conduct business on his behalf.[25] In 1855 Moritz reciprocated, giving Fleischl the honor of *sandek* (godfather) at the circumcision of his third son, Louis.[26]

The Hungarian Economy and the Jews

Economic historians of Central and Eastern Europe have traditionally viewed Hungary's economic development in terms of its "backwardness."[27] Not only in comparison to Western Europe, but also in comparison to the Western Crown lands of the Habsburg Empire (Lower Austria, Bohemia, Moravia), Hungary lacked the basic hallmarks of a modern, industrial economy in the first decades of the nineteenth century:

1. efficient communication networks (railroads, navigable rivers, roads)
2. modern financial institutions (banks, insurance companies)
3. factory production (e.g., textiles, glass)
4. indigenous middle class
5. large labor force (peasants were emancipated only in 1848)

Hungary's manorial economy was predominantly agricultural, with serfs working the vast noble-owned estates until the middle of the nineteenth century.

Due to inefficient farming methods, poor communication networks, the perishability of agricultural produce, and the nobility's traditional aversion to commerce, Hungary was slow to develop an export economy. As Andrew Janos has pointed out, only with the rising demand for grain during the Napoleonic Wars did Hungary begin exporting to Western European markets: "[F]or the first time in history," he notes, "financial gain became the acknowledged aim of farming," and the noble landowners "acquired a taste for making money."[28]

Hungary's Jews, many of whom worked as agents or managers on noble estates, played a central role in Hungary's burgeoning grain trade. Many of these Jews were recent immigrants from Bohemia and Moravia who had come to the Hungarian "Eldorado" to escape the occupational, residential, and marriage restrictions in their native lands. Their family and business connections proved indispensable in opening new markets, and their contacts with the great banking houses in Vienna often provided much-needed capital. As Péter Hanák has argued, these Jews "formed the backbone of the newly evolving entrepreneurial stratum in Hungary."[29] Unlike Western Europe (or the Western Crown lands), where the modern capitalist economy was built on the rational organization of labor in the *new industries* (especially textiles), in Hungary it was built on the rational organization of labor in *commerce*.[30] Furthermore, as Michael K. Silber has noted, it was typical of agrarian Hungary that "the foodstuffs industry (not textiles as in western and central Europe) ... inaugurated the industrialization of the country." The Jews were heavily involved in this agrarian economy, first as grain wholesalers, then as agricultural industrialists (grain milling or beet refining, for example).[31] Many nobles were happy to relegate these economic roles to Jewish merchants and entrepreneurs; others, such as Count István Széchenyi, believed that only the nobles could provide the conditions necessary for economic modernization.

Széchenyi, one of the most important landowners in Hungary, viewed economic modernization as part and parcel of the Hungarian national awakening. After traveling to England and France in the 1820s, he committed his energies and personal resources to bringing Hungary out of its economic backwardness. In 1825 he pledged a year's income from his estates to establish the Hungarian Academy of Sciences, a key institution for both economic and national revitalization. In 1830, he published a treatise entitled *Credit*, in which he laid out his plan for economic reform. He called for the abolition of entail and serfdom, the introduction of wage labor, the financing of development through foreign capital, and the establishment of a national bank. Most controversially, he called for the elimination of noble privileges, which he considered morally indefensible and economically detrimental to the nobles themselves. Indeed, he argued that economic modernization was impossible as long as the nobles paid no taxes and continued to squander their incomes on a lazy and frivolous lifestyle. It was incumbent on the nobility, he insisted, to invest their income in the common weal, and Széchenyi heeded his own words. He invested his income in building roads, improving the navigability of Hungary's rivers, and constructing a suspension bridge between Buda and Pest (the Chain Bridge, completed in 1849).[32]

Széchenyi's proposed reforms did not extend to the emancipation of the Jews, since he considered them totally inassimilable to Magyardom. In 1839 he questioned whether this "oriental tribe" could ever mix with the Magyars, and at the Hungarian Diet of 1844 he explained that Hungary—unlike France and England—could not emancipate its Jews, noting that a bottle of ink would leave no traces if poured into the ocean, but the same ink would render a bowl of Hungarian soup unpalatable.[33] While some scholars have emphasized the racial character of this quip, Széchenyi was primarily concerned about the caste-like character of Hungary's Jews—"a feudal estate in disguise," in Andrew Janos's felicitous terms.[34]

Széchenyi's views on Jewish emancipation, however, were at odds with many Hungarian liberals, who evinced great sympathy towards the Jews, not only because of their economic utility but also because of their readiness to learn the Hungarian language and adopt the national culture. As early as 1840, the Hungarian reformer and statesman Baron József Eötvös (1813–1871) argued for the emancipation of the Jews in Hungary, emphasizing utilitarian, and above all moral, grounds for granting them equal rights.[35] Another consideration was the demographic reality in Hungary, where Magyars were a minority in their own multi-ethnic kingdom and the middle class was dominated by Germans and other non-Magyars.[36] As George Barany has pointed out, liberal Magyar politicians—like József Eötvös and Lajos Kossuth—sought to "complete the social structure of the incipient Magyar nation-to-be" by building a new Magyar middle class and reinforcing it with magyarized Jews.[37] Many Jews proved willing and loyal allies of the liberal elite, and during the Revolution of 1848 they joined in the War of Independence against Habsburg rule, demonstrating their loyalty to the Hungarian national cause.[38] As a putative reward for this support, "citizens of the mosaic faith" were granted equal rights with all other denominations in Hungary on 28 July 1849—just before the Habsburgs quashed the revolution.[39] This last-minute emancipation, however, was never implemented, and the Jews of Hungary had to wait another two decades—until the Austro-Hungarian Compromise (*Ausgleich* / *kiegyezés*) of 1867—to receive equal civic and political rights.

Moritz Jellinek in Pest

Moritz Jellinek moved to Pest after the revolution, arriving at the outset of a decade-long period of neo-absolutism, which saw the reassertion of Habsburg rule over Hungary, the territorial dismantling of the Kingdom of Hungary, and the introduction of German as the language of administration. Despite the repressive policies, the neo-absolutist period also ushered in a period of economic prosperity, aided by the emancipation of the serfs (in 1848), the introduction of a unified customs area for the entire empire, the rapid growth of the railroad network, and, most importantly, the tremendous cereal boom of the 1850s.[40]

Moritz, a recent immigrant to Pest, managed to integrate himself into the Hungarian economic elite with surprising alacrity. Bettelheim and Fleischl certainly opened doors for him, but there were other factors that worked to Moritz's advantage as well. First, as brother of Hermann, a martyr to the revolution, Moritz was connected to a defining moment in the emerging Hungarian national narrative.[41] Secondly, as brother of Adolf, a celebrated rabbi, scholar, and preacher, he could hobnob with the Jewish elite of Pest with greater ease.[42] Thirdly, Moritz took pains to learn the Hungarian language, despite the fact that economic activity in Pest was frequently conducted in German. He understood the symbolic importance of learning Hungarian, especially in the period of neo-absolutism. He picked up the language in a couple of years, and was already publishing articles in Hungarian by 1860.[43]

Moritz was involved in almost all of the milestones in the modernization of the Hungarian economy in the 1850s and 1860s. He was a founding member of the Pester Lloyd Society (*Pester Lloyd Gesellschaft* / *Pesti Lloyd Társaság*), the most important commercial society in Pest, which was established in 1854.[44] He was accepted into Pest's privileged merchant class (*bürgerliche Handelsstand in Pest* / *Pesti polgári kereskedelmi testület*) in 1855, and in the same year he helped establish Pest's first Cereal Exchange (under the auspices of the Pester Lloyd), which aimed to centralize the grain trade, stabilize grain prices, and provide a single destination for wholesale buyers.[45] In 1857, as mentioned above, he was among the founders of the First Hungarian Insurance Company (*Ungarische allgemeine Asecurranzgesellschaft* / *Első magyar általános biztosító társaság*), one of the desiderata listed by Széchenyi in his 1830 treatise.[46] In 1861 he became a board member of the Trade Academy, which had opened its doors three years earlier. In the early 1860s, he compiled statistical reports for the Hungarian Academy of Sciences in an effort to rationalize the Hungarian economy.[47] He also became one of the few non-noble members of the Hungarian Agricultural Society, an organization that sought to modernize Hungary's agricultural economy in the spirit of Széchenyi.[48] His crowning achievement was the founding of Hungary's first (horse-drawn) tramway company in 1865. In this venture, which facilitated the physical expansion of Pest, he collaborated with a number of illustrious Hungarians, including Count Sándor (Alexander) Károlyi, a member of the upper nobility and an 1848er who had returned from French exile after the 1854 amnesty.[49]

Striking in their breadth, Moritz Jellinek's achievements are all the more remarkable when we consider that they took place *before* the emancipation of

Hungarian Jewry in 1867. Like the magnificent Dohány Street Temple, which was consecrated in 1859, Moritz's achievements in the 1850s and 1860s were a striking testament to the extraordinary economic and social rise of Pest Jewry, notwithstanding the myriad legal and political restrictions that were still in place.[50] When the twelve-year period of neo-absolutism came to an end in 1861, the question of Jewish emancipation returned to the public sphere and the legal status of the Jews was again debated in pamphlets, newspapers, and the newly convened Hungarian Diet. One pamphleteer adamantly opposed Jewish emancipation, arguing that the ascendancy of Hungarian Jewry—at the very time when Hungary was ostensibly suffering under the Habsburg yoke— was incontrovertible evidence that Jewish clannishness and self-interest was inimical to Hungarian national interests. "These were twelve golden years for the Jews," wrote the pamphleteer. "In these twelve years [of neo-absolutism], their number doubled through immigration to the promised land [i.e. Hungary], their wealth increased ten-fold, and the dull hatred—or foolish helplessness—of the [Hungarian] people also increased ten-fold."[51]

Jellinek was aware of this context of his own achievements—as well as the passions they could ignite. In this period, he penned a number of apologetic essays that presented the economic activities of Hungarian Jewry, first and foremost, as the fulfillment of their patriotic duty vis-à-vis the Hungarian state. Two of these writings—one published in German, the other in Hungarian—merit further examination.

In 1859 Moritz Jellinek published an article on Hungarian Jews and the economy that appeared in a curious almanac, *Illustriertes Israelitisches Jahrbuch für Ernst und Scherz* (Illustrated Israelite Yearbook for Seriousness and Jest).[52] Published in Pest, the yearbook attracted renowned Central European Jewish scholars, publicists, and literati such as Ludwig August Frankl, Max Letteris, Leopold Kompert, and Moritz's older brother, Adolf. At first blush, Moritz's article seems to descend into Enlightenment platitudes, deriding the Jews' penchant for petty trade (*Schacher*) and blaming it on centuries of oppressive laws and legal restrictions. Then it takes a novel approach, arguing that Hungarian Jewry shatters all the myths about the Jews' alleged proclivity for unproductive economic pursuits.

Jellinek begins with Hungary's educated and affluent Jews, pointing out that many of them engaged in farming and even managed large agricultural estates according to "the most rational principles." Others, he points out, had established modern textile, porcelain, and glass factories, a particularly significant accomplishment in light of Hungary's economic backwardness. The lower classes, while still highly concentrated in trade, were trying their best to learn "useful" handicrafts. As in other provinces of the Habsburg Empire, Hungary had its own society for "productivizing" the Jews by promoting handicrafts and agricultural labor, particularly among the impoverished classes. Jellinek was a member of this society, the Hungarian Israelite Handicraft and Agricultural Association (*MIKÉFE*), from at least 1862.[53]

Jellinek then arrives at the heart of his argument: while Hungary's Jews may have been heavily concentrated in trade, they were not engaged in unproductive *Schacher* like their coreligionists elsewhere, but in international commerce—the lifeblood of the modern Hungarian economy. Indeed, he claims that Jews introduced the export trade to Hungary, bringing about the crucial transition from *passive* to *active* trade. Previously, Hungary sold its surplus grain to foreign buyers, who came to Pest, Győr, and other Hungarian entrepôts, usually after poor harvests in Western Europe. Jewish wholesalers, in contrast, actively pursued markets abroad and—aided in the 1840s and 1850s by the expanding network of railways and navigable waterways—helped sell Hungary's grain in exchange for much-needed foreign capital. "We repeat with pride and self-confidence," Jellinek writes, "that Hungary's *active* trade is predominantly the work of Israelites, an accomplishment whose utility for the state as well as the private sector cannot be overestimated and for which the Israelites certainly deserve recognition."[54] It seems that Moritz Jellinek, a grain wholesaler at the time, was perfectly happy to identify himself as one of the most important engines of the Hungarian economy.

In 1863, Moritz Jellinek wrote a series of articles for *The Homeland* (*A Hon*), a political and economic daily that was edited by Mór Jókai, the celebrated Hungarian novelist, nobleman, 1848er, and moderate liberal.[55] Jellinek wrote regular columns on the Hungarian economy, one entitled "Retrospect" (*Visszatekintés*), which ran from January to March 1863, another entitled "National Economic Letters," (*Nemzetgazdasági levelek*), which ran from April to July. "Retrospect" covered a wide range of issues, from the poor grain harvest of 1862, to the effect of the American Civil War on the European cotton market, to Hungary's booming feather-bed industry.[56] "National Economic Letters" focused much more on the historical development of Hungary's modern economy, beginning with Count István Széchenyi's efforts to modernize Hungary's economy by attracting foreign capital and, most importantly, investing in the transportation infrastructure in Hungary.[57] In his descriptions of Széchenyi, Jellinek waxed patriotic about this "apostle of the nation" who led the Hungarians—like the Biblical "pillar of fire"—into a new era of economic progress.[58]

In a subsequent article, Jellinek, who signed his articles as Jellinek Mór (the magyarized form of his name), gave four reasons for the economic "backwardness" of the Hungarian economy.[59] The first three reasons could be found in much of the contemporary literature on Hungary's economic backwardness, but the fourth reason represented Jellinek's original—and rather revealing—contribution to this topic. The first reason was Hungary's perpetual struggle for political independence, which had left precious little time for the development of her material interests. The second reason was the past laziness of the inhabitants of Hungary, who had—until recently—lacked the motivation to work (cf. Széchenyi). The third reason was the prohibitive customs border, dating back to the late eighteenth century, which sealed Hungary off hermetically from the Austrian part of the Habsburg Empire. The fourth reason, according to Jellinek, was "socio-political relations," shorthand for state policy towards new immigrants to Hungary. "The country's economy," he wrote,

> was, to a large extent, in the hands of immigrants, and these merchants and craftsmen were overcome with such love and affection for our motherland—the kind of love that one usually feels only for his country of birth, a kind of affection that is occasionally indistinguishable from patriotism. Yet, the nation withheld from them the most important political rights. While the nation's characteristic hospitality and neighborliness did smooth over some of the roughness of the law, these traits did not engender the fervent moral sentiment (in the higher interests of our motherland), which aimed to make commerce more than just a tool for selfish purposes and advantages.
>
> . . .
>
> In our motherland ... it cannot be overemphasized that human beings as human beings should be accorded rights and freedoms; that the immigrant, after a certain number of years, should enjoy the same political and civil rights as those born with them.

Even a superficial reading of this fourth reason leaves little doubt that Jellinek is not concerned about immigrants per se, but rather about Jews—whether immigrants like himself, his wife and his daughter, or native-born Jews like his four sons—who were deprived of equal rights by virtue of their religion. By stressing that commerce should not be viewed as "just a tool for selfish purposes and advantages," Jellinek argues that the Jews in Hungary are not engaged in "pariah entrepreneurship," but rather in the building of a vibrant Hungarian economy.[60] The Jews' economic activities do not warrant the withholding of rights, but instead strengthen the case for complete civic and political emancipation.

Conclusion

The Jews of Hungary were finally emancipated in 1867, thanks in large part to the efforts of liberal politicians like Minister of Justice Ferenc Deák and Minister of Education and Religion Baron József Eötvös, both of whom were later featured in Gyula Benczúr's 1883 painting celebrating the twenty-fifth anniversary of the First Hungarian Insurance Company. Moritz Jellinek, whose peripheral position in this group portrait scarcely reflects his centrality in the modernization of the Hungarian economy, remained director of the Pest (and later Budapest) Tramway Company until his death on 13 June 1883, just a few months after the Benczúr painting was completed.

Jellinek's death came in the midst of the Tiszaeszlár blood libel trial, an anti-Semitic cause célèbre that divided Hungary in the 1880s just as the Dreyfus Affair would divide France a decade later.[61] In fact, the retrial—in which the accused Hungarian Jews were eventually acquitted—began in the Nyíregyháza, Hungary, courthouse just three days after Jellinek's burial in Pest's Jewish cemetery. Jellinek's funeral was attended by thousands of people "from the best classes" of Budapest society, including Budapest's mayor, Károly Ráth.[62] As Adolf Jellinek reported, not since the funeral of Ferenc Deák in 1876 had so many people gathered to pay their last respects—"without regard to confession."[63] Jellinek's death was front-page news in many of Budapest's dailies, and it received extensive coverage in the Habsburg Empire's various Jewish newspapers.[64]

Most of the obituaries hailed Jellinek's Hungarian patriotism, observing that the foreign birth of this "self-made-man of the best and noblest sort" ("*ein Selfmademan der edelsten und besten Art*") had in no way impeded his unflagging dedication to his adopted country.[65] "He was not born in this land," observed *Vasárnapi Újság*, "but his heart and tongue were fully magyarized (*megmagyarosodott*) and he reared his four sons in the Magyar spirit."[66] In the words of the *Pester Lloyd*, "Jellinek belonged to those who emigrated from abroad, found their homeland (*Heimat*) here, and served the land where they found their fortune (*Glück*) with the same degree of patriotism as those who were born here."[67] All of the obituaries, as well as Rabbi Sámuel Kohn's graveside eulogy, praised Jellinek's impeccable moral fiber, sublimely noble spirit, and exemplary industriousness. This was all the more noteworthy since at the time of his death many of Hungary's newspapers were not only lending credence to accusations of Jewish ritual murder, but also fulminating against the wave of largely impoverished, Yiddish-speaking Russian-Jewish immigrants who had arrived in Hungary after the 1881–1882 pogroms.

Moritz Jellinek, in contrast, had arrived more than three decades earlier, when Hungary still lacked the financial institutions to fuel a capitalist economy, an extensive railway network to facilitate international trade, a local public transport system to enable urban expansion, and indigenous, Hungarian-speaking entrepreneurs to modernize and industrialize the foodstuffs industry. In the 1850s and 1860s, Jellinek had found a hospitable political environment that not only valued the entrepreneurial skills he brought with him from Moravia, but also viewed his financial and commercial activities as an integral part of the nation-building process. By Jellinek's death in 1883, Gyula Benczúr could look back at the *Gründerzeit*, placing a young, red-headed Moravian Jew in the pantheon of great Hungarians—alongside Ferenc Deák and Baron József Eötvös—who had helped modernize the Hungarian economy and, in so doing, participated in the creation of modern Hungary.

NOTES

1. This portrait ("Az első magyar általános biztositó társaság alapitóinak első alakuló közgyülése 1857 julius 15") has been frequently reproduced. It was first published in *Vasárnapi Újság* (1 April 1883), 204, with 23 of the 28 men identified by name. Mór Jellinek is the second from the left, standing between Frigyes Harkányi and László Karácsonyi. The group portrait did not survive the Second World War. See Sándor Jeszensvky, *Háborús műkincsevszteségünk*, vol. 2 (Budapest: Magyar Művészet, 1948), 101, and Katalin Telepy, *Benzcúr* (Nyíregyháza: A Nyíregyházza Jósa András Muzéum, 1963), 27–28 and plates 89–90.

2. Buda and Pest were separate municipalities until 1873, when they were unified (together with Óbuda) to form Budapest. The unification of Budapest was facilitated, to a large extent, by the mass transport system that shortened travel times in this ever-expanding metropolis.

3. Michael K. Silber, ed., *Jews in the Hungarian Economy, 1760–1945* (Jerusalem: The Magnes Press 1992).

4. The most important of these works is Vera Bácskai, *A vállakozók előfutárai: nagykereskedők a reformkori Pesten* (Budapest: Magvető 1989), which takes a prosopographical approach to Hungary's largely Jewish entrepreneurial class in the first half of the nineteenth century. Among these individuals were Bernát Ferenc Weisz, Zsigmond Kornfeld, and members of the Goldberger, Wodianer, and Ullmann families. Zsigmond Kornfeld, Mór Wahrmann, and the Hatvany-Deutsch dynasty are treated in the recently published Marcell Sebők, ed., *Sokszínű kapitalizmus: Pályaképek a magyar tőkés fejlődés aranykorából* (Budapest: HVG Kiadói Rt. 2004).

5. Andrew Janos, *The Politics of Backwardness in Hungary, 1825–1945* (Princeton: Princeton University Press 1982), 79–80.

6. See his obituary: *Pesti Hírlap*, 14 June 1883.

7. For the most comprehensive work on the Jellinek brothers and the descendants of Adolf (including the Emil Jellinek-Mercedes of Mercedes-Benz fame), see Klaus Kempter, *Die Jellineks, 1820–1955: eine familienbiographische Studie zum deutschjüdischen Bildungsbürgertum* (Düsseldorf: Droste, 1998). Kempter deals only peripherally with Moritz Jellinek and makes only brief mention of his Hungarian career. For brief biographies of Moritz Jellinek, see Mór Gelléri, *A magyar ipar uttörői élet- és jellemrajzok* (Budapest, 1887), 251-254; József Szinnyei, ed., *Magyar irók élete és munkái*, vol. 5 (Budapest, 1897), 474–475.

8. Moses Rosenmann, *Dr. Adolf Jellinek; sein Leben und Schaffen. Zugleich ein Beitrag zur Geschichte der israelitischen Kultusgemeinde Wien in der zweiten Hälfte des neunzehnten Jahrhunderts* (Vienna: J. Schlesinger 1931); Klaus Kempter, *Die Jellineks*, 25–153, 207–260.

9. Da Costa was a Portuguese-born Marrano who, after returning to Judaism, was twice excommunicated by the Amsterdam Jewish community for his heretical writings. Hermann Jellinek, *Uriel Acosta's Leben und Lehre: Ein Beitrag zur Kenntniss seiner Moral, wie zur Berichtigung der Gutzkow'schen Fiktionen über Acosta, und zur Charakteristik der damaligen Juden* (Zerbst, 1847). Hermann dedicated this work to his brother Moritz.

10. Wolfgang Häusler, "Hermann Jellinek (1823–1848), ein Demokrat in der Wiener Revolution," *Jahrbuch des Instituts für deutsche Geschichte* 5 (1976): 125–175; Klaus Kempter, *Die Jellineks*, 25–104.

11. Articles by Moritz Jellinek appeared in *Der Orient* on 3 September 1844; 1 April 1848; 26 August 1848; 13 October 1848; 11 November 1848; 3 March 1849; 27 October 1849. They are signed "J," "Moritz," "M— z," or "M— tz."

12. Moses Rosenmann, "Ein authentischer Bericht über die letzten Tage Dr. Hermann Jellineks," *Die Wahrheit* (Vienna), 19 November 1926, 2–3.

13. Ibid.

14. The Jellinek correspondence can be found in the Adolf Jellinek Archive (Arc. 4° 1588) at the Department of Manuscripts and Archives of the Jewish National and University Library (JNUL), Jerusalem, Israel. The sons wrote all of their letters to their father in Judeo-German, with Hebrew occasionally interspersed. From March 1846 onward, Hermann wrote to Moritz primarily in German.

15. JNUL 4° 1588. Adolf Jellinek (Leipzig) to Moritz Jellinek (Napajedl), 20 November 1844: "Dein Fleiss und deine Betriebsamkeit freuen mich sehr und ich sage dir meinen herzlichsten Dank dafür, dass du endlich eine Stutze unseres Hauses geworden bist." Transcribed from the original Judeo-German.

16. JNUL 4° 1588. Hermann Jellinek (Leipzig) to Isaak Löbl Jellinek, 13 May 1845.

17. JNUL 4° 1588. Letter from Adolf Jellinek (Leipzig) to Isaak Löbl Jellinek, 13 May 1845.

18. JNUL 4° 1588. Hermann Jellinek (Leipzig) to Isaak Löbl Jellinek (Ungarisch-Brod), September 1846: "Ich bitte dich noch einmal in Bezug auf Moritz, das Verfahren einzuschlagen, welche ich dir angerathen habe. Seine Anlagen zum Geschäftsmann sind ausgezeichnet—nur behut noch die jenige Sparsamkeit, die ein jeder Geschäftsmann erst im Laufe seiner Geschäftsunternehmungen erlernt. Habe du nur Zutrauen zu ihm und ich hoffe du zufrieden sein wirst. Aber die Hauptsache bleibt immer dass er einen freien Spielraum haben muss … Mein ganzes Bestreben geht ja nur dahin, solche Vorschläge zu machen, wodurch dein Kapital recht gut verprozentirt werde…" (Transcribed from the original Judeo-German.) ("I ask you once again regarding Moritz to pursue the deal that I suggested to you. His abilities as a businessman are excellent—only protect that frugality, which each businessman learns only in the course of his business undertakings. Have faith in him and I hope that you will be pleased. But the main thing remains that he must have free room to act… All my efforts go to making such suggestions through which your capital will be well invested.")

19. JNUL 4° 1588. Hermann Jellinek (Leipzig) to Moritz Jellinek, September 1846: "Als Geschäftsmann darfst du nicht viel studieren—dass Geschäft muss immer die Hauptsache bleiben." ("As a businessman you should not study too much—the business must always remain the highest priority.")

20. Petitions to the Moravian Diet and Austrian Parliament in 1848 testify to the role of Jews in the Moravian cereal trade. Many petitioners wished to ban Jews from the cereal trade, due to the widespread belief that Jewish grain speculation was responsible for the famine and economic hardship of 1846 and 1847. See Jiři Radmiský and Milada Wurmová, *Petice moravského lidu k snemu z roku 1848* (Prague:

Archivní správa Ministerstva vnitra, 1955), and Haus- Hof- und Staatsarchiv (Vienna), Oesterreichischer Reichstag 1848/49, Faszikel 125.IX.24, "Petitionen von Juden um Emancipation, dann Petitionen dagegen."

21. JNUL 4° 1588. Hermann Jellinek (Leipzig) to Moritz Jellinek (Ungarisch-Brod), March 1846. On Moravian Jewish migration to Hungary, see Ernő Marton, A Magyar zsidóság családfája (Kolozsvár: Fraternitas, 1941), and Fülöp Grünwald and Sandor Scheiber, "Adalékok a Magyar zsidoság településtörténetéhez a XVIII. század első felében," Magyar-Zsidó Oklevéltár 7 (1963): 5–48.

22. Adolf Jellinek officiated at Moritz and Johanna's wedding, which took place in Ungarisch-Brod on 22 October 1849. His marriage sermon was published as a pamphlet: Adolf Jellinek, Trau-Rede bei der Vermählung seines Bruders, am 22. October 1849 in der grossen Synagoge zu Ungarisch-Brod (Leipzig: C.L. Fritzsche 1849). Adolf's marriage to Rosalie Bettelheim took place in Pest on 26 May 1850. Rabbi Löb Schwab, who was originally from Moravia, officiated.

23. Born in Óbuda in 1802 or 1806, Markus Bettelheim is listed as a fruit merchant (Fruchthandler) in the 1840 Pest Jewish conscription, and as a bread merchant (Brothandler) in the 1846 Pest Jewish conscription. Magyar Zsidó Levéltár, A pesti izr. hitközség 1840 évi lajstroma, f. 127; A pesti izr. hitközség 1846 évi lajstroma, f. 131.

24. For a biography of David Fleischl, see Hajnal: Arczképekkel es Életrajzokkal diszített Naptár (Pest, 1864), 109. See also Pester-Lloyd-Kalendar (Pest, 1859), 41. Oddly, Fleischl does not appear in the Magyar Zsidó Lexikon. Moritz Jellinek devoted an article to the goose-feather trade, in which he calls Fleischl "the first Pest wholesaler, who pioneered the large-scale export of feathers." See [Moritz Jellinek], "Visszatekintés. IV.," A Hon, 7 February 1863, 1.

25. JNUL 4° 1588. Moritz Jellinek (Pest) to Adolf Jellinek (Leipzig), 1 January 1854.

26. Louis (Lajos) Jellinek's birth record, which mentions David Fleischl's role, can be found at the Pest Jewish Community at Sip utca 12. Születési jegyzéke, 3 January 1855. The sandek at the circumcision of Moritz's second son, Heinrich (Henrik), was Moritz Fried, a native of Ungarisch-Brod and a resident of the Bettelheim house. See Születési jegyzék, 22 December 1853. No sandek is listed for his oldest son, Artur (b. 16 March 1852) or his youngest son, Marcell (b. 17 January 1858).

27. See Alexander Gerschenkron, Economic Backwardness in Historical Perspective: A Book of Essays (Cambridge: The Belknap Press of Harvard University Press, 1962), 5–30; Péter Gunst, "Agrarian Systems of Central and Eastern Europe," in The Origins of Backwardness in Eastern Europe, ed. Daniel Chirot (Berkeley: University of California Press, 1989), 53–91; Iván T. Berend and György Ránki, Economic Development in East-Central Europe in the 19th and 20th Centuries (New York: Columbia University Press, 1974).

28. Andrew Janos, The Politics of Backwardness, 35–36.

29. Péter Hanák, "Jews and the Modernization of Commerce in Hungary, 1760–1848," in Silber, Jews in the Hungarian Economy, 23–39, here 38.

30. Ibid., 33.

31. Michael K. Silber, "A Jewish Minority in a Backward Economy: an Introduction," in Silber, Jews in the Hungarian Economy, 19.

32. On Szécheny, see George Barany, *Stephen Szechenyi and the Awakening of Hungarian Nationalism, 1791–1841* (Princeton: Princeton University Press, 1969), and Andreas Oplatka, *Graf Stephan Széchenyi: Der Mann, der Ungarn schuf* (Vienna: Paul Zsolnay Verlag, 2004).

33. Walter Pietsch, "Deutsche, Juden und Ungarn vor der Revolution," in *Zwischen Reform und Orthodoxie*, Walter Pietsch (Berlin: Philo, 1999), 48; George Barany, *Stephen Szechenyi*, 90–93.

34. Janos, *The Politics of Backwardness*, 118.

35. See József Eötvös, *A zsidók emancipációjá* (Budapest: Magvető Könyvkiadó, 1981). This call for Jewish emancipation was first published in *Budapesti Szemle* (1840), 110–156. See also Paul Bödy, *Joseph Eötvös and the Modernization of Hungary, 1840–1870* (Boulder, CO: East European Monographs, 1985), 119.

36. In 1842, less than 40 percent of the population in the Kingdom of Hungary was Magyar. Slovaks, Germans, Romanians, Croatians, Serbs, Ruthenians, and Jews comprised most of the remaining 60 percent. See Paul Bödy, *Joseph Eötvös*, 24, and Walter Pietsch, "Deutsche, Juden und Ungarn," 41–51.

37. George Barany, "'Magyar Jew of Jewish Magyar?' Reflections on the Question of Assimilation," in *Jews and Non-Jews in Eastern Europe*, ed. Béla Vágó and George L. Mosse (Jerusalem: Keter Publishing House, 1974), 56.

38. István Deák, *The Lawful Revolution: Louis Kossuth and the Hungarians, 1848–1849* (New York: Columbia University, 1979), 115–116, and Béla Bernstein, *Az 1848/49-iki magyar szabadságharcz és a zsidók* (Budapest, 1898). On the integration of Jews into Hungarian liberal society, see Michael K. Silber, "The Entrance of Jews into Hungarian Society in Vormärz: The Case of the 'Casinos,'" in *Assimilation and Community: The Jews of Nineteenth-Century Europe*, ed. Jonathan Frankel and Steven J. Zipperstein (Cambridge: Cambridge University Press, 1992), 284–323.

39. Ambrus Miskolczy, *A zsidóemancipáció Magyarországon 1849-ben* (Budapest: Múlt és Jövő, 1999).

40. Éva Somogyi, "The Age of Neoabsolutism, 1849–1867," in *A History of Hungary*, ed. Peter F. Sugar (Bloomington and Indianapolis: Indiana University Press, 1990), 235–251.

41. On the role of 1848 in the formation of the Hungarian national narrative, see Alice Freifeld, *Nationalism and the Crowd in Liberal Hungary, 1848–1914* (Washington, D.C.: The Woodrow Wilson Center Press, 2000), 100–109.

42. In 1852, David Fleischl sought to hire Adolf Jellinek as preacher for the Pest Jewish community. Magyar Zsidó Levéltar (Pest), Protocoll des Kultus-Gemeindevorstand, 3 October 1852.

43. Jellinek's first article to appear in Hungarian was an overview of the international cereal trade, which was published in 1860. See Mór Jellinek, "Heti szemle," *Pesti Napló*, 26 July 1860, 1. In a letter from 29 July 1860, Moritz proudly told his brother Adolf about this article: "Das heutige 'Pesti Napló' hat von mir einen grossen Artikel über den Handel—der von mir gezeichnet ist—veröffentlicht. Lasse dir demselben von einem Ungarn vorlesen." (JNUL 4° 1588, 29 July 1860). ("Today's 'Pesti Napló' published a large article of mine about the trade that I described. Have a Hungarian read it for you.")

44. A *Pesti Lloyd Évkönyve 1856-ra / Jahrbuch des Pester Lloyd für 1856* (Pest, 1857). Moritz Jellinek is listed among "A pesti Lloyd rendes tagjai / Wirkliche Mitglieder d. Pester Lloyd," 69. See also Antal Deutsch, *A Pesti Lloyd Társulat 1853–1903* (Budapest, 1903). The Pester Lloyd Society also published the *Pester Lloyd*, a German-language liberal (Hungarian) nationalist daily, and a leading paper—particularly for business affairs—from 1854 onward. See Hedvig Újvári, "Die Geschichte des Pester Lloyd zwischen 1854–1875," *Magyar könyvszemle* 117 (2001): 189–203.

45. On the opening of the Cereal Exchange, see "Die Pester Kornhalle," *Pester Lloyd*, 30 September 1855, 2 and *Wiener Zeitung*, 4 October 1855, 2647. See also Gyula Szávay, ed., *A magyar kamarai intezmény és a budapesti kamara története* (Budapest: A Budapesti Kereskedelmi és Iparkamara, 1927), 99–100.

46. *Első Magyar Általános Biztositó Társaság 1857–1907* (Budapest: Pallas Részvénytársaság, 1908).

47. Mór Jellinek, "Magyarország gabonaforgalma az 1861-diki évben," *Statistikai Közlemények* 3, no. 1 (1862): 44–49, 257–259.

48. Of the 67 members in 1865, 26 were members of the upper nobility and many others were members of the lower nobility. Moritz Jellinek was one of only three Jewish members. See *Verhandlungs und Commisions-Bericht über billige Bahne: Aus der Staatswirtschaftlichen Abtheilung des ungarischen Landes-Agricultur-Vereines* (Pest, 1865). The members are listed on iii.

49. Sándor Károlyi (1831–1906) later became head of Hungary's Agrarian Party and founder of a cooperative movement, both of which had anti-Jewish tendencies. See János Gyurgyák, *A zsidókérdés Magyarországon* (Budapest: Osiris, 2001), 286–289, and Miklós Szabó, *Az újkonzervativizmus és a jobboldali radikalizmus története (1867–1918)* (Budapest: Új Mandátum, 2003), 125–133. For a brief biography of Károlyi, see Tibor Csík, "Károlyi Sándor," in Sebők, *Sokszínű Kapitalizmus*, 110–131. Oddly, Csík makes no mention of Károlyi's active involvement in founding the tramway.

50. See Lajos Venetianer, *A magyar zsidóság története* (Budapest: Fővárosi Nyomda, 1922), 235–238.

51. Baron Varicourt (pseudonym), *Die Juden und die Judenfrage* (Pest, 1861), 20. This also appeared in Hungarian in the same year as *A zsidók és a zsidók kérdése*. It was written in response to Count Kolloman (Kálmán) Majláth's pro-emancipation pamphlet, *Die Emanzipation der Juden* (Pest, 1861).

52. Moritz Jellinek, "Die Israeliten Ungarns auf ökonomischen Gebiete," in *Illustriertes Israelitisches Jahrbuch für Ernst und Scherz*, ed. Samuel Winter (Pest, 1859), 73–77.

53. Moritz Jellinek is listed as an "Ausschussmitglied" in 1862. See *Allgemeine illustrirte Judenzeitung*, 30 May 1862, 175. On MIKÉFE, which was established in 1842, see *Magyar Izraelita Kézműves és Földművelési Egyesület (1842–1949): Dokumentamok* (Budapest: Budapest Jewish Community, 2000).

54. Jellinek, "Israeliten Ungarns aufökonomische Gebiete," 77.

55. Moritz Jellinek is briefly mentioned in Jókai's correspondence. See Mór Jókai, *Levelezése II. (1860–1875)* (Budapest: Akadémiai Kiadó, 1975), 35.

56. Jellinek's "Retrospect" articles appeared in *A Hon* (1863) on 29 and 31 January; 4, 7, 13, 14, and 22 February; 1, 8, 11, 14, and 27 March.

57. Jellinek's "National Economic Letters" appeared in *A Hon* (1863) on 12, 16, 19, and 29 April; 1, 9, and 24 May; 2 and 21 June; 18 July.

58. Mór Jellinek, "Nemzetgazdasági levelek. II.," *A Hon*, 16 April 1863, 1. In his eulogy for Szechenyi (1860), Leopold Löw compared "the greatest Hungarian" to the prophet Samuel; see Lipót Löw, "Sámuel próféta és Széchenyi István: Történeti párhuzamban," in *Zsidó reformkor*, ed. János Kőbányai (Budapest: Múlt és Jövő, 2000), 280–287.

59. Mór Jellinek, "Nemzetgazdasági levelek. VI.," *A Hon*, 24 May 1863, 1.

60. The term "pariah entrepreneurship" is taken from Andrew Janos, *Politics of Backwardness*, 116.

61. For a narrative history of the Tiszaeszlár blood libel trial (and retrial), see Andrew Handler, *Blood Libel at Tiszaeszlar* (New York: Columbia University Press, 1980).

62. "Moritz Jellinek: Strassenbahndirektor," *Der Ungarische Israelit*, 15 June 1883, 193–196.

63. Adolf Jellinek, "Die Antisemiten strecken die Waffen," *Neuzeit*, 22 June 1883, 241–242.

64. Jellinek's death was front-page news in the *Abendblatt des Pester Lloyds* (13 and 14 June 1883) and *Pester Courier* (17 June 1883). It was also featured in *Pesti Hírlap* (14 June 1883); *Budapesti Hírlap* (14 June 1883), *Wiener Zeitung* (14 June 1883), and *Vasárnapi Újság* (17 June 1883). Among the Jewish newspapers, it was featured in *Der Ungarische Israelit* (15 June 1883), *Egyenlőség* (17 June 1883), and *Neuzeit* (15 and 22 June 1883).

65. *Abendblatt des Pester Lloyd* (13 June 1883). The *Pester Lloyd* erroneously listed his birthplace as Gaya, Moravia, instead of Drslawitz (or the nearby Ungarisch-Brod). This mistake—along with much of the accurate information from the *Pester Lloyd*—was repeated in most of the subsequent obituaries.

66. *Vasárnapi Újság*, 17 June 1883, 393.

67. *Abendblatt des Pester Lloyd*, 13 June 1883, 1.

JEWS, PLUMES, AND GLOBAL COMMERCE IN THE MODERN PERIOD

Sarah Abrevaya Stein

In August of 1911, a secret expedition sponsored by the government of the Union of South Africa set sail from Cape Town. Led by Russell Thornton, government agriculturalist of the late Cape Government, the party traveled to London, where participants were outfitted by Fortnam and Mason of Picadilly. From Britain, the group traveled by Elder Dempster steamer to and along the west coast of Africa, docking at Forcados, at the mouth of the Niger River. In Forcados, Thornton's crew shifted to paddleboat and navigated up river to Baro, where they employed ninety-four Hausa porters to help them cross overland—by train, horse, and on foot—to the camel caravan entrepôt of Kano.[1]

In Kano, Thornton's party intended to search the stock of all incoming caravans in search of the elusive Barbary plume, an ostrich feather coveted the world over for its dazzling fullness, width at the crown, and so-called "double fluff," that is, density or compactness along the flue.[2] The explorers' ambition was to trace the provenance of this plume backward along the feather commodity chain to its source: the so-called Barbary ostrich. With the support of their government and colleagues back home, they then intended to procure and smuggle back to South Africa 150 Barbary birds.

The thirst for ostrich plumes in the European and American metropole was the central catalyst for the bustling trade in ostrich feathers across the Atlantic Ocean and Mediterranean and Red Seas in the sixty or so years that bracketed the turn of the twentieth century. A variety of "fancy feathers," including those of the ostrich, adorned the hats and clothes of elite European and American women from at least the second half of the eighteenth century. But ostrich feathers were not widely employed by the fashion world until the 1880s, the

---

Notes for this chapter begin on page 182.

first of three decades in which women's hats were worn large and elaborately trimmed. Crucially, this was a time at which women were gaining ever more opportunity and desire to consume. The bevy of fashion choices they faced were outlined in new kinds of texts targeting the female shopper, fashion magazines among them, while the objects they coveted were displayed ever more alluringly in shopping neighborhoods like London's West End.[3] As consumers' buying power and thirst for feathers grew, so too did the global commerce in this luxury good: by the first decade of the twentieth century, Britain was importing nearly £2 million worth and the United States as much as $5 million worth of ostrich feathers annually.[4]

So valuable a commodity quickly caught the attention of Europe's imperial regimes and the American authorities. Beginning in the 1860s, the British imperial government actively facilitated intensive ostrich rearing by Boer, British, and some Jewish farmers in the Oudtshoorn district of the Cape Colony, an investment that ultimately resulted in feathers being ranked fourth in value among commodities exported from the Union of South Africa, following gold, diamonds, and wool.[5] The French and Ottoman regimes kept a careful eye on these proceedings. Both of these polities were interested in maintaining or expanding their holdings in North and/or Central Africa, and they too wished to capitalize on the trade in plumes in and across their colonies, if necessary by diverting traditional camel caravan routes to their advantage. At the same time, French and American consular agents, civil servants, and agricultural economists were debating whether, in imitation of the British, their own governments ought to facilitate intensive ostrich farming in Algeria or Senegal (in the case of the French) or in California, Arizona, or Florida (in the case of the Americans).[6]

British subsidies of Cape infrastructure had a positive and lasting effect on the ostrich industry. From the 1860s to the 1910s, the Cape produced the largest quantity of ostrich feathers consumed in Europe and the United States. And yet, throughout the feather craze, merchants in North Africa supplied the feathers most admired by European and American consumers, the elusive Barbary plume. Demand for Barbary feathers was so extensive that scholars of North and Central African trade credit the commodity with single-handedly reviving the institution of the trans-Saharan camel caravan in the last decades of the nineteenth century.[7]

Given the international demand for ostrich feathers in general and the Barbary plume in particular, we can appreciate why, in 1911, ostrich farmers, feather merchants, and government officials in South Africa theorized that if they could cross-breed the luminescent Barbary bird with the hearty Cape ostrich, they could produce an incomparable plume that would dominate the international feather market.[8] We next turn to what, precisely, this story has to do with Jews.

In turn-of-the-century North and South Africa, in Europe, and in the United States, Jews were the principal plume middlemen. In the Cape, over 90 percent of feather merchants were Yiddish-speaking immigrants from Russian Lithuania.[9] In North Africa, Sephardi Jews, most of whom were of Livornese origin, dominated feather sales and exports, while Maghrebi Jews dominated the local feather processing industry.[10] In London, where imported African plumes were sold to an international collective of feather merchants, Jewish women of Eastern European origin constituted the majority of blue-collar feather workers, while Jewish men made up 57 percent of dealers in ostrich feathers and 43 percent of ostrich feather manufacturers in 1883: a preponderance that rendered the ostrich feather trade one of London's "chief Jewish monopolies."[11] In New York, the American center of ostrich feather manufacturing, most feather workshops were owned by Jewish men and staffed, as in London, by a Jewish, female, Eastern European blue-collar workforce.[12] Across the global commodity chain, it seems, Jews were exceptionally fluent in feathers.

Despite Jews' significance to the global commerce of this luxury good, scholars of modern Jewish history lack the frame in which to situate this story. This is not, I would argue, due to accidental neglect. Scholars of Jewish culture have been understandably wary of linking Jews to the expanding global market in luxury goods—or, indeed, to the proliferation of capitalist markets in colonial settings—for fear of reiterating anti-Semitic stereotypes. As a result, though studies of Jews' investment in highly localized economies are numerous, there is little serious research on Jews' involvement in transnational commerce, particularly for the modern period.

And yet both Sephardi and Ashkenazi Jews were profoundly implicated in colonial and thus transnational economics in the eighteenth, nineteenth, and twentieth centuries: through the trade of precious stones and metals, women, opium and liquor, through their involvement in the fashion and textile industries and brokerage and financing. Using the Mediterranean Jewish feather diaspora as case study, this essay argues that we must write Jews into the imbricated histories of colonial economics and modern consumer culture: not simply as Zionist nation-builders in the service of Western colonialism, but as commercial liaisons of a consumption-hungry Europe.[13]

Second, this chapter grapples with ethnicity as a powerful force in the shaping of commodity networks. In this respect, it builds upon scholarship that demonstrates how gender and class norms shaped—and were shaped by—patterns of consumption in the modern period. I aim to suggest that our understanding of modern global commerce may be nuanced when we allow ethnicity to enter the picture. After all, the consumption of ostrich feathers, like the consumption of diamonds, women, and liquor, depended upon contact between gendered consumers in the metropole and Jewish merchants at home, in colonial markets, and beyond; and these relationships in turn fueled cultural assumptions about Jews' rootlessness and their inseparability from the portable, ephemeral, and luxury goods so central to the modern experience.

In addition to making these arguments, I will briefly compare the fates of the emergent ostrich feather industry of the Cape of South Africa, which was reliant upon the commercial dexterity of the Lithuanian Jewish diaspora, and the older, revived, but nonetheless fragile ostrich feather economy of North Africa that rested on Mediterranean Jews' mercantile expertise. As this comparison will demonstrate, while the Mediterranean Jewish feather network of North Africa was upended by the expansion of European imperial influence in the region, the Ashkenazi feather network of South Africa was abetted by it. For the purposes of this volume, this contrast is significant because it illuminates the variegated ways in which Jews were involved in modern flows of capital. Even within a single commodity chain, Jews' involvement in the supply of goods was mottled by local, national, and imperial politics, by sub-ethnicity, by gender and class, and by chronological happenstance.

"Barbary" Plumes and the Trans-Saharan Caravan

Although participants in the feather industry coveted "Barbary plumes," in fact the ostrich feathers that reached consumers in Europe and the United States via the Mediterranean were only shipped from the Barbary coast. They originated in the semi-arid Sahel, in the vicinity of Timbuktu, Niger, Housa, Bornu, Wadai, Kordofan, and Darfur, where ostriches were pursued by nomadic and settled hunters. Once hunted, the skins of ostriches, feathers attached, were purchased by three groups of merchants from the north: Ghadamasi merchants, Swiri (e.g., those from Essaouira) merchants, many Jews among them, and members of the Sanusiya Muslim Brotherhood. Ghadamasi and Swiri merchants operated on the three major trade routes that extended south from Tripoli and Essaouira (respectively), while the Sanusiya dominated commerce on the route from Beghazi to Wadai, though Jews, too, were represented on this route.

If Jews were among one of several groups that oversaw the sale and transport of ostrich feathers across the Sahara, the existing evidence suggests that they dominated the purchase, processing, and exportation of the feathers in the port cities of North Africa. Jewish feather traders operated across an unusually wide-reaching geographic terrain within North Africa (their extraregional connections will be described shortly). Jewish merchants who dealt in feathers could be found not only in the port cities of North Africa, but in smaller entrepôts throughout southwestern and eastern Morocco, in regional market towns along the Mediterranean coast and in the Tripolitanian mountains, at transit stations along the Nile, and between the Red Sea and Cairo.[14] In the words of an observer, writing in 1857: "The Jews are almost everywhere the purchasers [of ostrich feathers]; since it is they who venture afar, visiting the most distant markets or the most remote tribes from European centers. Furthermore, they know better than anyone the customs, language, and means of exchange suited to the style of the Arabs."[15]

In addition to serving as prominent feather buyers, Jews financed the conveyance of feathers from the Sahara and Sahel to port cities in the north. Given that trans-Saharan trade tended to operate on credit, the role of financiers was particularly crucial to the smooth operation of the feather industry. For much of the nineteenth century, commercial firms in Tripoli and Essaouira, many of them owned by Sephardi Jews of Livornese origin, advanced Ghadamasi merchants goods imported from Europe—primarily English calico, but including beads, mirrors, paper, spices, perfumes, tea, sugar, copper, and other goods—to sell on their return voyage south to Timbuktu, Kano, or Bornu. These firms would be repaid in ostrich feathers and other commodities that were subsequently carried northward.

Jews were also involved in the rather more blue-collar side of North Africa's feather industry. Once ostrich feathers were conveyed to Essaouira, Tripoli, Alexandria, and Cairo, the principal points of export for this commodity, they needed to be removed from the ostrich hide and prepared for sale overseas. There is evidence that the plucking, washing, sorting, and packing of ostrich feathers were the reserve of poor Judeo-Arab residents of North Africa's port cities, who, according to some accounts, undertook this work within the boundaries of Jewish quarters.[16] Astonishingly, when it became financially advantageous for the higher grades of ostrich plumes to be exported from the Sahel by parcel post and steamship, as was the case after about 1907, the feathers were reexported from London back to Tripoli for processing.

What allowed Jews to become influential in North Africa's feather industry? In what ways was their success as feather merchants dependent upon their being Jews? Mediterranean Jews succeeded as modern traders of feathers for many of the same reasons that Jewish merchants had prospered in the Islamic world since the medieval period: they had contacts across the Sephardi and Mediterranean world with whom they shared a language and family ties; they had the experience and skills required; and they capitalized on mutually beneficial relationships with the reigning authorities. Let us turn to these dimensions of Jewish feather merchants' "human capital" in turn.

The existence of a Sephardi—and, perhaps particularly, a Livornese Jewish—diaspora that stretched across the banks of the Mediterranean, athwart North Africa, and reached into Europe and the United States was a critical factor that enabled Jews to succeed in the feather industry of North Africa. This diaspora availed Jews with the overseas familial and commercial contacts that were so important for transregional trade. In the early modern period, Jewish feather merchants in Tripoli directed their feather exports to contacts in Spain, where they resold feathers to members of the aristocracy in the heart of the *juderia*.[17] As early as the seventeenth and throughout much of the eighteenth and nineteenth centuries, Livorno, Venice, Trieste, and Marseilles proved the most important import centers for the feather industry; in this period, Jews in North Africa's feather trade negotiated with Jewish-owned commercial houses in these Mediterranean ports.[18] This mercantile geography evolved just prior to the onset of feather mania. London had already begun to acquire a monopoly on feather sales in the 1850s, and this monopoly was more or less complete by the time the feather boom began in the 1860s.[19] After London acquired a monopoly on European feather imports, ostrich feathers from Essaouira, Tripoli, Benghazi, Cairo, and Alexandria were shipped directly to the British capital, and the number of North African Jewish family firms in London (and other port towns) grew accordingly.[20]

Shared language helped to cohere further the Mediterranean feather trading diaspora. Many Jewish feather traders—including those from Livorno, many of whom were by origin Marranos from Portugal—were speakers of Judeo-Arabic, and they tended to keep their account books in this language as well. So important was knowledge of Judeo-Arabic to the smooth operation of the feather industry that non-Jews in the trade (including European merchants and Muslim chiefs) corresponded in the language through Jewish interpreters and secretaries.[21]

Given what we now know of the prominence of Jews in the Mediterranean feather trade, it is not surprising that a representative of one of the most prominent North African Jewish feather families should be the crucial informant for the illicit North African ostrich feather expedition of 1911 with which this essay began. A clandestine meeting between the members of this expedition and a member of the Hassan family took place in Paris, while the South African poachers were en route from Cape Town to Forcados. With Hassan's advice, the explorers fulfilled their daring ambitions, though not without dramatic encounters with malaria, sand storms, French and American spies, and the emir of Katsina. After a year's time, the group managed to procure 156 Barbary birds, ferry them across desert and ocean, and, amidst much fanfare, safely transport them to an agricultural college in the Cape. There the cross-breeding of ostriches was begun—but alas, at an unfortunate juncture in the history of the feather trade. Mere months after these Barbary birds were introduced to Cape soil, the bottom fell out of the international ostrich feather market, rendering the birds and the once-coveted plumes they produced utterly worthless.

How Mediterranean Jewish traders managed the volatile feather market is suggested in a story retold by Nahum Slouschz, a Jewish scholar who conducted research on North African Jewry in the early years of the twentieth century:

> During the panic in the ostrich feather trade, a merchant was ruined. To meet the demands of the creditors he brought them even the jewels of his wife. The father of [Jewish feather merchant] M. L. had lent seventy-five thousand francs to one of his nephews, who had established himself in business somewhere in Africa. The [nephew] lost his entire fortune in speculation. M. L., uneasy about his loan, telegraphed his nephew, but received no reply. Months passed. He gave up the money as lost. Then, one day, he received a thick sealed envelope. He opened it, and found seventy-five thousand francs accompanied by a simple note in Judeo-Arabic: "Mine I have lost, but yours is sacred."

Slouschz's tale highlights so much of what was unique about the Mediterranean Jewish feather trading diaspora: it was conditioned by risk, sustained by credit, geographically peripatetic, contingent upon familial fidelity, and navigated in Judeo-Arabic. Language, ties of kith and kin, geographic dispersal, inherited and practical knowledge: these were among the most important resources that Jews in the feather trade commanded.

Certain extracommunal factors also pushed Jews into feather trading and allowed them to succeed in this capacity, in particular Jews' relationship with the old order of North Africa. This essay will not parse these relationships in detail, but will mention briefly that in precolonial Morocco and Ottoman Trip-olitania, Jews' relationship to the court was critical to their success as overseas traders. In both places, Jewish merchants were either subsidized and/or pro-tected by authorities who were interested in using trade to consolidate power and wealth.[22]

Because Jewish success in overseas trade was enhanced by the precolonial order in North Africa, Jews proved particularly vulnerable to the encroach-ment of European power, in a general sense, and to attempts on the part of Europeans to coopt the feather trade, specifically. Though commerce in plumes flourished after the formal colonization of North Africa had begun, ultimately the expansion of European influence in the region had a deleterious effect on the feather trade. This was because, first, colonial authorities encouraged the abrogation of advantageous treatment afforded certain merchants, many Jews among them. What is more, the expansion of colonial control also led to the introduction of political boundaries and provoked intraregional disputes, both of which rendered trans-Saharan travel dangerous and cumbersome. These factors—among others—contributed to the erosion of both the feather trade and Jews' status as the region's principal exporters of luxury goods, even before a slackening demand for plumes upended the international feather market ir-revocably in 1914.

Foreign competition represented an additional threat to North Africa's Jew-ish feather merchants wrought by colonial economics. As early as the 1860s, the ostrich industry of South Africa began to outpace North Africa as Europe's and America's principal ostrich feather supplier. By 1895, the Cape—which had once supplied a negligible quantity of Europe's ostrich feathers—was supplying Britain with fifteen times the value of feathers from North Africa. This figure rose to thirty-eight in 1900 and one hundred and seven in 1910.[23] The evolution in the landscape of the modern feather trade meant, rather ironically, that one Jewish mercantile economy—that is, the Lithuanian Jewish feather merchant diaspora of the Cape—began to supplant another: the Mediterranean Jewish feather merchant diaspora. Because of the relative success of the South African ostrich industry, North Africa's Jewish feather merchants experienced a financial bust precisely when the Jewish feather merchants of the Cape encountered a staggering boom.

This discrepancy was largely a result of imperial politics. If in northern Africa the encroachment of European powers threatened to erode a highly functional feather trading network in which Jews predominated, in southern Africa European imperialism facilitated the trade of ostrich plumes and Jews' involvement in the global exchange of this commodity. This contrast is significant to the Jewish historian in so far as it unsettles deeply rooted scholarly assumptions about Sephardi and Ashkenazi Jews' relationship to imperial power. This comparison suggests, first, that some Ashkenazi Jews were inextricably involved in the colonial project through their facilitation of the creation of capitalist networks in the colonies that served consumers in Europe's and America's metropoles.

If some Ashkenazim were more enfranchised by colonial systems and economics than has been acknowledged, Mediterranean Jewries were not, as has been assumed, necessarily beneficiaries of these phenomena. The existing scholarship on Sephardi, Levantine, and Mediterranean Jewries has emphasized the ways in which they served as cultural and commercial intermediaries between Europe, North Africa, and the Middle East in the colonial period, existing, per André Chouraqui's classic formulation, "between east and west."[24] However, if one focuses on the pre- and early colonial periods, and explores Mediterranean Jewry through the lens of commerce, it appears that Jewish merchants who benefited from being enmeshed in the old regimes of North Africa could also be adversely affected by encroaching European powers and by the transition from pre-colonial to colonial power. Seen through the lens of mercantile and consumer culture, the intrusion of European control in North and Central Africa upset rather than exploited Jews' ability to serve as commercial intermediaries, in a general sense, and as suppliers of luxury goods, in particular.

In tracing the ethnic constitution of a single global commodity chain, my ongoing research on Jews' involvement in the global ostrich feather market attempts to create a history of Jews circumscribed by the logic of commerce, which is to say, a history that is geographically uncircumscribed. If this threatens to confirm stereotypes about Jews' intimacy with capital, it must be remembered that it is also a story about failure, and about how elusive—and historically contingent—profit and expertise can be.

Weaving Jews into the history of modern capitalist and consumer culture, I would suggest, requires historicizing Jews' involvement in the expansion of transnational commerce in the modern period without viewing Jews as primordially destined to fulfill this role (that is, without falling prey to anti-Semitic stereotypes) and without erasing that which is unique about their involvement in or along particular commodity chains. This, in turn, requires paying more attention to ethnicity than have most scholars of consumption, and more attention to transnational commerce than have most scholars of Jewish studies. We need, in other words, to think about consumer, mercantile, and ethnic cultures as being shaped over time and in dialogue with one another, at once rooted in local contexts and enmeshed in a transnational socioeconomic web. What better metaphor to navigate this terrain than the feather of a bird that cannot fly.

NOTES

Thanks to the George L. Mosse Program, Department of History, of the University of Wisconsin, Madison, and to Gideon Reuveni for hosting the lively conference "Jewish History Encounters Economy," in which a preliminary version of this essay was shared. Appreciation is also due to Gideon, Nils Roemer, and the Institute of Jewish Studies at the University College of London, sponsors of "Jewish Longings and Belongings in Modern European Consumer Culture," a conference at which I delivered an additional portion of this work. My attendance at these events was enabled by the University of Washington's Graduate School, Department of History, Jackson School, and Jewish Studies Program, who I also thank for their support.

1. This article is a précis of my book, *Plumes: Ostrich Feathers, Jews, and a Lost History of Global Commerce* (New Haven: Yale University Press, 2008). My reconstruction of the Thornton expedition relies on a number of sources, including accounts by two of its participants, Frank Smith and Russell Thornton: C. P. Nel Archive (Oudtshoorn, South Africa), ASC 27/1-15 and 27/16-21, "Aschman, George documents: North African Expedition, 'Thornton Expedition.'" Thornton's memories of the expedition were published in: "Ostriches from the Soudan: Mr. R. W. Thornton's Story," *South African Agricultural Journal* (June 1912). The C. P. Nel Archive also holds an undated manuscript by H. J. Davin entitled "Three South Africans Risked Their Lives in Quest of the Golden Feather," which I have drawn upon here. Finally, this account utilizes Rob Nixon's summary of Thornton's unpublished memoir, the original of which proved inaccessible: Rob Nixon, *Dreambirds: The Strange History of the Ostrich in Fashion, Food, and Fortune* (New York: Picador USA, 2000), 78–87.

2. Edmond Lefèvre, *Le commerce et l'industrie de la plume pour parure* (Paris: L'auteur, 1914); Julius de Mosenthal and James Edmund Harting, *Ostriches and Ostrich Farming* (London: Trübner & Co., 1876).

3. Erika Diane Rappaport, *Shopping for Pleasure: Women in the Making of London's West End* (Princeton: Princeton University Press, 2000); Erika Rappaport, "Art, Commerce, or Empire? The Rebuilding of Regent Street, 1880–1927," *History Workshop Journal*, no. 53 (2002): 94–117; Judith R. Walkowitz, *City of Dreadful Delight: Narratives of Sexual Danger in Late-Victorian London* (Chicago: University of Chicago Press, 1992).

4. Lefèvre, *Le commerce et l'industrie*, 349, 42, 45; Carl Hayden, "Speech: The Ostrich Industry," Congressional record: proceedings and debates of the 62nd Congress, third session XLIX, no. V (1913), 57–61.

5. I explore this history, and Jews' unique role in the trans-Atlantic ostrich feather trade, in Sarah Abrevaya Stein, "Falling into Feathers: Jews and the Trans-Atlantic Ostrich Feather Trade," *Journal of Modern History* 79, no. 4 (Winter, 2007): 772–812. On the development of the ostrich industry in the Cape: Board of Trade and Industries, "Report No. 55: The Ostrich Feather Industry" (1925).

6. Early proponents of developing the ostrich feather industry in Central or Eastern Sahara included two Frenchmen, the civil engineer Jules Oudot and H. Mircher, who was an officer. Both published extensive reports on the matter. H. Mircher, *Mission de Ghadamès* (Algiers: Typ. Duclaux, 1863), Jules Oudot, *Le Fermage des Autruches en Algérie: Incubation Artificielle* (Paris: Challamel Ainé, 1880). In Britain, similar works by Julius de Mosenthal and Arthur Douglass were highly influential in inspiring and aiding the expansion of ostrich farming in the Cape. Arthur Douglass, *Ostrich Farming in South Africa* (London: Cassell, Petter, Galpin, 1881); Julius De Mosenthal, *Ostriches and Ostrich Farming* (London: Trübner & Co., 1879). On American efforts: *Ostrich Farming in the United States: Reports from the Consuls of the United States at Algiers, Cape Town, and Buenos Ayres, on Ostrich Raising and Ostrich Farming in Africa, in the Argentine Republic, and in the United States* (Washington, D.C.: Government Printing Office, 1882). On the Ottomans' investment in the feather trade: Ahmed Said Fituri, "Tripolitania, Cyrenaica, and Bilad As-Sudan Trade Relations during the Second Half of the Nineteenth Century," PhD diss., University of Michigan, 1982.

7. Scholarship in this vein is extensive: among the most influential sources are the following: Ralph A. Austen, "Marginalization, Stagnation, and Growth: The Trans-Saharan Caravan Trade in the Era of European Expansion, 1500–1900," in *The Rise of Merchant Empires: Long-Distance Trade in the Early Modern World, 1350–1750*, ed. James Tracy (Cambridge and New York: Cambridge University Press, 1990); Stephen Baier, *An Economic History of Central Niger* (Oxford: Clarendon Press, 1980); Stephen Baier, "Trans-Saharan Trade and the Sahel: Damergu, 1870–1930," *The Journal of African History* 18, no. 1 (1977); A. Adu Boahen, *Britain, the Sahara, and the Western Sudan, 1788–1861* (Oxford: Clarendon Press, 1964); A. Adu Boahen, "The Caravan Trade in the Nineteenth Century," *The Journal of African History* 3, no. 2 (1961); Dennis D. Cordell, "Eastern Libya, Wadai and the Sanusiya: A Tariqa and a Trade Route," *The Journal of African History* 18, no. 1 (1977); Ross

Dunn, "The Trade of Tafilalt: Commercial Change in Southeast Morocco on the Eve of the Protectorate," *African Historical Studies* 4, no. 2 (1971); Mark Dyer, "Export Production in Western Libya, 1750–1793," *African Economic History*, no. 13 (1984); Fituri, "Tripolitania, Cyrenaica, and Bilad As-Sudan Trade Relations," Marion Johnson, "Calico Caravans: The Tripoli-Kano Trade after 1880," *The Journal of African History* 17, no. 1 (1976); Paul E. Lovejoy, "Commercial Sectors in the Economy of the Nineteenth-Century Central Sudan: The Trans-Saharan Trade and the Desert-Side Salt Trade," *African Economic History*, no. 13 (1984); Jean-Louis Miège, "Le Commerce Trans-Saharien au XIXe Siècle: Essai de quantification," *Revue de l'Occident Musulman et de la Méditerranée*, no. 32 (1981–1982); Jean-Louis Miège, "Les Juifs et le commerce transsaharien au dix-neuvième siècle," in *Communautés juives des marges sahariennes du Maghreb*, ed. Michel Abitbol (Jerusalem: Institut Ben-Zvi, 1982); C. W. Newbury, "North African and Western Sudan Trade in the Nineteenth Century: A Re-Evaluation," *The Journal of African History* 7, no. 2 (1966); Terence Walz, *Trade between Egypt and bilad as-Sudan, 1700–1820* (Cairo: Institut français d'archéologie orientale du Caire, 1978).

8. Among those advocating this project was the agricultural expert J. Duerden, who published a number of works on the topic: J. E. Duerden, *Ostrich Feather Investigations* (Port Elizabeth: 1907), J. E. Duerden, "The Future of the Ostrich Industry," *Agricultural Journal of the Union of South Africa* 1, no. 3 (1911).

9. Leibl Feldman, *Oudtshoorn—"yerushalayim d'afrike"* (Johannesburg: The Sterling Printing Co. (Pty.) Ltd., 1940); Stein, "Falling into Feathers."

10. Sarah Abrevaya Stein, "Mediterranean Jews and Global Commerce in the Modern Period: On the Trail of the Feather Trade," *Jewish Social Studies* 13, no. 2 (Winter, 2007), 1–39.

11. On the preponderance of Jews in manufacturing and dealing: Joseph Jacobs, *Studies in Jewish Statistics, Social, Vital and Anthropometric* (London: D. Nutt, 1891), 37–38. These figures are usefully summarized by V. D. Lipman in: V. D. Lipman, *Social History of the Jews in England, 1850–1950* (London: Watts, 1954), 79–82. On the prevalence of Jewish women in manufacturing: "Chief Inspector of Factories and Workshops Report, October 1886–87," in *Command Papers; Report of Commisioners* (House of Commons Parliamentary Papers, 1888). These studies are confirmed by the archival records of Britain's Ostrich and Fancy Feather and Artificial Flower Trade Board, created in 1919 to monitor the industry, held by The National Archives of the United Kingdom, and include a general study of the industry conducted by the Board in 1919: LAB 2/723/15.

12. No study ever identified the ethnic breakdown of New York's ostrich feather trade nor specified what percentage of workers were immigrants or foreign-born. And yet the existing evidence suggests that the industry was disproportionately Jewish in makeup. This point was advanced in popular press accounts of the day, which casually called the trade "Jewish." In fact, many Italian women were employed as ostrich feather workers: indeed, their numbers seem to have risen over time. Still, throughout the feather boom Jews appear to have supplied the public face of the ostrich feather trade.

13. It is striking that what attention has been paid to Jews' involvement in transnational—and, in particular, trans-imperial—economic networks has tended to focus

either on the early modern period and/or on Sephardi or Middle Eastern Jewries. Strikingly, the few exceptions to this rule have been penned by scholars outside the field of Jewish studies, including Edward J. Bristow, *Prostitution and Prejudice: The Jewish Fight against White Slavery, 1870–1939* (New York: Schocken Books, 1983); Charles Van Onselen, "Jewish Marginality in the Atlantic World: Organised Crime in the Era of the Great Migrations, 1880–1914," *South African Historical Journal* 43 (2000), 96 - 137; Niall Ferguson, *The House of Rothschild* (New York: Penguin Books, 1998); Yuri Slezkine, *The Jewish Century* (Princeton: Princeton University Press, 2004). On linkages between Zionism and colonialism, see the work of Baruch Kimmerling, Ilan Pappé, Gershon Sharif, and Ronen Shamir.

14. As there was not a market for feathers in North Africa, itinerant merchants of the region were less likely to deal in feathers. Rachel Simon, "Jewish Itinerant Peddlers in Ottoman Libya: Economic, Social, and Cultural Aspects," in *Decision Making and Change in the Ottoman Empire*, ed. Caesar E. Farah (Kirksville: Thomas Jefferson University Press at Northeast Missouri State University, 1993), Harvey Goldberg, *Jewish Life in Muslim Libya: Rivals and Relatives* (Chicago: University of Chicago Press, 1990), 68-81, Fituri, "Tripolitania, Cyrenaica, and Bilad As-Sudan trade relations," 127.

15. Cited in Daniel J. Schroeter, "The Jews of Essaouira (Mogador) and the Trade of Southern Morocco," in *Communautés juives des marges sahariennes du Maghreb*, ed. M. Abitbol (Jerusalem: Institut Ben Zvi Pour la Recherche Sur Les Communautes Juives D'orient, 1982), 380.

16. Walz, *Trade between Egypt and bilad as-Sudan*, 38; Dyer, "Export Production in Western Libya," 126, Miège, "Le Commerce Trans-Saharien au XIXᵉ Siècle," 100; Fituri, "Tripolitania, Cyrenaica, and Bilad As-Sudan Trade Relations," 127; Baier, *An Economic History of Central Niger*, 71.

17. Jonathan Irvine Israel, *Diasporas within a Diaspora: Jews, Crypto-Jews and the World Maritime Empires (1540–1740)* (Leiden: Brill, 2002), 173.

18. On the centrality of Livorno—and Livornese Jewish merchants—to Mediterranean and extraregional trade see, especially, Francesca Trivellato, *The Familiarity of Strangers: The Sephardic Diaspora, Livorno, and Cross-Cultural Trade in the Early Modern Period* (New Haven: Yale University Press, 2009).

19. Other contemporary observers of the feather trade suggested that London's monopoly on feather trading emerged only in the 1870s, but primary sources indicate otherwise. See, for example: Lefèvre, *Le commerce et l'industrie de la plume.*

20. As Daniel Schroeter has demonstrated, during the nineteenth century the "Berberisco" population of London was growing in number and visibility. Daniel J. Schroeter, *The Sultan's Jew: Morocco and the Sephardi World* (Stanford: Stanford University Press, 2002), especially 55–76.

21. Daniel J. Schroeter, *Merchants of Essaouira: Urban society and imperialism in southwestern Morocco, 1844–1886* (Cambridge: Cambridge University Press, 1988), 115.

22. Schroeter, *Merchants of Essaouira*, esp. chap. 10; Schroeter, *The Sultan's Jew;* Minna Rozen, "The Leghorn Merchants in Tunis and Their Trade with Marseilles at the End of the 17th Century" and Rachel Simon, "The Socio-economic Role of the Tripolitanian Jews in the Late Ottoman Period," both in *Communautés*

juives des marges sahariennes du Maghreb, ed. Michel Abitbol (Jerusalem: Institut Ben-Zvi,1982).

23. Lefèvre, *Le commerce et l'industrie de la plume.*
24. André N. Chouraqui, *Between East and West: A History of the Jews of North Africa,* trans. Michael M. Bernet (Philadelphia: The Jewish Publication Society of America, 1968).

✍ 10 ✍

TRADING IN TORAH

Bootleg Bibles and Secondhand Scripture
in the Age of European Imperialism

Adam Mendelsohn

Historians have long been interested in the position of Jews in commodity chains—slaves, spices, grain, cattle, diamonds, coral—in the early modern period. For the most part these networks were closed to those without capital and consanguinity. By contrast we still know surprisingly little about Jewish participation in international trade in the modern period. The limited literature on Jews and commerce in the age of European imperial expansion and colonization in the nineteenth century focuses almost exclusively on the Jewish position as links in an extractive commodity chain that shipped raw materials from colonial sources to metropolitan markets.

Sarah Abrevaya Stein's recent book on the Jewish dominance of the supply of ostrich feathers from South and North Africa is the best of this breed.[1] The Jewish middlemen who are the subjects of her study were involved in purveying feathers from farms to colonial ports, on to London for grading and sorting, and finally to consumers in Europe and the United States for sale. While Stein adds substantially to the existing literature on colonial commodity chains by inserting ethnicity as a unit of analysis, her choice of subject reinforces the conceptualization of imperial trade as a hub and spoke model, with agents on the periphery supplying the metropole with colonial resources. The flow of feathers was unidirectional, with Jews opportunistically filling middlemen roles along a supply chain that might otherwise have been performed by others. This model sees the colonies and informal empire primarily as a site of extraction, overlooking reverse flows that traveled from the metropole outward.

Notes for this chapter begin on page 196.

Although the feather trade was in many ways characteristic of extractive commodity chains in the long nineteenth century, Jews were involved in several other branches of international commerce that did not follow this capital-intensive and linear pattern. While plumes were a passing fancy—the elaborate chain that linked farmers with consumers withered when feathers fell out of fashion—other modern Jewish commercial networks were both more durable and involuted.

This chapter offers a case study of the Jewish role in the trade of an unlikely commodity that was shipped from the metropole outward: Christian missionary Bibles. Unlike the ostrich feather trade, in which Jewish businessmen served as conduits for a commodity from periphery to metropolitan market, Jewish businessmen in the Bible business in Lebanon, Syria, and Palestine, with ready access to cheap missionary texts supplied from London and New York, trans-shipped cut-price scripture to their coreligionists elsewhere in Britain's informal and formal empire, sending Bibles to Yemen, Kurdistan, the Ottoman Empire, Persia, and India. Most likely these businessmen introduced missionary Bibles into an existing circulatory system for distributing Jewish sacred objects. This unexpected trade highlights the role of ethnic minorities in bridging informal and formal empires, shipping colonial commodities to Europe for processing, but also importing and adapting merchandise to meet local and ethnic demand.

The case study also suggests that by focusing exclusively on traditional colonial commodities we lose sight of the exchange of cultural cargo that crossed imperial boundaries. Much of this cargo—newspapers, books, and certain luxury goods—supplied the wants of settlers pining for a distant homeland, as well as those who aspired to emulate metropolitan ways. Other objects were imported and sometimes repurposed by ethnic middlemen to satisfy particularistic local markets. This process was aided by rapid advances in the technologies of transportation and communication. Imperial expansion created new pathways for exchange and strengthened some existing connections. Growing Western influence in the Ottoman Empire, for example, facilitated flows of remittances and philanthropy, ideas and fashions, books and newspapers, and sacred objects between Ottoman Jewry and the larger Jewish diaspora. Yet as the Bible trade demonstrates, trading links could bypass the metropole. Bibles moved great distances at the edges of empire, passing laterally between Jewish middlemen and consumers along a circulatory system that was largely independent of the vertical commodity chains of colonial commerce.

The opportunistic sale of bootleg Bibles by Jews in the 1840s and 1850s is thus a striking example of a distribution system very different from the archetypical colonial commodity chain. The shipping and sale of secondhand scripture does not fit neatly into traditional understandings of imperial commerce. Study of this phenomenon therefore promises a more dynamic portrait of colonial trade, and complicates notions of "center" and "periphery" in Jewish and imperial history.

The emergence of the Jewish trade in bootleg Christian missionary Bibles required the confluence of several factors. Firstly, British imperial trade policy sought to encourage and safeguard the entry of industrial manufactures—primarily textiles—into Persia, Morocco, and the Ottoman Empire. Britain and its imperial rivals pursued this policy aggressively from the 1830s onward, winning extraterritorial rights for their subjects in the Ottoman Empire, stationing their representatives and consuls across Persia, the Levant, and the Balkans, breaking manufacturing and trading monopolies, and extending their military and financial presence. Britain wielded substantial influence via consuls and other imperial agents in the zone outside of its formal area of control.[2]

Secondly, enterprising Christian missionaries, sponsored by European and American missionary societies, marched in lockstep with the expanding influence of the Great Powers, establishing beachheads in the Ottoman Empire and Persia with protection provided by the assertive imperial powers.[3] Mission societies embarked on an aggressive expansion campaign in the 1840s. The London Society for Promoting Christianity among the Jews, the largest of a constellation of Christian mission societies focused on converting Jews, opened at least eight new stations (Oran, Beirut, Safed, Jaffa, Baghdad, Aleppo, Cairo, and Salonica) during this decade alone. In the 1840s, Jews, along with the Eastern churches, were a favored missionary target. The latter somewhat admiringly labeled their nemeses "Bible men" because of the zeal with which scripture-toting evangelists distributed their wares.[4] This mock reverential title points to a third factor critical to the emergence of a Jewish trade in bootleg Bibles: the mass availability of cheap Bibles produced in vernacular translation.

In the first decades of the nineteenth century the cost of printing the Bible dropped substantially. The Christian Bible became cheap and ubiquitous in United States and Britain by the middle decades of the century as declining printing costs made mass publishing possible. Christian Evangelicals had been among the first to grasp the implications of mass publishing, skillfully utilizing the printing press to communicate with their followers and win new converts. Tracts, pamphlets, catechisms, sermons, and Bibles were printed cheaply and in unprecedented quantities, supplying a vast market of devoted readers.[5] These religious, instructional, and inspirational texts were distributed by an army of colporteurs, Bible readers, and itinerant agents, operating independently or representing tract and Bible societies.

By contrast, at mid century Hebrew Bibles from Jewish sources were expensive in London and New York, particularly when compared with the mass produced subsidized volumes distributed by Christian mission societies.[6] Missionaries quickly discovered that even if their spiritual message was rebuffed by

Jews, one of their earthly wares was warmly welcomed. Hebrew Bibles—particularly those with a vernacular translation—gave missionaries a point of access to Jewish communities that were otherwise suspicious and often hostile. That the Bible translation was tendentious, pointing the reader toward a Christological interpretation of the text, only encouraged this initiative.[7] Although no figures are available for the extent of the distribution of the King James version, the use of this Bible in Jewish schools in the United States and Britain, and the considerable efforts made by Jews at mid century to supply a rival English translation, point to its penetration. Rebecca Gratz, unable to find an appropriate alternative, struggled to adapt the Christian translation for use in her Hebrew Sunday School in Philadelphia in 1838. According to her niece, objectionable portions of the text were torn out or covered over with scraps of paper.[8] As late as 1860 the Jews' Free School in London rejected Isaac Leeser's translation on the grounds that the King James version "has become such a component part of the literature, is so much embraced public feature in all what is English, and forms such an element in the language, that the [school] committee will not do without it."[9] Perhaps this preference for an inexpensive and freely available text should not be surprising. The London Society claimed that Jewish schools in Jerusalem—a city in which the Jewish community went to great lengths to avoid contact with missionaries—also relied on its Hebrew Bible for use in the classroom.[10] The success of initiatives to print and distribute cheap Bibles among Jews in Britain and the United States encouraged the mission societies to extend their field of focus abroad to the Jewish communities of Eastern Europe, Persia, and the Ottoman Empire. This program formed part of a vast Protestant project that produced new translations in over one hundred languages and dialects by 1850.[11]

The London Society for Promoting Christianity among the Jews published its first edition of the Tanach in Hebrew in 1823, and over the next seventeen years distributed 61,620 copies and 167,034 portions of this Bible at home and abroad.[12] In 1827 it printed a Yiddish translation of the Pentateuch and three years later the Tanach for distribution in the slums of London and at its missions stations in Central and Eastern Europe.[13] American mission societies were particularly active in this translation drive. The American Bible Society printed a cheap English translation for mass circulation among Jews.[14] American missionaries in Bombay translated the book of Genesis into Marathi in 1819—intended for use among the Bene Israel—and finally finished the whole Bible in 1855.[15] Agents of the British and Foreign Bible Society translated the Bible into Persian and printed it using Hebrew script.[16] William Schauffler, a missionary in Constantinople supported by the Female Jews Society of Boston, appears to have found more reward in translation than arduous daily interaction with potential converts. Between 1835 and 1842 Schauffler completed the translation of the entire Hebrew Bible into Judeo-Spanish, also preparing a lexicon and school textbooks and producing early scholarship on Sabbatai Zevi. Eight thousand copies of his Bible translation were printed and distributed from Constantinople with the aid of substantial grants from the American Bible Society and the Church of Scotland.[17] The American Bible Society again drew on Schauffler's linguistic skills for the preparation of a Judeo-German Bible translation, which it printed in 1847.[18]

If the mission societies found a market eager for inexpensive vernacular translations in London and New York, the demand was even greater abroad, particularly in the Levant, North Africa, and India. Although missionaries distributed some Hebrew Bibles for free, they also sold substantial numbers, albeit almost always at a subsidized rate. John Nicolayson, the London Society representative in Jerusalem starting in 1826, had sold roughly 5,000 by the time the missionary Andrew Bonar visited at the end of 1839. Missionaries in Damascus, Baghdad, Bombay, and Salonica also reported no shortage of eager buyers. In Constantinople, missionaries reported that the Judeo-Spanish translation "was much sought after" by local Jews.[19] Attempts to sell the New Testament, however, were less successful. Bonar described how the Jewish buyers of one shipment of Bibles sold with the Hebrew and Christian texts printed side by side tore out the New Testament and replaced it with Rashi's commentary. Jacob Sappir, who visited Yemen in 1858, reported that rural Jews found a better use for the unwanted text. Reluctant to throw away copies of the New Testament they had received from Joseph Wolff in 1836 because of its Hebrew script, some entrepreneurial Jews instead extracted portions of the text to use for making amulets for sale to Muslims.[20] Whatever their disdain for the Christian version, there was considerable demand for the Hebrew Bible in Yemen. C. L. Lauria, the London Society missionary in Cairo in 1847 sent a stream of Bibles in response to requests from visitors that a "large supply" be sent.[21] This demand was sustained into the late 1860s, evidenced by the ban imposed by Yemenite rabbis on the purchase of Bibles from missionaries in 1866.[22]

The discovery of this seemingly endless reservoir of demand beyond the borders of Britain's formal empire had two important consequences. Firstly, some enterprising Jews developed a secondary market for Christian Bibles, purchasing Bibles imported by the missionary societies cheaply and reselling them at a profit in distant markets, a process best described as scriptural arbitrage. Once disbursed by missionary colporteurs, some of these Bibles had an extraordinary second life as commodities. Andrew Bonar describes how copies of the Hebrew Bibles printed by the British and Foreign Bible Society and sold at subsidized rates by missionaries in Jerusalem and Damascus were purchased in bulk by enterprising Jews who in turn sent the texts to be resold on the secondary market in Baghdad, Mosul, Aleppo, Kurdistan, Yemen, and India. (Joseph Frey claimed that Königsberg acted in the same way as a Bible entrepôt for the Russian Empire.) The missionary Henry Aaron Stern provides some corroboration for this astonishing Tanach-trade, recording his surprise at finding missionary texts in "some of the most remote places" in Persia and Kurdistan. He found, in his own words, "that they had been scattered thus far by the Jews themselves, beyond the sphere of the labours of the missionaries."[23] Most likely, missionary Bibles entered an existing Jewish circulatory system for distributing sacred objects within the Ottoman Empire. This resale of cheap bootleg Bibles may have not been not motivated solely by profit. Another account describes a wealthy Syrian Jew purchasing over 500 Bibles from the London Society and selling them at a low price in Baghdad in order to discourage Jews from approaching missionaries directly.[24] This initiative appears not to have had the desired effect. Stern, who spent a lengthy stint in Baghdad in the 1840s, reported being stopped in the street and besieged at home by Jews "enquiring for books."[25]

Whatever the motives of the participants, the trade involved more than the shipping of missionary Bibles by Jews from an area of relative surplus to one where Bibles commanded higher prices. It involved the appropriation, commoditization, and repurposing of an article for a use very different from that which its metropolitan producers had originally envisaged. This trade was thus unusual for several reasons. For one, the missionary Bibles that were resold by Jews were never intended by the mission societies who produced them to become commodities, never mind to be shorn of the proselytizing intent. Secondly, Jewish businessmen identified and exploited a secondary market among their coreligionists elsewhere. In effect, Jewish businessmen discovered a product that could be commoditized and sold at profit to Jewish consumers through arbitrage. Thirdly, this trade involved a Jewish informal economy far removed from the neat colonial commodity chains described by some scholars. Not only did this trade involve the appropriation and repurposing of a missionary text for Jewish purposes, and the shipping of Bibles by Jews to Jewish consumers, but it also involved trade along the margins and across the borders of formal and informal empire that completely bypassed the metropole.

The second major consequence of the discovery of this pent-up demand among Jews for vernacular Bibles was reactive. The success of mission societies in uncovering and then satisfying demand among Jews for Bibles galvanized a Jewish response. The mission societies proved that profitable publication was viable, throwing down the gauntlet to Jewish religious leaders who had been slow to produce vernacular translations. It was no coincidence that in the middle decades of the century, Jews in Britain and America produced four new translations of the Bible into English, the first such efforts since 1780. Similar programs were conceived by Jews elsewhere.

Among Jews in England and United States, the King James translation reigned almost unchallenged until the 1830s. The two rival editions of the Pentateuch produced by Jewish publishers in Britain in the 1780s—and thereafter widely used for the next fifty years—adopted the authorized version as the English translation, providing supplementary notes but otherwise leaving the text unchanged.[26] Ironically, the missionary drive to print and distribute thousands of copies of this and other translations among Jews from the 1820s onward provided evidence to Jewish publishers that a substantial market for Bibles existed among Jews. Beginning in the late 1820s, several efforts were made to supply this market with a new Jewish translation.

The first initiatives came from two English scholars, Solomon Bennett and Selig Newman.[27] Both promised to correct the mistranslations of the King James version; Bennett aimed to produce an entirely new translation. Even if primarily motivated by scholarly priorities, Newman (if not Bennett) may have been at least partly inspired by the goal of supplying a text with a shallower Christological imprint more appropriate for Jews. Although he publicly denied any polemical intentions, Newman's variant version would inevitably enable Christian and Jewish readers to "separate the chaff from the wheat" in very different ways when interpreting the Biblical text. Newman certainly recognized the importance of providing a revised translation at a time when Bible distributions "far surpass those of any other age and country," leaving readers ever more vulnerable to misapprehension and misdirection.[28] Newman, who had taught Hebrew at Oxford, had a history of confronting conversionists in print and in person. In 1827 he attended weekly meetings of the Philo-Judaean Society, on one occasional verbally sparring with the apostate missionary Joseph Wolff about the Christian interpretation of the Hebrew Bible.[29] (In a stroke of irony, The Eclectic Review of London recommended Newman's 1832 Hebrew-English dictionary as "extremely useful in the preparation of Hebrew exercises, especially to any who may be desirous of translating any English books, tracts, &c., into Hebrew, with a view to effect the conversion of the Jews."[30]) Newman returned to print two decades later and a continent away—he moved to New York in the 1840s—publishing an anti-missionary polemic that returned to the turf he had earlier disputed with Wolff.[31]

A third pretender to the King James throne—who also began the daunting task of providing a complete new translation in the 1830s—proved far more successful. While Bennett died before publishing (and most likely completing) his ambitious project, and Newman confined his efforts to a 72-page notation of variant readings, Isaac Leeser, a pioneering preacher and publisher in Philadelphia, produced a wholly new translation that broke substantially with the Anglican version.[32] Inspired by Zunz's landmark translation of the Bible into German—and probably by parallel efforts in Philadelphia to produce a Bible suitable for Catholics—Leeser began work on his own translation in 1838.[33] He finished the Pentateuch seven years later, and the entire Hebrew Bible in 1854. While Leeser opted not to discard the old English prose and spellings familiar to readers of the King James Bible, he was forthright in challenging the primacy of the Protestant text. The authorized Bible, he wrote in his preface, had long been "looked upon with deep veneration almost bordering on super-stitious dread." Rather than an act of lèse-majesté, his "improved translation" would rightfully unseat the King James version.[34] In England at least, Leeser's sanguine expectations were thwarted by deep-seated attachment to the Prot-estant text. As noted earlier, the Jews' Free School declined to purchase his translation precisely because the authorized Bible had become a "much em-braced public feature in all what is English." He had more success in America. This was in large part due to Leeser's own assiduous salesmanship, including a fifteen week cross-country trip starting in November 1851 to drum up sub-scriptions.[35] Rosa Mordecai reported, with some grumbling about a stylistically tone-deaf translation, that Leeser's Bible replaced the King James version at the Hebrew Sunday School in Philadelphia by 1854.[36] By the 1860s, the Leeser translation had become "the standard Bible for English-speaking Jews" in the United States.[37]

The Leeser Bible was not the only new translation that struggled in Brit-ain. There was certainly no shortage of calls for a Jewish Bible to pry loose the steely grip held by the authorized version and to satisfy growing pressure for reform and modernization in synagogue worship. In May 1843 the Lon-don *Jewish Chronicle* editorialized on the urgency of a "corrected translation of the Bible."[38] Three years later Grace Aguilar was still lamenting the want of a translation by a "faithful Hebrew" and discussed the feasibility of writing and publishing such a work.[39] There were a number of false starts.[40] A triumvirate of prominent hazans—David Aaron de Sola of Bevis Marks, Israel Linden-thal of the New Synagogue, and Morris Raphall of the Birmingham Hebrew Congregation—produced a new translation of Genesis in 1844 that discarded the distinctive idiom of the authorized version. (Raphall later offered to assist Leeser with his Bible translation.[41]) Again they sought "faithfulness"—a man-tra of Jewish detractors of the authorized translation—and made pointed refer-ences to the energy of British missionaries in distributing Bibles to "every part of the globe." Although the volume was heralded with great excitement—the *Jewish Chronicle* gushed that when completed, the new edition would "be the most important publication that ever emanated from the Jews of Great Brit-ain"—their plan to translate the entire Pentateuch fizzled, seemingly for lack of demand.[42]

Abraham Benisch, a scholar, newspaper editor, and teacher in London at the Jews' and General Literary Institution (and occasional correspondent with Isaac Leeser) made much more headway.[43] Like his American counterpart, Benisch saw himself as walking in the footsteps of Mendelssohn and Zunz. Cru-cially, he had more savvy and stamina than his predecessors in England, win-ning the coveted sanction of the Chief Rabbi (important for sales in Britain and its empire) and ready access to the pages of the London *Jewish Chronicle*, which, like Leeser's *Occident*, was a crucial tool for encouraging sales. He completed the Pentateuch in 1851 and printed the fourth and final volume a decade later. Benisch marketed his translation as a Family Bible, a counterpart and rival to the popular Christian Family Bibles, not as an alternative to the inexpensive editions produced by the British and Foreign Bible society. Family Bibles were designed to appeal to women, typically providing a more appealing format that spoke to an aspiration to domestic piety and respectability.[44] (The original edition of Leeser's Bible also had this market in mind.[45]) Like Leeser, Benisch intended his Bible to replace the King James version as the benchmark within the Jewish community. While he promised a fresh and "faithful" translation more attuned to "characteristics peculiar to Judaism," he cleaved much closer to the authorized version.[46] Yet even this more limited goal was anathema in Britain. By 1854 popular pressure forced Benisch to retreat. Readers accustomed to the authorized Bible complained that his new renderings "grate upon their ears." Despite its "manifest unfitness for Jewish families and schools," the Anglican text was "invested with a kind of semi-sacredness" by the Jewish public. Benisch reluctantly restored the Anglican translation in instances "where it could be done without doing violence to the principle of fidelity." While he regretted this "sacrifice," his decision was pragmatic. To do otherwise would doom his translation to commercial failure.[47] This pragmatism paid off. When the Jews' Free School in London rejected Leeser's translation in 1860, they seem to have preferred Benisch's revised version.[48] The King James translation continued to hold sway among the Jews of Britain for at least another three decades.[49]

Leeser and Benisch competed to sell their Bible translations abroad, courting Jewish buyers across America and the British Empire. Both used the newspapers they edited to promote and advertise their Bible translations to potential buyers at home and abroad. They were aided by the dramatic growth of the English-language press. As early as 1845, Leeser's *Occident* had subscribers in Canada, Barbados, St. Thomas, Grenada, Jamaica, Venezuela, England, Brazil, Puerto Rico, New Zealand, New South Wales, and Tasmania. The London *Jewish Chronicle* also boasted subscribers across Britain's formal and informal empire and beyond. Their Bibles, along with competing missionary translations, were among the cultural commodities that traveled along Jewish supply chains from the metropole outward.

The Bible trade also forces us to reevaluate the impact of Christian missionizing in the nineteenth century. The missionary movement has often been assessed in terms of the total number of converts won to its cause. This narrow parameter, wielded by critics of the mission societies in the nineteenth century, distorts the extent of their impact. Measured in baptisms, Jewish missions had very limited success, particularly given the resources expended.[50] Measured in terms of the agitation and anxiety that they aroused among Jewish communities, and the fevered efforts adopted to counteract their perceived menace, the equation is altered entirely. Missions were engines for innovation within

Anglophone Jewry, persuading Jewish communities from New South Wales to New York to mimic their methods in areas a diverse as education, publishing, and communal welfare.[51] There is ample evidence that missionaries were also agents of cultural revival in the Ottoman Empire and Persia, contributing to the spread of Judeo-Spanish and Judeo-Persian culture, and pressuring communal elites to modernize Jewish schooling.[52] In this way, missionaries were carriers of modernity, catalyzing cultural and social change within the Jewish communities they encountered and stimulating unprecedented cooperation between Jews across imperial and national boundaries.

Thus, in summary, the missionary program of printing and distributing cheap Bibles to Jews had two unexpected consequences. Christian missionary Bibles sent from Britain and America to Palestine, Lebanon and Syria were turned into commodities by entrepreneurial Jews who shipped the Bibles eastward to satisfy demand among communities who had little access to cheap scripture. Meanwhile, the missionary push to distribute Bibles to Jews revealed to Jewish communal leaders the extent of popular demand among Jews for cheaply available scripture. The new Jewish translations published from the late 1830s onward were stimulated both by a perceived need to counter missionary efforts, and by a realization that the market for a new Jewish translation was large and potentially profitable. This contrasts substantially with historians' current understanding of Jewish involvement in colonial trade. While undoubtedly Jews were instrumental in some colonial commodity chains, this example demonstrates both how Jews at the edges of empire opportunistically supplied their own ethnic market by appropriating and repurposing metropolitan articles, bridging informal and formal empires, and how those at the center shipped cultural cargo in reverse along the same supply chains that facilitated the extraction of colonial commodities. Bibles, both bootleg and legitimate, therefore reveal the dynamism of Jewish involvement in colonial trade. Jewish businessmen involved in colonial trade were not only, to borrow Stein's phrase, "falling into feathers," but also, when it suited them, trading in Torah.

Notes

An earlier version of this essay was presented at the "Jews, Commerce & Culture" Colloquium organized by the Herbert D. Katz Center for Advanced Judaic Studies at the University of Pennsylvania in April 2009. My thanks to the center for the year-long fellowship without which this research would have been impossible, and to my colleagues at the center for their friendship and generous advice.

1. See Sarah Abrevaya Stein, *Plumes: Ostrich Feathers, Jews, and a Lost World of Global Commerce* (New Haven: Yale University Press, 2008).

2. On Britain's informal empire, see John Gallagher and Ronald Robinson, "The Imperialism of Free Trade," *The Economic History Review* 6, no. 1 (1953), 1–15, here 11; John Darwin, "Imperialism and the Victorians: The Dynamics of Territorial Expansion," *The English Historical Review* 112, no. 447 (1997), 614–642; Martin Lynn, "British Policy, Trade, and Informal Empire in the Mid-Nineteenth Century," in *Oxford History of the British Empire*, ed. Andrew Porter, vol. 3 (Oxford: Oxford University Press, 1999), 101, 108–109. For the forced opening of the Moroccan and Ottoman economies see Daniel Schroeter, *Merchants of Essaouira: Urban Society and Imperialism in Southwestern Morocco, 1844–1886* (Cambridge: Cambridge University Press, 1988), 125–129; Donald Quataert, "The Age of Reforms, 1812–1914," in *An Economic and Social History of the Ottoman Empire*, ed. Halil İnalcık (Cambridge: Cambridge University Press, 1997), 825–842.

3. On the expansion of missionary activity in the middle of the nineteenth century, see Adam Mendelsohn, "Tongue Ties: Religion, Culture and Commerce in the Making of the Anglophone Jewish Diaspora, 1840–1870," PhD diss., Brandeis University, 2008, 49–89.

4. Jeremy Salt, "Trouble Wherever They Went: American Missionaries in Anatolia and Ottoman Syria in the Nineteenth Century," *Muslim World* 92, no. 3 (2002), 287–307.

5. For the revolution in religious publishing see David Nord, *Faith in Reading: Religious Publishing and the Birth of Mass Media in America* (Oxford: Oxford University Press, 2004), 41–97; Richard Altick, *The English Common Reader: A Social History of the Mass Reading Public, 1800–1900* (Columbus, OH: Ohio State University Press, 1998), 99–128; Paul Boyer, *Urban Masses and Moral Order in America, 1820–1920* (Cambridge, MA: First Harvard University Press, 1978), 22–33; Nathan Hatch, *The Democratization of American Christianity* (New Haven: Yale University Press, 1989), 125–133, 141–146; Joseph Kett, *The Pursuit of Knowledge under Difficulties: From Self-Improvement to Adult Education in America, 1750–1990* (Stanford: Stanford University Press, 1994), 55–59, 67–73; Robert Ellison, *The Victorian Pulpit: Spoken and Written Sermons in Nineteenth-Century Britain* (Selinsgrove, PA: Susquehanna University Press, 1998), 15, 46–47; Leslie Howsam, *Cheap Bibles: Nineteenth-Century Publishing and the British and Foreign Bible Society* (Cambridge: Cambridge University Press, 1991).

6. In 1841, the entire New Testament was available for purchase at the unsubsidized rate of 9 shillings in London. A copy of the Hebrew Bible could be bought from a Christian purveyor for 10s 6d in 1847. In 1860, 25 shillings could buy the Old and New Testament in English and Hebrew. By contrast, a reprinted English and Hebrew translation of David Levi's Bible was sold for 30 shillings in 1845. Isaac Leeser's translation of the Pentateuch was advertised in London for £2 7s 6d in 1848. Raphall, Lindenthal, and De Sola's translation of the Book of Genesis sold for 7s 6d. Each of the four volumes of Abraham Benisch's translation were sold in 1855 for 15 shillings, or 10s 6d each if bought as a complete set. *Voice of Jacob* (*VoJ*), 5 December 1845; *Jewish Chronicle* (*JC*), 25 February 1848, 28 January 1853, 15 January 1855; *The Baptist Magazine* 33 (January 1841): 69; Bishop Pamphili

Eusebius, *The Greek Ecclesiastical Historians* (London, 1847), 3; *The Gentleman's Magazine,* December 1860, 20. See also Henry Mayhew, *London Labour and the London Poor,* vol. 1 (London: G. Woodfall, 1851), 87.

7. For a discussion of the Christological content of the King James Version—composition and ordering of the canon, chapter headings, etc.—see Joseph H. Hertz, *Jewish Translations of the Bible in English* (London: Jewish Guardian, 1920), 4–5; Jonathan D. Sarna and Nahum M. Sarna, "Jewish Bible Scholarship and Translations in the United States," in *The Bible and Bibles in America,* ed. Ernest S. Frerichs (Atlanta: Scholars Press, 1988), 86–87; Jonathan Sarna, "Jewish-Christian Hostility in the United States: Perceptions from a Jewish Point of View," in *Uncivil Religion: Interreligious Hostility in America,* ed. Robert N. Bellah and Frederick Greenspahn (New York: Crossroad, 1987), 13.

8. Dianne Ashton, *Rebecca Gratz: Women and Judaism in Antebellum America* (Detroit: Wayne State University Press, 1997), 152–153; Hebrew Sunday School Society, *Celebration of the Seventy-Fifth Anniversary* (Philadelphia, 1913), 6–7; Lance Sussman, *Isaac Leeser and the Making of American Judaism* (Detroit: Wayne State University Press, 1995), 101.

9. "The almost unanimous wish of the Committee is that the [King James] version should be retained as now as it harmonizes with Jewish Doctrines and Principles." Adler to Leeser, 26 November 1860, ACC/2805/01/01/006, London Metropolitan Archives.

10. This claim is made in Thomas D. Halsted, *Our Missions: Being a History of the Principal Missionary Transactions of the London Society for Promoting Christianity amongst the Jews, from its foundation in 1809, to the present year* (London: William Macintosh, 1866), 184.

11. For the scale of this translation initiative, see William Strickland, *History of the American Bible Society* (New York: Harper and Brothers, 1850), 142, 158–163; Peter Wosh, *Spreading the Word: The Bible Business in Nineteenth-Century America* (Ithaca: Cornell University Press, 1994), 151–174.

12. The society published a complete translation of the New Testament in Hebrew in 1817. By 1840 it had distributed 55,745 copies. See Harvey Newcomb, *Cyclopedia of Missions* (New York: Charles Scribner, 1860), 492; Robert Michael Smith, "The London Jews' Society and Patterns of Jewish Conversion in England, 1801–1859" *Jewish Social Studies* 43, no. 3/4 (1981), 275–290, here 283.

13. William Thomas Gidney, The *History of the London Society for Promoting Christianity Amongst the Jews* (London: London Society for Promoting Christianity Amongst the Jews, 1908), 71–72, 151–152, 640.

14. Henry Dwight, *The Centennial History of the American Bible Society* (New York: Macmillian, 1916), 329.

15. See *Memorial Papers of the American Marathi Mission, 1813–1881* (Bombay, 1882), 80–84.

16. William Canton, *A History of the British and Foreign Bible Society* (London: John Murray, 1904), 353; Harvey Goldberg, ed., *Sephardi and Middle Eastern Jewries: History and Culture in the Modern Era* (Bloomington, IN: Indiana University Press, 1996), 37.

17. *Report of the Board of Commissioners for Foreign Missions, Presented at the Thirty Third Annual Meeting* (Boston, 1843), 91; Gidney, *History of the London Society*, 252; David Bunis, "Modernization and the Language Question among Judezmo-Speaking Sephardim of the Ottoman Empire," in Goldberg, *Sephardi and Middle Eastern Jewries*, 228–229.

18. See William Schauffler, *Autobiography of William G. Schauffler* (New York: Randolf and Company, 1887), xxi, 128–129, 185–186; William Schauffler, "Shabbathai Zevi and His Followers," *Journal of the American Oriental Society* 2 (1851): 3–26; *Report of the Board of Commissioners for Foreign Missions, Presented at the Thirty Fourth Annual Meeting* (Boston, 1844), 247; Andrew A. Bonar and R. M. M'Cheyne, *Narrative of a Mission of Inquiry to the Jews From the Church of Scotland in 1839* (Edinburgh, 1842), 352; Ridley Haim Herschell, *Visit to My Fatherland: Being Notes of a Journey to Syria and Palestine in 1843* (1844), 54; Strickland, *History of the American Bible Society*, 270–271, 283; Bunis, "Judezmo-Speaking Sephardim of the Ottoman Empire," 228–229; Salt, "Trouble Wherever They Went," 287–313.

19. See Herschell, *Visit to My Fatherland*, 54–55.

20. Jacob Sappir, *Sefer Masa 'Teiman* (Tel Aviv, 1941), 119–120.

21. *Historical Notices of the London Society for Promoting Christianity amongst the Jews* (London, 1850), 25, 29; Bonar and M'Cheyne, *Narrative of a Mission of Inquiry*, 172; Gidney, *History of the London Society*, 255, 301, 305; *Memorial Papers of the American Marathi Mission, 1813–1881* (Bombay, 1882), 80.

22. JC, 9 November 1866; see also Gidney, *History of the London Society*, 306.

23. See *Historical Notices of the London Society*, 25; Bonar and M'Cheyne, *Narrative of a Mission of Inquiry*, 172, 527; Joseph Wolff, *Journal of the Reverend Joseph Wolff* (London, 1839), 391–392; Joseph Frey, *Judah and Israel* (New York, 1840), 190. For demand for the Bible among the Bene Israel, see Canton, *British and Foreign Bible Society*, 378; *Report of the Board of Commissioners for Foreign Missions, Presented at the Thirty Third Annual Meeting* (Boston, 1842), 133. For Jews buying and reselling missionary Bibles in Posen, see *VoJ*, 23 March 1844, 110. For Stern's mission to Kurdistan, see Erich Brauer, *The Jews of Kurdistan* (Detroit: Wayne State University Press, 1993), 45–46; Henry Stern, *Dawnings of Light in the East* (London, 1854), 206–225.

24. *Historical Notices of the London Society*, 24.

25. Gidney, *History of the London Society*, 257–259.

26. See David B. Ruderman, *Jewish Enlightenment in an English Key: Anglo Jewry's Construction of Modern Jewish Thought* (Princeton: Princeton University Press, 2000), 219–221.

27. Ibid., 228–230; Solomon Bennett, *Critical Remarks on the Authorised Version of the Old Testament, containing some examples of its Errors, with Specimens of an Amended Translation* (London, 1834). Bennett is best known for his feud with Chief Rabbi Solomon Hirschell. For an explanation of their disagreement, see Ruderman, *Jewish Enlightenment in an English Key*, 251–256; Todd M. Endelman, *Jews of Georgian England, 1714-1830: Tradition and Change in a Liberal Society* (Ann Arbor, MI: University of Michigan Press, 1999), 142–145.

28. Selig Newman, *Emendations of the Authorized Version of the Old Testament* (London, 1839), iii–iv.

29. Confrontations at mission meetings between missionaries and hostile Jews in the audience were not uncommon. See, for example, *JC*, 26 April 1861.

30. *The Eclectic Review* (December 1838): 721–722.

31. Selig Newman, *The Challenge Accepted; a Dialogue between a Jew and a Christian: The Former Answering a Challenge Thrown out by the Latter, Respecting the Accomplishment of the Prophecies Predictive of the Advent of Jesus* (New York, 1850); Endelman, *Jews of Georgian England*, 28; Sarna, "Jewish Responses to Christian Missions," 39–40; C. S. Monaco, *Moses Levy of Florida* (Baton Rouge: Louisiana University Press, 2005), 124–125.

32. For Leeser see Sussman, *Isaac Leeser.*

33. Leeser believed a Jewish Bible translation would confer legitimacy and honor on the Jewish community, affirming their claim to equality with Protestants in the United States. See Sarna and Sarna, "Jewish Bible Scholarship," 87.

34. Quoted in Hertz, *Jewish Translations of the Bible in English*, 14. Sussman, *Isaac Leeser,* 151; Sussman, "First Jewish Translation of the Bible," 174–179; Sarna and Sarna, "Jewish Bible Scholarship," 87–89.

35. Sussman, "First Jewish Translation of the Bible," 168.

36. Jacob Rader Marcus, *The Jew in the Modern World: A Sourcebook* (Detroit: Wayne State University Press, 1996), 154–155.

37. Sussman, "First Jewish Translation of the Bible," 159.

38. *JC*, 12 May 1843.

39. See Sussman, "First Jewish Translation of the Bible," 185.

40. For an example of one such stillborn translation project see *VoJ*, 8 December 1843 and 12 April 1844.

41. Morris Raphall to Isaac Leeser, 16 March 1854, Microfilm 199, American Jewish Archives.

42. *JC*, 10 January 1845; David Aaron De Sola, *A Prospectus of a New Edition of the Sacred Scriptures* (London, 1840); David Aaron De Sola, I. L. Lindenthal, and Morris Raphall, *The Sacred Scriptures in Hebrew and English, volume 1, Genesis* (London, 1844). The project may have become mired in the controversy that surrounded de Sola and Raphall's *Eighteen Treatises on the Mishna* (London, 1842), which was published by Benjamin Elkin, a prominent advocate of religious reform, without the authors' permission. For a discussion of the dispute, see Benjamin Elkin, *Letters Addressed to the Editor of the "Voice of Jacob," being replies to the observations contained in Nos. xxxvii., and xxxix., of that publication* (London, 1843); Joseph Jacobs and Lucien Wolf, *Bibliotheca Anglo-Judaica: A Bibliographic Guide to Anglo-Jewish History* (London, 1888), 113.

43. On Benisch as a newspaper editor see David Cesarani, *The Jewish Chronicle and Anglo-Jewry* (Cambridge: Cambridge University Press, 2005), 32–49; J. M. Shaftesley, "Dr Abraham Benisch as Newspaper Editor," *The Jewish Historical Society of England—Transactions* 21 (1967): 214–231. On his correspondence with Leeser see Sussman, "Jewish Translation of the Bible," 187, fn. 88; Abraham Benisch to Leeser, 23 September 1858, 27 July 1864, 26 October 1864, P-20, American Jewish

Historical Society. On the birth of Sussex Hall and the spread of Jewish literary societies in the United States and the British Empire, see Mendelsohn, "Tongue Ties," 174–218.

44. See Mary Carpenter, *Imperial Bibles, Domestic Bodies: Women, Sexuality, and Religion in the Victorian Market* (Athens, OH: Ohio University Press, 2003), xviii, 4–7.

45. The original Leeser Bible left pages blank for recording births and deaths. Sussman, "First Jewish Translation of the Bible," 168.

46. While "fully admitting of the great merits of the Anglican version," he disputed its suitability for Jewish readers. The "translators appointed by King James cannot be considered as free agents, they have been bound in this work partly by the positive injunctions of that monarch, and partly by the less obvious but more powerful influence of Christian authorities." Abraham Benisch, *Jewish School and Family Bible* (London: James Darling, 1851 and 1854), preface.

47. See the translator's preface of Abraham Benisch, *Jewish School and Family Bible.*

48. See Adler to Leeser, 26 November 1860, ACC/2805/01/01/006, LMA.

49. Two new Jewish revisions of the King James version were printed in the 1880s: Hermann Gollancz, *The Holy Bible* (London, 1880) and Michael Friedländer, *The Jewish Family Bible* (London, 1884). For complaints about the continued reliance on the King James translation, see *JC*, 15 June 1860; Hertz, *Jewish Translations of the Bible in English*, 6.

50. By one estimate, the London Society converted 664 Jews between 1809 and 1851. Mel Scult, for example, calculated that each London Society convert between 1809 and 1816 cost the society £500 in total expenditure. To his mind, the missionary enterprise was "a fantastic exercise in futility and we can not help but wonder how the missionaries persisted with such vehemence in the face of so little success." Mel Scult, *Millennial Expectations and Jewish Liberties* (Leiden: Brill, 1978), 97. For other estimates of the numbers of converts won by missionaries, see Gidney, *History of the London Society*, 216; Harvey W. Meirovich, "Ashkenazi Reactions to the Conversionists, 1800–1850," in *Transactions of the Jewish Historical Society of England* 26 (1979), 20. Missionaries also had very limited success converting eastern Christians in the Ottoman Empire. See Salt, "Trouble Wherever They Went," 308.

51. For a detailed discussion of this argument, see Mendelsohn, "Tongue Ties," 90–141.

52. In Constantinople, the Protestant mission "contributed to the diffusion of Judaeo-Spanish culture" through its extensive publications of textbooks, dictionaries, and religious works in the language. The same pattern was evident elsewhere. Esther Benbassa, "The Process of Modernization of Eastern Sephardi Communities," in Goldberg, *Sephardi and Middle Eastern Jewries*, 92; Minna Rozen, *Jews in Turkey and the Balkans* (Tel Aviv: Tel Aviv University, 2002), 66, 70; Harvey Goldberg, "Introduction," in Goldberg, *Sephardi and Middle Eastern Jewries*, 37.

⤜ 11 ⤛

CUT TO ZIONISM

The Emergence of the Diamond Industry in British-Ruled Palestine

David De Vries

For quite some time it has been a well-known fact that Palestine was transformed between the late 1930s and the late 1940s. The rise of Fascism in Europe and the Second World War changed the character of the country's economy, and the Holocaust transformed its demographic and cultural horizons. The retreat of the British Empire had an impact on Palestine politically, and by the end of the 1940s a bloody civil war had resulted in the birth of the state of Israel and the statelessness of thousands of Palestinians. Historians have fittingly dedicated considerable effort to unraveling these vicissitudes. However, only in recent years have economic and social historians begun to draw attention to the fact that the British-backed maturation of capitalism in Palestine, particularly in the economy of the Jewish polity (the *Yishuv*), was a major part of the transformation. Indeed, after years of capital import and slow economic growth, the 1940s saw a remarkable economic boom, a flourishing of industry largely at the expense of agriculture, and the unprecedented activity of private manufacture, aided as it was by the economic policies of the British Palestine government.[1]

As contemporaries readily recognized, this period of industrialization was also expressed in the strengthening of the heretofore weak organizations of manufacturers and merchants who aspired to translate economic achievement into social and political power. An integral part of the transformation was the destabilization of the representational power of Jewish organized labor (the Histadrut), particularly in industry. The latter was also related to an unprecedented upsurge, between the years 1941 and 1946, in workers' strike action, at times independent of and occasionally against the authority of the organized labor movement. State-sponsored efforts at strengthening private capital formed the basis of a contemporary Middle Eastern pattern, and in Palestine as elsewhere it laid the infrastructure for subsequent social change.[2]

Less perceptible, however, was the growing integration of private capital and entrepreneurship in the life of the *Yishuv* by groups seeking to enhance the legitimization of capitalism as a way of thinking and of social practice. Built in the 1930s on the integration of capital's national role in Zionist state-building, and pushed further to the center of economic activity by Palestine's economic boom and British wartime protective economic policies, Jewish industrialists and manufacturers could, in the 1940s, claim a victory over the suspicion and even derogation they had experienced earlier regarding their social and Zionist roles—their "national egoism," as Labor's leader David Ben-Gurion had phrased it in the mid 1920s.[3]

The central economic role of private capital in Palestine and its social acceptance have gradually advanced since the early rise of manufacturing in the mid 1920s, despite contemporary ambivalence toward Jewish participation in a capitalist economy and toward the urbanization of the Zionist project. It further intensified during the invigorated industrialization of the first half of the 1930s, as reflected in the concomitant maturation of the industrial activity of the private sector in Palestinian towns, the rhetoric of a national role that capitalism came now to fulfill, and the recognized capacity of capital to work for the "Zionist social good." What was novel in the latter part of the Mandate period was that capitalism and its legitimization gradually became far from an internal *Yishuv* affair and much more tightly linked to outside forces and events. Furthermore, during the war particular standard-bearers of the process were able to grow, operate, and struggle to carve a recognized place in society because they were located at the juncture of local and international contexts created and shaped by changes wrought by Fascism and war. In both senses, the economic and social boundaries of Palestine's Zionist polity were blurred, integrated not only into larger political and military systems, but also into imperial networks and rival international economic interests. The significance of this process in the formation and advancement of capitalism in modern Palestine would seem self-evident. But only by analyzing the specificity of the ties woven by these groups in the context of the war can we uncover the meaning of this blurring and explain its relation to the British presence. A study of the formation of the diamond industry is particularly instructive in unraveling this process.[4]

The Making of a Production Center

The diamond industry is illuminating in this case because of the long-standing historical association of Jews with diamond cutting and trading. The central role played for many years by Jews in the diamond industry in the Dutch and Belgian economies was indicative not only of Jewish integration in particular economic niches, but also of the importance of ethnic ties and trust relations in modern economic development.[5] However, examining the diamond industry is even more instructive both because the industry arrived in Palestine so late, and because its emergence was less in diamond trading than in production itself. During the first thirty years of the twentieth century, there had been some scattered attempts to establish a diamond industry in Palestine. The social climate of professional induction and "skilling" of youth had developed in Palestine already by this time, and Dutch and Belgian diamond merchants and cutting experts showed a willingness to transfer capital and polishing machines from the traditional diamond centers in the Netherlands to Palestine. The diamond industry in Antwerp, globally dominant as it had been since the decline of Amsterdam after the First World War, would not encourage rival cutting centers, however, and in this competitive stance it was greatly assisted and backed by the De Beers diamond cartel. Moreover, most of the Jews who dominated diamond cutting and trading in Amsterdam and Antwerp between 1870 and 1930 hardly conceived of Palestine as an option in which to develop an industry that was heavily dependent on Jewish ethnic networks and on Europe as an entrepôt for the international diamond business. Finally, and no less significantly, the customs duties that the British Mandate in Palestine placed on the import of rough diamonds from Europe were too high to allow cutting and polishing in the country to become profitable. None of the historical forces that shaped the presence of Jews in the European diamond production and business as a middlemen minority and occupiers of an occupational niche could overcome these limitations. Palestine would only become a part of the historical continuum of relocations that had characterized the diamond industry in the past (and still do) when a tremendous shift began to crack Antwerp's domination.[6]

Two separate processes contributed to this shift. One was the rise of Fascism in Europe, the other the strengthening of business ties between the British Empire and the De Beers diamond cartel. On Hitler's assumption of power, the world diamond industry was in the midst of a recovery from the economic slump of the early 1930s. The industry in Antwerp was also expanding, partly due to the movement in Europe of merchants, capital, and expertise that National Socialism provoked. More significant was the new German policy of enlarging the diamond cutting industry (located in Hanau and Idar-Oberstein) for export, and acquiring industrial diamonds essential for the armament economy. By the beginning of the war, the German diamond cutting industry surpassed that of the Netherlands and had positioned itself as a competitive threat to Antwerp. Belgium's Jews, a majority of whom were involved in trading and polishing diamonds, were also beginning to experience instability and a rise in anti-Semitism.

From 1936 to 1938, a small number of Jewish diamond merchants and experts left Antwerp for these reasons, some even going to Palestine. The majority stayed and even took part in the flourishing diamond trade with German diamond dealers, who now offered diamond cutting at much cheaper prices than those in Antwerp. The Second World War broke out against this ambivalent backdrop of the destabilization of Jewish life in Belgium on the one hand, and the continuity of a vibrant diamond business on the other, which threatened the very existence of the industry in Belgium.[7]

De Beers was likewise destabilized. Its recovery from the world economic crisis of the late 1920s and the development of its sales organization in London (the Diamond Trading Company) in 1934–1935 were based on expanding diamond mining in Africa. Its ties with the British government and imperial presence in South Africa and Sierra Leone were improving, demonstrated by the mining concession given in 1935 to the De Beers–British subsidiary company, the Sierra Leone Selection Trust. At the same time, however, the German threat to the Netherlands and to the Belgian Congo (a key source for industrial diamonds) endangered the cartel's capacity to keep up its sales of rough diamonds. The British too felt threatened by the potential decline of the cartel and the consequent implication this might have on their business interests in Africa. When war broke out, De Beers and the British strengthened their ties in a joint effort to find alternative cutting locations to the Netherlands and to counter the advancement of the German diamond industry. These ties would be central to the part played by diamonds in the Allied economic warfare and the context in which Palestine's cutting industry emerged.[8]

The search by the British and the diamond cartel for an alternative to Antwerp opened a window of opportunity for an initiative that originated in Palestine and was backed by the Colonial Office and the Ministry of Economic Warfare in London. Behind the initiative stood Oved Ben-Ami, the head of the Netanya town council, while the argument in favor of British support was designed by Frederick Albert Mathias, the director of the Sierra Leone Selection Trust and at that time the main diamond advisor to the Ministry of Economic Warfare. Ben-Ami, a local liberal politician, ardent Zionist, land and urban developer, and upholder of the capitalist road to Zionist state-building argued that the threatened diamond industry in Antwerp and its Jews could be transferred to Palestine in order to save the Jews, to industrialize the largely agricultural town of Netanya, and to serve the anti-German Allies. For his part, Mathias was an enthusiastic believer in cultivating government support for the diamond business. The argument he developed in supporting Palestine combined, on the one hand, anti-German economic warfare with the distance of Palestine from the diamond-seeking Germans, and on the other, the British need for American dollars with the selling interests of De Beers. In a larger perspective Mathias, in siding with the Ben-Ami campaign, practically orchestrated the forging of networks along a complex diamond chain—starting with the mining of rough diamonds in Africa, to sorting and distributing them in London, then cutting and polishing the stones in Palestine and exporting the finished diamonds to the United States.[9]

The marriage of Ben-Ami's and Mathias's approaches was predicated on the industry in Palestine serving the interests of the British and Allied war needs while remaining a Jewish-only industry. Furthermore, it guaranteed Palestine a steady supply of rough diamonds from the Diamond Trading Company in London. This would be mediated by a Jewish broker and a known and trusted sightholder with De Beers. For its part, the cartel was assured by the Colonial Office and the Palestine government that it would be Palestine's sole seller of stones and that moves against illicit trade in diamonds in the Middle East would be accelerated.

The British protective intervention in establishing the diamond industry and its operation as a controlled capitalist venture meant endowing the initiators of the industry with monopoly status. The British supervised the selection of the experts chosen to move from Antwerp to Palestine, the authorization of the manufacturers in Palestine itself, and the import-export operation to New York, Cairo, and Bombay. In agreeing to make the small town of Netanya the center of the industry in Palestine, the British bowed to the pressure of Oved Ben-Ami, the town's mayor and the key figure in this private-capital project. The British ordered all the polished stones to be exported, thus promising themselves a steady income in American dollars. Furthermore, all trading and exporting were inspected and in effect left to the manufacturers, thereby curtailing free trade.

However, a caveat was added that the expansion of the diamond industry in Palestine was to be limited in terms of the quantity cut and polished. According to the reasoning of the time, while the transference of the industry to Palestine was based on trustworthy relations between state, capital, and skilled experts, nothing was to be done in Palestine that would hamper the future recovery of the Belgian diamond industry—not even a Jewish-only diamond cutting center that espoused anti-German warfare, a capitalist venture and a Zionist goal. The notion of trust, so prevalent in the historical and ethnic-based diamond trade, was now applied by imitation to international commitments but had to be buttressed (uncommon in the diamond trade) by bureaucratic arrangements and official stipulations. In view of Belgium's dominant position in the world of diamond production and trade, and of the British imperial and business interest in maintaining good relations with the Belgian Congo and De Beers, these understandings and arrangements harbored a strong claim for legitimacy. It was now considered a private industry in the service of the war, the Empire, and the Zionist cause.[10]

Legitimization

Confronting a different source of authority produces some variations on this theme. Indeed, the institutions that ran the *Yishuv*, and in particular the Jewish Agency (dominated since the early 1930s by Mapai, Labor's leading political party), were no less instrumental in the establishment of the industry. The department of trade and industry of the Jewish Agency had been involved in the 1930s in an attempt to introduce diamond capital and expertise from Antwerp to Palestine, and to persuade the British government to reduce the customs on imported rough diamonds. The department was also in contact with diamond dealers in Tel Aviv who ran a small diamond exchange, as well as with Zionist activists in England and South Africa who helped with contacts to the De Beers cartel. But the diamond industry, designed by the British and the manufacturers linked to Ben-Ami, was to be a private affair. It was an independent capitalist venture under the auspices of the British government and free of the national-oriented control of the Zionist institutions. No matter how involved the national institutions in Jewish industry were, and how crucial in their eyes the industrialization of the *Yishuv* economy, from the outset they were kept outside the sphere of decision-making and control over diamond production.[11]

By barring Zionist institutional control over an industry that linked Jewish capital, the Palestine government, and international business interests, the Zionist political and industrial elites slung a barrage of historical and social stereotypes against the manufacturers and the character of their project. The independence of the capitalists was criticized for displaying a lack of allegiance to national institutions; they were charged with preferring their profits and independence over Zionist state-building and over cooperation with the more loyal Palestine Manufacturers' Association. The diamond industry produced luxury items, mainly for the American middle class. They were nonproductive in the Zionist view, which valued agricultural and industrial work and production. As such, they were seemingly steeped in an unbridled indulgence of the acquisitive spirit and thus were anathema to Zionist values. If the great profits of the industry were harnessed to the Zionist project, if they were not solely to benefit the capitalists and the British, the industry would be legitimized. Moreover, the problem was less with the capitalist nature of the industry and more with how it highlighted the incapacity of Zionism to fully engineer its social forces and control its actions, in particular when the capitalists' autonomous action was supported politically by the Palestine government and economically by growing demand in the United States for stones polished in Palestine. This sense of marginalization only affirmed that state-backed capitalism, which the diamond industry reflected, was taking root in Palestine.[12]

The anti-diamond rhetoric seemed to Ben-Ami and his circle of diamond manufacturers and diamond factory owners an empty diatribe that could be overturned swiftly once their independence was compromised. And indeed, the more the Jewish Agency realized the powerful economic performance of the industry during the war, the more it was willing to overcome its estrangement from the industry. For Ben-Ami, the introduction of a diamond industry to his small town was to industrialize it, to attract the young, to urbanize the town. This was part and parcel of his idea of Zionism, earlier founded on land acquisition, territorial expansion, and the designation of land and rural plantations for the Jewish people. But while the earlier vision was local, the diamonds had widened the horizons. They would serve a national cause, but they would do so by modernization, international networking, and world trade. The earlier sense of the capitalist road to Zionist realization could now reach maturity in the Jewish polity by moving out of the local confines and joining in world capitalist competition. All was to be harnessed to this cause—efficiency, productivity, regimentation. The tradition of skilled cutting, cleaving, and polishing was a clear case in which novelty and technological advancement could flourish.[13]

The diamond industry in Palestine therefore emerged, Janus-faced, in the early 1940s. It became Britain's "special native" in the Middle East, a standard-bearer of capitalist entrepreneurship and the servant of Zionist goals. This quid pro quo arrangement, happening as it did in the context of a very restrictive British white paper policy in Palestine, was a particularly useful means for legitimating requisitions. It joined service to the empire and the fight against the Germans. It promised the Belgians self-restraint and gave De Beers an outlet for its unsold merchandise. It added to British finances in the Middle East and greatly supported the cooperation between the Colonial Office, the Ministry of Economic Warfare, and the De Beers cartel. In Palestine itself it structured Ben-Ami's posture as a capitalist entrepreneur and liberal municipal activist, a Zionist in the service of the empire and the war, a savior of Jews otherwise forced to serve the German interest in diamond cutting, and, last but not least, a great contributor to the Zionist cause of industrializing the *Yishuv* economy. The long-standing historical association between Jews and the diamond industry in the Diaspora now became, in Palestine, and with the direct assistance of the British and the international diamond cartel, a component of the economic infrastructure of the Zionist polity.[14]

International Politics

The diamond industry aspired to independence and autonomy from Zionist institutional control and went about materializing these aspirations through the guardian intervention of the British (now militarized) rule of Palestine. However, as previously noted, the diamond manufacturers were deeply dependent on external forces and considerations—that is, the Belgians, with whom the British wished to cultivate good relations, and the Diamond Trading Company, without which rough diamonds would not have reached the diamond factories. To add to this complex situation, the Diamond Trading Company needed the Belgians for their access to mines in the Belgian Congo, and the Belgians needed good relations with the United Kingdom—the host of their exiled government and of many Belgian and Jewish refugees. Early in the war, when Belgian and Jewish diamond circles established, with the direct assistance of the cartel, a special diamond reserve to aid in the recovery of the diamond industry in Antwerp at the end of the German occupation (COFDI), the British government was compelled to approve it. Belgian diamond interests in wartime London ran what can be called a "politics of supply" aimed at regulating the distribution of rough diamonds from De Beers to the alternative cutting centers, mainly in Palestine.[15]

Indeed, the greatest ambivalence besetting the diamond industry in Palestine was toward Belgium. On the one hand, this was where the diamond experts and know-how originated. Amsterdam was significant also as a legacy of the networks between the diamond industry, Jewish communal life, and trade union organization. Antwerp, however, especially since the First World War, was closer kin. It had specialized in cutting small stones as Palestine was now doing; it served as a model for the industry's organization, internal relations, and ethics; and the entire network of which the Palestine manufacturers were a part stemmed from and revolved around Antwerp and its exiled communities in other places. On the other hand, however, Belgium was the reason why the British wished to limit expansion of Palestine's diamond productive capacity. As much as its diamond industry had been paralyzed since mid 1940, Antwerp was Palestine's main future competitor. And as much as its leaders, such as the socialist Camille Huysmans, were pro-Zionist, the shadow that the Belgians cast, exemplified by COFDI's activities in London, worried the manufacturers in Palestine and forced their deep involvement in the politics of supply.[16]

The international bargaining revolved around Palestine's expansion in the cutting of small stones (otherwise known as sand), which was also Antwerp's prewar professional specialty. If Belgian interests held the upper hand, the cartel's Diamond Trading Company would curtail the supply of small stones for Palestine and force its factories to reorient themselves to bigger stones (e.g., brilliants and baguettes), and guide the workers and the labor process accordingly. If Palestine had its way, the postwar recovery of Belgium's diamond industry was endangered. One aspect of these political maneuverings was the development of arguments aimed at assuaging Belgian concerns. Whereas for the British, the Palestine diamond manufacturers were the "special native" and for Zionism they exemplified "capitalist nationalism," for the Belgians they car-

ried the weight of the victim's moral right. Palestine wanted neither to compete
with Belgium, so the manufacturers argued, nor to hamper its postwar recovery.
It had, though, the moral right to "inherit" the Germans and their prewar diamond cutting industry.

Indeed, during the 1930s Amsterdam was in decline, other cutting centers were not yet born, and the German diamond industry was Belgium's fierc-
est contender. Germany was to be blamed for the war, for the occupation of
Antwerp, for the looting of diamonds, and for forcing Jews to continue cutting diamonds in the concentration camps in Vught (in the Netherlands) and
in Bergen-Belsen (in Germany). It confiscated reserves of rough diamonds for
industrial use and aimed at acquiring mineral-rich African colonies, such as
the Belgian Congo. The suffering that Germany caused the Jews, exemplified
in the demise of their occupational communities and trading centers, was no
less harsh and horrendous than the fall of Belgium, the German challenge of
Belgian colonies, and German economic exploitation of the Netherlands. Palestine was, therefore, fully justified in claiming a place in the diamond production, not as a challenge to Belgium but as part of an international diamond
community of which Belgium was the recognized leader. More significantly,
Palestine was entitled to inherit the German diamond industry for the purpose
of economically building the Zionist polity, as if thereby being compensated for
the crimes committed against the Jews. Diamonds were now endowed not only
with the international mission to counter German economic warfare and revive the economy of the Netherlands, but also with the idea of serving Zionism.
The logic was naturally also tailored to the desires of the national leaders in the
Zionist institutions in Palestine who opposed the industry's independence but
also recognized the meaning of its success for economic state-building in Palestine. In the late 1940s, this logic would resurface when the Palestine diamond
industry, the Jewish Agency, and diamonds circles in Belgium cooperated in a
concerted action to limit the revival of the diamond industry in Germany.[17]

Working Diamonds

The "Zionization" of the historically Jewish-dominated diamond industry was,
however, far from a straightforward matter, even within the confines of the
Yishuv. The Labor Movement was politically a dominant force in the *Yishuv,* but
it accepted capitalist Zionism as long as it was controlled and directed by the
national institutions. When the diamond industry arrived in Palestine, it had
to confront what some diamond manufacturers defined at the time as an institutional "triangled thread" of economic and political cooperation between the
Jewish Agency, the Palestine Manufacturers' Association, and the Histadrut.
As a nationally oriented labor movement, the latter, however, not only objected

to capital's quest for total institutional independence (in which it joined forces with many of the *Yishuv*'s industrialists), but also couched it in exclusionist terminology that made some diamond manufacturers sense that they were politically and socially marginalized and fittingly imagined as "bastards."[18]

In such a highly skilled occupation as diamond cutting and polishing, work and workers were the keys to the industry's capacity to establish itself and survive. In the Netherlands the diamond worker spent many months in apprenticeship, being supervised and nurtured, which served to foster interest, pride, and ambition between the manufacturers and the workers. This was encouraged by the domination of the occupation by Jews and by a common sense of distinctiveness. This coalescence did not exclude social conflict, and the strength of the diamond workers' unions in Amsterdam and Antwerp seemed to testify to the need to challenge the manufacturers and at the same time to regulate unrestrained conflict. In Palestine, though, organized labor posed a much greater challenge to the manufacturers; this confrontation itself was an expression of the capitalist transformation the war wrought on Palestine.[19]

First and foremost, the diamond industry in Palestine was managed and controlled by adherents of a liberal tradition in employment relations that objected to the total domination of the diamond workplace by the Histadrut. These liberal forces, headed by Ben-Ami and the manufacturers (some Belgian, some local), did not oppose collective bargaining so much as the excessive intervention of organized labor in the affairs of the diamond factories. This referred in particular to the issue of the "Taylorization" of the cutting and polishing labor process. Contrary to tradition, Palestine asked De Beers to specialize in one type of stone, namely the small stone, or sand. This had also been Antwerp's specialty, and it catered to the diamond cartel's need to dispose of large reserves of such stones, which had been provoked by the paralysis of the Netherlands. Specialization in the small stone turned Palestine into one of the world's leading suppliers. Furthermore, while in the Netherlands it took at least three years to induct an apprentice cutter and polisher, and apprenticeship usually covered all types of stones and all cutting and polishing skills, in Palestine the labor process was fragmented into a system called the "chain" or "phases," in which the apprentice learned just one phase of the polishing process. This "Taylorization" of production helped shorten the learning process to six months and speeded up a cutter's entry into production and earning.

The "Taylorization" of the labor process not only accentuated the supplanting of home work by the factory, it also accounted for a new kind of paternalism in the diamond industry that was less known in the Netherlands. A blatant expression of this paternalism was the bonding of the apprentice to the factory and to the manufacturer until all the apprenticeship tuition was paid. In both the matters of "Taylorization" and bondage as well as the process of selecting the apprentices, the Histadrut remained excluded. Piecework, which was so

characteristic of the occupation and anathema to the Histadrut, was maintained, even though most work was done in factories. Finally, and crucially,
workers' representation was structured by the manufacturers in such a way that
the Histadrut could never claim a majority among the workers and was forced
to renegotiate regularly with four or five other trade unions to achieve a common stance against employers. This fragmentation of representation amounted
to a lack of Histadrut control in the factories.[20]

The Histadrut activists among the diamond workers attempted to surpass
the other unions by recruiting unorganized labor. Its position among the workers was, however, weakened by the intensity of strike action in the diamond
industry, partly due to the intermittent supply of rough diamonds from London,
which often left the piecework workers without work and pay. The Histadrut's
incapacity to force restraint on workers was also a cause for wildcat militancy.
To challenge the diamond manufacturers, the Histadrut could either join any
strike that broke out in any small factory, or mobilize the Zionist institutions to
act against the manufacturers' autonomy of action.[21]

The latter option was usually chosen. The recruitment of the national institutions was reflected in the enhanced role the labor movement assigned to
the Jewish Agency, and in particular to its Departments of Trade, Industry, and
Labor, in bargaining over working conditions and in resolving conflicts over
workers' representation. National intervention in disputes and strikes followed,
resulting in significant involvement in the industry's general economic survival.
Recruitment was, however, buttressed by a political language that grouped the
national institutions and the Histadrut together with the diamond manufacturers and better-off diamond workers on the opposite side. The manufacturers were derided as exploitative capitalists reminiscent of the worst in Jewish
history, dedicated to producing goods for luxury consumption, deceiving the
workers, and refusing to cooperate with labor Zionism. This derogatory imagery
well illustrated the criticism vented by the Zionist political elite against the
non-national independence of the diamond manufacturers.[22]

Cut to Zionism

The terminology the diamond manufacturers used to challenge the negative
images labor had of them naturally alluded to the twenty-year-old controversy
in the Zionist movement regarding the correct path (public or private) for Zionist state-building. In focusing on the efficiency of private capital and on the
imperative to postpone socialist experimentation to the period after a Zionist
entity in Palestine had materialized, the diamond manufacturers reproduced
those elements of the 1920s debate that provided the diamond industry with

an image of a worthy economic project, risky yet successful, promising and real. Their independence was justified, because it was Zionist. The manufacturers rationalized the specialized fragmentation (even Taylorization) of the labor process and the consequent paternalism of the workplace; this was a paternalism based not simply on the role of the owner and employer as a capitalist, but also his role as the source of inspiration for the linking of capital with the nation, and the harnessing of capital accumulation to the Zionist cause. This merging of capitalist efficiency with considerations of time and international competitiveness interested the Zionist economists who propounded the association between Herzl and Taylor, coupling a national home for the Jews with efficiency, and could thus be referred to as the Zionization of the labor process. It also attracted the attention of the diamond trade in London, of whom some members were Jewish Belgian exiles, fearful that Palestine's subsequent specialization in small stones would not only surpass Belgium's prewar supremacy but also hamper its postwar recovery.[23]

At the same time, however, this terminology introduced novel utilitarian conceptions aimed at legitimizing capital's roles in the wartime economy. The argumentation focused on the industry's high productivity and income from foreign trade, both part of the tremendous boom Palestine experienced during the war. The Palestine diamond industry was part of the Allies' war effort and had a role to play in absorbing refugee cutters and polishers from the Netherlands; those not so fortunate as to escape were forced to labor in the diamond cutting workshops in Bergen-Belsen. It advanced the moral legitimacy of the Zionist economy in Palestine in inheriting the German industry, and played a key role in relaxing economic competition with Belgium by weaving international connections among the manufacturers and the diamond workers' unions. In its self-presentation, the diamond industry imagined therefore a world in which Zionism, despite the war and the Holocaust, did not reject its Jewish and European pasts. In this local politics of identity, the external and international played a key role, and the more successful the industry in Palestine, the more legitimate it became.[24]

Nothing was more powerful in this process than the dramatic growth of the Palestine diamond industry. In the absence of competition from Belgium between 1940 and 1944, and with the strong impact of rising demand for diamonds in the American middle classes during the war, the Palestine industry expanded far beyond the limits designed for it in 1940 by the Colonial Office and the Ministry of Economic Warfare. Despite the restraints applied to the industry in late 1943 (by forcing it to move to cutting larger stones), growth continued unabated. While the number of diamond factories did not change from 1942, the number of workers acquiring cutting and polishing skills increased consistently, and by 1945 the industry could boast some 4,500 workers (see Appendixes 1 and 2). In Palestine's industrial context, this was more than an ordinary change, highlighting as it did the technological capacity and managerial skill that made good use of the uncompetitive international environment.[25]

Economic advancement and an international reputation convinced the suspicious leaders of the Zionist institutions, and of the Jewish industrialists organized in the Zionist Palestine Manufacturers' Association, of the diamond industry's economic viability. Furthermore, it provided work for many Jews, raised the standard of living of the young diamond cutters and polishers, and provided Palestine with an international economic legitimacy that impressed the local *Yishuv* leaders. The high levels of strike action among diamond workers affected this image, mainly among British officials in Palestine, but this could scarcely tarnish the emerging image of economic prowess and its global resonance. Criticism would shift now from the autonomy of the manufacturers to their profitability and the coalescing of interest with the British authorities. When the British authorities decided after the war to liberalize control of the industry and ease the restraints on the local diamond trade and world destinations, the manufacturers quickly adapted; more workers were employed in the cutting factories, and much of what was left of the opposition to the industry among the *Yishuv*'s economic and political elites evaporated.[26]

At the end of 1946 the competition between Belgium and Palestine along with the seething unrest in Palestine's diamond workshops coincided with a sharp decline in American demand for Palestine's polished diamonds. After the war, De Beers reoriented its supplies toward the Netherlands, and the economic nationalism of Belgian manufacturers and unions tolerated little overseas competition. The Zionist claim that its diamond industry had the moral legitimacy to inherit the German prewar diamond industry went unheeded by the Europeans. In parallel, the British authorities in Palestine who were about to withdraw from the country withdrew their protection of the local diamond industry.[27]

The grave crisis that the local diamond industry experienced in 1947 as a result of these factors, and the prolonged period of recovery that extended to the early 1950s, demonstrated again the blurred boundaries between the local and the external. The withdrawal of the British Mandate from involvement in the industry was replaced by the growing presence of the *Yishuv* institutions and later by the state of Israel. The dependence on, and almost patrimonial relationship with, one state structure was replaced by another, and the diamond capital owners and manufacturers readily transferred their claims for help in the international competition and attainment of resources to this state-in-the-making. For the latter, the diamond industry would soon serve the expansion of Israel's foreign trade and state-sponsored attempts to erect a private-capital infrastructure in Israel's newly built development towns.[28]

An Emerging Diamond Community

The question of the historical predominance of Jews in the world diamond industry has been posed many times in the past. Often it invoked the economic advantages of an ethnic group able to mobilize its internal mechanisms and social institutions to cut commercial transaction costs and advance a highly profitable trading business based on informal dimensions of reputation and trust. While the notion of trust relates in these discussions to diamond trading, and to capitalism's search for efficient middlemen groups to maintain global low-cost commerce, it also affected diamond production itself. The disciplinary systems that owners and manufacturers developed to oversee the cutters and control the polishing labor process testified to the failure to replace trust as the defining factor in the ecology of the diamond workplace. Along the same vein, the ties and "reputational knowledge" that workers and experts wove and created during their apprenticeship and work experience served them well when they later turned to business and trading, and to creating familial lineages of diamond merchants and bourse traders. In this sense, the possibility of a diamond-cutting center, which the British allowed to materialize early in the war, reproduced the social basis of a Jewish diamond trading group that would later cultivate the older reliance on communal ties and trustworthy relations.[29]

However, beyond these aspects of the diamond trading culture and the economic advantages Jewish diamond dealers traditionally enjoyed, it must be remembered that the diamond industry in Palestine started first and foremost as a diamond cutting and polishing center, and that the world trading prowess of the Palestine and Israeli diamond-merchant community developed only much later. That the Israeli community of diamond dealers and merchants and the national involvement of the state of Israel in its affairs were a corollary, not the precondition, of the country's production center and its backing by the De Beers cartel and the British government, problematizes the origins of such commercial networks.[30]

The diamond industry in Palestine of the 1930s and 1940s took off largely due to an intertwining of external factors and local motivation. Quickly finding itself along a global commodity chain temporarily distorted by the war and relocated by war aims and international business interests, it then recuperated after it. Furthermore, it developed local and national characteristics of the diamond cutting labor process and of employment relations exactly because it was so linked internationally and had to survive in competition with international forces. The language the manufacturers and the diamond entrepreneurial organizers used created essential slots of meanings that would later legitimize the unshackling of capital and the weakening of the Zionist labor movement. The terminology idealized both the private-capital road to the materialization of Zionism and service to the British Empire as a cultural means for securing the

state's sheltering and espousal of capital. More specifically, it revered entrepreneurial capital and its independence to the point of actually presuming to
surpass other social forces as main builders of Zionist sovereignty. Not impeding
capital's path, facilitating its ambitious search for markets and skilled work,
culturally legitimizing its social individualism, institutional independence, and
high living standards—these were increasingly becoming routine claims and
accepted norms.[31] Indeed, as the nationally oriented derogation of the diamond industry gradually faded, its cosmopolitan images would be conveniently
adopted by the state of Israel for national use, and the small group of capitalists
in diamond manufacturing and trading would help pave the way for Israel's
later liberal-ideological and social shifts.[32]

Appendix 1

The Diamond Industry in Palestine, 1940–1948

	Factories	Employed
1940	5	200
1941	12	1,200
1942	23	2,500
1943	33	3,570
1944	33	3,600
1945	33	4,000
1946	34	5,000
1947	30	3,000
1948	30	800

Sources: David Gurevich, *Workers' Wages in the Jewish Diamond-Polishing Industry in Palestine, 1944* (Jerusalem: Department of Statistics of the Jewish Agency,
1945) (H); Avraham Friedman, "The Diamond Industry in Palestine's Economy,"
Hameshek Hashitufi, 23 February 1947 (H); Oved Ben-Ami, "Die Diamantindustrie
in Palästina," *Schweizer Goldschmied* 5 (May 1948).

Appendix 2

Diamond Cutters and Polishers 1939 and 1946

	Early 1939	Early 1946
Belgium	25,000	15,000
Holland	8,000	1,000
Germany	8,000	—
France	3,500	450
United States	500	4,000
South Africa	400	1,000
UK	—	800
Palestine	60	5,000
Brazil	100	4,000
Cuba	—	3,000
All	45,460	34,250

Source: *Report of the Proceedings of the First Congress after the Liberation of the Universal Alliance of Diamond Workers*, Antwerp, 2–6 September 1946, The George Meany Memorial Archives, Silver Spring, MD, RG 18—005/12.

Notes

1. The chapter is based on David De Vries, *Diamonds and War: State, Capital and Labor in British-Ruled Palestine* (New York: Berghahn Books, 2010). Hebrew sources are marked (H).
2. Ian W. Gaskin, "Palestine 1939–1945: A Study of Economic Colonial Policy," PhD diss., University of Oxford, 1992, 45–115; Jacob Metzer, *The Divided Economy of Mandatory Palestine* (Cambridge: Cambridge University Press, 1998), chap. 5; Robert Vitalis and Steven Heydemann, "War, Keynesianism, and Colonialism: Explaining State-Market Relations in the Postwar Middle East," in *War, Institutions, and Social Change in the Middle East*, ed. Steven Heydemann (Berkeley: University of California Press 2000), 100–148.
3. David Ben Gurion, "The National Destiny of the Working Class [1925]," in *From Class to Nation*, ed. David Ben Gurion (Tel Aviv: Davar, 1933), 231–234 (H); Hagit Lavsky, "Is There an 'Essential' Link between Jews and Capitalism? The Case of

Eretz Israel," in *Religion and Economy: Connections and Interactions,* ed. Menachem Ben-Sasson (Jerusalem: Zalman Shazar Center, 1995), 387–399 (H).

4. Robert R. Nathan, Oscar Gass, and Daniel Creamer, *Palestine: Problem and Promise,* (Washington, D.C.: Public Affairs Press of the American Council on Public Affairs, 1946), 506–514; Werner Feilchenfeld, *European Post-War Economics—and Palestine: Impressions of a Palestinian Traveller* (Tel Aviv: Export Union of Palestine, 1946); Economic Research Institute of the Jewish Agency, *The Economic War Effort: Facts and Figures* (Jerusalem: Department for Trade and Industry of the Jewish Agency, 1946), 3–22.

5. Lisa Bernstein, "Opting Out of the Legal System: Extralegal Contractual Relations in the Diamond Industry," *Journal of Legal Studies* 21, no. 1 (1992): 115–157; Renee Rose Shield, *Diamond Stories: Enduring Change on 47th Street* (Ithaca: Cornell University Press, 2002), 1–42; Abe Michael Shainberg, "Jews and the Diamond Trade," *Jewish Directory & Almanac* 1 (1984): 301–311; Jacob Arnon, "The Jews in the Diamond Industry in Amsterdam," in *Dutch Jewish History,* ed. Dan Michman (Jerusalem: Tel Aviv University and Hebrew University of Jerusalem, 1984), 305–313; Salvador E. Bloemgarten, "Henri Polak: A Jew and a Dutchman," in Michman, *Dutch Jewish History,* 261–278.

6. Editor, "Infant Diamond Industry of Palestine," *Diamond Fields Advertiser* (Kimberley, South Africa), 12 August 1940; David Rothblum, Memorandum on the Prospects of the Diamond Industry in Palestine, 21 September 1943, Central Zionist Archive in Jerusalem (hereafter CZA), S40/269/2; Walter A. Aronheim, "The Development of Diamond Industry and Trade in Peace and War," MA thesis, New School for Social Research, New York, 1943; Joshua Hadari, "The Diamond Industry in Palestine," *The Palestine Tribune,* 31 May 1945; Gedalia Yogev, *Diamonds and Coral: Anglo-Dutch Jews and Eighteenth-Century Trade* (Leicester: Leicester University Press, 1978), chap. 12; Henriette Boas, "Jews and the Amsterdam Diamond Trade," *Studia Rosenthaliana* 26, nos. 1–2 (1992): 214–222.

7. Sidney H. Ball, "The Diamond Industry in 1936," *Gems and Gemology* 2, no. 4 (1936): 67–68; Sidney H. Ball, "Recent Developments in the Diamond Industry," *Gems and Gemology* 3, no. 6 (1940): 85–86; Editor, "The European Diamond Cutting and Polishing Industry," *Foreign* Commerce Weekly 3, no. 3 (19 April 1941); Herbert Binneweg and Jan Walgrave, *Beurs voor Diamanthandel: A Hundred Brilliant Years 1904–2004* (Antwerp: Beurs voor Diamanthandel, 2004), 58–70.

8. Mildred Berman, "The Location of the Diamond-Cutting Industry," *Annals of the Association of American Geographers* 61, no. 2 (1971): 316–328; Colin Newbury, *The Diamond Ring: Business, Politics, and Precious Stones in South Africa, 1867–1947* (Oxford: Oxford University Press, 1989), chaps. 10–11; Eric Laureys, *Meesters van het Diamante De Belgische Diamantsector tijdens het Nazibewind* (Tielt: Lannoo, 2005), 175–177.

9. Frederick A. Mathias to Gerard Clauson, 27 March 1940, The National Archive, London (hereafter TNA), CO 852/289/1; Frederick A. Mathias, Palestine–Diamond Cutting Industry, 27 March 1940, TNA CO 852/289/1; Oved Ben-Ami, The Diamond Cutting Industry in Palestine: A Report presented to His Majesty's Principal Secretary of State for the Colonies, October 1942, TNA CO 852/457/2;

Frederick A. Mathias, Memorandum—The Diamond Industry—Post War Issues, 20 May 1943, TNA BT 96/159.

10. Albert Ehrenfeld, Memorandum for the Diamond Control Board, February 1944, CZA, S40/269/2; Albert Ehrenfeld, The Problem of Reorganization of the Diamond Industry in Palestine in the Light of the Present Crisis, December 1946, CZA, S8/2566.

11. Internal Report of the Trade and Industry Department of the Jewish Agency on the Diamond Industry, May 1940, CZA, S8/315 (H); Correspondence between Oved Ben-Ami and Dr. Emil Schmorak, December 1940, CZA, S8/315 (H); Nachum Tischby to Arieh Schenkar, 31 March 1941, CZA, S8/1390/1 (H).

12. T.A., Diamond Industry—Note on its Present Situation, submitted to the Jewish Agency, 13 October 1943, CZA, S40/269/2; see also Ronen Shamir, "The Jewish Bourgeoisie in Mandatory Palestine: Guidelines for Research," Israel Sociology 3, no. 1 (2001), 133–148 (H).

13. Deliberations of the Palestine Diamond Manufacturers Association in May 1945, Netanya City Archive (hereafter NCA), 126/1045; Oved Ben-Ami, "The Palestine Diamond Industry: Retrospect and Outlook," The Diamond News and the South Africa Watchmaker and Jeweller (February 1948); Oved Ben-Ami, "The Palestine Diamond Industry," The Palestine Economist Annual (1948): 96–97.

14. Pinchas Smagarinsky to the Universal Alliance of Diamond Workers, 27 February 1946, Archive of the International Institute of Social History, ANDB, 6553; Yehoshua Mazur, "The Diamond Industry," in Palestine's Economic Future: A Review of Progress and Prospects, ed. Joseph Burton Hobman (London: Perey Lund Humphries, 1946), 229–237.

15. Louise London, Whitehall and the Jews, 1933–1948 (Cambridge: Cambridge University Press, 2003), chap. 7; Robert W. Allen, Churchill's Guests: Britain and the Belgian Exiles During World War II (Westport: Praeger 2003), chaps. 3–5; on COFDI (Correspondence Office for the Diamond Industry) see Laureys, Meesters van het Diamante De Belgische Diamantsector, 285–290.

16. Minutes of the 2nd Meeting of the Diamond Control Board, 24 November 1943, NCA, 101/764; John L. Fletcher to the Palestine Diamond Manufacturers' Association, 25 November 1943, NCA, 62/346; H. McErlean, Ministry of Economic Warfare, to R.H. Burt, 26 November 1943, TNA CO 852/527/2; Eric Laureys, "The Plundering of Antwerp's Jewish Diamond Dealers, 1940–1944," in Confiscation of Jewish Property in Europe, 1933–1945: New Sources and Perspectives (Washington, D.C.: United States Holocaust Memorial Museum, Center for Advanced Holocaust Studies, 2003), 57–74.

17. Chaim Danhirsch, "The Diamond Industry toward a Transition Period," Hayahalom 1, no. 5 (February 1945): 5–6 (H); "Diamond Conference," Palestine Post, 11 July 1946, 3.

18. See articles in Misgav: The Bulletin of the Diamond Workers Union in the Histadrut, April-May 1943 and September 1943 (H); The Diamond Worker in Palestine: Submitted to the International Congress of Diamond Workers by The Executive Committee of the General Federation of Jewish Labor in Eretz-Israel (Tel Aviv: Histadrut, 1946), 7–15.

19. Henri Polak, *A Short History of the Diamond Cutting Industry* (London: The Diamond Workers Section Committee of the Society of Goldsmiths, Jewellers & Kindred Trades, 1950), 37–43; Paul Grodzinsky, *Diamond Technology: Production Methods for Diamond and Gem Stones* (London: N.A.G Press, 1953, originally published 1942), 414–420; David Rothblum, Evaluation on the Prospects of the Palestine Diamond Industry, 1943–1947, CZA, S25/7302 (H).

20. Moshe Shapira (at the Histadrut Executive) to the Palestine Diamond Manufacturers Association, 23 April 1941, NCA, 111/897 (H); The Five Diamond Workers' Unions to the Palestine Diamond Manufacturers Association, 8 June 1942, Labor Movement Archive in Tel Aviv (hereafter LA), IV-250-49-175-a (H); Joint Circular of All the Unions to the Workers' Committees in the Diamond Industry, 9 June 194, LA, IV-353 (H); Minutes of the 1st Session of the Central Committee of the National Union of Diamond Workers, 9 September 1946, LA, IV-208-1-4551 (H).

21. *The Diamond Worker in Palestine*, 12.

22. Editor, "The Background of the Diamond Crisis," *Palnews* 16, no. 5/6 (1947); articles by Moshe Ben-Yehuda, Pinchas Smagarinsky, and Avraham Friedman in *Niv Poalei Hayahlomim* (the bulletin of the Histadrut's Diamond Workers' Union), on 2 February and 3 August 1947 (H).

23. Derek Penslar, *Shylock's Children: Economics and Jewish Identity in Modern Europe* (Berkeley: University of California Press 2001), chap. 6.

24. Editor, "Palestine Diamond Cutting Industry," *Diamond Industrial Review*, June 1945; Moshe Schnitzer, "The Revolution in the Diamond Industry," *Hayahalom*, October 1947 (H); Report of a Committee Appointed by the Government to Examine the Question of Post War Regulation of the Palestine Diamond Industry, 11 December 1945, NCA, 66/380.

25. David Gurevich, *Workers Wages in the Jewish Diamond-Polishing Industry in Palestine, 1944* (Jerusalem: Department of Statistics of the Jewish Agency, 1945) (H); Avraham Friedman, "The Diamond Industry in Palestine's Economy," *Hameshek Hashitufi*, 23 February 1947 (H); Oved Ben-Ami, "Die Diamantindustrie in Palaestina," *Schweizer Goldschmied* 5 (May 1948); Yoel Estheron, The Development of the Diamond Industry in Palestine during World War II, unpublished seminar paper, Department of Economics, Hebrew University, 1975 (H).

26. Elhanan Halperin, Moshe Schnitzer, *Diamonds* (Tel Aviv: n.p., 1946), 72–89 (H).

27. Walter Feilchenfeld, Gaston Loebel, "Diamond Industry and Trade in Palestine," in *Palestine Export Annual 1946/47*, ed. Walter Feilchenfeld (Tel Aviv: Export Union of Palestine, 1947), 64–75; Oved Ben-Ami, "The Palestine Diamond Industry: Retrospect and Outlook," *The Diamond News and the South Africa Watchmaker and Jeweller*, February 1948; Oved Ben-Ami, "Diamonds in Palestine," *Haaretz*, 24 March 1948) (H).

28. Yaakov Arnon, "The Diamond Industry," *Haaretz*, 8 June 1955 (H).

29. Barak. D. Richman, "How Community Institutions Create Economic Advantage: Jewish Diamond Merchants in New York," *Law and Social Enquiry* 31, no. 2 (2006): 383–420.

30. See the introduction in Ina Baghdiantz McCabe, Gelina Harlaftis, and Ioanna Pepelasis Minoglou, eds., *Diaspora Entrepreneurial Networks: Four Centuries of History* (Oxford and New York: Berg, 2005).

31. See Moshe Ben-Yehuda, "In the Diamond Industry," *Hapoel Hatsair*, 14 May 1947 (H), and "In the Diamond Industry in Tel Aviv," *Hapoel Hatsair*, 24 September 1947) (H).

32. On the Israeli diamond industry after 1948, see Editor, "The Diamond Industry," in *Israel's Industrial Future: Outlook 1960–1965* (Jerusalem: Ministry of Commerce and Industry, 1965), 228–232; Michael Szenberg, *The Economics of the Israeli Diamond Industry* (New York: Basic Books, 1971).

CONTRIBUTORS TO THE VOLUME

Susanne Bennewitz is the author of *Basler Juden—französische Bürger: Migration und Alltag einer jüdischen Gemeinde im frühen 19. Jahrhundert* (2008). She studied German literature and Jewish studies in Berlin and was an assistant curator in the Jewish Museum in Basel. Currently living in Saarbrücken, Germany, she works on economic history.

Helen M. Davies is a fellow in the School of Historical Studies at the University of Melbourne. Her doctoral dissertation, *Jewish Identity, Social Justice and Capitalism: The Making of the Pereire Brothers* (2005), has been the basis of articles on Emile and Isaac Pereire, nineteenth-century French railway magnates and bankers, as well as of her current project, a biography of the Pereires.

David De Vries is an associate professor at the Department of Labor Studies at Tel Aviv University, Israel. His primary research interests are modern labor and business history of Palestine and Israel. His publications include *Idealism and Bureaucracy in 1920s Palestine: The Origins of 'Red Haifa'* (1999, in Hebrew), *Dock Workers: International Explorations in Labor History, 1790–1970* (2000, co-edited), and most recently *Diamonds and War: State, Capital, and Labor in British-Ruled Palestine* (2010). Currently he is writing on strikes in Israeli history and is involved in a project on new perspectives in the business history of the modern Middle East.

Anthony D. Kauders is a lecturer in modern European history at Keele University, England. He is the author of *German Politics and the Jews* (1996), *Democratization and the Jews* (2004), and *Unmögliche Heimat: Eine deutsch-jüdische Geschichte der Bundesrepublik* (2007). He is currently working on the reception of psychoanalysis in Germany from1900 to 1985.

Jonathan Karp is an associate professor in the Judaic Studies and History Departments at Binghamton University of the State University of New York. He is the author of *The Politics of Jewish Commerce: Economic Thought and Emancipation in Europe* (2008) and co-editor of *The Art of Being Jewish in Modern Times: Essays on Jews and*

Aesthetic Culture (2007). Currently he is working on a book entitled *The Rise and Demise of the Black-Jewish Alliance: A Class-Cultural Analysis.*

Paul Lerner is an associate professor of history at the University of Southern California. He is the author of *Hysterical Men: War, Psychiatry and the Politics of Trauma in Germany, 1890–1930* (2003) and co-editor of *Traumatic Pasts: History, Psychiatry and Trauma in the Modern Age* (2001). His current research concerns the political, cultural, and psychological responses to department stores and mass consumer culture in modern Central Europe and focuses, above all, on the construction of department stores as a Jewish phenomenon.

Adam Mendelsohn is an assistant professor of Jewish studies at the College of Charleston, where he is involved in creating the Center for Southern Jewish History and Culture. His article "Tongue Ties: The Emergence of the English-language Diaspora in the Mid-19th Century" won the Wasserman Prize for best article in American Jewish History in 2009, and his "Two Far South: Rabbinical Responses to Apartheid and Segregation in South Africa and the American South" won the Quadrennial Prize for Best Article in Southern Jewish History in 2005. His reader, *Jews and the Civil War* (co-edited with Jonathan D. Sarna), will be published by New York University Press in 2010.

Michael L. Miller is an associate professor in the Nationalism Studies Program at Central European University in Budapest, Hungary. His research focuses on the impact of nationality conflicts on the religious, cultural, and political development of Central European Jewry. He has published articles in the *Slavic Review, Austrian History Yearbook, Simon Dubnow Institute Yearbook,* and *Múlt és Jövő,* and he has contributed entries to the *YIVO Encyclopedia of Jews in Eastern Europe.* His book, *Rabbis and Revolution: The Jews of Moravia in the Age of Emancipation,* was just published by Stanford University Press.

Kirill Postoutenko is currently a DAAD guest professor of macrosociology at the University of Constance, Germany, and an associate professor of history, sociology, and anthropology at Smolny College (Saint-Petersburg, Russia). He is the author of *The Onegin Stanza in Russian Poetry* (1998) and *Soviet Culture: Codes and Messages* (2009). Presently he is completing a project on discursive performance of political leadership in the Soviet Union, Nazi Germany, and the United States.

Gideon Reuveni is a lecturer for modern European and Jewish history at the University of Melbourne. He is the author of *Reading Germany: Literature and Consumer Culture in Germany before 1933* (2006) and the co-editor of several other books on different aspects of Jewish history. His current area of research is the intersection of Jewish history and economics. Presently he is working on a book on consumer culture and the making of Jewish identity in Europe.

Sarah Abrevaya Stein is Professor of history and Maurice Amado chair in Sephardic studies at the University of California, Los Angeles. Co-winner of the 2010 Sami Rohr Prize for Jewish literature, she is the author of *Making Jews Modern: Yiddish and Ladino Press in the Russian and Ottoman Empire* (2003) and *Plumes, Ostrich Feathers, Jews, and a*

Lost World of Global Commerce (2008). With Julia Cohen, she is currently editing *The Sephardic Studies Reader: 1730–1950* and working on a book manuscript provisionally entitled *Mediterranean Fever: Classifying Jews in a Century of Decolonization*. With Aron Rodrigue, she is co-editor of the forthcoming *An Ottoman Rebel: Sa'adi Besalel Ha-Levi and Jewish Salonica in the Nineteenth Century* (2011).

Sarah Wobick-Segev is a Jim Joseph postdoctoral teaching fellow at Syracuse University. Her doctoral dissertation examined Jewish sites of sociability in Paris, Berlin, and St. Petersburg/Leningrad from the 1890s to the 1950s. She has several articles currently in press and has most recently published, "Une place pour l'amour? Le mariage juif à Paris et à Berlin dans une ère transitionnelle, 1890–1930" in *Expériences croisées. Les juifs de France et d'Allemagne aux XIXe et XXe siècles* edited by Heidi Knörzer (Éditions de l'éclat, 2010).

SELECTED BIBLIOGRAPHY

Abraham, Gary A. *Max Weber and the Jewish Question: A Study of the Social Outlook of his Sociology*. Urbana: University of Illinois Press, 1992.

Andreau, Jean. *Banking and Business in the Roman World*. New York: Cambridge University Press, 1999.

Arbell, Mordechai. "Jewish Settlements in the French Colonies in the Caribbean (Martinique, Guadeloupe, Haiti, Cayenne) and the 'Black Code.'" In *Jews and Expansion to the West*, edited by Norman Fiering and Paolo Bernardini, 291–308. New York: Berghahn Books, 2001.

Auslander, Leora. "'Jewish Taste?' Jews, and the Aesthetics of Everyday Life in Paris and Berlin, 1933–1942." In *Histories of Leisure*, edited by Rudy Koshar, 299–318. Oxford: Berg Press, 2002.

Baer, Yitzchak. "A Social and Religious History of the Jews (Comments on S. Baron's New Book)" [in Hebrew]. *Zion* (1938), 277–299.

Baranowski, Shelley. *Strength through Joy: Consumerism and Mass Tourism in the Third Reich*. New York: Cambridge University Press, 2004.

Barkai, Avraham. *From Boycott to Annihilation: The Economic Struggle of German Jews, 1933–1943*. Translated by William Templer. Hanover, NH: Brandeis University Press, 1989.

———. "Judentum, Juden und Kapitalismus: Ökonomische Vorstellungen von Max Weber und Werner Sombart." *Menora* 5 (1994): 25–38.

Baron, Salo W. *A Social and Religious History of the Jews*, vol. 2. New York: Columbia University Press, 1937.

———. "Modern Capitalism and Jewish Fate." In *History and Jewish Historians*, edited by Salo W. Baron et al., 43–64. Philadelphia: The Jewish Publication Society, 1964.

Barzilay, Isaac E. "John Toland's Borrowings from Simone Luzzatto: Luzzatto's *Discourse on the Jews of Venice* (1638) the Major Source of Toland's Writing on the *Naturalization of the Jews in Great Britain and Ireland* (1714)." *Jewish Social Studies* 31 (1969), 75–81.

Ben Sasson, Menahem, ed. *Economy and Religion* [in Hebrew]. Jerusalem: Shazar Centre, 1995.

Berlanstein, Leonard R., ed. *The Industrialization and Work in Nineteenth-Century Europe.* New York: Routledge, 1992.

Bernfeld, Tirtsah Levie. "Financing Poor Relief in the Spanish-Portuguese Jewish Community in Amsterdam in the Seventeenth and Eighteenth Centuries." In *Dutch Jewry: Its History and Secular Culture (1500–2000),* edited by Jonathan Israel and Reiner Salverda, 62–102. Leiden: Brill, 2002.

Biale, David. "Jewish Consumer Culture in Historical and Contemporary Perspective." In *Jewish Longing and Belonging,* edited by Gideon Reuveni and Nils Roemer. Leiden: Brill Publications, 2010.

von Böhm-Bawerk, Eugen. *Karl Marx and the Close of his System.* Translated by Alice M. McDonald. London: T.F. Unwin, 1898.

Botticini, Maristella, and Zvi Eckstein. *From Farmers to Merchants: A Human Capital Interpretation of Jewish Economic History.* London: Center for Economic Policies, 2002.

Braudel, Fernand. *The Mediterranean and the Mediterranean World in the Age of Philip II,* vol. 2. New York: Harper & Row, 1973.

———. *Civilization and Capitalism, 15th–18th Century.* 3 vols. New York: Harper & Row, 1982–1984.

Brenner, Michael. *The Renaissance of Jewish Culture in Weimar Germany.* New Haven: Yale University Press, 1996.

Brentano, Lujo. *Die Anfänge des modernen Kapitalismus.* Munich: Verl. der K.B. Akademie der Wissenschaft, 1916.

Caro, Georg. *Sozial- und Wirtschaftsgeschichte der Juden im Mittelalter und der Neuzeit.* Hildesheim: G. Olms, 1964, first published in 1908.

Carter, Erica. *How German Is She? Postwar Reconstruction and the Consuming Woman.* Ann Arbor: University of Michigan Press, 1997.

Chiswick, Carmel U. *The Economics of American Judaism.* London: Routledge, 2008.

———, Tikva Lecker, and Nava Kahana, eds. *Jewish Society and Culture: An Economic Perspective.* Ramat Gan: Bar Ilan University Press, 2007.

———, and Tikva Lecker, eds. *The Economics of Judaism and Jewish Observance*: Special Issue of *Contemporary Jewry* 20 (1999).

Cohen, Robert. "Passage to the New World: The Sephardi Poor of Eighteenth-Century Amsterdam." In *Neveh Ya'akov: Jubilee Volume Presented to Dr. Jaap Meijer,* edited by L. Dasberg and J. N. Cohen, 31–42. Assen: Van Gorcum, 1982.

———. "The Edgerton Manuscript." *American Jewish Historical Quarterly* 62 (1973): 333–347.

Cooperman, Bernard Dov. *Trade and Settlement: The Establishment of the Jewish Communities of Leghorn and Pisa.* Unpublished PhD dissertation, Harvard University, 1976.

Crew, David, ed. *Consuming Germany in the Cold War: Consumption and National Identity in East and West Germany.* Oxford: Berg, 2003.

Crossick, Jeffrey, and Serge Jaumain, eds. *Cathedrals of Consumption: The European Department Store, 1850–1939.* Ashgate: Aldershot, 1999.

Dubnow, Simon. *Weltgeschichte des jüdischen Volkes,* vol 1. Berlin: Jüdischer Verlag, 1928.

Endelman, Todd. *The Jews of Georgian England, 1714–1830: Tradition and Change in a Liberal Society.* Philadelphia: Jewish Publication Society of America, 1979.

Frankel, Jonathan. *Prophecy and Politics: Socialism, Nationalism, and the Russian Jews, 1862–1917*. Cambridge: Cambridge University Press, 1981.

Frevert, Ute, ed. *Vertrauen: Historische Annäherungen*. Göttingen: Vandenhoeck & Ruprecht, 2003.

Fuchs, Christian. "Transnational Space and 'Network Society.'" *21st Century Society* 2 (2007): 49–78.

du Gay, Paul, and Michael Preke, eds. *Cultural Economy*. London: Sage, 2002.

Godeleir, Maurice. *Rationality and Irrationality in Economics*. New York: Monthly Review Press, 1972.

Goldscheider, Calvin, and Alan S. Zuckerman. *The Transformation of the Jews*. Chicago: University of Chicago Press, 1984.

Graetz, Heinrich. *Geschichte der Juden von den ältesten Zeiten bis auf die Gegenwart*. Leipzig: O. Leiner, 1897–1911.

de Grazia, Victoria, ed., with Ellen Furlough. *The Sex of Things: Gender and Consumption in Historical Perspective*. Berkeley: University of California Press, 1996.

Greif, Avner. *Institutions and the Path to the Modern Economy: Lessons from Medieval Trade*. Cambridge: Cambridge University Press, 2006.

Gross, Nachum. *Jews in Economic Life* [in Hebrew]. Jerusalem: Shazar Centre, 1985.

Gross, Nachum et al., eds. *Economic History of the Jews*. New York: Schocken Books, 1975.

Hart, Mitchell B. *Social Science and the Politics of Modern Jewish Identity*. Stanford: Stanford University Press, 2000.

Heinze, Andrew. *Adapting to Abundance: Jewish Immigrants, Mass Consumption and the Search for American Identity*. New York: Columbia University Press, 1990.

Holmes, Colin. "J.A. Hobson and the Jews." In *Immigrants and Minorities in British Society*, edited by Colin Holmes. Boston: Allen & Unwin, 1978.

Horowitz, Hayyim D. "The Economic Question" [in Hebrew]. *Hashiloach* (1920), 15–32.

Hume, David. *Essays, Moral, Political and Literary*. Edited by Eugene F. Miller. Indianapolis, IN: Liberty Classics, 1985.

Israel, Jonathan. *Diasporas within a Diaspora: Jews, Crypto-Jews and the World Maritime Empires (1540–1740)*. Leiden: Brill, 2002.

———. *European Jewry in the Age of Mercantilism, 1550–1750*. Oxford: Clarendon Press, 1985.

Kahan, Arkadius. *Essays in Jewish Social and Economic History*. Chicago: University of Chicago Press, 1986.

Kaplan, Yosef. *An Alternative Path to Modernity: The Sephardi Diaspora in Western Europe*. Leiden: Brill, 2000.

———. "The Self-Definition of the Sephardic Jews of Western Europe and Their Relation to the Alien and the Stranger." In *Crisis and Creativity in the Sephardic World, 1391–1648*, edited by B. R. Gampel, 121–145. New York: Columbia University Press, 1997.

Karp, Jonathan. *The Politics of Jewish Commerce: Economic Thought and Emancipation in Europe, 1638–1848*. Cambridge: Cambridge University Press, 2008.

———. "The Mosaic Republic in Augustan England: John Toland's 'Reasons for Naturalizing the Jews.'" *Hebraic Political Studies* 1 (2006), 462–492.

Kisch, Guido. "The Jews' Function in the Medieval Evolution of Economic Life: In Commemoration of a Great Scholar and His Theory." *Historia Judaica* 6 (1944): 1–12.

König, Wolfgang. *Volkswagen, Volksempfänger, Volksgemeinschaft: 'Volksprodukte' im Dritten Reich: vom Scheitern einer nationalsozialistischen Konsumgesellschaft.* Paderborn: Schöningh, 2004.

Koshar, Rudy, and Alon Confino, eds. *Regimes of Consumer Culture*: Special Issue of *German History* 19, no. 2 (2001).

Kramnick, Isaac. *Bolingbroke and His Circle: The Politics of Nostalgia in the Age of Walpole.* Ithaca, NY, and London: Cornell University Press, 1992.

Kuznets, Simon. "Economic Structure and Life of the Jews." In *The Jews: Their History, Culture and Religion,* edited by Louis Finkelstein, 1597–1666. New York: Schocken, 1960.

Landes, S. David. "The Jewish Merchant: Typology and Stereotypology in Germany." *Leo Baeck Institute Year Book* (1974), 11–30.

Leach, William. *Land of Desire: Merchants, Power, and the Rise of a New American Culture.* New York: Vintage, 1993.

Lefèvre, Edmond. *Le commerce et l'industrie de la plume pour parure.* Paris: L'auteur, 1914.

Levin, Mordechai. *'Erkhe hevrah ve-kalkalah ba-'ideologyah shel tekufat ha-Haskalah.* Jerusalem: Bialik Institute, 1975.

———. *Social and Economic Values: The Idea of Professional Modernization in the Ideology of the Haskalah Movement* [in Hebrew]. Jerusalem: Bialik Institute, 1975.

Levine, Gary Martin. *The Merchant of Modernism: The Economic Jew in Anglo-American Literature, 1864–1939.* New York: Routledge, 2003.

Litman, Jacob. *The Economic Role of Jews in Medieval Poland: The Contribution of Yitzhak Schipper.* Lanham: University Press of America, 1984.

Luzzatto, Simone. *Discorso circa il stato de gl'Hebrei in particolar dimoranti nell' inclita Citta di Venetia, di Simone Luzzatto, Rabbino Hebreo.* Venice, 1638.

Marx, Karl. *Capital: A Critique of Political Economy,* vol. 3. Translated by Ernest Untermann. Chicago: Charles H. Kerr and Co., 1909.

Marx, Karl, and Friedrich Engels. *The Communist Manifesto.* London and New York: Penguin Books, 1998.

Mayhew, Henry. *London Labour and the London Poor.* London, 1851.

Mendes-Flohr, Paul. "Werner Sombart's *The Jews and Modern Capitalism*: An Analysis of Its Ideological Premises." *Leo Baeck Institute Year Book* (1976), 87–107.

Miller, Michael. *The Bon Marché: Bourgeois Culture and the Department Store, 1869–1920.* Princeton: Princeton University Press, 1981.

Mitzman, Arthur. *Sociology and Estrangement: Three Sociologists of Imperial Germany.* New York: Knopf, 1973.

Morris-Reich, Amos. "The Beautiful Jew Is a Moneylender: Money and Individuality in Simmel's Rehabilitiaon of the the the 'Jew.'" *Theory, Culture and Society* 20 (2003), 127–142.

Muller, Jerry Z. *The Mind and the Market: Capitalism in Modern European Thought.* New York: Knopf, 2002.

———. *Capitalism and the Jews.* Princeton, Princeton University Press, 2010.

Musgrave, Peter. *The Early Modern European Economy.* New York: St. Martins, 1998.

Nelson, Benjamin. *The Idea of Usury: From Tribal Brotherhood to Universal Otherhood.* Chicago: University of Chicago Press, 1969.

Neusner, Jacob. *Why Does Judaism Have an Economics?* New London: Connecticut College, 1988.

Oelsen, Toni. "The Place of the Jews in Economic History as Viewed by German Scholars." *Leo Baeck Institute Year Book* (1962), 183–212.

———. "Wilhelm Roscher's Theory of Economic and Social Position of the Jews in the Middle Ages." *Yivo Annual of Jewish Social Science* 12 (1958/59), 176–195.

Penslar, Derek J. *Shylock's Children: Economics and Jewish Identity in Modern Europe.* Berkeley: University of California Press, 2001.

———. "The Origins of Jewish Political Economy." *Jewish Social Studies* 3 (1997), 26–60.

Penso de la Vega, Joseph. *Confusion de confusiones; dialogos curiosos entre un philosopho agudo, un mercador discreto, y un accionista erudito descriviendo el negocio de las acciones, su origen, su ethimologia, su realidad, su juego, y su enredo.* Amsterdam, 1688.

Philipp, Alfred. "Die Juden und das Wirtschaftsleben. Eine antikritisch-bibliographische Studie zu Werner Sombart: "Die Juden und das Wirtschaftsleben." PhD dissertation, University of Berlin, 1929.

de Pinto, Isaac. *Reflexoëns Politicas, Tocante à Constitutiçam da Naçam Judaica, Exposiçam do Estado de suas Finanças, Causeas dos Atrasos, e Desordens que se experimentam, e Meyos de os prevenir.* Amsterdam, 1748.

Porter, Roy, and Mikulás Teich, eds. *The Industrial Revolution in National Context: Europe and the U.S.A.* Cambridge: Cambridge University Press, 1996.

Postone, Moishe. "The Holocaust and the Trajectory of the Twentieth Century." In *Catastrophe and Meaning: The Holocaust and the Twentieth Century,* edited by Moishe Postone and Eric Santner, 81–116. Chicago: University of Chicago Press, 2003.

Raphael, Freddy. *Judaïsme et capitalism: essai sur la controverse entre Max Weber et Werner Sombart.* Paris: Presses Univ. de France, 1982.

Rappaport, Erika Diane. "Art, Commerce, or Empire? The Rebuilding of Regent Street, 1880–1927." *History Workshop Journal* 53 (2002): 94–117.

———. *Shopping for Pleasure: Women in the Making of London's West End.* Princeton: Princeton University Press, 2000.

Ravid, Benjamin. *Economics and Toleration in Seventeenth Century Venice: The Background and Context of the Discorso of Simone Luzzatto.* Jerusalem: American Academy for Jewish Research, 1978.

Reuveni, Gideon. *Reading Germany: Literature and Consumer Culture in Germany before 1933.* New York: Berghahn Books, 2006.

———, and Nils Römer, eds. *Longing, Belonging, and the Making of Jewish Consumer Culture.* Leiden: Brill Publications, 2010.

Ripperger, Tanja. *Ökonomik des Vertrauen.* Tübingen: Mohr Siebeck Verlag, 1998.

Rivkin, Ellis. *The Shaping of Jewish History: A Radical New Interpretation.* New York: Charles Scribner's Sons, 1971.

Roscher, Wilhelm Georg Friedrich. "Die Stellung der Juden im Mittelalter, betrachtet vom Standpunkte der allgemeinen Handelspolitik." *Zeitschrift für die gesamte Staatswissenschaft* 21 (1875): 503–526.

Roth, Cecil. "The Economic History of the Jews." *Economic History Review* 14 (1961): 131–135.

Rubinstein, W. D. "Jews in the Economic Elites of Western Nations and Antisemitism." *The Jewish Journal of Sociology* 42 (2000): 5–36.

Ruderman, David B. *Kabbalah, Magic, and Science: The Cultural Universe of a Sixteenth-Century Jewish Physician.* Cambridge: Harvard University Press, 1988.

Schipper, Ignaz. "Anfänge des Kapitalismus bei den abendländischen Juden im frühen Mittelalter." *Zeitschrift für Volkswirtschaft, Sozialpolitik und Verwaltung* 15 (1906), 501–564.

Scholem, Gershom. "Wissenschaft vom Judentum einst und jetzt." In Gershom Scholem, *Judaica* vol. 1, 147–164. Frankfurt a.M.: Suhrkamp Verlag, 1963.

Sennett, Richard. *The Culture of the New Capitalism.* New Haven: Yale University Press, 2006.

Shelton, George. *Dean Tucker and Eighteenth-Century Economic and Political Thought.* London: St. Martin's Press, 1981.

Sinkoff, Nancy Beth. *Out of the Shtetl: Making Jews Modern in the Polish Borderlands.* Providence: Brown University Press, 2003.

Skinner, Andrew S. "Adam Smith: An Economic Interpretation of History." In *Essays on Adam Smith*, edited by Andrew Skinner and Thomas Wilson, 154–178. Oxford: Clarendon Press, 1975.

Slezkine, Yuri. *The Jewish Century.* Princeton: Princeton University Press, 2004.

Smith, Adam. *The Wealth of Nations.* Edited by Edwin Cannan. Chicago: University of Chicago Press, 1976.

Sombart, Werner. *The Jews and Modern Capitalism.* Translated by M. Epstein. New Brunswick: Transaction Books, 1997.

———. "Das Warenhaus, ein Gebilde des Hochkapitalistischen Zeitalters." In *Probleme des Warenhauses: Beiträge zur Geschichte und Erkenntnis der Entwicklung des Warenhauses in Deutschland*, Werner Sombart, 77–88. Berlin: Verband Deutscher Waren- und Kaufhäuser, 1928.

———. *The Jews and Their Participation in the Creation of the Present-Day Economy.* Translated into Hebrew by Israel Shalom Bauhauslauwizsky. Kiev: Globermann Print, 1912.

Soyer, Daniel. "Class Conscious Workers as Immigrant Entrepreneurs: The Ambiguity of Class among Eastern European Jewish Immigrants to the United States at the Turn of the Century." *Labor History* 42, no. 1 (2001), 45–59.

Stein, Sarah Abrevaya. *Plumes: Ostrich Feathers, Jews, and a Lost History of Global Commerce.* New Haven, Yale University Press, 2008.

Strauss, Raphael. "Jews in the Economic Evolution of Central Europe." *Jewish Social Studies* 3 (1941), 15–40.

Sumberg, Theodore A. "Antonio Serra, A Neglected Herald of the Acquisitive System." In *American Journal of Economics and Sociology* 50, no. 3 (1991), 365–373.

Sutcliffe, Adam. "Can a Jew Be a Philosophe? Isaac de Pinto, Voltaire, and Jewish Participation in the European Enlightenment." In *Jewish Social Studies* 6 (2000), 31–51.

Sutherland, Lucy Stuart. "Samson Gideon: Eighteenth Century Jewish Financier." *Transactions of the Jewish Historical Society of England*, 17 (1951–52), 78–92.

Tamari, Meir. *The Challenge of Wealth: A Jewish Perspective on Earning and Spending Money.* Nothvale, NJ: J. Aronson, 1995.

———. *"With All Your Possessions": Jewish Ethics and Economic Life.* New York: Free Press, 1987.

Teller, Adam. *Money, Power, and Influence: The Jews on the Radziwill Estates in 18th Century Lithuania* [in Hebrew], Jerusalem: Shazar Centre, 2005.

Toland, John. *Reasons for Naturalizing the Jews of Great Britain and Ireland on the Same Foot as All Other Nations.* London, 1714.

Trivellato, Francesca. *The Familiarity of Strangers: The Sephardic Diaspora, Livorno, and Cross-Cultural Trade in the Early Modern Period.* New Haven: Yale University Press, 2009.

Tucker, Josiah. *A Second Letter to a Friend Concerning Naturalizations.* London, 1753.

Veltri, Guiseppe. *Renaissance Philosophy in Jewish Garb: Foundations and Challenges in Judaism on the Eve of Modernity.* Leiden: Brill, 2009.

———. "Alcune considerazioni sugli Ebrei e Venezia nel pensiero politico di Simone Luzzatto (Some Reflections on the Jews of Venice in the Political Thought of Simone Luzzatto)." In *Percorsi di storia ebraica. Atti del XVIII convegno internazionale dell'AISG, Cividale del Friuli-Gorizia, 7/9 settembre 2004* (Pathways in Jewish History. Proceedings of the 18th International Convention of the Italian Association for the Study of Judaism), edited by Cesare Ioly Zorattini, 247–266. Udine: Forum, 2005.

Waibl, Elmar. *Ökonomie und Ethik.* Stuttgart: Frommann-Holzboog, 1985.

Weinryb, Bernard D. "Prolegomena to an Economic History of the Jews in Germany in Modern Times." *Leo Baeck Institute Yearbook* 1 (1956), 279–306.

———. "Jewish Economy" [in Hebrew]. *Moznayim* 7 (1938), 336–344.

Wiles, Richard C. "Mercantilism and the Idea of Progress." *Eighteenth-Century Studies* 18, no. 1 (1974), 56–74.

Williams, Rosalind H. *Dream Worlds: Mass Consumption in Late Nineteenth-Century France.* Berkeley: University of California Press, 1982.

Wittrock, Bjorn. "Modernity: One, None, or Many?" *Daedalus* 129, no. 1 (2000), 31–60.

Wolf, Lucien, ed. *Menasseh ben Israel's Mission to Oliver Cromwell.* London, 1901.

Yerushalmi, Yosef Hayim. *From Spanish Court to Italian Ghetto.* New York: Columbia University Press, 1971.

Zemon Davis, Natalie. "Religion and Capitalism Once Again? Jewish Merchant Culture in the Seventeenth Century." *Representations* 59 (1997), 56–84.

Zenner, Walter P. *Minority in the Middle: A Cross-Cultural Analysis.* Albany: State University of New York Press, 1991.

Zunz, Leopold. *Etwas über die rabbinische Literatur.* Berlin: In der Maurerschen Buchhandlung, 1818.

INDEX